LO:

THE
CONSERVATIVE
NATION

The preservation of freedom is intimately related to economic and social progress. The cultural gains of the past can only be carried over into the future if the essential changes in the structure of society can be accomplished by peaceful means. When social evolution slows down, the tide of revolution rises. . . . We must look, therefore, not merely for a makeshift policy to deal with the immediate and most pressing needs, but for an imaginative plan of social reconstruction which will lay the basis for a long period of social peace.

Harold Macmillan

To understand a limited historical epoch we must step beyond its limits, and compare it with other historical epochs. To judge Governments and their acts, we must measure them by their own times and the conscience of their contemporaries. Nobody will condemn a British statesman of the seventeenth century for acting on a belief in witchcraft, if he find Bacon himself ranging demonology in the catalogue of science.

Karl Marx

Now beneath the Fertile-Land-of-Reed-Plains lay a kami in the form of a great cat-fish, and by its movement it caused the earth to quake, till the Great Deity of Deer-Island thrust his sword deep into the earth and transfixed the Kami's head. So, now, when the evil Kami is violent, he puts forth his hand and lays it upon the sword till the Kami becomes quiet.

Jorge Luis Borges
The Book of Imaginary Beings
Cape, London 1970

THE CONSERVATIVE NATION

ANDREW GAMBLE

ROUTLEDGE & KEGAN PAUL
London and Boston

First published in 1974
by Routledge & Kegan Paul Ltd
Broadway House, 68–74 Carter Lane,
London EC4V 5EL and
9 Park Street,
Boston, Mass. 02108, USA
Set in Monotype Bembo
and printed in Great Britain by
W & J Mackay Limited, Chatham
© Andrew Gamble 1974
No part of this book may be reproduced in
any form without permission from the
publisher, except for the quotation of brief
passages in criticism

ISBN 0 7100 8008 5
Library of Congress Catalog Card No. 74–83001

Contents

Preface

This book is a study of opinion in the Conservative party since 1945. It is not a study of how particular decisions were taken, nor does it describe in any detail how party policy developed. Similarly, there is no attempt to provide a full-scale analysis of either the structure of power or the social composition of the party. Instead, I have tried to focus attention on the manner in which leading Conservatives perceived and adjusted to political reality.

Political reality in the modern political system has several dimensions, marked out by the constraints imposed on political practice by the necessary involvement of politicians in both electoral politics and government. At various stages in the book, notably in the first and final chapters, I sketch out the nature of these constraints. The purpose of this theoretical analysis, however, is not to establish any causal relationships between the structure of the political system and the patterns of ideological response described in this book, but rather to provide a framework for interpreting the ideology and practice of the British Conservative party in recent times. All histories are fictions, reconstructions of the past, never the past itself. The quality of the fiction depends on how it is constructed—the methods and the framework of interpretation that are employed. It is a mistake to suppose that the necessity of choosing between frameworks can ever be dispensed with, and some standard of objective truth and objective method enthroned to guide research. Too much academic rigour in this direction leads to rigor mortis in the social sciences. Though there are good grounds for choosing between theoretical frameworks, there are no absolute objective ones.

This book is concerned with very recent events, and the difficulties and biases of writing such history are sufficiently well known. The crucial limitation is the absence of many documents, such as Cabinet papers, that later become available. That is why I have avoided a detailed chronological account of events and policies, which could only be incomplete, and tried instead to analyse and interpret the changing role of the Conservative party in British politics. The material I have drawn upon is predominantly the public utterances and reflections of Conservatives, and it is selected and presented against a background of developments in the political market and the organization of the state.

This book does not claim therefore to be in any sense exhaustive. It merely supplies one interpretation from a particular perspective of the political practice of the British Tories and the ideological difficulties they have encountered during the post-war period. The first two chapters give a theoretical and historical account of the Conservative party and the British political system. Chapters 3, 4 and 5 analyse the electoral perspective of the leadership in the period 1945–70 and the opposition to it within the party. Chapters 6 and 7 look in more detail at two areas central to this electoral perspective, which were the subject of major debates in the party. Chapter 8 recapitulates the historical and theoretical argument of the book and adds a postscript on the Conservative Government of 1970–4.

I would like to thank Professor Philip Abrams, who first interested me in the Conservative party as a subject for research, and Professor John Barnes, for much friendly advice, criticism, and encouragement. I am also indebted to Mrs Crisp and Mr G. D. M. Block of the Conservative Research Department for permission to use the Library there, and to the Library staff at the London School of Economics.

Much of the research and writing for this book was done while I was teaching remedial kids at Thomas Calton School in Peckham and living in Brixton. These surroundings provided many welcome and often bizarre diversions from the peculiar and solitary routines of academic research, and I would like to thank staff and pupils at Thomas Calton and my friends in Brixton, particularly the toilers in the Brixton Food Co-op.

Friendship with Paul Walton over the last five years, and the work we have done together, (particularly our book, *From Alienation to Surplus Value*, Sheed & Ward, London 1972), has been a constant source of new understanding, inspiration, and mental exhaustion. It has greatly altered and developed my thinking on many subjects, and has shaped many of the methodological and theoretical assumptions that underlie this present work.

I am also very grateful for discussions with friends and colleagues in the Politics Department at Sheffield University, especially Patrick Seyd, who read through and commented on an early draft of the manuscript. His own book on the Conservative party is due to be published shortly.

Finally, I have to thank Mary Beckinsale, Chris Flavin, Paul Ginsborg, and Pat Slowe, for their conversation, cooking, political commitment, and improbable stories; Miss A. M. Lyall, for typing the manuscript with such care; Sorrel for sitting under the lamp; and Chris for her unwavering scepticism.

A.G.

Abbreviations

CAP	Common Agricultural Policy
CBI	Confederation of British Industry
CPC	Conservative Political Centre
CPC SC	Conservative Political Centre—Summer School
CRD	Conservative Research Department
CUCO	Conservative and Unionist Central Office
EEC	European Economic Community
FBI	Federation of British Industries
FCS	Federation of Conservative Students
FUCUA	Federation of University Conservative and Unionist Associations
GATT	General Agreement on Tariffs and Trade
IEA	Institute of Economic Affairs
IRC	Industrial Reorganization Corporation
NAC	National Advisory Committee
NEDC	National Economic Development Council
NIC	National Incomes Commission
NOP	National Opinion Polls
NUCUA	National Union of Conservative and Unionist Associations
OECD	Organization for Economic Cooperation and Development
ORC	Opinion Research Centre
SET	Selective Employment Tax
TUC	Trade Union Congress
UNO	United Nations Organization
VAT	Value Added Tax
YC	Young Conservatives

Chapter 1
INTRODUCTION. THE CONSERVATIVE UNIVERSE: THE POLITICAL MARKET AND THE STATE

For practical politicians, as practical politicians well know, can do little
more in politics than give the names to what is happening anyway and
smooth the path of the inevitable by persuading people to vote for it.

Christopher Hollis[1]

1 THE TORY TRADITION

British Conservatism has many roots. Some historians trace Conservative ideas and the conservative disposition in a lengthy chain as far
back as Charles I and King Canute. Professor Hearnshaw even discovered Conservatism at work in the Garden of Eden:[2]

> In that visionary abode of bliss Adam was the person who repre-
> sented the qualities of contentment and stability. Eve was the
> innovator, eager for novelty, ready for reckless experiment, liable
> to be led away by any such seductive slogan as 'Eat More Fruit' or
> 'Free Figleaves for all'.

Conservatism's future adversary, Karl Marx, cast in the supporting role
of the serpent, made a brief first appearance on the stage of history,
sowing discord and discontent among the unwary.

Much modern academic discussion of the Conservative party still
concentrates, although not normally in so extravagant a fashion, on the
abstract ideas and principles that are held to underly the practice of
Conservatives. Conservatism is thus presented as one of the great Ideas
that stride across History, pushing men and nations before it, and only
pausing when confronted by another of the great Ideas, such as
Liberalism or Socialism, storming along in the other direction. This is
certainly one way of picturing history and the evolution of societies,
but it is hardly very fruitful. It requires that the historian always seeks
the origin and significance of the beliefs and actions of those he studies
in the general principles that are assumed to underlie and inspire them.

It is very difficult, however, even to connect the ideas and actions of
Conservative politicians with beliefs in original sin or the organic nature
of society, still harder to show that they are directly inspired by them.[3]
Philosophical reflection on politics should not be confused with the

practice of politics, and it is in vain that armies of researchers set out to discover whether Conservative practice reflects a coherent 'philosophy'. Michael Oakeshott, one of the more independent of modern Conservative thinkers, has indeed poured scorn on such a quest. 'Reputable political behaviour,' he writes,[4] 'is not dependent upon sound philosophy. . . . In general, constitutional tradition is a good substitute for philosophy.' Oakeshott argues that to be Conservative in politics does not mean that one has to believe in the existence of a natural law, or a providential order that reflects divine purpose in nature and history, or the organic composition of society, or the absolute value of individual personality, or original sin. It is not logically connected with any particular beliefs about the universe, the world in general, or the nature of man, but only with beliefs about the activity of governing and the instruments of government.

This must be the starting point for any study of the modern British Conservative party, particularly as it is the attitude of many Conservatives themselves. Rationalist Conservatism in the grand continental manner has never flourished in the ranks of the English Tories, who have generally preferred scepticism and philistine common sense. One of the more intellectual of their leaders, Lord Salisbury, once remarked[5] that a gram of experience was worth a ton of theory and professed to distrust the 'German mania for barren metaphysics'. British Conservatives in general have not normally bothered to justify their beliefs in private property and social hierarchy by appealing to natural law and revealed truth.

The Tory tradition, therefore is not best understood as a tradition of 'ideas'.[6] It is primarily a tradition of political practice, and ideas are only important in so far as they are part of that practice. To understand a political practice we must understand the political system in which it takes place. In Britain since the nineteenth century the political system has been radically transformed by the introduction of universal suffrage, and there is little meaningful continuity across this divide.

The new system was not heralded by any great symbolic event. No Constitution or Bastille inaugurated it. The change occurred gradually, in stages. Politicians began to learn the realities and the requirements of their new situation. Many ideas, attitudes and practices belonging to earlier times survived for a while, but gradually they have faded away. The different rationality imposed by the new politics has taken over.

In this system political practice has two main aims: to carry on the government and to win the right to office in a competitive election. The practice of politics has always required a mediation between the source of power to which the politician owes his appointment and the execution of policy. What is desired by the 'sovereign' and what proves possible to achieve may diverge to the point where the politician disappears in the chasm he meant to straddle. What is novel about universal suffrage and mass democracy is the extent of the wedge which has been driven between the two. It becomes legitimate to speak of two kinds of politics—a politics of power and a politics of support.

Mass democracy has weakened the direct control of the 'sovereign' over policy, and at the same time has greatly increased uncertainty about the nature and desires of this new 'sovereign', and therefore about what the politician has to do to win power. The conventional notion of the sovereign electorate implies that the politician is helpless before the demands and pressures of the electors. His only function is to translate the popular will into effect by legislation and administration. The real position is more nearly the reverse of this. The politician acts in the name of the people and the nation, but the very institutions of mass democracy ensure that he is no mere spokesman or delegate for his electors. He is a spokesman for his party. That is a very different matter.

At the same time, even if the politician strove to be simply the spokesman of those who elected him he could not guarantee to carry out their wishes. For while political leaders may control and direct the parties, they cannot control the state in the same way. They are elected to form a government, and the world of government is the world of organized interests, of realities and necessities, of checks and balances. The policy of any government is tightly circumscribed and constrained by relationships and forces that are not of its own making. The modern state is not a neutral agency to be fought for and occupied by the stronger party after an election, then used as an instrument for whatever purposes it sees fit. Politicians find certain policies and priorities imposed on them regardless of their 'mandates' and the size of their electoral majorities.

2 THE POLITICS OF POWER

The modern political system is thus founded on the separation of the state and the nation. But what is the state? From one standpoint it comprises certain major institutions—the state system or state apparatus. This is the machinery that discharges the functions of the state. The state system must be distinguished from the political system on the one hand, and the government on the other. The government is only one part of it. The state system also includes the civil service, the judiciary, the police and the army, and the various organs of local government.[7] The government is at the apex of both the state system and the political system, and occupies the point where they overlap.

The modern state is furthermore a nation-state. Nationality is the basis of sovereignty, and the political nation that is thus formed, is founded on the equality of all its members before the law. This has eventually produced equal representation in a political market. All citizens have the right to vote and all votes are intended to carry equal weight. State and nation combine in the nation-state, a state whose government is in principle representative of the nation because it is accountable to it through democratic institutions.[8]

Presiding over the state, however, and winning the support of the nation are two separate activities in the modern political system. This is because the state does not consist merely of the machinery of the state system. The idea of the state also covers the general social, economic and political arrangements that are found in a community and which the state system exists to uphold. Any given state, therefore, expresses the particular priorities of the prevailing politics of power. It is essential to grasp that the state at any one time is not just a set of institutions but a set of priorities, and that these priorities do not reflect primarily the 'will' of the nation in the political market, but rather the organization of the 'nation' in the economic market and the situation of the 'nation' in the world market. The state, through the government and the rest of the state system, expresses and maintains the relationships of economic power and social class that comprise the social relationships of production in the national economy. The interests thus represented in the state set limits to the foreign policy of governments, which is aimed at fortifying the strength and safeguarding the security of the nation-state abroad.

The concept of a politics of power therefore implies that there are at any one time certain realities and constraints which all governments must accept. Ultimately, any politics of power is founded on the ruling mode of production, the manner in which economic activity is socially organized. This gives rise to a particular form of property, and through it a particular class structure which determines the distribution of both income and of economic power. A mode of production cannot be legislated away by the government. It is the objective structure on which the state rests, and which the state exists to uphold.

The constraints, however, which a mode of production imposes on the politics of power are general and unspecific. The state obviously has to ensure the continued existence of the social relationships that constitute the mode of production. To call a society feudal or capitalist implies that the politics of power cannot infringe the 'fundamental interests' of the ruling feudal or capitalist class without a revolutionary transformation of that society. But a ruling class, the class that has economic power, is not the same as the government. Indeed a ruling class never governs directly. Government always falls to other groups which may be more or less representative of the ruling class. So, beyond the physical preservation of its property, it is rarely clear what the 'fundamental interests' of a ruling class may be in any concrete situation, partly because any such class is likely to be split into many groups with different immediate interests, and partly because of the uncertainty and lack of information inherent in practical affairs, and brought about in this case largely by the existence of other classes. Such factors make an objective, scientific assessment of political reality by governments impossible. Instead, it must always be interpreted and explored, through ideologies and by political parties.

Some modes of production last for centuries without changing very much. Capitalism is unique for the scale and speed of the changes which it generates in all societies throughout the world. One result is that capitalism as a world system passes through definite epochs and periods, in which each individual nation-state faces new problems and new opportunities. In every period, the prevailing politics of power is always concerned with the maintenance of the capitalist mode of production and the class structure. But this concern has to be expressed in terms of a particular set of strategic priorities, assumptions and goals of government. The maintenance of free trade, economy, and the gold standard, objects of British government for so long, comprised such a set of priorities. Frequently they constitute a consensus, which all parties adhere to when in office. At bottom such a consensus reflects a compromise between the interests of capital in accumulation and its interests in political stability. The former are bound up essentially with profitability, the rate of return on capital and the place of the national economy in the world economy. The latter means that concessions may sometimes have to be made in response to pressure from other classes, and to solve problems that private capital cannot solve for itself. Such pressure in Britain has largely been channelled through electoral institutions and the political market. It is through the prevailing priorities of government that the balance of interests and classes in the state can be assessed. The state, in the wider sense in which I am using it here, is thus the sphere of the politics of power, whilst the nation is the arena for the politics of support.

In general, the politics of support are concerned with how support can be won for political parties that intend to stick to 'practical' politics, and accept the 'realities' and the constraints of the prevailing politics of power. The limits within which an effective British economic policy or foreign policy is discussed are laid down by social and international relationships, normally outside the control of politicians. For a politician or a political party to go beyond these limits and break with the 'consensus' in a radical way requires either an indifference to gaining the spoils of office, or a revolutionary movement to transform society. Only if the balance of power between social classes is altered can a new politics of power be created.

Without such a radical transformation, a split opens between the politics of power and the politics of support, and the party that breaks with the consensus no longer appears as an alternative national government, but only as the mouthpiece of one section of the electorate. Reformist and left-wing parties that do win elections generally achieve less in office than is expected, because they usually conceive their task in terms of the politics of support rather than the politics of power. They tend to believe that control of the government through victory at the polls gives them the power to implement the policies on which they were elected. When the realities of government present themselves, such parties frequently succumb to prevailing orthodoxies even faster than their political opponents.

3 THE POLITICS OF SUPPORT

The politics of support in the modern political system takes place in three main arenas—Parliament, the party organization, and the mass electorate. The last is organized as a market. Like most markets, however, the political market does not function as some had intended and others had feared. Advocates of democracy used to imagine a democratic state to be one in which all citizens participated actively and continuously in the running of their community. Democracy was meant to develop and educate all men as citizens, in addition to providing peaceful means of satisfying their particular interests and grievances. The main components of the modern political market are three; the existence of a mass electorate; competition between two or more parties for the votes of this electorate; and a set of rules governing this competition. The old democratic ideal of the political market was the marketplace of ideas and opinions, where every man could have his say, and at the end of the discussion the citizens would vote for what they considered to be the best policy that had been proposed. But such 'perfect competition' has rarely existed, least of all in national democracies. In practice, democracy has been transformed from a political goal into a political method by the centralization of political power and decision making in the government; by the growing domination of legislatures by executives; and by the rise of political parties. It has become an 'institutional arrangement for arriving at political decisions in which individuals acquire the power to decide by means of a competitive struggle for the people's vote.'[9]

The actual working of mass democracy has divided the political market into two camps. There are those that compete for office and those that vote. Like the producers and consumers in economic markets it is a mistake to believe that these two functions are of equal importance. One is active, creative and continuous; the other is passive, receptive and intermittent.[10] Equal representation in the political system grafted on to a class society, in which economic and political power are concentrated in a few hands, has perpetuated, not abolished, inequality. In such a society, mass democracy serves to limit participation rather than to secure it.

The political market also lays down a standard of rational behaviour.[11] The goal of parties and politicians that compete in it is not arbitrary or a matter of choice. It is inherent in the way their roles are defined by the market. They must win election, which carries with it the right to office. 'Rational' behaviour is behaviour most likely to gain this end, and must therefore seek the most effective means of achieving it. The politician faces the mass electorate across the political market. His task is so to express it, mould it, lead it, frighten it, deceive it, dazzle it and persuade it, that it, or at least a sufficient part of it, confers on him and his party enough votes to win election.

The politician of course does not have a free hand. The way in which he competes for office is limited by the rules and procedures of electoral competition that are in force,[12] and by the character of the electorate. The rise of a political market does not mean that there is a sudden disappearance of ideologies, pressure groups and classes. These are the raw material with which the politician must work.

From the politician's point of view, a major aim of the politics of support is to build an organization that will enable his party to compete successfully in the political market, and that will reduce the uncertainty that universal suffrage brings to politics. But to realize that aim, important constraints are placed on the politician's freedom. For he must keep the support of his party in Parliament, and of his party in the country, whilst he is wooing a majority of the mass electorate. To some extent, therefore, every politician in Britain is a prisoner of his party and its traditions. In addition, they are all prisoners of the structure of the mass democracy. In Britain, a unified national electorate requires that parties to be successful must become national parties and pursue national politics.

The only way, therefore, to understand the role that general principles play in the political practice of Conservatives is to see them in relation to the politics of the nation which the party has found itself obliged to develop. Conservative ideas and principles at any one point in the history of the party will be found to be a ragbag drawn from almost every conceivable intellectual tradition. This is not surprising, however, and these differences in philosophy are not a good guide to how Conservatives will divide on particular issues. The party sometimes appears a huge coalition, a giant museum of the political movements of the past. Angus Maude has argued that[13] 'The Conservative party . . . still contains within itself, perfectly preserved and visible like the contents of archaeological strata, specimens from all its historical stages and of all its acquisitions from the Liberals.' He detected landed gentry, Anglican believers in the union of Church and State, Grand Whigs, Young England romantics, Tory Democrats, businessmen, municipal social reformers, and imperialists.

Despite this babel of conflicting voices, however, the Conservative party is renowned for its unity and cohesion, the absence of factions in its ranks and loyalty to its leaders. But this is no paradox, for, overriding the particular ideologies of different sections of the party, has been its need to develop a politics of the nation. Rarely have the politics of support been the only concern of Conservative politicians. The Conservatives have always prided themselves on being a party of government. This has made electoral ideologies subordinate to the electoral perspective of the leadership.

Electoral perspectives are the ideology of the leadership. Through them the leadership attempts to reconcile the conflicting demands of the politics of power and the politics of support, the state and the nation. But they do not seek to strike an equal balance. In an electoral perspective, political questions are always viewed from the standpoint of the state and the requirements of the politics of power. The task of this kind of political perspective is to reconcile such requirements with winning support in the political market.

Electoral perspectives, like the politics of support itself, have several dimensions. Two are of crucial importance—how to win support in the mass party and in the mass electorate. The first dimension means involvement in electoral ideologies, for these are what bind party organizations together. Electoral ideologies are used, fostered, and developed by political leaders, but they cannot be controlled by them. Indeed, they can be used by groups or aspiring leaders within the party against the incumbent leadership, and sometimes such challenges are successful either in toppling the leaders, or in making them alter their policies. The situation is always complex because political leaders themselves see the world through the ideologies of their party, and therefore themselves share conceptions of the Conservative Nation. But their task as political leaders is to subordinate their idea of the nation to their knowledge of the state. Their followers naturally feel no such constraint. They typically seek to shape and transform the prevailing politics of power to fit their conception of the Conservative Nation.

These perspectives and ideologies are termed 'electoral' because their form and content is conditioned by the existence of the political market. Each, however, has a different emphasis. The electoral perspective of the party leaders seeks the best way of securing support for the party in the mass electorate, and sees the party organization as an indispensable means for achieving this. By contrast, the electoral ideologies of the rank and file in the party strive to build a party that is ideologically and not just organizationally strong. From such a base, programmes for government that can secure the endorsement of the electorate can be launched.

Electoral ideologies express the nation; electoral perspectives reflect the state. To party leaders in such a political system, there appears a constant tension between the claims of party and the claims of the mass electorate. The latter, being unorganized, passive, and inarticulate, can be much more easily harnessed to the business of government. Yet leaders cannot harness this support, cannot in fact expect to compete effectively at all in the political market without their mass party organization. The central task of party management becomes striking a compromise between the two, and thus determining whether the state should be subordinate to the nation, or the nation to the state.

The Conservative party has been organized to ensure the latter, but that does not mean it has always been successful. The main channel by which leaders address the mass electorate is the party organizations. They must accordingly employ the electoral ideologies that command most support in their own party to recommend themselves to the electorate. More recently, politicians have sought ways of bypassing their party organizations to some extent and reaching the electorate directly, using market research, opinion polls, and new media like television, in an attempt to reduce their dependence on their parties.[14]

Since the politics of power has always come first for Conservatives, the politics of support is generally interpreted in terms of its requirements. This accounts for many well attested features of the party, especially the emphasis on strong leadership,[15] the rare emergence of factions,[16] and the lack of a coherent doctrine and philosophy.[17] Division into solid right and left wing factions is characteristic of parties more devoted to the politics of support than the politics of power. So too are very elaborate and coherent ideological doctrines. Conservatives are content to draw their arguments for particular policies from many different sources and political traditions.

Factions,[18] in the sense of close-knit groups organized to replace either the leadership or the policies of the party over a period of time on a whole range of issues, have existed within the Tory party but not very often. Since 1940 the two best examples of factions have been the Tory Reform Committee and the Monday Club. Alliances between MPs to fight over particular issues, such as Suez, Rhodesia, immigration, or resale price maintenance, have been more common. They dissolve when the issue is settled, and the members of such alliances do not usually act together on subsequent issues. These alliances and factions do not arise in a vacuum, but, like electoral ideologies, out of broad tendencies of opinion.[19] In the postwar party there have been three main tendencies—the right progressive, the diehard, (which had two wings—whig and imperialist) and the new right. They are marked out by different attitudes to the postwar settlement and the politics of power it established.

Such tendencies are rarely given an organizational form, and it is not surprising that Conservatives are so loud in celebrating the unity of their party and the absence of enduring splits.[20] The substance of these tendencies can be studied in the activities of the factions and alliances they inspire, and more generally in debates at party conferences. The existence of such tendencies often gives rise to conflict between the electoral perspective of the leadership and electoral ideologies in the party that seek to replace or modify it. The party may not often split, but that does not mean that Conservative leaders can escape the politics of support, or that there are no major controversies in the party.[21] The leadership has to explain and justify its policies, and this often proves difficult when the requirements of the politics of power and the demands of the politics of support in the party diverge. In general, electoral ideologies carry most weight when the party is in opposition; a weak leadership can be propelled by forces within its own party and by the need to separate their programme from that of their electoral opponents into accepting policies that conflict with the realities of government.

This is not necessarily disastrous, however, for the prevailing politics of power is not fixed and immutable. Policies that can advance both the dominant interests of property and maintain political stability have to be forged. They do not drop from the skies. Nothing is ever finally settled in politics. For this reason, even in the Conservative party, individual leaders and groups sometimes choose to leave the ground of the politics of power for the politics of support, and challenge the established leadership. Although they are generally unsuccessful over the issues on which they fight, such a move can pave the way for their eventual leadership of the party.

The Conservatives have developed such a strong identity as the party of government because they have generally been the party in government. Out of the 18 general elections since manhood suffrage was established in 1885, the Conservatives have won 12, and have ruled either alone or in coalition for 60 of those 88 years. Much ingenuity has been devoted to explaining this remarkable performance, but it should not be overrated. It is largely accounted for by the accidents of electoral politics.[22] For a large part of this period the party owed its success to the splits among its opponents and the electoral advantage of such a situation in a system resting on single member constituencies. Between 1886 and 1906, the Liberals were split over Home Rule for Ireland, and the Conservatives, as a direct result, were almost continually in office. Between 1918 and 1945, the rise of the Labour party and the decline of the Liberals meant that there was no single dominant party in opposition to the Conservatives, who again, as a result, virtually monopolized the government, usually with a substantial minority vote.

In the post-war period, when Labour was at last firmly established on an equal electoral footing with the Conservatives, the Conservatives were still thought of as the natural party of government, especially after their third successive election victory in 1959. But if we take the twenty-five years from 1945 to 1970, we find the Conservatives in office in thirteen of them, and Labour in office in twelve. Both had won four elections, if the 1970 result is included. Since the war, therefore, the

Conservatives have not had a monopoly of government, and have had to compete on almost equal terms with their electoral opponents.[23] This is one reason for the new strength of the politics of support within the party, and the growing importance of the party organization.

4 THE PARTY CONFERENCE

As the suffrage was widened, the political parties were faced with a quite new electoral task. No longer was it feasible to win election through bribery and patronage. Instead the parties were obliged to cast around for some means of organizing bodies of support within the electorate in order to shape and control the votes of as many electors as possible. The response of both major parties after 1867 was to form mass organizations, to appoint national agents, and to create a professional party secretariat. In this way a separate sphere was created for the politics of support outside Parliament as a bridge to the new mass electorate. It acquired its own institutions and procedures.

There seemed a danger, much fastened upon by the opponents of democracy, that the old parliamentary parties might come to lose their independence and be dominated by the caucus that controlled the party organization.[24] The priorities of the politics of support would override the prevailing politics of power, and Parliament would dwindle in importance as the sphere of public speech, public action, and public decision. In fact, Parliament has indeed severely declined since the nineteenth century.[25] But although power has passed to party, it has not passed to the party organization, but to the party leadership. The rise of modern parties in Britain has been a history in which party leaders have used their mass organization to discipline and control their MPs, and have used their parliamentary supporters to preserve themselves from the demands of the party rank and file.[26]

Once the electorate began to be enlarged, party affiliation and party labels became the main way of simplifying the choice before electors in the political market. The national image and national policy of the party grew to be more important than the personality and views of the individual MP. MPs therefore became primarily representatives of their parties. In return, those who controlled the parties demanded increasing conformity and loyalty from their MPs. Independents in Parliament began to disappear, party lines became more tightly drawn and the power of the whips increased. The electorate and not the House of Commons now 'chose' the government. Prime ministers began resigning immediately if they lost their parliamentary majority at a general election, without waiting to be defeated in the new Parliament.

In the meantime the mass organizations were also brought under the control of the party leaders. This was especially true of the Conservative party, whose mass organization, the National Union, was formed as an adjunct to the party in Parliament.[27] It never acquired, and hardly ever asserted, any rights to determine policy independently of the leadership's direction. The campaign launched by Lord Randolph Churchill and the Fourth Party to make the Tories more responsive to their new middle class constituency was short-lived. Conservative leaders often boasted of their independence from the party organization. Balfour even suggested that his valet would be a better adviser on policy than a Conservative party conference.

In dealing with their supporters in Parliament and in the country, the Conservative leaders were greatly strengthened by their control of the party's secretariat—Central Office. The most important positions in Central Office have always been filled through direct appointment by the leader of the party. In addition, the leader has the major responsibility for making policy in the party, so he appoints the committees that advise on policy and has to approve the research done by the Conservative Research Department. Central Office is accordingly oriented more towards the leadership than towards the National Union, the constituency associations, or the parliamentary party. It seeks to coordinate the work of the party by disseminating information, expertise, literature and speakers, and naturally tends to reflect the priorities of the leadership rather than those of any section of the membership. Central Office's chief aim has been to maintain the party organization as an effective electoral and competitive organization in the political market. The organizational tasks assume priority; how to win victory in elections, how to attack electoral opponents, how to improve administration, and how to keep up the morale of the party workers.

Yet it is quite wrong to imagine the mass organization as monolithic, tightly controlled from the top, breathing with one breath, and chanting in unison.[28] The party leaders need their party organizations. They could not otherwise win elections, and this imposes important constraints on their political practice. The value of a party organization is two-fold. On the one hand, it provides a committed body of support in every constituency, a way of raising funds, a means of distributing propaganda, and of canvassing the electorate; on the other it provides a crucial channel of communication between the leaders and the mass electorate. A great part of politicians' information about the electorate comes through their party organization. Recently the parties have tried to supplement this information by using new techniques of market research, partly in an effort to reach the mass electorate directly and gain a more 'objective' picture, partly to distance themselves from their party workers' embrace. But for all the sophistication of the new electoral techniques, the party organization cannot be dispensed with. A solid base of electoral support for the Conservatives, reflected in the morale and the number of party workers, is a necessity so long as the party seeks to remain electorally competitive. The party in the country, like the party in Parliament, may rarely determine policy directly. Yet both impose major constraints on what policies can be put forward. The policy of the party must always be explained and justified by the leaders to their supporters. It must be sold twice over, first to the party and then to the mass electorate. For the party in the country this occurs above all at the party conference.

Conservative conferences are thus important because they are the most obvious arena in the party where the politics of support meet the politics of power. No-one doubts that the latter predominates. The conferences are not sovereign assemblies but party rallies, and the scales are weighted in favour of the leadership by the procedural rules that are in force. The leadership controls the agenda and thus chooses which resolution out of all the resolutions submitted on a topic to call for debate. Delegates can now vote in a ballot for two resolutions that they want debated in addition to the official programme, but often only one is actually called. The time allowed each speaker is short, the decision on whether to call amendments is in the hands of the Chairman of the conference, and a member of the party's front bench always winds up the debate, and has a much longer time in which to speak. The delegates do not instruct their leaders, they petition them.

Yet the Conservative conference has undoubtedly grown in importance since 1945. Each constituency association is allowed to send seven delegates, none of whom are formally elected or instructed to support particular policies. If all attended, the conference would be around 5,600. In fact it usually numbers 3,000. The system of selection of delegates means that the more enthusiastic of the rank and file are likely to be present at the conference. Before the war few MPs attended it. The Woolton reforms, however, by strengthening the party organization in the country, gave a new status to the conference. Since then the great majority of Conservative MPs have attended as a duty. The leader of the party continued to stay away, only arriving after all the debates were over to deliver a speech to the delegates. This was once intended to keep the party organization in its place, and to underline that the leader alone was responsible for party policy. It became anachronistic and unwise, however, for a modern party, and Heath began attending the whole of the conference after his election as leader in 1965.

It is still a widely held view that the conference is so deferential to the leaders that the debates are meaningless and never decide anything. Christopher Hollis described it thus:[29]

> A Conservative party conference is intended to be, and is, the dullest thing that ever happened . . . the delegates have not come to hear their rulers but to see them, and one is often tempted to wonder whether it would not be the best plan to cut out the speeches altogether.

Taper, writing in the *Spectator* in 1958 was even more caustic:[30] 'At the slightest reference to Mr Macmillan the entire conference has a prolonged seizure; at the sight of Lord Hailsham, the air is thick with bursting blood vessels.'

But the real significance of the conference lies elsewhere. Its function is to enable the Conservative party in the country to become a support of government, to reconcile the politics of support to the politics of power. The debates are not in fact irrelevant.[31] Conservative leaders have to win support at the conference for the policies they are pursuing, and that means they must justify them in terms of an ideology of the Conservative Nation that the conference will accept. A central purpose of this book is to examine how Conservative leaders negotiate the politics of support against a background of changing circumstances and realities in the world of power. Ideologies provide, amongst other things, maps of problematic reality,[32] and so long as reality remains problematic, ideologies are indispensable to the politician in his bid to explore it and bridge the gulf between power and support, administration and legitimation. If ideology were at an end, so would politics be.

It could be objected that a study of opinion in the party as it is revealed in the debates at the annual conference reveals nothing at all, because there is a complete separation between ideology and administration.[33] According to this view, Conservative leaders make whatever ideological pronouncements they are called on to make at the conference, but disregard party ideology and party opinion when it comes to making policy. It is true that on only one occasion since the war has Conservative policy been modified by direct pressure from the conference. That was in 1950 when a pledge to build 300,000 houses a year was inserted in the party manifesto against the advice of the leaders.

It is a very superficial view of influence, however, that measures it only by such dramatic and relatively unimportant incidents. The Conservative conference is not after all a policy making body. What is of much greater significance is to assess how far opinion in the party, as reflected in the conference debates, has both initiated and inhibited new directions in policy. During the thirteen years of Tory rule examples of such influence include the bringing forward of legislation on immigration and the hindering of an earlier approach to the EEC. After 1964, when the party was in opposition, the politics of support naturally claimed still greater attention. Party policy on government intervention in the economy, incomes policy, selectivity in welfare, overseas defence spending, Rhodesia, law and order, immigration, and trade unions, were all either launched or revised in deference to the sustained pressure of the party rank and file. A sign of this growing importance of the mass organization, and the party conference in particular, was the permission that was granted in 1967 for ballots to be held after debates if a substantial minority of the conference desired it.

None of this should be exaggerated. The National Union is not about to make a bid to assume control over policy. The mass organization has been a constraint upon leaders ever since the politics of support and the political market became the context of political action. If its power has grown since 1945 that is because the party has been busy adapting itself more and more to the special requirements and techniques of the politics of support in a political market.

5 CONCLUSION

If then we are searching for the real Tory tradition, we shall not find it in long, profound meditations on the origin of evil and the principles of social order. It resides instead in the history of the Conservative party and its political practice in the modern era; its attempts to reconcile the politics of support and the politics of power, and to make the Conservative Nation a reality, by finding a majority in the nation to support the Conservatives' claim and evident desire to manage the affairs of the British state.

The political settlement in Britain after the end of the Second World War involved a major restructuring of the politics of power—the creation of a new consensus. The development of the implications of this new politics of power and the new state it created, and the attempts by Conservative leaders to harmonize it with their politics of support, is the subject of the rest of this book. Firstly, however, the development of the Conservative party and its political practice before 1945 will be briefly outlined.

Chapter 2
THE CHANGING TORIES: THE ROAD TO THE POLITICAL SETTLEMENT

At that time we had not thoroughly learnt by experience, as we now have, that no reform, no innovation—experience almost justifies us in saying, no revolution—stinks so foully in the nostrils of an English Tory as to be absolutely irreconcilable to him. When taken in the refreshing waters of office any such pill can be swallowed.

Anthony Trollope[1]

1 DISRAELI AND ONE NATION

The Conservative and Unionist party originated as one grouping in the unreformed House of Commons. The original Tories were a loose coalition of landed interests, attached to causes many of which failed to survive into modern times.[2] The purpose of the old constitution was to provide strong and stable government. Tories were more attached to this tradition than to reforming the House of Commons, because however unrepresentative Parliament might be, it did guarantee the continued supremacy of landed property. In the early nineteenth century the Tories were identified overwhelmingly with landed interests and opposition to reform of the franchise. Reform was, however, victorious in 1832, and brought the first step towards the political market.

The question of parliamentary reform involved not merely the extension of the franchise but the recognition by the state of the claims of industrial property. For the Tories, Peel accepted the new politics of support made necessary by the 1832 reform, and re-established his party in government. His implicit acceptance at the same time of the new strategic priorities of the politics of power and thus the new state that was required by the growing predominance of industrial over landed property, was confirmed most dramatically by the repeal of the corn laws in 1846.[3] This destroyed Peel politically, however, for he could not carry the support of his party. Disraeli and Lord George Bentinck ably exploited the gap which Peel had allowed to open up between his policies in government and the interests of his immediate supporters. They toppled their lost leader, but at the price of making the party the mouthpiece only of landed interests. The narrowing of support in the new political nation that this implied proved no longer sufficient to win elections, and the party was condemned for almost thirty years to be a party of opposition, and its politicians to be practitioners only of the politics of support. Whigs and Liberals ruled.

By the 1860s it had become clear to many that if the Tory party was ever to reestablish itself as an alternative party of government, then it needed to become more independent of the landed interest, and rid itself of the commitment to restore Protection. Any practical politician would have been forced to that conclusion. It has always been the special task of the politician to perceive and respond to the conditions for effective political action. Thus it is no surprise to find Disraeli, who had helped turn the party against Peel, leading the Tories away from their principles of 1846 and along the road which Peel had been exploring before him. A new kind of politics was necessary to prise the Tories loose from their dependence on the agricultural community and its special interests, in order to win a majority of the new political nation that was being created.

Disraeli's role in creating the new Conservative party has been much exaggerated.[4] In most things he was pretty lethargic. But he did possess many insights into the future shape of the new politics. He saw that the gradual widening of the suffrage inevitably made electoral politics national politics. Parties were forced to compete for the votes of the whole nation, and not merely in a geographical sense. They had also to put forward 'national' policies and begin to act as brokers for many different groups and interests. Instead of politics being mainly a matter of coalitions between individual political leaders and their followers, who drew their support from distinct regional communities, a new pattern was beginning to emerge, the rise of party. In time the new national base of electioneering, which mass parties made possible, helped to separate the gathering of support from the business of government by preventing the parties from seeking any too close identification with particular groups of electors.

For Disraeli, the reasons for leading the Conservatives to embrace national politics were particularly compelling. In the 1870s, close to 70 per cent of their MPs were still directly connected with the land. Once their leaders had accepted the inevitability of further reform in the franchise, then the key strategic question for the Tories became how they could win sufficient support in the new mass electorate to become a party of government again. Many doubted that such a rebirth were possible, especially if the franchise were extended still further. It was Disraeli who, however much his immediate reasons for supporting reform in 1867 were governed by particular circumstances,[5] also saw deeper, and realized that an enlarged electorate, properly handled, could in fact aid and not destroy the Tory party. The principles and the old politics of power to which the Tories had been committed he knew were lost whatever happened. The only question, therefore, was whether the Conservatives could seize their opportunity and become an alternative government party again. Reforming the franchise appeared in this light to be not so much a further step in the progress of Liberalism, as a way of overturning the automatic domination of the political system which the Liberals had enjoyed since 1832. An injection of greater uncertainty into politics could aid the Tories and restore them to power.

One of Disraeli's key contributions was to develop the slogan and strategy of One Nation.[6] No claim perhaps has been made more often by Conservatives, or disputed more hotly by their electoral competitors, than that they are a truly national party whose policies seek to create national unity, and to benefit all groups in the national community.[7] This Conservative wish to base their appeal to the electorate on a national rather than on a class perspective is central to their whole electoral strategy. For, as the party of property, they could scarcely hope otherwise to secure the votes of the most industrialized, urbanized, and proletarian nation in Europe, which is without any major racial, regional, religious or ethnic division of its working class that a party of the right could exploit.[8] Since 1885 the votes of propertyless manual workers have dominated the political market. The Conservatives have been obliged by this reality of the modern political system to adapt and become flexible, to learn how to combine what is necessary in government with what is necessary to win power. One Nation is thus not an ideological frill for Conservatives. It expresses one of the conditions for their survival as a political force.

The practice of politics for the Conservative means that he must continually take part at some level in the debate over the kind of national politics the Conservative party ought to pursue or, in other words, over what the Conservative Nation is. He must marry the nation to the state and identify, as circumstances change, the role the Conservative party is to play in national affairs—the institutions it should defend, the aims it should pursue, and the supporters it should seek to attract.

Disraeli's own solution to these problems was to proclaim the Conservatives the party of imperialism on the one hand, and the party of social reform on the other. It is a conception that has exercised enormous fascination for later Conservatives, not only for its particular content, but also for its attempt to combine a positive programme for government directly with winning electoral support. Disraeli's own efforts to weld this idea into a concrete programme proved not very vigorous. More important at this stage was his skill in drawing the party away from exclusive representation of the landed interests, making it appear more and more the party which stood for the defence of property interests in general. This image was to be consolidated by the sober and prudent administration of Lord Salisbury.

Disraeli was less original in his political practice than has sometimes been imagined because circumstances 'did not yet warrant sweeping changes. The inertia of traditional political practice proved strong, and the terrible catastrophe which many Conservatives, including Salisbury, had predicted would follow from the 1867 Reform Bill never arrived. The 1885 reform was to be a far greater step towards the modern political system. It is true that under Disraeli's leadership the National Union was formed, a party secretariat appointed, and efforts made to start constituency associations.[9] But recent research has shown that many of these steps were tentative and made little impact at the time.[10] Certainly they did not mark any sudden transformation of politics from the old to the new. A greater watershed in British politics came in the 1880s.

2 JOSEPH CHAMBERLAIN AND TARIFF REFORM

The period after 1885 saw the real rise of the modern Conservative party and the real construction of the political market and the modern party system. Accidents played their part too. The Conservatives were in office almost continuously until 1906, not because they had found the best way of applying Disraeli's precepts, but because the Liberals split over Home Rule for Ireland in 1886, and the Liberal Unionists under Joseph Chamberlain deserted to form a coalition with the Conservatives. The Conservatives now found themselves unexpectedly dominating British politics, the natural party of government. Their complete conversion to the prevailing politics of power was shown by their resolute indifference to the decline of British agriculture in the 1880s and 1890s, despite the overwhelming support they now enjoyed from landed interests. Most of the remaining landowners in the Liberal party, like the Duke of Devonshire, allied with the Tories on the issue of keeping the kingdom united. Many representatives of industrial and commercial property remained with the Liberals, but the Conservatives were to show themselves competent stewards of the general interests of property. Lord Salisbury's ministries built on the fodauntion of Disraeli's, and there could be no doubt, as he himself declared, that the chief object of government in England—the protection of property —was not neglected when the Conservatives were in office.

It was at this time that the party began to build a solid base amongst the middle classes—professional men, clerks, teachers, shopkeepers, small manufacturers, farmers, lawyers, and stockbrokers. It was to such groups that the imperialist sentiment that raged in the 1880s and 1890s particularly appealed. The party became strongly identified with the Empire. The Conservative Nation almost from its very beginning was an imperial nation. National greatness became one of the distinctive themes of the party's image and ideology.[11]

This identification was encouraged by Joseph Chamberlain, Colonial

Secretary after 1895 and a leading representative of the industrial capitalists of Birmingham. It was Chamberlain who tried to widen the base of the party's support still further, by making a direct appeal to the working class. A policy of imperial expansion abroad was to be linked to social reform, including old age pensions, at home. The one would pay for the other, whilst leaving the share of property in national income untouched. Chamberlain attempted to put forward a new electoral ideology that would attract working class votes to the Conservatives by appealing simultaneously to their self-interest and their patriotism. This went far beyond Disraeli who had merely sketched out the possibilities of such an appeal. Armed with the new pamphleteering resources of Central Office Chamberlain sought to put it into effect.[12]

The force of Chamberlain's proposals lay in the growing awareness by politicians of the electoral power that the working class now had. A middle class base was insufficient for the Tories to win elections, and a conservative peasantry was conspicuously absent. There were some in the party that longed for a revival of peasant proprietorship and small land-holding to bring into the political system a 'mob' to counter the industrial 'mob'.[13] But such a thorough-going reaction was no longer possible. However well it might have suited the electoral interests of the party to resettle the industrial proletariat on the land, it ran right against the property interests which the prevailing politics of power upheld.

In the first decade of the twentieth century the working class finally erupted into the political market. The character of the new electorate that had existed since 1885 belatedly made itself felt. The parliament of 1900 was accordingly the first parliament in which economic affairs predominated over constitutional and religious issues.[14] The period up to the outbreak of the First World War is thus of major importance in understanding the inter-relation between the politics of power and the new politics of support. The political market began to assert itself more, by forcing the old parties to face the requirements of electoral competition and the rise of a new competitor, the Labour party. This occurred during a time of new and serious problems for the British state. Despite the consolidation of Britain's imperial strength after victory in the Boer War, Britain faced increasing imperialist rivalry from France, Germany, and the USA. At the same time, the state was threatened at home by labour unrest, and constitutional crisis over the budget and Home Rule for Ireland.[15]

In Parliament a major rift developed between the parties over policies that touched a central plank of the prevailing politics of power; the question of free trade versus tariff reform.[16] This was in no way a revival of the old argument of 1846. The terrain was completely different. What it brought was a major division within the Conservatives, a division that found expression in a conflict between the established electoral perspective of the leadership and a new conception of the Conservative Nation.

Central to the dispute was Chamberlain's belief that imperial preference for trade between countries in the Empire was essential to keep the Empire strong and safeguard it against growing economic and military competition from Germany and America. In his view, the interests of British industry demanded protective tariffs. At the very least, Britain should have the option of imposing retaliatory tariffs if other countries imposed them against British goods. Chamberlain expected tariff reform, however, not only to protect British interests and increase the pace of industrial advance, but also to provide a source of revenue to the Exchequer which could be used to finance schemes of social reform. Thus tariff reform was intended to secure not only the essential interests of the British state in the world market as Chamberlain conceived them. It would also secure broad-based electoral support for the Unionists. It seemed a perfect balance between the requirements of the politics of power and the requirements of the politics of support.

Chamberlain was, however, opposed from within the Unionist coalition by the Unionist Free Traders, many of them his old allies, and also naturally by the Liberals who discovered a new unity in fighting his proposals. The supporters of free trade were firmly convinced that free trade remained in the interest of British capital and the British state, in particular City finance capital. It was linked as well in their minds to the spread of civilization, enlightenment and peace, and more particularly to keeping down the cost of living and maintaining prosperity. Many firmly believed that the support of the nation for the existing state could only be kept if the political parties were seen to govern justly, inside the limits set by natural economic laws.

The Liberal electoral counter-attack against tariff reform stressed its cost to the people in the form of higher food prices if Britain were prevented from importing food from the cheapest source; at the same time they brought forward their own proposals for social reform, which planned to raise the money for pensions and unemployment benefits by direct taxation, most of which would fall on property. Thus although Liberal Free Traders and Conservative Tariff Reformers agreed on the need to increase government intervention and the size of the state sector in the field of welfare provision, they disagreed fundamentally on how the increase should be financed.

Chamberlain resigned in 1903 from the Cabinet to campaign for tariff reform in the country, but after some initial successes, he found he could not reverse the electoral tide that was flowing towards the Liberals. At the election of 1906 there was a Liberal landslide, and Labour achieved its first representation in the House of Commons.

In the years of opposition that followed, the Unionist party was captured by the Tariff Reformers, though Chamberlain himself was paralysed by a stroke in 1906. The key to the Tariff Reformers' success lay in their virtual monopoly of the Unionist Press and their campaign in the constituencies. This campaign was organized by a body known as the Confederacy, one of the most successful factions in the history of the party. It hounded Free Traders out of the parliamentary party. Many, like Churchill, crossed over to the Liberals or left politics altogether. By 1910 the pragmatists in the leadership, notably Balfour himself, had bowed to the inevitable and accepted a full tariff reform programme. It is the clearest example of Conservative leaders capitulating to pressures from their supporters on a major policy, and abandoning their electoral perspective.

Which policy, tariff reform or free trade, was in the real interests of British capital before 1914? Undoubtedly, especially once the pre-war boom got under way after 1909, it was free trade that still served best the short-term interests of most sections of capital, particularly finance capital. Tariffs were sought mainly by declining industries, and some branches of iron and steel. Most of the Tariff Reformers that had industrial interests tended to be drawn from these groups, whilst Free Traders tended to have City interests.[17] So long as the world market was still expanding, then free trade made most sense. In 1913, Britain still had 30 per cent of the world trade in manufactures. Tariff reform and imperial preference would only have been to Britain's advantage in a world recession or trade war.

If, however, the Conservatives had won the 1906 election, would tariff reform have become their policy in government as it became in opposition? The answer is almost certainly no, and this gives another clue to how the politics of power and support are interrelated in the state. The Conservative Cabinet in 1903 had rejected full-scale tariff reform, and chose instead only a few minor measures that infringed free trade. There is no doubt that had the Tories won the election, the arguments of supporters of free trade within the party would have been enormously strengthened by support from the Treasury, the Bank of England, and the representatives of leading industries and banks that wanted free trade to continue.[18] A political leader is far more able to negotiate the politics of support and harmonize its demands with prevailing realities when he is in power than when he is in opposition. The Tariff Reformers owed their victory to the fact that the Tories were out of office after 1906. In the circumstances of the pre-war years capital was more ready to see the maintenance of free trade, combined with a small increase in direct taxation, than tariff reform, which would have necessitated a major reorganization of the British state, turning it away from the world market towards a self-supporting Empire. A rapidly expanding export trade made the taxation that came with the free trade policy a small price to pay for political stability. If the Conservatives had won the election, they might well have maintained free trade and not increased taxation. But such an apparently ideal world for the interests of property might have carried greater dangers of social upheaval.

As it was, the bitterness with which the Conservatives fought the Liberals over Ireland and the Budget almost exploded the nation into civil war. The forces of the right in the party gained in strength after the electoral defeats of 1910 and 1911, and their analysis of the causes of Britain's malaise sharpened.[19] There were strong attacks on how Parliament worked, and considerable alarm about the activities of separatist and anti-national groups, the wave of labour unrest, the Suffragettes' campaign, the flood of aliens (mostly Jews) into Britain, and the growing international challenge from Germany. The Ulster Volunteer movement set up to fight Home Rule became a model for what many of the right wanted. Its military organization, its patriotic ethos, and its inclusion of men from all classes provided a political vehicle for the right outside the constitutional political market. Many Unionists now found this preferable to parliamentary games at Westminster. A major challenge from the right to the constitution and the prevailing politics of power was probably only averted by the outbreak of world war. This has so far been the only occasion when the Conservatives have been ready to abandon their wooing of the nation through the political market, and leave the prize of constitutional legitimacy to their electoral rivals, so keen became their desire to recapture and remould the state.

3 CLASS CONFRONTATION AND THE DEFENCE OF THE STATE

A new stage in the development of the political market in Britain opened in 1918. The Representation of the People Act brought full manhood suffrage and votes for women who were over thirty and owned property. An extra two million men and six million women were added to the electorate. Lloyd George's Coalition Government had speedily recognized the need to secure the full cooperation of organized labour in the war effort, and this was one result.[20]

Whilst the organized strength of the working class was becoming an increasingly important influence on the state, it was even more rapidly transforming the politics of support. Following the war-time split in the Liberal party, Labour was suddenly established, when the war ended, as the major party of opposition. In this situation the Liberals found it increasingly difficult to combine being a capitalist party of free trade with being the party of radical social reform financed out of redistributive taxation. The Conservatives appeared more and more

23

as the only serious defenders of the interests of property and the existing state against the threat of confiscation represented by Labour.[21]

The first decade of the peace, therefore, saw steady advance by Labour and dwindling support for the Liberals. Yet, as in the period after 1886, when the Conservatives owed their ascendancy to the split in the Liberals, so in the 1920s the Conservatives were almost continually in office because the non-Conservative vote was split between the Liberals and Labour. The Conservatives almost always polled many fewer votes than the other two parties combined. The electoral pact between the two parties which had kept the Tories out in 1910 lapsed after 1918. Labour had to make its own way.

The dominant political question of the interwar years became, therefore, how Labour was to be handled. The possibility that the party might win an electoral majority menaced the stability of the prevailing politics of power. Apart from Ireland, Liberals and Tories had for long adhered to a consensus about essentials—the protection of capitalist property—and had disagreed only over strategic priorities. Labour's attitude to the British state, however, was still uncertain.

Since the British constitution put such stress on strong government, Conservatives feared that a Labour government, backed by a majority in Parliament, would feel able to embark on a wholly new course that could threaten the very basis of the state. In the Conservative interpretation of the constitution, unlimited power was only bestowed on governments which intended to uphold existing arrangements and institutions. They thoroughly rejected the doctrine of the mandate, which suggested that parties in office should implement programmes on which they fought elections.[22] For that would mean subordinating the politics of power to the politics of support, and making the organization of the state subordinate to the whim of the nation. Electoral ideologies would triumph over electoral perspectives.

From their experience of the political market, Conservatives firmly believed that the task of parties was to win support for policies and politicians that would abide by the limits laid down by the prevailing politics of power. They had felt justified in their extra-parliamentary opposition to Home Rule, because self government for Ireland threatened the very unity of the kingdom, and they argued that the Liberals had had no constitutional right to embark upon it. They were merely appeasing the Irish MPs that kept them in office after 1910. It is not surprising, therefore, that the Conservatives viewed Labour too as a grave threat to the Constitution, because its leaders, and still more its rank and file, insistently declared that policy should be decided not by government in consultation with its advisers in the civil service, the City, the press, industry, and the major pressure groups, but by a mass organization outside the network of established institutions.[23]

Two main strands may therefore be isolated in Tory reactions to

Labour up to 1940. One was direct confrontation, aiming at the destruction of the Labour movement and the Labour party. The second sought to delay Labour's advance, and win the leaders of the Labour movement, both in politics and in the unions, to 'constitutional methods'. The first was represented above all by Churchill, and the second by Baldwin.

Conservatives supported the Coalition under Lloyd George's leadership after 1918, because of the need to resist any further advance by Labour and to ride out the very serious industrial unrest that was spreading through the country, affecting even the army and the police. In time, as the danger passed, the Conservative party in Parliament, and to a lesser extent in the country became uneasy about the continuance of the Coalition, because its opposition to socialism was so negative. They doubted if such an electoral strategy could hold back the advance of collectivism in the long run.[24] The leaders of the party still believed, however, that a united front under Lloyd George's leadership, was the best available political instrument for fighting Labour. The resulting split in the party led to the famous Carlton Club meeting, and one of the most dramatic revolts in the history of the party. Almost the entire leadership was displaced, and the Government of 'the second eleven' took over. But many of the rebels, like Leo Amery, were disappointed by the outcome. Restoring independence to the Conservatives did not bring any great new scheme of imperial preference and social reform. The overall political strategy of the party under Bonar Law and Baldwin did not change, and those leaders in the Coalition, such as Churchill and Birkenhead, who felt that Labour's challenge to the Constitution was the central dividing line in domestic politics, were soon numbered in the ranks of the Conservative party again.

During the interwar period, the Conservatives were in power for all but three years. Their politics were defensive, aimed at protecting the economic system and the constitution that legitimated it. These years saw few departures or innovations in policy, and little reorganization of the state. During the war there had been a prolonged struggle between those political leaders who wanted to fight the war with a minimum of interference in the economy, and those who favoured mobilization of all national resources and energies by the state. This conflict, which concerned the whole management of the war, had precipitated the fall of Asquith.[25] The new Coalition Government, headed by Lloyd George, and supported by the Conservatives, swiftly imposed stringent economic and financial controls, including the power to fix prices, direct labour, plan capital investment, organize transport, and distribute food. Imperial preference was also introduced. But this great extension of the state was not continued after the war. The pressure for collectivism was successfully resisted and contained.

In part, this was because policy after 1918 was guided by the desire to return to the era of pre-war prosperity. In part, it was because the predominance of the Conservatives and the split in the opposition supplied no political instrument, short of working class revolution, that could change the prevailing politics of power. Once the war emergency was over, most Conservatives saw more dangers than advantages in a new interventionist state, since there was no guarantee that they would always be running it. The Coalition Government and the Conservative administrations that followed it made a dogged defence of all property interests, and at the same time tried to recreate the conditions that were believed to have underpinned the prosperity of British capitalism in its golden age. This meant financial orthodoxy, balanced budgets, a return to the Gold standard and free trade, and repeated attempts to revive Britain's export industries.

Retrenchment and the cutback in government expenditure started under the Coalition Government when it accepted the proposals of the Geddes committee. The 1922 budget reduced expenditure below £1000 million, and cut income tax. Further reductions were to follow. The cutbacks did not reduce the State sector to its pre-war size, but it gave evidence of government priorities in coping with unemployment. Intervention to raise demand was not among them. The level of state spending barely altered during the interwar years.

The most dramatic attempt to restore the pre-war politics of power came under the Conservative Government elected in 1924. The return to the gold standard which it announced in 1925 was intended to re-establish free trade and Britain's commercial and financial supremacy. It was a policy supported overwhelmingly by the Treasury and City opinion. Its consequences were to price many of Britain's exports out of world markets, and thus contributed to the continuing high level of unemployment in many of the traditional export industries in the late 1920s, and to the General Strike of 1926.[26]

The General Strike illustrates very well the priorities to which government was committed. Its immediate cause was the strike of the miners, who struck not for a wage increase, but to prevent their wages being reduced and their hours of work lengthened by the mineowners. The need for wage cuts was that coal was no longer competitive in overseas markets, following the return to the gold standard and the consequent over-valuing of sterling. So the mineowners looked to reductions in wages to restore their profits. The miners' union demanded a subsidy from the Government to the industry in order to keep wages and hours at their existing levels. The Government's attitude, however, and the nature of the state it administered, had already been expressed by Baldwin: 'All the workers of this country have got to take reductions to help put industry on its feet.' The Government agreed to a subsidy only for six months, during which it conscientiously prepared to meet and defeat a general strike. Its position was plain. There could be no extension of the state sector to finance unprofitable sectors of private industry. If the workers would not make industry profitable again by accepting wage cuts, they would have to endure unemployment. The response of the TUC was to threaten, and subsequently was forced by the Government to carry out, a massive sympathy strike in support of the miners. The Government treated this as an attempt by the union to dictate government policy, and to alter the assumptions on which the politics of power was based. They proclaimed the strike a challenge to the Constitution. The TUC persisted throughout the Strike in regarding it as another limited industrial dispute. When the union leaders realized that the Government was not prepared to bargain at all, and that therefore their only alternative was to overthrow it, they capitulated. The Government won a complete victory. The miners were eventually forced back to work on the owners' terms, and the 1927 Trade Disputes Act was passed into law. Sympathy strikes were made illegal, picketing restricted, and an attempt was made to curb the growth of the Labour party by sabotaging its finances.

The complete collapse of industrial militancy after 1926 soon found its political parallel in the debacle of 1931. The 1929 Labour Government, with no great popular support or industrial militancy behind it, never wavered in its acceptance of the prevailing politics of power. In the financial crisis of 1931 they succumbed to its dictates to the extent of recommending cuts in the dole and rigid financial orthodoxy in the face of the world slump.[27] Its measures were widely seen as the prelude to another great round of wage reductions. As in 1926, cuts in wages were regarded by industry, the City, and the Treasury as the only lasting solution to the crisis. That the leaders of the party of the Labour movement should have accepted so completely the most favoured capitalist solution to the crisis was a remarkable fulfilment of Baldwin's hopes that the Labour leaders could be educated in the realities of power and brought to accept the existing state. At the same time, Churchill's strategy was also to triumph. The Conservatives happily accepted office in a reconstructed administration under Ramsay Macdonald because it split the Labour party from its leaders, and destroyed it as a serious electoral competitor for a decade by encouraging a massive shift of Liberal voters into the Conservative camp.

On both the industrial and political fronts, the Labour movement was crushed and supine during the 1930s. This was the background against which the Conservatives rode out the Depression. Their policies were defensive, ad hoc responses to the crisis. Britain was at last taken off the gold standard, tariffs were imposed, rationalization on corporatist lines was encouraged in many industries.[28] But no radical departures in policy were made. The changes that were made to established policies were forced on Britain by the world slump. No political forces existed which could create a new course to solve the problems brought by the Depression. Radical measures, and politicians to carry them through, were not lacking. But they were isolated in the political market, because of the collapse of Labour and the Liberals. Besides, it was not capital that bore the ill-effects of the Depression. On the contrary, profits boomed during the slump.[29]

In Germany and the USA, revolutions in policy were accomplished. The New Deal and the Nazi programme both tried to remove the obstacles to faster capital accumulation that lay at the root of the Depression, and both did so by using government in a new way to restructure capital and provide new markets and new demand.[30] This was accompanied in Germany by ruthless measures to hold down wages in order to raise profits.[31] In Britain, the most that was achieved, by way of new policies, was the final victory of the tariff reformers. 1932 saw both an Imports Duties Bill, which imposed a 10 per cent tariff, and the Ottawa Conference, which increased preferences for British goods selling in Empire markets in return for free entry of Dominion products to the British market.[32] But this was a hollow triumph, for it was not achieved, as Joseph Chamberlain had intended, from a position of strength, and was meant only as a cushion against the world recession. In this it partially succeeded, but a programme to end unemployment by increasing government expenditure on public works, as advocated by Lloyd George and Oswald Mosley, was not adopted. Britain slumbered on.

Her long sleep was not to be broken until world war broke out again between the leading industrial nation-states. Like the First World War before it, such a struggle could not avoid being simultaneously a struggle between nations and a struggle for control of different parts of the world market. Among the reasons that drove Germany and Japan to war was their desire to break into the spheres of influence and colonial strongholds of their rivals. Eventually they were defeated. Britain shared in the victory, but she did not secure many of the fruits. The continuity of her institutions and traditions stayed unbroken, but her relative power in the world shrank. The real victors were the Americans and the Russians. The Russians gained Eastern Europe, whilst the Americans won potential mastery over the rest of the world, including the opportunity to break up the old colonial Empires like Britain's they disliked so much.

4 THE POLITICAL SETTLEMENT

If a man were asked to name the greatest single achievement of the British Labour party over the past twenty five years, he might well answer, the transformation of the British Conservative party. (John Strachey)[33]

The situation faced by the Conservatives as the 1945 election approached was not an easy one. The war had wrought many changes in the attitudes and expectations of the electorate; it had brought about the full employment that no government in the interwar years had achieved; and it had stimulated a sense of unity and common purpose by its demonstration of the collective power of the nation to achieve its ends through better organization of the state. Most political leaders came to accept that social reform and reorganization must take place when the war was over. Indeed an explicit condition for the wholehearted participation of the Labour movement in the war effort had been that this should be so.[34]

The party that benefited electorally from the war was Labour. Since the Conservatives had been almost continually in office from 1918 until 1940, they were inevitably identified with the bad times of appeasement and slump. There was little confidence that a Conservative government, if re-elected, would actually change anything. The chief asset of the party was Churchill, and it may be that if he had been standing in a presidential election in 1945, he would have been returned to power. As it was, his prestige and popularity were not enough to save the Conservatives. Churchill the party leader reawakened many memories, not least of his former career as hammer of the working class, supporter of Fascism in Italy and Spain, and implacable opponent of self-government for India.[35] In several respects, Churchill represented many of the features of pre-war Conservatism that were widely feared and distrusted in 1945.

It is a mistake, however, to imagine that the Conservative party at this time was preparing to restore the glad days of the Depression. The Conservatives' acceptance of what became the post-war settlement had already made great strides by 1945. Nowhere was this clearer than in the work of the Coalition Government, which had set up numerous committees to plan social and economic policy after the war. Most famous of these was the Beveridge Committee, appointed in 1941 to conduct a comprehensive survey of existing schemes of social insurance.[36] There was also the Fleming report on education, a committee investigating the coal industry, a Population Commission, and white papers on a National Health Service, full employment, industrial injuries, and family allowances. Many of these produced legislation in the last years of the war.

Churchill had wanted the Coalition to continue after the war was over, and carry through the whole of its projected social programme. This the Labour party would not agree to, and so forced an election in July 1945. With the exception of nationalization, the parties fought the election on virtually the same policies. The real division lay between the Conservatives' declared policies in 1945, and their actual policies in the interwar years. The essence of this change was the commitment

29

in 1945 to a permanent level of government spending and therefore of taxation that was much higher than before the war, and to government intervention in the economy to maintain full employment. This change was of course disguised because of the size of the state sector in the war economy. What the social programme of the Coalition Government proposed was to maintain the state sector at something like its war-time level, but to shift the bulk of spending from arms to welfare. There was to be no retrenchment.

Thus the war brought about in Britain what the Depression had not —the political will to transform the relationship between the state and the economy. There was a big extension of the state sector and collectivist controls on the economy during both wars, but it was only consolidated after 1945, not after 1918. In 1918 there had been a strong desire to recreate the conditions of pre-war prosperity. Few desired in 1945 to recreate the 1930s. Another reason was that a political instrument to establish the new state now existed in the form of the Labour party, able for the first time to form a majority government.

The new system that emerged in 1945 is often referred to as a quite new system, a mixed economy, a post-capitalist society that had finally overcome the blemishes of laissez-faire. But it is foolish to imagine that laissez-faire ever existed, or that there was ever a time when the state was somehow not involved in the economy. On the contrary, the relation of the state to the economy has always been of the utmost importance. Under capitalism, the function of the state has been to guarantee the best possible conditions for economic activity. In this sense the state has always exercised general control over industry as such; it is the form that has changed. This overall control is expressed through the central policies of the government, in particular those concerning the money supply and the exchange rate. The state has also of course always upheld the legal basis of capitalist property; it enforces the law of contract and defends the rights of property during strikes, lockouts, and picketing. Finally, the state has come to play a more active role in the economy, both by providing services to industry and by operating certain parts of industry directly. The form of state that exists, and the politics of power that maintains it, reflects the kind of economy that exists, and the key to the organization of the state is how it is financed.[37]

The post-war political settlement certainly involved a new relationship between the state and productive industry. But to judge the matter properly, it has to be remembered that the revolution that was effected was a modest one. The state certainly emerged after 1945 as the largest unit in the economy. But 80 per cent of productive capacity stayed under the control of private capital. The mixed economy remained a capitalist one. If it was to be healthy, then production and investment had to be made profitable. The basic laws upholding capitalist relationships of ownership and production were unchanged and continued to be enforced. What was changed by the post-war settlement were the general policies by which the state controlled the economy, and the overall size of the state sector.

The state sector was enlarged in three ways. Government spending was greatly increased, the number employed in the state sector rose, and the state took into public ownership all the natural monopolies in the economy that were still outside the public sector. The new, higher level of government spending (40 per cent of GNP, compared with 27·5 per cent in 1923, and 13·5 per cent in 1913),[38] was intended to be permanent and required a much higher level of taxation to finance it. This was especially necessary, since, far from falling, it was to rise to over 50 per cent of GNP by 1970. This was partly because the new spending was linked to the new policies with which the government sought to regulate the economy. The commitment to balanced budgets and financial orthodoxy was replaced by acceptance of the principle of budget deficits and the management of the overall level of demand by the government. The aim was to ensure that through the government's credit and spending policies full employment was maintained.

In part the new state was organized to overcome some of the weaknesses of the capitalist economy. In part, it was designed to increase political stability. What it also involved, however, was a big enlargement of the unproductive sector in the economy, and therefore a big increase in the burden that had to be carried by industry.[39] In one sense, therefore, the new state represented the cost of social peace, full employment of resources, and an expanding domestic market. The government now took over directly the responsibility for formulating the 'national interest' in economic matters, and undertook to promote by its policies not merely full employment, but stable prices, economic growth, and a trade surplus.

The ability of any government to deliver such goods, however, did not depend merely on some injection of Keynesian wizardry into economic management. It was also powerfully affected by Britain's place in the world market. No politics of power is carried on in a vacuum. It always operates within constraints laid down by the division of the world into nation-states that claim and enforce their sovereignty over particular territories. Contradictions naturally abound between the distribution of the world's territory, resources, and population between rival nation-states, and the driving force of capitalist production towards a market embracing the whole world, that promotes specialization on an international scale. This erodes the self-sufficiency of even the largest states, and weakens their ability to work out their own arrangements and destinies undisturbed.

Whether Britain would be applying Keynesian policies, therefore, in the midst of a renewed world slump or a boom, was a matter of crucial importance for their impact, but a matter outside the British government's control. By 1970, 29 per cent of Britain's GNP had to be exported to pay for the food and raw materials she needed for her industries and her population. Britain could not afford to opt out of the world market. All governments needed a strategy for trade and the balance of payments, just as they were soon to find they needed one for inflation. This need supplied the major external constraints to the policies any government could adopt. It was ironic that the state should have assumed powers to control the domestic economy at a time when Britain's new isolation and vulnerability in the world market left British governments with less freedom of manoeuvre than ever before.[40]

British wealth and industrial superiority in the past had been based upon her lead in productivity and her command of world markets. Britain's early industrial start had permitted far-reaching specialization, a high level of foreign investment and the acquisition of the largest world Empire. Her wealth and superiority were not, however, founded on the Empire or dependent on it. Rather the Empire had symbolized and consolidated the hold Britain's export industries and export of capital had already won over the world market.

The substance of the Empire in the 1930s, when it was used to cushion Britain against the full effects of the slump, was the Sterling Area, the colonies, and the preference system that linked the economies of the self-governing Dominions with Britain's. All these were still intact in 1945. The British economy was no longer able, however, to sustain Britain's old imperial role in the world market. This was partly due to the direct impact of the war. British investments abroad were depleted, sold off to pay for arms, whilst her industrial capital and inventories were run down. But it was also due to the belated recognition of the new economic might of America, the only country whose industrial plant had not been destroyed in the war, and which now pressed for freer trade and the break-up of the old colonial Empires. Free Trade had been a policy which naturally favoured the country whose industries achieved the highest productivity. This was no longer Britain.

Thus by 1945, Britain had lost the special advantages from her early industrialization, but still suffered from the consequences—in particular the need to import the greater part of her food and raw materials, and therefore the need to sell her manufactured goods on the world market.

It was clear that the world market after the war would be dominated by America. The new international monetary system established at the Bretton Woods conference was founded on the supremacy of the dollar. The abiding interest of the British national economy and the British state was for a secure place in the expanding sectors of the world market. One of the legacies of her past success, however, was institutions and policies that sought to conserve Britain's old place in the world market, built around the retention of the colonies as markets and sources of raw materials, a continuing export of capital, the preservation of sterling as an international currency. These involved safeguarding Britain's traditional investments and markets by a military presence abroad, and protecting the City by maintaining the exchange rate for the pound, despite the extra burdens on the balance of payments which overseas military spending and the export of capital imposed. A clear incompatibility was to develop between these policies and policies aimed at encouraging domestic investment and growth.[41]

5 THE RIGHT PROGRESSIVES

The conversion of the Conservative leadership to the need for a political settlement and a new politics of power when peace came proceeded fairly smoothly during the war. The party organization was quiescent, so there was little overt opposition from that quarter. A Post-War Problems Committee was established, chaired by R. A. Butler and David Maxwell-Fyfe. It spawned sixteen sub-committees and produced six reports. Meanwhile, the Coalition Government was preparing its plans for reconstruction.

These quiet deliberations by the party leaders did not satisfy a group of young Conservative MPs who, during 1943, rapidly coalesced into the Tory Reform Committee.[42] It grew to include forty-one MPs, among them Hugh Molson, Peter Thorneycroft, David Gammans, Quintin Hogg, and Lord Hinchingbrooke. From the formation of this committee may be dated the appearance of the Right Progressive tendency in the party—opinion pledged to support a new political settlement. The Tory Reform Committee was originally founded to urge the Government to take speedy action on the Beveridge Report, but it developed into an organized faction, trying to change Conservative thinking about government management of the economy and the desirable level of government expenditure and taxation after the war.

Whilst Butler's committees went about their work methodically and unobtrusively, the Tory Reform Committee under the flamboyant leadership of Hinchingbrooke launched a broadside against what they took to be the policies of the party in the past. They declared themselves violently opposed to the 'Whigs' and 'money barons' in the party, and called for a revival of Disraelian Toryism. In his pamphlet (*Full Speed Ahead—Essays in Tory Reform*) Hinchingbrooke argued that Baldwin's Conservative party had forsaken the strategy of One Nation. Revolutionary trade unionism in the 1920s had allowed the extreme right to seize the party and convert it into an instrument for defending financial and commercial interests. The subservience of the Tories to big business in the 1920s and 1930s had caused grave social divisions, and the party had to shake itself free:[43]

> I hope you are aware of the desire that exists in the Progressive Right to be rid of the incubus of finance and the control of big business, to make money the servant of enterprise, not its master, to rebuild our country after the war not with the thought of money gain but with the thought of social purpose.

Nor did he intend social purpose as an empty phrase. It meant specific commitments. The state had to retain a general measure of control over transport, aircraft, manufacturing, coal, milk, agriculture, banking, finance, and investment. Unbalanced budgets and a measure of state planning had to replace outworn economic theory and 'a return to the old ways of laissez-faire.'

Hinchingbrooke felt confident that such commitments would cement the new unity that the nation had discovered in the fight against Germany. 'The old tug of war between capital and labour,' he wrote[44] 'is ending in a happy draw.' The condition that old conflicts would not reopen lay in government readiness to plan the economy. Britain could only survive as a great power if full employment of her resources were maintained. Full employment required national unity and national unity required social reform. In Hinchingbrooke's eyes it was a simple equation.

Hinchingbrooke's vehemence may have been his own, but his views were shared by the members of the Tory Reform Committee. Quintin Hogg, their other main spokesman, spoke in similar terms. Hogg had returned from the army in 1942 with clear objectives—to instil a new spirit into the Conservative party, and to advocate a 'national policy', a guide to Britain's role in the post-war world. He too called for a return to One Nation politics and demanded[45] that the Tory party speak to the electorate 'in its true accents of progressive reform.' In a famous speech in the House of Commons, he declared that some Conservatives were inclined to overlook one or two 'ultimate facts' about social reform:[46] 'The first is that if you do not give the people social reform, they are going to give you social revolution.' Referring to Disraeli, he argued[47] that the 'wise man' who made maintenance of established institutions the first Conservative principle, had made the improvement of the condition of the people the third.

Like Hinchingbrooke, Hogg did not contemplate cautious, half-hearted measures of reform. He called for planning, an extension of public ownership, and a new consensus that would supplant the class war. The New Conservative, he argued, in a revealing passage in one of his pamphlets,[48]

> will not engage in the dispute between Nationalization and private enterprise. He sees in the modern extra political form of public control a Nationalization which has lost its terrors, and in the larger

joint stock companies with limited liability a private enterprise which has lost its meaning. He is not impressed by the fear of schemes for social security as destructive of enterprise. On the contrary, he sees in them the basis for social stability necessary to the restoration of industry. He recognizes that privilege based on birth or wealth has served its end, and he looks forward to a classless democracy in which differences of education and technical skill have taken their place.

The watchwords for the future, Hogg announced, had to be 'work for all' and 'social democracy'. Such improbable Tory slogans found a great deal of support not only in the Tory Reform Committee, but also in the pages of the party's monthly magazine, *Onlooker*. In August 1944, it carried a profile of Hogg and told its readers that, although Hogg had sometimes been accused of 'meeting Socialist policies half way', his attitude was in fact 'entirely in accord with the progressive Conservatism of today' as expounded by the reports of the Post War Problems Committee and other literature issued from the Conservative Central Office.[49] In a later issue, another young Tory, David Eccles, contributed an article on 'The ideas of Quintin Hogg'. We are waiting, said Eccles,[50] for someone to tell us 'how to reconcile the necessities of the two-party system . . . with the mechanics of planned unemployment and a just distribution of the resulting national income.' As far as Eccles was concerned evidently, Hogg's arrival meant the waiting was over.

During the last years of the war, *Onlooker* was filled with demands for social reform and progressive Toryism. Books by two older opponents of 'laissez-faire' policies and the whig tendency in the party, Leo Amery and Robert Boothby, received glowing reviews from Quintin Hogg and Hugh Molson. A typical article was that by Henry Brooke:[51] 'The Dragon of Unemployment—the Government's Historic plan for its destruction.'

The only sour note in this progressive beehive was provided by A. G. Erskine-Hill, MP, in a review of Hinchingbrooke's pamphlet, *Full Speed Ahead*. Under the title 'Full Speed to Where?' Erskine-Hill warned[52] that although the condition of the people must be 'elevated' after the war, nothing should be done which would be 'at the expense of the personality, dignity and character of the individual, however humble.' Significantly, he complained about the financial recklessness of Hinchingbrooke's proposals and his apparent taste for authoritarian power. His own view of the future was very different:[53]

I am confident that no matter what may happen in the short run after this war, the people of this country will be only too glad to find that there is still a party which has not lost its moorings by going full speed ahead on an uncharted course, and which continues to believe in the continuity and stability of customary life, so far as that will be possible in a world buffeted by post-war difficulties.

Erskine-Hill was not a lone voice. There was substantial opposition within the parliamentary party to the enlargement of the state sector and the new government policies envisaged by the plans of the Coalition Government. There was still more to the ideas of the Tory Reform Committee. The Progress Trust[54] was set up by Erskine-Hill and others specifically to oppose the influence of the Right Progressives. They attracted considerable support. The Signpost booklets, for example, a series on post-war problems, many of which were written by Conservative MPs, generally reflected the priorities of pre-war Conservatism and the old whig tendency in the party. Certainly the Tory Reform Committee failed to convert the bulk of the existing parliamentary party to their views before the election.

The parliamentary party, however, did not control policy. The party's election manifesto reflected the programme of the Coalition Government. Full employment had been achieved during the war and it was inconceivable that any post-war government would permit the slump to return, by refusing to use the new powers of the state. The Conservative party had indeed lost its moorings. There would be no return to 'customary life', even if the inspiration for the change hardly lay in 'alien Russia', as some thought.[55] Its real origin was more immediate—the opportunity for a far reaching political settlement between labour and property which the war had provided; a settlement which could ensure both political stability and business prosperity. This was the electoral perspective which the Right Progressives in the Tory Reform Committee had begun to forge. There had been fore-runners in the party during the 1930s—isolated reform groups such as the 'YMCA'[56] to which Macmillan and Boothby had belonged. It was only the war, however, with its tremendous social upheaval and its practical demonstration of the power of state planning and intervention that made a new political settlement and so a new politics of power both possible and necessary. Lord Woolton, shortly before his appointment in 1943 as Minister of Reconstruction, declared in a speech to the Constitutional Club that the war had shown the capacity of a united people to make itself the master of circumstance. Steps must now be taken, he urged, to ensure that the unemployment, poverty, and malnutrition of the inter-war years never returned:[57]

Is there any difficulty about us agreeing that this nation, recreated in war into one that is spirited and adventurous, will organize itself with equal adventure in the world of commerce to secure full employment; and that we will underwrite the risk for one another, so that there shall be some reasonable security that people shall work in worthy conditions?

Full employment and social security—these were what the new political settlement had to guarantee, and they pointed inexorably to a changed role for the state. On other questions, however, particularly Britain's future place in the world market, her relationship to the Empire, to America and to Europe after the war, little was said.[58]

Chapter 3
REORGANIZATION AND
RECOVERY: OPPOSITION 1945-51

My present feeling is not so much one of depression as of waking up
bewildered in a world completely strange to me. I feel that my entrails
have been pulled right out of me.

James Stuart, Conservative Chief Whip[1]

1 THE AFTERMATH OF THE 1945 ELECTION

The size of the 1945 defeat staggered Conservatives. Among their
leaders only Butler seems to have predicted it.[2] The London Press,
mesmerized by Churchill's personal ascendancy could not imagine that
the vast Conservative majority in the House of Commons could melt
away to nothing, still less that there would be a Labour landslide.[3]
The result was naturally compared with that other great rout of the
Conservatives, the 1906 Election, and although the margin was not so
great, 1945 was indeed to prove a major turning point in the British
political system. Labour won an outright majority for the first time,
and the achievement of the new political settlement foreshadowed in
the Coalition Government's plans and measures was assured.

This was in part, however, because the election result had as
important consequences for the Conservatives as it did for Labour. It
ensured the dominance of the Right Progressives in the party. Sixty per
cent of the pre-war Conservative MPs retired or lost their seats in 1945,[4]
and the size of the defeat gave the opportunity for a major reorganization of the party.

There were two main political options open to the Conservatives
after the election. Either they could accept in broad terms the political
settlement and the new politics of power that Labour was engineering,
or they could reject both and risk plunging the country into open class
war and constitutional crisis. There was overwhelming pressure in the
party for the first option. Electoral calculation, business interests,[5] and
political stability all demanded it. This was partly obscured by the
election campaign, because Churchill chose to emphasize not the
Conservatives' plans for reconstruction, but the Red Peril. His enthusiasm
for confrontation, which had been displayed throughout his career, did
not desert him in 1945. He therefore returned to the themes which he

knew so well, not least from his days as editor of the *British Gazette*.[6] Electors learnt to their astonishment that Churchill's colleagues in the Coalition Government were planning to establish a Gestapo in Britain after the election. Harold Laski, sinister chairman of the Labour party's national executive, was accused of biding his time, dreaming all the while of overthrowing Attlee as Lenin overthrew poor moderate Kerensky in 1917. Such extravagant claims, however, seem only to have revived old suspicions about Churchill's lack of judgment and remoteness from domestic political reality.[7] However much Churchill himself was already preparing for the cold war, a Red scare in 1945 was premature, so long as Russia remained a gallant ally, and such strong pressure for social reform existed.

The Conservative campaign caused general dismay in the ranks of the Right Progressives. Butler lamented in his Memoirs that the work of the Post-war Problems Committee played little part in the Conservatives efforts. The small gap between the parties' official policies was thereby obscured. Both promised Food, Work, Homes and Welfare, including a reformed educational system, a National Health Service and the implementation of the Beveridge proposals on national insurance.[8] The main difference between them was over nationalization. At this stage, the Conservatives were prepared to admit the need for reorganization and greater state control of some industries, but no more. They put greater emphasis on the ability of private enterprise to provide full employment after the war, whilst Labour was committed to state planning through public ownership. But this was still a side issue in 1945. It concerned the implementation of the post-war settlement—the best way of achieving its goals—rather than its substance—maintaining the extension of the state sector.

After the defeat, many scapegoats were found. The Conservatives, it was said, had patriotically allowed their organization to run down during the war, whilst the Socialists had kept and even extended theirs. It was claimed that all the army education posts had been filled by Leftists, who had poured out red propaganda to the forces. Churchill's charisma was allegedly weaker among the troops than among the home population. Their demands for a new and better life after the war were the strongest and most deeply felt. Both Macmillan and Butler later recognized how powerful had been the appeal of socialism in 1945. It had provided a doctrine and a vision to which the Conservatives had no 'authoritative answer or articulated alternative.'[9] Macmillan believed[10] that the electorate had been persuaded in the last years of the war that an 'automatic utopia' awaited once the struggle was over. A Socialist state would bring about 'unexampled prosperity in a world of universal peace.' Yet, at the same time, neither were unduly despondent. If the party could be rebuilt and the Right Progressives established more firmly in control, then the Conservatives could confidently await the turn of events. Butler resolved that the party should not go into another election with the propaganda victoryalready lost,[11] whilst Macmillan was afterwards to reflect:[12]

> The immediate post-war years were bound to be a period of serious economic and financial difficulty at home and of grave problems abroad. In both spheres it may well be that by a sound instinct the British people felt that it would be wiser for a Government of the Left to be in control.

Perhaps he recalled the brief period after 1918, when the Coalition Government, headed by Lloyd George, was menaced by militant sections of the working class.[13] In any case, he correctly saw the political problem in 1945 to be harnessing the revolutionary mood and reaching a settlement with the Labour movement. At the same time it was necessary to drive further the wedge between Socialism and Communism. A Labour Government, led by such men as Attlee, Bevin, and Morrison, would help achieve these aims. Then the Conservatives could resume their rightful place. There were indeed some changes introduced by Labour, thought Macmillan,[14] that were valuable and could not be reversed. But at the same time, the electors were to have many 'salutary lessons' from the experience of a Labour government, and would soon be ready for a 'more pragmatic and less doctrinaire approach to the nation's difficulties.' A very similar conclusion was reached by Alec Douglas-Home, at that time isolated within the party because of his association with the Munich policy. In a letter to J. C. Masterman he wrote:[15]

> If the Socialists had to come to power there is much to be said for the present. If they had lost they would have been sullen, resentful, and out to queer the pitch of the Conservatives in foreign and domestic affairs. There might well have been a degree of violence which would have been very bad for us all.

2 REORGANIZATION

The 1945 defeat precipitated a major reorganization of the party. Its effect was to consolidate the grip of the Right Progressives. Butler, one of the chief architects of the reorganization, has described how[16] 'the overwhelming electoral defeat of 1945 shook the Conservative Party out of its lethargy and impelled it to rethink its philosophy and reform its ranks with a thoroughness unmatched for a century.' The philosophy had in fact already been rethought before the 1945 election by the Tory Reform Committee and its allies in the leadership. What was now required was the consolidation of that section's grip on the party machine. This is how the main changes in the organization of the party should be seen. They were more important for extending the control of the Right Progressives than for increasing directly the electoral effectiveness of the party.[17]

The main changes were as follows:

1   The establishment of a new Conservative youth movement, the Young Conservatives, in place of the Junior Imperial League. The Chairman of the Young Conservatives was to be one of four vice chairmen of the NAC of the National Union.[18]

2   The overhaul of Central Office. A greatly expanded role for the Conservative Research Department (CRD). The setting up of the Conservative Political Centre (CPC) to organize political education.

3   The Maxwell Fyfe committee.[19] Its most important recommendation was the abolition of the candidate's contribution to his election expenses. This greatly reduced the purchase of constituencies by gentlemen and others, and increased the scope for professional career politicians.

4   Woolton's appointment as Chairman. Woolton introduced several changes that became permanent features of the party's organization. Most important were the efforts made to recruit far more individual Conservative members (Operation Doorknocker), and the appeal for funds on a greater scale than ever before. The two were naturally interrelated. Woolton correctly saw that to maintain a professional central and local party organization that could compete successfully in a two party system, a secure financial base was essential.[20]

The result of these changes was that for really the first time the Conservative Party created an adequate professional bureaucracy to service its mass organization. It also greatly extended the scope of its organization in the country and improved its network of communication. Information flowed more freely in both directions. The Conservative electoral machine was now in certain respects independent of the party in parliament. The reorganization of the party after 1945 was thus a further stage in the recognition by the Conservatives of the institutional separation of the politics of power from the politics of support required by the political market.

A familiar feature of the spread of bureaucracy is that an activity previously regarded as a whole is split into several parts, which then become provinces for experts. The main immediate result of extending bureaucracy in the Conservative party was the recruitment of professionals to staff the new organs of Central Office. Central Office now offered the best way to start a political career in the Conservative party for men without connections, and several of the men Butler recruited for Central Office after 1945 did indeed go on to become leaders of the party. They included Macleod, Heath, Powell, and Maudling. A professional career structure began to be established.

3 THE NEW ELECTORAL PERSPECTIVE

The basic assumption that lay behind the reorganization of the party and the new approach to the electorate was that elections were won or lost before the actual election campaign commenced. This meant that not only had the Conservatives to strengthen and extend their organization of the electorate. They had also to win the propaganda war. Butler therefore resolved that the dissemination of Conservative ideas and policies should receive much greater direction from Central Office.[21]

The new propaganda had two aims. One was to further consolidate the grip of the Right Progressives on the party—the other was to provide the party with an image and a policy that would wrest the political initiative from Labour. These two aims were not always compatible, and after 1947 there was increasing emphasis on the tactical requirements of fighting Labour, rather than on the refinements of progressive Toryism, but by that time the Right Progressives were firmly entrenched in the leadership of the party. The symbolic seal of their victory was the 1947 Conference when the Industrial Charter was approved by a great majority, only three voting against it. As Macmillan wrote in the November issue of *Tory Challenge*:[22] 'Between the two wars there was always a progressive element in the party; but it never dominated the party. Now it has seized the control, not by force or palace revolution, but by the vigour of its intellectual and spiritual power.' The party, he said, had overcome its defeatist mood. It was back in the tradition of Disraeli, Randolph Churchill, and Joseph Chamberlain.

1832 afforded another historical parallel for the party leaders seeking to rally their supporters. After the crushing Whig victory and the enactment of the Reform Bill, and despite general belief that the Tories were at last buried, the party had rallied under Peel and adjusted to the new political situation that they faced. Peel's Tamworth Manifesto of 1834 was the public expression of the Tories' acceptance of 1832, and there was strong pressure from Conservatives after 1945 for a similar statement to signify the party's changed course. Quintin Hogg called specifically for a new Tamworth Manifesto:[23] 'As in the days of Peel, the Conservatives must be seen to have accommodated themselves to a social revolution.'

Another prominent Conservative, W. W. Astor, writing in *New English Review*,[24] argued that the party could not begin to win back support in the electorate until the leaders produced clear and authoritative statements of party policy. He agreed with an American assessment that the party would disintegrate unless it found a new leadership and philosophy to counter its great defeat.

That leadership and philosophy were to be provided by Butler,

Macmillan and the other leaders of the Right Progressives. Butler became one of the chief ideologues of the right progressive tendency. In a famous statement he summed up the changed political situation and the substance of the postwar political settlement:[25]

> It is the task of the present generation of Conservatives to found our modern faith on the basis of two features of this age, namely the existence of universal adult suffrage and the acceptance by authority of the responsibility for ensuring a certain standard of living, of employment and of security for all.

Throughout these years of opposition Butler hammered away at these themes. His speech to the first postwar Conference on political education in March 1946 was typical. In it he made five main points:[26] (1) the Conservatives had lost the election because they had no positive alternative to socialism to put before the electorate; (2) such an alternative had to recognize that circumstances were changing, so that it was no longer possible to 'sit in entrenched positions or rely on holding old-fashioned fortresses'; (3) there was a need for a total reorganization of the social structure on which the Conservative party rested; (4) redistributive taxation had to be accepted to reduce the extremes of poverty and wealth; and (5) laissez-faire economics had to be repudiated in favour of a system in which the state acted as 'a trustee for the interests of the community and a balancing force between different interests.'

The fruits of Butler's efforts and the work of the new party professionals were most visible in the series of Charters that the Tories sprang upon the world while they were in opposition.[27] The Industrial Charter was undoubtedly the most important of these. Under all the platitudes about creating a new understanding between employers and workers lay the commitment to the new level of state spending. Nigel Harris has pointed out that the Industrial Charter represented the high water mark of 'etatiste' corporatist thinking in the party, and was largely ignored as a guide to policy when 'neo-Liberalism' swept through the party after 1947.[28] This is no doubt true. But what Harris ignores is the political significance of the Charter. It reflected the new dominance of the right progressive tendency, of those forces in the party who welcomed the extension of the state sector on political and economic grounds. 'Neo-Liberalism' did not erode this, it merely changed the emphasis of the Tories' electoral offensive, and it gained a hold on the party not merely through the revival of confidence in prosperity, but also because of the electoral requirements of fighting Labour.

So there is no need to question Butler's judgment on the Industrial Charter. He argued[29] that it succeeded just as Peel succeeded in adapting the thought of the Tories of his day to the post-Reform Bill era. It showed the Conservatives had come to terms with the 'present day problems of an island economy,' or, in other words, with the political settlement and the new politics of power. The party was seen to be changing course, and to be recapturing the national image so essential to its electoral fortunes, and so badly dented by the image of the 1930s successfully pinned on it by Labour in 1945. As Charles Hill has written:[30]

> The health and strength of Conservatism depend on its capacity to attract and to hold the reluctant vote and the reluctant candidate . . . it was between 1945 and 1950 that the Conservatives first gave convincing evidence that they were a national party.

This 'convincing evidence' was the party's official acceptance of the political settlement, and it brought into their ranks important recruits like Hill, Woolton, and Monckton.

Signs that the Industrial Charter was more a political document than a bromide which stifled controversy in the party comes from the sharp attacks that were made upon it by remnants of the old Whig tendency in the party. The Beaverbrook press solemnly warned the Tory Party that if the Left failed, then the electorate would turn Right but never half Right. This was a common criticism, expressed most forcibly by Sir Waldron Smithers, who called the Charter, 'milk and water' Socialism. Tribune confidently predicted big splits within the party.

Such attacks were inevitable, given the conflicting aims of the Charter. According to Butler it was intended firstly to counter the idea that the Conservatives were the party of laissez-faire, and so would not maintain either full employment or the Welfare State; secondly to provide a recognizable alternative to the reigning orthodoxies of socialism; and thirdly to make a new approach to the adjustment of human relations within industry.[31] The first two aims were clearly in conflict. But the opposition to the Charter had no alternative electoral perspective to suggest to the leadership, and contented itself by grumbling about the changes within the party. One article in Truth, for instance entitled 'Conservatism's Opportunity' complained in October 1948:[32] 'The nation cries aloud for leadership, and all that the Conservative Party can offer it is a series of "charters" drawn up by "political experts".' Next year in January, 'Truthful Tory' claimed there were deep divisions in the Tory party, and asked despairingly:[33]

> Does official Conservatism wish to conserve the great tradition that the individual citizen and his family are the sound unit of society, or does it wish to agree that the State is the sole unit to which the citizen and his family must be serflike in their subservience? Does Toryism teach that it is right and just that a man or woman should have special rewards for special services, or does it believe in a sentimental egalitarianism whatever its effect on productivity and the human character?

Alas for Truthful Tory, the gap between what Toryism taught and what Tory leaders now felt it necessary to do was not to be closed. The editors of *Truth* had no difficulty in uncovering the source of the cancer. They denounced the party's new obsession with planning as Fabian, and lambasted the party's policy document *The Right Road for Britain*, which was intended to form the basis for the Conservative election campaign. There was no striving for the middle ground here:[34]

> The truth of the matter is that it is cowardly, because only by title
> and in occasional moments of remembrance is it Conservative. It is
> not Mr Churchill's blinding vision of a renaissance of Toryism; it
> is merely what the Butler saw. It offers in short the planning of Mr
> 'Rab' Butler and his friends in place of the planning of our present
> collectivist governors.

The essence of this planning as far as *Truth* was concerned was the existence of an enlarged state sector. *The Right Road for Britain,* it complained, promised no reduction of government expenditure. Indeed new 'channels' were to be added.

But the Right Progressives were unmoved. The opposition to the charters was labelled the Liberal and Whig element in the party, foreign bodies that should be expelled so as to allow Toryism to re-emerge. Macmillan in particular enjoyed this. He told a meeting at Westminster:[35]

> All the forces of reaction in the country, the *Daily Herald,* Lord
> Beaverbrook, Sir Waldron Smithers, and Co., are united in saying
> that this Industrial Charter is not Tory policy. What they really
> mean, all of them, is that they wish it were not Tory policy.
> Fortunately, their wishes cannot be granted. In any case, important
> as our critics may be, I prefer to rest upon the tradition of Disraeli,
> fortified by the high authority of Churchill.

Like Butler, Macmillan was quite clear about the importance of the Industrial Charter as a political document. In his Memoirs,[36] he wrote that it proved the party's determination to maintain full employment, to improve the social services, and to keep overall control of the economy in the hands of the government.

The 'Whigs' were isolated in the party at this time, because the Right Progressives managed to pin the label of laissez-faire on them. Laissez-faire was synonymous with slump, depression, unemployment, dole queues, malnutrition. Although the Tories spent considerable energy combating Socialist 'lies' about the 1930s and the Conservative interwar record, the 'myth' of the 1930s played an important role in the struggle to influence opinion within the party. With such associations hardly anyone could be found to defend laissez-faire. Even *Truth* disowned it.[37]

45

The idea that the Conservative party should be born again and return to its 'authentic' tradition was not confined to Right Progressives. This was shared by a staunch anti-progressive like Aubrey Jones. The cast of Jones' thought at this time was profoundly pessimistic and religious. The rise of socialism and the cult of progressivism he regarded as a rupture in Nature. A belief in progress, he wrote,[38] makes a man either a Liberal or a Communist. The true Conservative, on the other hand, sees man trudging 'round and round very much on the same spot.' The abiding problem of politics for the Conservative is the suppression of evil, which can only be achieved, thought Jones, by conserving the essential meaning of the institutions whose function is to suppress evil. He attacked the progressive label of modern Conservatism. There was something seriously wrong with the party and with the country, he thought, because it had ceased to respect the word, diehard. He warned that there were two sides to Conservatism, Reform and Tory:[39] 'without Toryism Conservatism becomes a mere hanger-on to "progressivism", applauding tendencies which are pernicious, but which it feels it can condone because they are gradual and imperceptible.' An uncorrupted Conservatism, he believed,[40] would not seek power by 'extending to an eager electorate promise after promise of bigger state benefits.'

But this kind of analysis of Conservatism did not lead Jones to advocate a return to laissez-faire and customary life. On the contrary, he outdid the Right Progressives themselves in his condemnation of Liberal capitalism and the Conservative record in the 1930s.

He believed[41] that England was undergoing a great crisis and declining as a world power. But for him the causes did not lie in material factors and the effects of two wars. On the contrary, it was a spiritual crisis within Britain's own mind and arising from her own thought. It was a crisis brought about by one hundred and fifty years of Liberalism, which had inexorably destroyed all the institutions and principles for which Conservatism stood, by its emphasis on extreme individualism, until finally it had begun to destroy itself and had prepared the way for collectivism:[42]

> Liberalism contained within itself the seed of its own destruction. It rested everything on the individual, turned everything on individual wealth and individual achievement. And at the same time, it corroded the old corporate loyalties, opposed servant to master, class to class, scattered self-assertion, suspicion, mistrust, stored for the future perpetual rebellion and perpetual instability, and so made it inevitable that one day individual property would itself be attacked. That day has now come.

With his outlook Jones could hardly be expected to recognize that the association between capitalism and Liberalism was not accidental, or that the consequent erosion of traditional institutions and authority he so much lamented could not be halted by a revival of Conservative thought. What was practically important, however, was that his analysis of the political situation after 1945 made him a political ally of the Right Progressives in their bid to oust the 'liberal' invader from the party ranks. He was against negative opposition or opposition that merely defended the status quo, or alternatively tried to outbid the Government in material pledges, such as for instance, the Conservative call for an easing of austerity. He was convinced[43] that while the Conservative party might regain office because the electorate turned to them as a 'refuge from maladministration', if it were to reassert an 'enduring sway' it must 'strike deeper roots.' It must defeat the opposition by the power and moral strength of its thought. Jones therefore was a strong supporter of the Industrial Charter, because it aimed to close the gulf between 'masters and men' and to reconcile state guidance with individual initiative.

When the smoke clears, therefore, Jones stands out as a supporter of the New Conservatism, ready to accept the political settlement in the interests of political stability. This was expressed in terms of ideological opposition to Liberalism and laissez-faire capitalism, which he considered[44] had gone too far in 'repelling the state.' The government had been kept from supervising the economy. The doctrine of free trade had led to the 'exaltation of the economic, the belittlement of the nation . . . a sterile materialism, and an abstract cosmopolitanism.'

Aubrey Jones was rare among Conservatives because he based his acceptance of the New Conservatism on an ideological analysis of the party's policies in the past. The enthusiasm for intervention and planning of many other Conservatives vanished overnight when the capitalist economy began to grow again. Aubrey Jones, however, continued to support the extension of the state sector in the hope that it would lead to a regulated, stabilized capitalism, in which the class conflicts of Liberal capitalism would be shut out, and the institutions essential to social order and moral health protected from the corrosive influence of unchecked individualism.[45] He failed to see that the modern state itself was an instrument and an expression of that very rationalization he disliked so much. His writings in this period belong to that tradition in British Conservatism which seeks to base the party's electoral strategy on moral authority, and spurns electoral opportunism. This is at the root of Jones's attacks on facile progressive thinking, and it is a critique that reappeared among some Conservatives in the 1960s.

Who could be found to defend laissez-faire? Apart from the *Daily Express* and Sir Waldron Smithers, there were few indeed within the party who were ready to reject planning, welfare and the post-war world. This was no doubt partly because laissez-faire was a fiction and had certainly never existed in any real sense between the two wars.

47

Slump and unemployment there had been, however, and it was the apparent connection between full employment and government spending, now sanctified by Keynesian economic theory, that made the postwar settlement so hard to contest politically. There was a certain inevitability about the triumph of 'progressive' ideas. As Henry Fairlie wrote later[46] of Butler's success in persuading the Conservative party to accept the Welfare State, 'this has never seemed to me a much more impressive achievement than persuading Harriet Martineau to accept the universe.'

Root and branch opposition to the New Conservatism, therefore, was confined mainly to a few intellectuals amongst leading Conservatives. The two most important critics in this respect were Michael Oakeshott and Richard Law. Oakeshott's views may best be studied in a review he wrote of Quintin Hogg's book *The Case for Conservatism*. His main disagreement with Hogg lay in the attitude to central planning which he described[47] as 'the product of an academic ignorance of how the business world works, and a common ignorance of how society lives which have been growing on us for many years.' He contested Hogg's belief that a laissez-faire economy had ever existed, because if it had, then there could be no objection to central planning. What had existed, he claimed, was the rule of laws that had laid down duties as well as rights to be the framework for economic life. Conservatism, he warned, had resisted the pressure for a centrally planned society, but not with absolute conviction: 'If there ever comes a time when two parties compete for power on the basis of rival plans, an even larger lunacy than that from which we at present suffer will have established itself.' Oakeshott detected in Hogg just such a lunacy, because Hogg held a Liberal view of political obligation. Instead of regarding the collection of duties and rights enshrined in the common law as 'the very structure of our freedom', Hogg chose to regard all the social laws and conventions as limitations on the absolute freedom of the individual. Any law, and therefore any change in the law, were equally interfering with individual freedom. Oakeshott argued that such a notion prevented Hogg from seeing any difference between the kind of limitation and interference arising from laws that had grown out of social tradition and living communities, and the limitation and interference perpetrated by the central planning of the state:[48] 'The step from these ideas of limitation and interference to the idea of adjustment by means of overhead planning, with physical controls, is as short as it is disastrous.' Hogg's approval of social adjustment by means of 'the rearrangement of incentives in industry' confirmed Oakeshott's fears: 'The bug of rationalistic politics has bitten the Conservative.'

Oakeshott pleaded for a politics of power that confined itself at home to breaking up concentrations of power and reforming 'current mischiefs and maladjustments' according to recognized legal procedures.

Such an account of the business and aims of the politician was no doubt a more accurate rendering of the Tory tradition than that of the Right Progressives. But it carried no political weight. Rationalistic politics, the natural companion of the enlarged state sector, was seeping through the party. By accepting the new state, Conservatives were obliged more and more to turn away from social tradition towards social engineering.

Richard Law took up very different ground. His religious pessimism was even more extreme than Aubrey Jones's. He announced that his generation was witnessing something more terrible than the mere collapse of a civilization:[49] 'It is the collapse of all absolute moral values, the end of man as a moral being.' The New World was marked first of all by the changed status of Britain within it: Britain had fallen from the summit of power and influence into a 'trough of impotence', from which there might be no recovery. Labour's victory in 1945 was both the symbol and the instrument of this ruin.

Law explained Labour's success by the moral and intellectual climate in 1945. This had nourished the false belief that all the difficulties and setbacks which Britain suffered between the wars, and finally even the war itself, had been caused not by forces outside Britain's control, but by the self-interest of the ruling class in Britain and the anarchy of a competitive economic system. So widespread had this view become, among politicians of all parties, that it encouraged grave delusions. It was believed that[50] some 'wizardry of governmental organization' could sweep away all Britain's problems, and the operation of the 'normal laws' of economics could be suspended provided only 'a sufficiently determined attack' were made upon them.

The weakness of Law's case politically was the evident success that tampering with the workings of natural economic laws brought. No-one in politics, so soon after the war and the memory of the slump, was in favour of unemployment. No-one believed that a return to 'laissez-faire' would not bring just that. To the electoral arguments were added the economic arguments. Productive industry, fearful though it might be of further nationalization, had no interest in seeing the state contract to its pre-war size, still less to its size in the nineteenth century.[51]

At one point, Law carried his views into the letter columns of *The Times*, and denounced the direction of Conservative policy. He was answered by Boothby.[52]

T. E. Utley, who became one of the most prominent Conservative journalists in the post-war years, reflected on the debate in the *Spectator*. It was clear, he said, that in future the Conservative party would have to operate within a new social and economic framework. But it was also clear, he noted, that many Conservatives in the old whig tendency in the party still believed, like Law, that socialism would fail because of its disregard for natural economic laws, that reaction would come, and that the Conservatives would be swept back to power, to overturn the post-war settlement and restore the old politics of power. Utley, how-ever, held out little hope for them or for the survival of the whig tendency:[53]

> The present, or some future, Socialist Government may fail, but the Socialist economic system which it has created will remain, and the public will demand not a government of Liberal revolutionaries to restore the economic system of the nineteenth century, but a competent technocracy to apply the ultra revolutionary and coercive measures necessary to rescue a Socialist economy from disaster.

What these ultra revolutionary measures might be Utley did not specify, but certainly the spokesmen for the Right Progressives felt themselves more than able to supply a 'competent technocracy'. They emphasized the 'empirical' approach of Conservatism as opposed to the dogmatism of their opponents. The Conservative party existed to steer a middle way between extremes and maintain political stability by controlling the impact of change.

The notion of a 'Middle Way' supplied an interpretation of the Conservative party's place in British history that appealed most strongly to many of their leaders, for it permitted great flexibility in dealing with changing circumstances. It emphasized the essential solidarity of the nation and the widespread consciousness of national unity. The Con-servatives were the party that stood out against extremes, and protected the nation against the attacks of sectional interests. It was a mould into which many electoral perspectives and ideologies could be poured. It appeared in classical form in the writings of Professor Hearnshaw. Any theory of national unity and consensus had to account for the many examples of the opposite. Hearnshaw had no doubts:[54]

> Of course unhappily, from time to time, some sections of the English people become disgruntled by adversity, or poisoned by the virus of alien dogma. These misguided sections under the impulse of misery or of madness, turn against their mother-country and try to injure or destroy her. They divide the nation in hopeless schism; they attack their fellows with merciless ferocity; they temporarily break the unity of the people, threaten the continuity of the constitution, and menace the very life of society. Such were the fanatics of the Puritan Reformation; such were levellers of the Stuart rebellion; such were equalitarian demagogues of the eighteenth century period of revolution; such are the Marxian socialists and Communists. It has been, and is, the special task of English Conservatism to maintain the organic unity of the nation and the living continuity of its institutions, together with the kindly and genial English spirit, as against all the destroyers.

Such a politics of confrontation was not what the leaders of the

Right Progressives needed after the war. Instead they had to show how the Conservative party could be a party which accepted the post-war settlement, yet remain distinct from Labour in its aims and principles. The Middle Way[55] became an important part of the new electoral perspective. Conservatives, it was held, had always been concerned to defend national unity and national interests. The French Revolution had spawned Jacobinism, a moving spirit of disorder and destruction, forever taking on new shapes and disguises. In England it had breathed life into two political movements—Liberalism and Socialism. (It was no accident that these were also the creeds of the two political parties that have been the main electoral opponents of the Conservatives in the political market). They were essentially alike, although superficially they appeared as opposites—Liberalism stressed the importance of the individual, whilst Labour emphasized collective action. Their similarity lay in their 'Jacobin' approach to politics. They tried to achieve a complete realization of their 'idea', and to succeed in this they were unable and generally unwilling to follow policies that took account of all interests and classes in the nation. So always they pursued policies that were unjust to some.

In less mystifying terms, such parties always threatened to upset the existing balance of power between classes and between interests within classes. This could destroy the organic unity of the nation and more concretely it could undermine the prevailing politics of power. In contrast, the Conservatives proclaimed One Nation. They strongly believed, according to John Boyd-Carpenter,[56] that 'it is not possible in the long run for one section of the community to be benefited at the expense of another.' Armed with a truly 'national' policy, one that advanced the interests of all sections of the community, Conservatives had steered a middle way between the Liberals and the Socialists, performing, in Quintin Hogg's words,[57] 'a timeless function in the development of a free society.' This was to prevent new ideas 'held in the passion of the moment' from causing irretrievable error, by shaping them in accordance with the country's institutions and traditions, accepting what was good, and discarding what was bad.

Stripped of its rather exotic ideological trappings, the meaning of the notion in the post-war context was clear enough.

The middle way was a middle way between the laissez-faire of nineteenth-century Liberalism and the collectivism of twentieth-century Socialism. Parties were defined by their attitude to the role of the state in the economy. Macmillan had expressed such ideas in his writings during the 1930s. Later he wrote[58] that his aim had been to devise

> some coherent system, lying in between unadulterated private
> enterprise and collectivism. It was a policy which I afterwards called
> 'the Middle Way'; an industrial structure with the broad strategic

control in the hands of the state and the tactical operation in the hands of private management, with public and private ownership operating side by side.

By arguing that the Conservatives had opposed 'laissez-faire' capitalism, the child of the Liberal party, The Right Progressives hoped to show their own supporters that Conservative acquiescence in the post-war settlement was principled as well as opportunist. Against the Liberals, so their argument ran, the Tories had been compelled to oppose the state to the community, to pass factory acts, legalize trade unions, and propose social legislation to counter unbridled capitalism. Now, against the socialists, they were forced to oppose the community to the state, to stop the reaction to Liberalism swinging over to wholesale collectivism, with the loss of individual freedom which that entailed.

In certain respects, the Middle Way interpretation of Conservatism assigned the party a very passive role, always reacting to the excesses of its opponents, and trying to moderate them in the national interest, rather than steering new courses. It did, however, place an enormous value on ideological flexibility, and on an empirical, undogmatic approach to political problems. That meant accepting existing priorities. As such it was a valuable aid in assisting the accommodation of the party to new circumstances, and above all to the new politics of power. It also provided a platform from which the leadership could stifle the remnants of the old whig tendency in the party.

4 THE ELECTORAL STRUGGLE

Side by side with the organization of the New Conservatism, the party was engaged in the party political struggle with Labour. Electoral considerations helped to weaken the opposition to the post-war political settlement and to strengthen the determination of the Right Progressives to win the party over to its acceptance, but it was necessary too for the party to reassure its active and its traditional supporters. As the Labour Government encountered serious economic difficulties, so the confidence of the Opposition increased. They began to emphasize the bankruptcy of Socialism more than the virtues of the New Conservatism.[59]

The extent of political uncertainty in a mass democracy is always very great, so it is not very surprising to find politicians of all parties projecting their own prejudices and fantasies onto the electorate. Such opinions as politicians express about the state of feeling in the country are generally more revealing about politicians than about the electors. In a political system where passivity rather than participation is the normal condition of the electors, talk about the views of the electorate is usually inappropriate. The electorate as an entity with a mind of its own does not exist, yet so often is it made the subject of the political process by politicans and political observers that they end up believing their own fictions. We learn that the electorate experienced this, was persuaded of that, and decided to eject this or that government from office.

Conservatives, for example, frequently overestimated the swing back towards them in the last years of the Labour Government. The idea grew in Conservative mythology that most people who had voted Labour in 1945 voted not for 'socialistic doctrinal measures', but to get things done. In this sense, wrote David Maxwell-Fyfe,[60]

> there was a fatal lack of understanding between the Labour voters of 1945 and the men they elected to office. . . . It was essentially this feeling that they had been betrayed which caused such a profound and permanent effect upon the people who swept Labour into office in 1945.

Yet he admitted that it took the Conservatives not five or six years to win a clear majority of the seats in Parliament, but ten years.[61]

In his memoirs, Butler too, remarked how, despite all its setbacks, the Labour Government remained popular; it lost not a single by-election, and two General Elections were required to oust it from power. Butler explained this by pointing to the cohesion of the Labour Ministers and the predicament of the Conservative party:[62]

> our need to convince a broad spectrum of the electorate, whose minds were scarred by inter-war memories and myths, that we had an alternative policy to Socialism which was viable, efficient and humane, which would release and reward enterprise and initiative but without abandoning social justice or reverting to mass unemployment.

In the end, however, the Conservatives won the election more because of the loss of direction and disintegration of the Labour Government and the weakness of the Liberals in 1951, than to any great inroads they made into the Labour vote. The Labour share of the poll was 47·8 per cent in 1945, and it declined only to 46·1 per cent in 1950. The Conservative share rose from 39·8 per cent in 1945 to 43·5 per cent. In both elections the Liberal vote stayed steady at around 9 per cent. The Labour lead of 2·6 per cent in 1950, however, meant a majority of only five seats, whilst a lead of 8 per cent in 1945 had given them a majority of 146. Such were the realities of landslides and come-backs. In 1951, the Liberals could afford to put up only 109 candidates, compared with 405 candidates in 1950. Their percentage share of the vote dropped accordingly from 9·1 per cent in 1950 to 2·5 per cent in 1951, and their total votes from 2,621,548 to 730,556. This was the decisive factor in the Conservatives' success. Their share of the poll rose 4·5 per cent in 1951 to 48 per cent and they received 13,717,538 votes. What was still more remarkable, however, was that Labour did even better, polling 48·8 per cent and 13,948,605 votes, the party's highest total ever.[63] Owing to the bias of the British electoral system, the Conservatives were returned with a majority of 18 seats.

This was no triumphant vindication of the New Conservatism, nor was it very plausibly a massive repudiation of Labour and Labour's programme.[64] It seems certain that had the Labour Government managed to survive until the effects of Korea and post-war austerity had been swallowed up by the world boom of the 1950s, it would not have lost the election.[65]

So the real achievement of the Conservatives in opposition was not that they caused a massive defection from Labour, but that they rebuilt their party after the defeat of 1945 until it was an effective electoral organization again by 1950, able to challenge Labour as the alternative government. The New Conservatism played its part in this, but of great importance also was the ideological war against Labour. This rallied Conservative supporters, dispelled defeatism, and ultimately restored the political initiative to the Tories when Labour went back on the defensive.[66]

In their ideological offensive, the Conservatives had to mark out the dividing line between themselves and the Socialists without rejecting those parts of the postwar settlement that were endorsed by the New Conservatism. In foreign policy Bevin's cold war strategy left the Conservative leaders little to disagree with,[67] although they continued to cast doubts on Labour's competence to handle defence and security. The real battle, therefore, came over home affairs, and nationalization was made the central issue in dispute. All the evil tendencies of Socialism were symbolized for the Conservatives by nationalization, although in practice they had little objection to the early measures of public ownership.[68]

Nationalization was brought to the fore in all the attacks on Socialism. Conservative leaders stressed that it was the great dividing line in British politics, both in Parliament and the nation. Macmillan called it the 'prime socialist dogma', which would bring about the 'grim nightmare of a totalitarian state.' Eden predicted that this issue, which dominated British electoral life, would determine Britain's economic future.[69]

Conservatives were well aware that the kind of nationalization the Labour party carried through involved neither expropriation of property owners nor a radical reorganization of the structure of authority in these industries. The significance of nationalization to them was that it meant further encroachments of the state sector into productive industry, which they believed would damage its efficiency and profitability.

Butler analysed these questions in an article he wrote on Conservative policy in 1949. Many criticized Conservative policy for just being Socialism under another label, he admitted:[70] 'It is true that, apart from nationalization, both parties agree on certain objectives. . . . Agreement on fundamentals is in the tradition of our Constitution. But between the parties there are great differences of method.' These differences of method proved to be closely linked to the disagreement over nationalization. Butler pledged that a Conservative Government, whilst retaining some controls, would cut government expenditure and taxation by a significant amount to restore 'incentives' and would remove from industry the threat of more nationalization. He shrewdly assessed the dilemma of the Labour party to be whether to accept the perpetuation of the mixed economy, or whether to adopt a policy of progressive nationalization. If they chose the former they had to accept the consequences:[71]

> It is vain to attempt to run a mixed economy with all the trappings of a socialised State. If free enterprise is not merely to be allowed to continue, but is expected to make the major contribution to the British economy, it must be given the conditions in which it will work and the stimulus to which it can respond.

Butler already saw that the real issue that lay behind nationalization was not totalitarianism versus laissez-faire, but whether the state sector was to support or swallow productive capital. Labour, he complained, treated private enterprise as something to be let out on licence and rigorously controlled.

Meanwhile nationalization spread out its tentacles—bureaucracy, centralization, regimentation, drab uniformity, and Conservatives readily imagined the Nation's tree of life itself was menaced by the rigid application of an alien dogma. Major Proctor expressed this traditional Conservative idea at the 1946 Conference:[72] 'Liberalism and Conservatism have grown out of the life and experience of the British people, unlike Socialism which is no more rooted in English soil than a toffee apple on a Christmas tree.'

But since the programme of the New Conservatism prevented any uncompromising opposition to Socialism, Conservatives were forced to define which parts of Socialism were particularly alien to the English way of life. Nationalization was a long way in front for Conservatives. It was the heart of the Socialist programme, the Socialist philosophy, and the Socialist threat. The Conservative Research Department laid claim to the rest of Labour's policies. Nationalization had been the only idea, one of its staff declared in *Notes on Current Politics*,[73] which the 'Socialist' party had ever contributed to the political life of the nation. All Labour's other measures for which it claimed credit, including food subsidies, national health, social security and family allowances, had apparently been worked out long before Labour came to office. The party had merely inherited them. Conservatives further argued that an economic policy governed by nationalization put at risk not only growth and prosperity, but also the new levels of expenditure on welfare, which the Conservatives imagined they had bequeathed to Labour. This was the general theme of the two manifestos of 1950 and 1951. The 1950 manifesto attacked the 'Socialist Failure' and the 'Socialist Deception'—they had promised prosperity but had caused inflation and devaluation. At the same time, 'they spread the tale that social welfare is something to be had from the state free, gratis and for nothing.' In 1945 the Socialists, it was said, had promised that national-ization and planning would make the British people 'masters of their economic destiny', but had laid on instead a series of spectacular economic crises. The burden of taxation had been greatly increased, enterprise and effort had been stifled:[74] 'Success has been penalised. Thrift and savings have been discouraged. A vote for Socialism is a vote to continue the policy which has endangered our economic and present independence both as a nation and as men and women.' Whilst committing the Conservative party to maintain the Welfare State and full employment, the manifesto emphasized[75] that 'Britain can only enjoy the social services for which she is prepared to work.' It pledged that the Conservative aim would be not 'enviously to suppress success, but to release energy and enterprise.' Conservatives sought to create unity and would not pursue a 'doctrinaire and ill-considered theory', but would help the British people to lead their 'traditional way of life.' The same call was made by the 1951 manifesto. The traditional way of life that Socialism threatened was clearly outlined:[76] 'The attempt to impose a doctrinaire Socialism upon an island which has grown great and famous by free enterprise has inflicted serious injury upon our strength and prosperity.' Stress on the absolute opposition between nationalization and free enterprise reached remarkable intensity during these years. The real meaning of the debate was about how the enlarged state sector should be related to the rest of the economy, but free enterprise and nationalization became much larger ideological symbols than that. When they spoke of free enterprise, Tories meant simul-taneously individual freedom, initiative, and traditional liberties. The 1951 manifesto announced:[77]

> we must guard the British way of life, hallowed by centuries of tradition . . . However well meaning many of the present Socialist leaders may be, there is no doubt that a Socialist state, monopolising production, distribution and exchange, would be fatal to individual freedom.

Churchill spoke of the British people being reduced to a 'mass of state directed proletarians'; Eden foresaw that the spread of Marxist materialism would ultimately reduce society to a single drab, dull monotone, whilst Macmillan warned that a Socialist state would treat human beings as 'cogs in a vast machine.'[78]

The theme of the Tories' election campaigns in 1950 and 1951 was therefore Churchill's call, 'Set the People Free'. The Socialist state was to be destroyed or at least rolled back. Above all, this meant an end to nationalization, and as some Tories imagined, a programme of denationalization.[79] For only if productive industry were free could the people be free; and prosperous. Churchill dramatized the issue in typically stark terms. Neither Socialism nor Communism, he said, 'will enable—or indeed allow—the fifty million inhabitants of this small island to earn their living in these modern times, or to hold our position as one of the leading powers of the world.' As a result the next General Election faced the British people with a momentous choice:[80]

> The choice is between two ways of life; between individual liberty and state domination; between concentration of ownership in the hands of the state and the extension of ownership over the widest number of individuals; between the dead hand of monopoly and the stimulus of competition; between a policy of increasing restraint and a policy of liberating energy and ingenuity; between a policy of levelling down and a policy of opportunity for all to rise upwards from a basic standard.

It needed Tory sceptics like Christopher Hollis to put the overblown antagonism between nationalization and free enterprise into proportion. He pointed out that there was no future for a purely negative, reactionary Conservatism, which believed in halting and then rolling back nationalization, and allowing free enterprise to blossom in its place:[81] 'There is no future for such a creed, not because we are necessarily better or more humane than our ancestors, but because the conditions for the restoration of such a society do not exist.'

This was merely one sign that traditional Conservative ideology was not very well adapted to the requirements of the new politics of power. The stress on individual freedom and the evils of centralized control and state domination only made sense if the party were preparing to cut back the new state in a drastic manner. They had no such plans. The leaders talked one language to their supporters, and prepared to learn another when they returned to power. Their commitment to the post-war settlement was too deep to permit otherwise.

5 THE CHANGING SOCIAL BASE

The core of the Conservative Nation during these years was still the middle classes. The middle class for Conservatives contained all the unorganized 'little men' in the community; and was the guarantee, not just of social stability, but of the 'British way of life.' In an article entitled 'Why the £600-a-year man is so important' Walter Elliott wrote in 1947:[82] 'The middle class man, the £600 a year man, respected both by those above and those below him, has always been the particular strength and product of our island.' These men were 'the NCOs' of British society, the bulwarks of local communities. He reminded his readers that another word for bourgeois was burgher, which simply meant citizen. Now these citizens were under attack. They were threatened by inflation, 'the hall-mark of a system under which the middle classes are brought to extinction,' and by direct confiscation.

But Socialism was not merely destroying the financial independence of this class. By its policies of centralization and state direction it was removing all the opportunities for enterprise and initiative. David Gammans, MP, considered that this was one of the most serious charges against the Labour Government; they were destroying the means whereby Britain could recover:[83]

> the general stifling of brains, initiative and enterprise, the declaration of war on the middle classes and industrialists, the increasing and over-centralization in Whitehall, the destruction of credit and the general feeling of hopelessness which is causing people to emigrate.

So Conservatives pictured the middle class as the class of small, independent men, able and willing to stand on their own feet, who were the source of enterprise and invention in the economic field, and at the same time the guardians of customary life. This image of the ideal Conservative Man found actual embodiment in the Marshall family from Guildford, whose picture adorned the 1949 policy document, *The Right Road for Britain*. The picture showed Mr and Mrs Marshall with their two children, striding happily up the middle of a main, country road. Central Office was overwhelmed with questions about the family: were they real? or were they actors hired for the job? where did they live? and so forth. As a result, *Tory Challenge* carried their picture again, on the front of their issue for December 1949, and an article inside with more photographs, showing the Marshalls 'at work and play', entitled 'The family on the cover.' It revealed that the family lived in Guildford in a modest home of their own, that Mr Marshall was self-employed as a builder and decorator, and that they were firm Conservatives. For as the article pointed out:[84]

> They are completely representative of the great majority of those who comprise the Conservative party, those who work with their hands as well as with their brains, who neither demand state help nor need state interference, but only ask to be able to do a fair day's work for a fair day's pay, and to accumulate steadily sufficient property and savings to enable them to be independent.

The Marshalls belonged to the middle class because they strove to be independent of the state. Their property and savings came out of their earnings. They were not part of the middle class because of their inherited wealth, or education, or professional training, but rather because of their attitude to work and the state.

Conservatives thus naturally believed strongly in the virtues of the small businessman—'sturdily independent, freely enterprising, serving the public'—the ideal small shopkeeper symbolizes many of the virtues which Tories most value in society.[85] Yet they were aware that the opportunities for men to be self-employed and therefore independent of both the trade unions and large firms, were dwindling rather than increasing in the modern economy. A community of small producers was not on the agenda of reality, so the Tories' electoral net had to be cast further afield.

Conservatives were therefore obliged to define independence in a rather different form from strict economic independence, in order to attract support from the mass of clerks and professional workers who staffed the great bureaucracies of state and industry. The delineation of this class began soon after 1945. At the 1947 Conference, Robert Carr, proposing a motion that dealt with the lower salaries and fixed income groups, asked:[86]

Why was it that so many of this class voted Socialist in 1945? . . . this class must surely at heart be Conservative. Our aim is to establish a property-owning democracy—this class is the nucleus of that structure. Our ideals are individual liberty coupled with individual responsibility. This class is rich in a spirit of independence, of responsibility for themselves and their families, and in a determination to build up this independence even at the cost of great sacrifice and effort.

Independence thus came to be extended by Conservatives to mean those who were prepared to save and collect a small amount of property, yet remain independent of the state. The slogan, a property-owning democracy,[87] did not concern policy. It identified what already existed; a large class of white collar and salaried workers, who owned or aspired to own their houses and to build up reserves of savings. But the notion implied other things as well. For if independence was no longer primarily economic independence, then initiative and enterprise would have to come from somewhere else in society. It was no use expecting them from bank clerks and civil servants. The new field where property-owning democrats were expected to exercise their independence was welfare provision. Thus the slogan of a property-owning democracy assisted the growing interest of the party in managers and technologists (and in the big corporations as opposed to small business) as the 'dynamic' force in the economy. It also reinforced the crusade for selective rather than universal welfare benefits that took root in the party during the 1950s.

In his speech—'The New Conservatism'—David Eccles identified the electoral fortunes of the Conservatives very clearly with an expanding economy. He denied that the party was any longer the representative of the old governing class and Colonel Blimps. 'Education and universal suffrage have opened new doors and recruited new forces.' The base of the party had been greatly widened:[88] 'Today we represent all those men and women of talent and energy, wherever they were born, whatever their accent, however they started in life, who can be trusted and relied upon to put back that word "Great" in front of Britain.' These social forces were not hidden away. On the contrary, 'they stand out. They are easily recognised'; for they comprised all the 'active producers of wealth': skilled workers; managers; trade union officials that were 'more interested in productivity than keeping Socialist politicians in office'; professional men and women; 'in short, anyone who is able and willing to show the way up the ladder.' As far as Eccles was concerned, it was now more important to earn than to inherit. Conservatives could win electoral support by encouraging a socially mobile society in an economy in which wealth and opportunities were constantly expanding. This was a programme that could be expected to appeal to the new middle classes and to affluent workers. Angus Maude, writing on the changing class structure,[89] cited a Gallup poll which showed that 49 per cent of the population called themselves middle class, and 46 per cent working class. 'If people want to be middle class,' said Maude, 'and begin to feel middle class, they or their families are likely to become middle class if they stick at it.' Above all, he implied, they might acquire that most important badge of middle-class status—a Conservative voting habit.

Thus, already by 1951, Conservative leaders had begun to explore the shape of the post-war consensus and the new social patterns emerging under it. The old appeals to the electorate remained, but new ones had also to be found, to keep the party leaders attuned to new possibilities to win support. Conservative leaders were convinced that the new state could not be dismantled except at grave risk to prosperity and to constitutional politics. With the return of the party to government, therefore, the leaders required more than ever an electoral perspective that would help them keep their place in the political market and reconcile their supporters in the constituencies and in Parliament to the new politics of power.

Chapter 4
THE STALEMATE STATE:
POWER 1951–64

This is not a time for ideological convulsions.

Winston Churchill, 1954[1]

1 POWER AND PROSPERITY

The 1950s were the golden years for the Conservatives. They dominated British politics again. Two convincing electoral victories stemmed the hitherto inexorable advance of the Labour party, and seemed to confirm the Tories as the normal governing party. The strategy of the Right Progressives appeared to have been justified. It had revived the party as an electoral organization and restored it to government, committed not to overturning the work of its predecessors but to maintaining it. The ease and smoothness with which the new electoral perspective had been established and the supporters of 'laissez-faire' dispersed surprised many observers. In the Labour party it was thought inconceivable that the Conservatives should have changed so much, and many suspected that they were showing one face to the electorate and and would show another when they returned to power. But they were wrong. With a few modifications the Conservatives continued Labour's policy. So alike did the parties seem, especially in their economic policies that it appeared indeed as though Mr Butskell[2] had taken over the affairs of the nation.

Yet the 1950s were paradoxical for the Conservatives. For whilst they were years of electoral success and renewed political ascendancy at home, abroad Conservatives had to preside over the steady decline of British power and influence and to define afresh the essential interests of the British state in the world. This had always to be reconciled with the existing support for Conservatism, in Parliament, in the party, and in the country. This involved a still greater reorientation of Conservative politics than that involved in the acceptance of the New Conservatism after 1945, since for so long Conservative ideology had revolved around the maintenance of British Greatness. A slow pace was thus imposed on the transformation, and contributed to the festering of a deep-seated economic disorder, which began to show itself most clearly in the 1960s.

In a perceptive article written in 1959, Peregrine Worsthorne analysed the dilemma that had been forced upon Conservative leaders:

> The Right is acutely aware that the kind of Britain it wishes to preserve very largely depends on Britain remaining a great power. Certainly the Conservative party's main appeal to the great mass of the voters is its close association with national greatness. It is as the 'conserver' of the Land of Hope and Glory . . . that it wins elections. . . . The decline of Britain as a great power, therefore, would undermine the basic Conservative appeal far more effectively than socialist legislation. . . . Everything about the British class system begins to look foolish and tacky when related to a second-class power on the decline.[3]

In dissolving the Empire and redirecting British policy towards Europe, Conservative leaders were thus putting at risk the very ideological supports on which the political hegemony of Conservatism had been built and the interests of British capital protected. This new political vulnerability of property was, however, partly masked by the concord with the Labour movement during these years. The shock of Britain's decline was also softened through the adroit leadership of Macmillan, whose aristocratic pose and unflappable manner managed to suggest that nothing was changing at the very moment the most radical developments were taking place.[4]

At home, the contrast between the years of 'austerity' under Labour and the years of 'affluence' under the Conservatives was apparent enough to seem a vindication of the Conservatives' claim that they could run a welfare capitalist system better than Labour. This then was a time for the celebration of the New Conservatism and the new vigour of capitalism that made the defensive positions of the 1930s seem obsolete. The revival of a free market ideology,[5] reflected faith in the institutions of capitalism as engines of prosperity, in particular the market and private ownership of the means of production, and their superiority to any alternative. Capitalism could again be justified on pragmatic grounds—Conservative Freedom works—rather than on moral grounds —the spiritual necessity of inequality and private property for the good life. The boom also threw the Labour party into disarray, since much of their case for controls and planning and nationalization in the past had been that they offered a more efficient and less wasteful method of running the economy. The boom helped the Conservatives keep power and it also froze the political settlement. Openings to the left no longer seemed relevant. The new politics of power worked, so no fundamental changes in priorities were felt necessary.

Conservative domestic policy was based on two main assumptions after they returned to power in 1951; the state sector was to be administered, not dismantled, and the unions were to be appeased. The acceptance of such priorities for the politics of power imposed powerful constraints on their policies, regardless of their ideological commitments.

There was considerable discussion among Conservatives in these years of these new constraints on government policy that had been established by Labour and inside which the Conservatives had to govern. As T. E. Utley described it:[6]

> The central problem of British home policy since the war has been the problem of how to combine full employment with low prices and a production great enough to make the welfare state safe.
> Everything that any political party says or does in home affairs must be referred back to that.

These new constraints, in his view, had come about from the disappearance of overseas assets combined with unprecedented 'demands' for state welfare and the maintenance of full employment by government action. Such a shift in priorities, however, brought about by the 'demands' of the electorate was viewed with gloom by others. For Worsthorne,[7] it meant the arrival of the Stalemate State, a product of the post-war revolution, which had weakened but not replaced the old upper class. This 'revolution' had accompanied the decline, not the rise of British power, and so remained 'unheroic', not a source of inspiration and energy, but a reflection of the dwindling authority and ability of the old British upper class. The working class had strengthened its economic position, but had not won real political power. Such a situation, he believed, was unstable, and had to give way to a further realignment of political forces.

Such notions were not, however, greatly entertained by the Conservatives. The 1950s were not a period when the party was much given to reflection. The post-war settlement worked, and it was Conservatives who were making it work. Yet already an emptiness behind the glitter of the new electoral perspective was becoming apparent. Against the progress of collectivism it was mainly defensive, and rested heavily on practical success in economic management.

Although Conservatives talked the language of neo-Liberalism in the 1950s, with its emphasis on competition, markets and consumer choice, this made little impact on the politics of power which the New Conservatism required. The Right Progressives did not see the revival of capitalism as an argument for going back to 'laissez-faire', but as a vindication of the post-war settlement, and the new techniques of demand management. On the other hand, it marked out a welcome frontier to defend against Labour. The renewed expansion of private enterprise meant that no further extension of the state sector would be necessary.[8]

Particularly was this true of the social services. The Conservatives fully accepted the principle that the state should provide for all a basic *minimum* of security, housing, opportunity, employment, and living standards. That had been a central pledge in the *Right Road for Britain*. But they were now anxious to ensure that the commitment of the state to provide welfare was not unlimited. Aided chiefly by Tories in the One Nation Group,[9] and later *Crossbow*, the party felt its way towards a new definition of the social services. This regarded them as belonging to the sphere of distribution rather than to costs of production. Tory spokesmen, therefore, stressed that production must precede distribution—the social services could not be expanded faster than the economy expanded. They accordingly strongly opposed benefits that were universal in scope, and were given to everyone, because of the expense involved. They further suspected that one of the motives of the socialists in advocating universal benefits was to promote egalitarianism by redistributing wealth through the tax system. In other words, Conservatives accepted the new social services and the level of taxation needed to finance them, but only as a once-for-all increase, and not as an expanding share of the national income. They sought to contain expenditure by keeping provision down to a minimum standard, and by trying to keep benefits limited and specific. Above the minimum standard individuals were encouraged to provide for themselves.[10]

The Right Progressives were now no longer on the defensive. It was their system and their faith that had triumphed. Their undimmed confidence was expressed by David Eccles, MP, in a speech to the CPC meeting at the 1954 Conference, entitled 'Popular Capitalism'. He argued[11] that Britain was working towards a social system which would solve all the conflicts and problems of the past. The Conservatives were the leaders in the search for such a system. The Socialist 'experiment' of 1945–51 had not been 'in the mainstream of British history, but like the Protectorate of Oliver Cromwell was one of those deceptive shortcuts which turn out to be circuitous and bring you back not far from where you left the high road.'

The task had therefore fallen to the Conservatives, to find a new way of providing orderly expansion, while maintaining full employment. Capitalism, freed from daily interference by Ministers and civil servants, could rival a planned economy. The continued success of capitalism (and therefore by implication of Conservatism) depended for Eccles on the answers to three questions. Can capitalism, he asked,[12] 'not only produce the goods most efficiently but continue to produce them at a rising rate, maintaining employment and increased earnings'; secondly, 'distribute what it produces with that rough justice which will make men loyal to the system itself'; and finally, 'provide something which goes beyond the pursuit of wealth and helps to satisfy man's desire to serve a cause outside himself?'

These were critical questions. The New Conservatives had no doubt how they should be answered, and the answers meant that Socialism was now not so much a grave threat as an irrelevance. The end of ideology was at hand and for Conservatives, and some political scientists, it meant the end of Socialism.[13]

Conservatives felt they had at last blunted the appeals and demands of Labour. By conceding social services and guaranteeing full employment the central demands of the Labour movement had, in their view, been met. Further attacks on property could be ruled out. For, as Butler announced to the CPC Summer School in 1960,[14] the chasm between the Two Nations had been bridged. The post-war settlement had created an affluent, open, and democratic society in which the 'class escalators are continually moving.' People were no longer divided between haves and have-nots, but between haves and have-mores. As a result, 'the old materialist canon of Socialism, the demagogic appeal to grudges and grievances, in a word the politics of poverty, has lost its old relevance and pith.' Quintin Hogg went still further:[15]

> The fantastic growth of the economy, the spectacular rise in the standard of living, the substantial redistribution of wealth, the generous development of social welfare, and the admitted humanizing of private industry, have rendered obsolete the whole intellectual framework within which Socialist discussion used to be conducted.

The old slogan, Tory men and Whig measures, had acquired a new meaning.

Such ideas were fully reflected in the election manifestos and the electoral message of the Conservatives. In 1955 the chief slogan was 'Invest in success'; in 1959 'Conservatives give you a better Standard of Living—Don't let Labour Ruin it.' The 1955 manifesto asked the British people a simple question:[16] 'Which were better for themselves, for their families and for their country? The years of Socialism or the years of Conservatism that have followed.' In case there was any doubt, it told them that to vote for Socialism was to vote for a policy which was tried and which failed. A vote for the Conservatives would be to 'invest in success.' The dividing line between Conservatism and Socialism in ideology came over the economy and the role of the state within it. The economy had been rebuilt, the manifesto stated. Now the need was for a new surge of national effort:[17]

> Socialism would merely hinder this task. Instead of thinking how to expand wealth in which all can share, the Socialists continue to 'plan' the equal division of scarcity. Instead of looking forward to the next twenty-five years, they are still parroting the untruths and half-truths of twenty-five years ago. Instead of learning from the many

mistakes they made when in office, they are obstinately preparing
to repeat them. Their partisan attitudes would create disunity
among the people and undermine business confidence. . . . We
offer the nation a programme for prosperity; they offer a blueprint
for disaster.

This analysis was amplified for the bonanza election of 1959. As the
manifesto *The Next Five Years* stated:[18]

Eight Years ago was a turning point in British history. The Labour
Government had failed in grappling with the problems of the post-
war world. Under Conservative leadership this country set out
upon a new path. It is leading to prosperity and opportunity for all.

The appeal once again was overwhelmingly pragmatic. A victory
for the Conservatives would guarantee future prosperity. Labour would
ruin it because of their incompetence and outmoded ideas. Like the
dinosaur their party had failed to adjust. It was now a sad irrelevance,
more deserving of pity than fear:[19] 'The Socialists have learned nothing
in their period of Opposition save new ways to gloss over their true
intentions. Their policies are old-fashioned and have no relevance to
the problems of the modern world.'

The Conservative victory in 1959, the first time a party had won
three elections in a row in the twentieth century, convinced many
that the Labour party was doomed, because more and more of its
traditional supporters were being tempted by affluence to identify
themselves with the middle class and vote Conservative.[20] Macmillan
declared after the election, 'The class war is over and we have won it,'
a theme he pursued more soberly in a letter to the Queen:[21]

The most encouraging feature of the Election . . . from Your
Majesty's point of view, is the strong impression that I have formed
that Your Majesty's subjects do not wish to allow themselves to be
divided into warring classes or tribes filled with hereditary animosity
against each other. There was a very significant breakdown of this
structure of society which, in spite of its many material advantages,
was one of the chief spiritual disadvantages of the First Industrial
Revolution. It will be curious if the Second Industrial Revolution,
through the wide spread of its amenities of life to almost every
home in the country, succeeds in destroying this unfortunate
product of the first.

At the same time he confided in his diary: 'The great thing is to keep
the Tory party on *modern* and *progressive* lines.' It did seem for a time
that provided the Conservatives continued their successful administration of the Welfare State and the economy, opposition would wither
away.

The 1950s saw the full development of the political market. Constituencies were now stabilized at around fifty thousand electors, and the Labour party was firmly established as the main electoral competitor of the Conservatives. The Liberals had never been weaker. Elections appeared to show a marked pattern; each party commanded around 40 per cent of the electorate, and competed fiercely for the remaining 20 per cent—the floating vote, or the middle ground of politics as it became known. Politicians could never quite make up their minds whether this middle ground was full of reasonable, moderate men who weighed up the parties' promises, personalities, and past records, before casting their vote, or whether it contained all the most ignorant and apathetic sections of the electorate. It remained true that party strength was amazingly constant, and very small swings made and unmade governments.[22]

The combination of such an equal balance in the political market with the consensus on the new state led to a declining interest in 'ideology' and a growing interest in 'rational' electioneering in both parties. It became plausible to suppose that the consensus between the parties on the state reflected a consensus in the nation. In the spectrum of political opinion from right to left, the majority of the electors had moved towards the middle, the breeding ground of the floaters, leaving only minorities clustering at the extremes.

Such a notion was clearly a fiction, but it was an important fiction. For it suggested a particular electoral strategy. Success in the political market now seemed to depend on capturing the centre and winning the support of the floaters. In bidding for their votes the parties would have to allow their programmes and their images to converge, in order to appear less ideological. At the same time, even though ideology was less and less 'rational' for politicians to be seen flaunting, they still needed to have sufficient ideological luggage to keep the loyalty of solid supporters and to distinguish themselves from their electoral rivals. As one of the theorists of the political market has expressed it:[23]

> Even in a certain world political parties are caught in the dilemma of all competitive advertisers. Each must differentiate its product from all near substitutes, yet it must also prove this product has every virtue that any of the substitutes possesses.

The gradual recognition by the party leaders that in their electoral capacity they resembled less bodies of citizens seeking to articulate the needs, demands, and identity of the nation, and more giant firms confronting a mass market of uncertain extent and character, prompted the spread of new electioneering methods. The whole process of the politics of support in the mass electorate—drawing up programmes and manifestos, canvassing, distributing propaganda and holding meetings —was increasingly viewed as similar to the marketing campaign of a firm. The notion supplied a perfect legitimation for the eager acquiescence of both parties in the political settlement and the new politics of power.

Many barriers existed to full campaign rationality. The nature of the product gave some difficulty. Professional staffs devoted full-time to electoral strategy were mostly lacking. Politicians still obstinately retained other views of their role in the political market. Nevertheless, innovations went ahead. Television began to be used more as access to it spread.[24] Party political broadcasts became an important feature of the election campaign. Poster advertising received greater professional advice.

The major innovation, however, was the use of opinion polls and market research. A rational campaign strategy clearly required sound information about the electorate. All the information the politician received through traditional sources was unreliable, because it was unmethodical, often partisan, and impressionistic. Polls on the other hand were apparently objective. What they could tell a politician was how strong or weak was his party's image; which issues appealed to particular social groups; how the party should organize its campaign; and how voters reacted to different campaign strategies.[25]

Polls provided a new map of the mass electorate, by isolating different audiences.[26] They could therefore show the party how to go about building an electoral majority, by 'identifying the preferences of the majority, if a majority exists, but also of evaluating the intensity of voters' preferences on particular issues.'[27] The goal behind political market research is to make voters consumers of politics: 'They "buy" political labels and allegiances as they would any brand image—because of the pleasurable associations it promises to afford.'[28] An article in *Impact*, the YC magazine, explained the new politics in a similar fashion:[29]

> From a marketing point of view, there is no difference between
> selling a commercial product or service—and persuading the electorate to support a particular candidate or party when given an opportunity to do so in the polling booth.

The growing use of polls, however, marked no great triumph of electoral manipulation. Manipulation had always been built into the political market from the fact that power was centralized in the state and in the parties that competed to control the state. Rational campaigning only made this relation between politicians and electors more explicit. Little more certainty was gained thereby. The results of pollsters' work could not be measured, and at best they provided a new interpretation for politicians of how to influence the mass electorate and win its support.

It fitted in well with the electoral perspective of the Right Progressives, and certainly aided the leadership in by-passing the party organization—the normal channel for information about the electorate. In this way the use of polls and market research were a device that helped to counter-balance the pressure on the leadership from supporters in the party organization and the parliamentary party.[30] Despite the much greater finances of the Conservatives, however, and their business links, the development of the new techniques by the party was uneven. The party hired an advertising agency, Colman, Prentis, and Varley, as early as 1948, but it only began to use polling and advertising systematically after Lord Poole became party chairman in 1955. Under his supervision, two main target audiences were identified; 'activists' and 'affluent young workers with families'. Television was little used, but the 1959 election campaign certainly reflected Poole's influence. After he left Central Office in 1959, the new chief of publicity, George Hutchinson, was far less keen on the new techniques for gathering electoral information and resorted to older methods. The publicity staff did, however, number thirty-seven by this time (twenty-five in London, and twelve in the constituencies). National Opinion Polls were commissioned to do a survey in time for the 1964 election, and ten thousand interviews were completed, but very little use was made of them in the 1964 campaign.

Scientific politics had thus made only a small penetration by the early 1960s. But for a while it did seem as though scientific management of the economy would be combined with the scientific management of the electorate to establish a one-party state. In 1959, the Conservative party had come back from what seemed almost certain defeat after the Suez fiasco to win a still more convincing electoral victory, and raise its parliamentary majority yet again. It appeared that a new electoral cycle was replacing the old business cycle,[31] and bringing together again the politics of power and the politics of support. Armed with their new powers, governments could control the economy and engineer booms just before elections, and postpone recessions and tax increases until just after. So, provided a government was not visited with crass incompetence, it should always be able to ensure its re-election, especially since its period of office was not a fixed term. The Prime Minister still decided the date of dissolution of Parliament.

Material well-being seemed the major influence on the floating vote, and the best way of achieving prosperity was demonstrably the prevailing politics of power. A successful challenge to the governing party either through the nation or the state, grew more and more unlikely. Ideology was at an end, because only the electoral perspective that was based on the existing politics of power seemed viable. As a result, politics grew increasingly administrative, the search for technical solutions to problems thrown up by the running of the social and economic machine.[32] The Labour party's deep split after 1959 on

69

'ideological' questions—whether to drop Clause IV from the party constitution, and with it the commitment to public ownership altogether, and whether to renounce unilaterally Britain's nuclear weapons —only seemed to underline their irrelevance to the emerging pattern of British politics.[33]

2 THE ELECTORAL PREDICAMENT

The rapidity with which the Conservative sun sank after 1960 is therefore remarkable. Many of the reasons for the defeats in 1964 and 1966 belong simply to the accidents of electoral politics; the Profumo scandal, the leadership mêlée at Blackpool in 1963, and the new unity of the Labour party after 1962 all played a part. But there were deeper causes too, which underlay Labour's new competitive strength in the political market. One of these was the abruptness of decolonization and the failure at the beginning of 1963 of the bid to enter the EEC. The latter wrecked Macmillan's Grand Design. He had worked since the beginning of his premiership in 1957 to rebuild the alliance with America, to disengage Britain from her Empire, and to gain entry to the Common Market. De Gaulle's veto thoroughly disorganized and disoriented all sections of the party. The modern wing—the Right Progressive tendency—was utterly dismayed by the collapse of the European policy, and lost a good deal of energy and purpose as a result. The party suddenly found itself without an anchorage, yet still buffeted by all the accumulated bitterness and bewilderment amongst its traditional supporters which the withdrawal from the Empire had aroused.

To these problems was added economic misfortune. The 1961 balance of payments crisis was the most serious since the war. Selwyn Lloyd, the Chancellor of the Exchequer, imposed a Pay Pause, a credit squeeze, and higher taxes. The crisis raised serious doubts about the Conservatives' ability to manage the economy. Britain's economic problems after ten years of Conservative rule seemed to be growing worse, and the ability of the Government to control the situation less certain.

This crisis triggered off a great debate amongst the talking classes about the poor performance of the British economy compared to the other advanced capitalist nations since 1950.[34] So at the moment that the Grand Design was depriving the Tories of many of their strongest images of the Conservative Nation, their claims to be the party of good management and prosperity were severely dented. Even unemployment began to rise. The New Conservatism suddenly started coming apart at the seams, for the party was facing problems it could not cope with, whilst at the same time it had alienated and confused many of its traditional supporters by its foreign policies.

So by 1963, the party found itself in a grave electoral predicament.

How could it rebuild the support which, on the evidence of by-elections and opinion polls was flowing away from it so fast? Party intellectuals were divided on this question. In 1962, before the collapse of the EEC negotiations but after the disastrous Orpington by-election in March 1962 (when a leading Right Progressive, Peter Goldman, a former director of the CPC, was heavily defeated by the Liberal candidate, Eric Lubbock), doubts on the adequacy of the party's existing electoral perspective began to be raised. Julian Critchley asked in his column in the *Spectator* whether 1963 was likely to be another 1906.[35] In his view, the new electoral weakness of the party lay in the increasing bankruptcy of its electoral perspective. The party had succeeded in winning and holding power because it was an alternative to the Labour party, and because it was widely believed that the Conservatives could manage the economy more efficiently than anyone else. Time, however, said Critchley, had diminished the first; performance had weakened the second. He acclaimed Macmillan's skill in readjusting Britain to her 'changed position in a changed world,' but pointed out that the electoral risks involved had often been underrated. The trend of by-elections was a sign that traditional support had been alienated. Yet Critchley did not urge retrenchment and a return to old landmarks. There was a more serious danger—that the party was losing its ability to keep up with changing circumstances on the domestic front:[36] 'There have been times when, however skilfully it has managed its support or however efficiently it has governed, events have begun to move too quickly for it.'

Critchley's recommendation at this stage, therefore, was for the 'progressive forces' in the Cabinet to be further strengthened. To regain control of the political business cycle was the first priority for recapturing the electoral initiative. The *Spectator* agreed with him. When Macmillan carried out the greatest Cabinet purge of modern times on 13 July 1962, a leading article welcomed it enthusiastically:[37] 'The new liberal wing of the party is now unmistakably in the ascendant, both in the Cabinet and outside it, with no more than a minimum of reassurance handed out to the more cautious and traditionally Conservative.'

Apart from Selwyn Lloyd, the most prominent of the victims was David Maxwell-Fyfe, Earl of Kilmuir. He was also the most aggrieved. He no doubt appreciated the irony that the direction of the purge was an outcome of the reforms in the party that he himself had helped to set in motion after the war. The new cabinet reflected more than any other group in the party the professional bureaucracy. The promotion of Maudling, Powell, Joseph, and Boyle in a Cabinet presided over by Macmillan and Butler, and already containing Heath, Macleod, and Hogg, signified the complete predominance of the Right Progressives. Henry Fairlie wrote[38] that since 1945 the combined influence of such men had 'killed the Right within the party: it is now hardly possible to discern it.' Unknown to Fairlie, the hydra of the Right did not lack other heads.

By 1963, the concern over Britain's failing performance in the world market was made worse for the Conservatives by the abrupt curtailment of the main policy they had for remedying it. This re-opened the debates of the intellectuals. Under the onslaught of the 'State of England' writers, Conservatives were forced to re-assess their thirteen years of rule. Many now began to see these years less as a triumphant progress, and more as a holding operation within a 'socialist' framework.

In March 1963, Angus Maude contributed three important articles on the Conservative crisis for the *Spectator*. The party's dilemma in his view was how to appeal to its traditional supporters and to the floating voters at the same time, when both were now wanting different things, and when the requirements of the politics of power was pushing Conservative policy away from conservatism. Conservative leaders, said Maude,[39] were being

> forced by logic of circumstances to proclaim themselves the party
> of radical economic and social change . . . the Conservative party
> may well find itself committed to the advocacy of some most un-
> Conservative measures. How far this has been grasped by the party
> in Parliament, and how far it will prove acceptable to the party in
> the constituencies, remains to be seen.

Traditionally Maude argued, the electorate had not turned to the Conservatives for radical change, but for consolidation and a slower rate of change. But the results of Conservative rule since 1951 had led to an entirely new situation. There was much bewilderment that after twelve years of Conservative Government Britain's international status had declined; that Government expenditure had vastly increased compared with its pre-war level; and that taxation was still high. What this meant, according to Maude, was that most of the old familiar Tory slogans were now meaningless and irrelevant. Such slogans as Free Competitive Enterprise, Sound Finance, The Commonwealth and Empire, Keeping Britain Strong, Cut Government Spending, and the expectations they raised, no longer matched the goods that were produced. The new electoral perspective, he implied, could no longer be justified by older electoral ideologies.

T. E. Utley shared some of Maude's diagnosis, but he advocated a quite different strategy. He agreed[40] that there was a certain incoherence in calling for reliance on the spontaneous efforts of the people in opposition to Wilson's brand of technocratic socialism, if only because 'it appears to bear surprisingly little relation to anything which the Tory Government has done since it came to power.' But, he still insisted,[41] the fault of this did not lie with the Conservative party, but with the politics of power which the Conservatives like Labour had been obliged to pursue, and which depended upon reconciling 'the conflicting demands of the public for full employment, extensive social services, constant economic expansion, unrestricted trade union-ism and stable prices.'

So all the criticism of Tory rule was misplaced. It was wrong to see it as a 'succession of muddles and makeshifts, hesitations and evasions.' Utley believed that Tory freedom of action was limited by the power of the trade unions and that the only alternative to Stop-Go was Labour's policy of high expenditure, high taxes and administrative controls. In a second article, written just before the Tory Conference, Utley returned to this theme. The Tory party had not been a free agent during its period of power. The leaders should tell the party that their government had been compelled like all governments to work with the materials at its disposal, in particular 'a public opinion already half-Socialist.' For the last twelve years, the Government had fought a 'containing operation' against the forces of collectivism, and had succeeded in winning back some valuable ground.

The hosannas of victory of 1959 were no longer echoing very loudly in 1963. The way ahead for the Tories was ambiguous. Should they become the party of 'radical' social and economic change, the party of modernization, accepting that the state sector could not be cut back, and hoping that rapid social change would further undermine the traditional working class electoral support for the Labour party? Or should the party turn away from the middle ground and the treacher-ous floating vote and reassure its traditional supporters? The latter course would entail definite commitments, and it was the one that Utley now favoured. The time had come for a Tory offensive. The Blackpool conference, he wrote,[42] should demand a decisive assurance that 'the dominant theme of the Tory manifesto will not be the need to temper public planning with administrative prudence, but the need to fight it with the ideas of private opportunity and personal duty.' Like so many of the ideological demands put forward by Conservatives, the essence of this was that state expenditure should be cut back: The electorate would want to know, said Utley, how the Tories would change British institutions to enable Britain 'to depend less on her Government and more on herself.'

This choice, between modernization and retrenchment dominated the politics of support in the party at this time. It identified different parts of the electorate to which the party could direct its main appeal. Thus the protagonists of modernization were also those who believed the party's future to lie in attracting the floating votes of the affluent workers and the new middle class; whilst those who now took a more critical view of the Tory record and of their administration of the enlarged state sector, stressed that the party could not stay in power

73

unless it rebuilt its support in the 'solid' middle class and to a lesser extent among the Tory working class. The different approach to the political market arose from the different vantage points from which it was assessed. The electoral perspective of the leadership clashed with the electoral ideologies of the party. The former was based outside the politics of support; the latter were firmly rooted within it.

3 MODERNIZATION, THE AFFLUENT WORKER, AND THE NEW MIDDLE CLASS

The policy of modernization was pushed most strongly by the Bow Group,[43] which saw itself as the vanguard and chief exponent of the right progressive tendency within the party.

The Group was founded in 1951 to play a similar role within the Conservative party as the Fabian society fulfilled for Labour. The main activity of the Group has been its numerous research groups which provide a constant stream of pamphlets, normally highly specialized with detailed policy recommendations. In 1957, a quarterly journal, *Crossbow*, was launched. It became the chief disseminator of Bow Group ideas in the party. In a statement of intent published in the first issue, the basic principles of the Bow Group were set out:[44]

> *Crossbow*, like its sponsors the Bow Group, is a sign of change in British politics since the war. Formerly the number of people willing to give time and energy to promoting ideas from the Right was remarkably few. Now the pendulum is swinging the other way.

But it was a particular kind of right wing ideas that *Crossbow* was eager to promote:[45]

> Toryism . . . is usually on the point of entering a long period of decline and apathy. . . . In the minds of many Conservatives today, illogically and stubbornly, there are still 'certain landmarks too sacred to be disturbed, certain questions which it is not permitted to reason about.'

The task the Bow Group set itself was to open up debate about some of these landmarks. Conservatism it regarded as 'an empirical force', seeking change where it was due, and discriminating between good change and bad change. What such vague formulations might mean was suggested by an editorial in the following issue:[46]

> The editorial policy of *Crossbow* is to reflect and express the griev- ances and the hopes of the generation that has grown to adulthood since the war; a generation that is not wedded to a view of this country and its place in the world that is politically antediluvian or financially unreal.

This meant chiefly opposition to the electoral ideology of national greatness,[47] still entertained by many surviving 'Die-Hards' in the imperialist wing of the party, and commitment to an ideology of economic growth:[48] 'An expanding economy is no idle slogan; growth makes all policies easier, both at home and abroad.'

The Bow Group functioned as a workshop for the Tory leadership, engaging in fairly detailed research on different policies and problems. Their interest was thus primarily in the politics of power, but they also developed the electoral perspective of the leadership, and worked out some of its implications for electoral strategy.

This perspective had two main aspects. The first was that a revived capitalism made the old argument between free enterprise and Socialism irrelevant. The only real question was how to make the economy grow faster. This implicitly took for granted the size of the state sector, although many qualifications were added. The second aspect was that economic growth dissolved the old class structure and created new social groups, in particular affluent workers and the technical intelligentsia, whom a dynamic Toryism could attract.

A dominant theme of Bow Group writing was that Toryism must be separated from conservatism. Gordon Pears in an article called 'Down with Conservatism',[49] stressed that conservatism was not a patent of the Tory party, but a basic human instinct. Institutions that were riddled with it included the trade unions, the Civil Service, and the Labour party. The latter suffered from an 'obsession with the problems of the past.'

In 1959, just before the election, a *Crossbow* editorial hammered home the same message:[50] 'It is a truism today that the Tories are the progressive party and that the Socialists are stuck in the past.' The editorial went on to analyse the predicament of the Labour party if it lost the election. It saw two alternatives. Either the party could move Left, or it could recognize that its dogmas were out of date, and that 'the people of this country are not interested in social revolution but in prosperity and freedom.' If it did this it would have to appeal to the 'radical' rather than the 'class' vote. According to *Crossbow*, this would mean emphasizing colonial and moral issues, but little hope was held out for a Labour revival by this means, for it argued that the ground was already monopolized by Tories and Liberals.

The same issue carried a review of the three Penguin Specials on the election. The reviewer, Bryan Cartledge, was enthusiastic about Roy Jenkins's book, *The Labour Case*, which he described[51] as 'unquestionably the best', and as 'more like a series of Bow Group pamphlets than a statement of Labour policy.' In Cartledge's view the book provided 'a bold indication of what the party of the Left must become if it is to survive as a political force.' By contrast, he had nothing but dismay for the contribution of that erstwhile Tory radical, Quintin Hogg, *The*

Conservative Case. Battered once before by Michael Oakeshott, Hogg came under fire again, this time from a different quarter. 'The image of the Conservative party which his book creates should not be allowed to remain unchallenged,' wrote Cartledge.[52] He thought the book's chief flaw its attempt to erect a 'new quasi ideology or metaphysic', which divested pragmatism of all meaning: 'The central problem of the future of the Welfare State is allowed only six pages, whereas twelve are devoted to a windmill-tilting attempt to lay the moribund bogey of the interwar myth.'

The Bow Group too, however, did not remain unmoved by the rapid decline in Tory fortunes in the 1960s and the onset of new economic difficulties. It burst some of their confidence in the inevitable triumph of their ideas. Their response was to turn the searchlight onto their own party. *Crossbow* acknowledged[53] that the crisis was a serious one, and had more deeply disturbed 'the British people' than any crisis since the war. The prospect was a Britain that might become a 'weak link' in the world struggle against Communism. Britons, complained *Crossbow*, were losing confidence in the country's capacity to save itself. This indicated that the Conservatives had not yet learnt how to manage the economy with sufficient skill, and the reason, for *Crossbow*, was plain: 'Both parties have been driven by their own slogans into a doctrinal argument over more or less State control, more or less capitalism.' This was now irrelevant. The real priority should be to concentrate 'the best brains in the country . . . on the single task of streamlining the economic machine, so as to make capitalism work.' It also meant a quite new attitude to the state sector. Conservatives should no longer seek at all costs to contain its growth, but should be ready to expand it when necessary:[54]

> The aim of 'Setting the People Free' has probably been followed as far as, if not further than, is possible in many fields of policy. In other directions the pursuit of 'freedom' should certainly mean an extension of the role of the state.

Conservative planning was under way. There were naturally proposals for an institution like the French Commissariat du Plan, which would work 'within the framework of an overall consensus of a high growth rate.' It was this consensus that was needed and which made all other 'ideological' questions a waste of time:[55]

> In the field of economic planning the question is not 'has the State a role?' but 'what kind of role must it play?' . . . in a complex industrial society the government is in fact deeply involved in the business of making capitalism work.

This led on to pleas for a radical reform of the Tory party, in order to remedy the 'most important weakness of a complex democratic society' —its delay in implementing new ideas:[56]

Have we not here an ideal opening for a modern Conservative party—for Mr Macleod's Conservative party? Is it not time to establish within the party some really effective policy committees who can set about building the bridges between problems and solutions—bridges that can in due course be incorporated in a dynamic Tory programme.

The basic fault lay in the way politicians still approached their task. The failures had been failures of analysis. Political debates continued to be conducted in 'slogans irrelevant to the complex and often substantial problems of our age.'[57]

A year later, despite the Cabinet reshuffle, the setting up of the NEDC—which did receive a welcome—and the evident conversion of the Government to the new ideology of growth through planning, the analysis was much the same. *Crossbow* was still impatient. Politicians, it complained,[58] were still perpetuating the ideological lag between doctrine and reality. They fostered 'the illusion that the battle is still between fundamentally different philosophies, between a society of individual conflicting interests (which does not exist) and State control (which nobody wants).' Modernization could not tolerate old electoral ideologies.

The other aspect of an ideology of growth was that it allowed a new restatement of One Nation politics. The slogan of One Nation, *Crossbow* explained,[59] meant that Conservatives must be the party of all the people, not just of one class. But it had new ideas of how this could be done. What was important, it argued, was not that the party should cover all classes, but that class should be taken out of politics. Their way to do this was to commit the Conservative party to the ideology of economic growth, trusting to the engines of prosperity to do the rest. But Bow Groupers were aware that they had to fight against the older electoral ideologies. As Henry Vane put it:[60]

We are . . . not in the least preoccupied with the idea of national 'greatness'. Yet to judge from the speeches of Tory politicians, that is one of the party's main ideals, nebulous as it may be. We are not interested in 'greatness', we are interested in 'success'.

The protagonists of the ideology of growth were aware that its pursuit entailed political risks. As *Crossbow* put it:[61] 'The task of reconciling change with traditional interest groups will demand more and not less subtlety.' For while it regarded the commitment to growth as part of the consensus between the parties, it acknowledged that both parties had large and deep-rooted interest groups, 'for whom greater efficiency and faster expansion are not the prime objectives, and who find the new techniques required to achieve them objectionable.'

Crossbow's message, however, was emphatic.[62] Not only must these interest groups be resisted; upon their successful containment hung electoral success too. The new politics of power was creating a new constituency in the political market, whose allegiance was undecided. It lay in between the great traditional interests and owed its formation to

> the common desire for greater prosperity, greater efficiency, and a more direct and less doctrinaire approach to the major domestic issues of a free society. The party that can win the vote of this new generation, that can bring the brains of the nation to bear on their problems, that can avoid becoming bogged down in its attempts to appease traditional interests, is the party that will hold power in this country.

These people were the people of the escalator; in Charles Curran's words:[63] 'an army of young men and women . . . risen out of the working class. They are the managers, executives and administrators of our changing society—a parvenu élite picked for their brains.' Toryism, Curran told *Crossbow* readers, must provide 'a vehicle and an outlet' for the aspirations of this new class. What they wanted was more in-equality to help distance themselves from the working class which for them was made up of 'failures who are left at the bottom because of their innate shortcomings and deficiencies.'

What the people of the escalator disliked most about the working class, however, was its life-style:[64]

> It is a life without point or quality, a vulgar world whose inhabitants have more money than is good for them, barbarism with electric light . . . a cockney tellytopia, a low grade nirvana of subsidised, supervised houses, hire purchase extravagance, undisciplined children, gaudy domestic squalor, and chips with everything.

The sober, patriotic, deferential working men of the Conservative Nation are hard to discern in these children of affluence. Nor at this time did Curran stop to question whether there were enough places on the escalator to ensure the return of a Conservative Government at a General Election.[65]

4 THE DISAFFECTION OF THE MIDDLE CLASSES

Whilst Curran and the Bow Group identified a new area of electoral support, others were more concerned that the party was losing its traditional support in the middle classes.[66] These 'middle classes' erupted into open revolt on two main occasions during Conservative rule. Special middle-class associations were formed,[67] and safe Conservative seats were sometimes in danger. The most dramatic by-election reverse suffered by the Tories was at Orpington in 1962. But they had been rattled before by the size of the swing at Tonbridge in 1956. One of the main sores of middle-class discontent that showed itself in the debates at party conferences was resentment at the level of Government expenditure and the consequent rate of inflation. This theme recurred again and again. The middle classes were being squeezed out of existence, ground between the grindstones of Capital and Labour, both of whom were able to protect themselves against the effects of inflation. During the post-war Labour Government, middle-class rage was naturally directed at the Socialists, who seemed bent on despoiling them of their wealth and depriving them of their privileges. A pointed cartoon of the period by Illingworth entitled 'On the Beach at Margate',[68] showed clean cut Middle-Class Man leaping up from his deckchair shouting in pain as two savage little dogs—Shinwell and Morrison—plunge their teeth into his leg. In the next deckchair, their wizened owner, Mrs Clement Attlee, smiled indulgently from under her bonnet, saying 'Aren't they sweet!'

With the return of a Conservative Government in 1951 loudly proclaiming that it would set the people free, these Conservative supporters were confident that the state would be rolled back, the unions curbed, and their prosperity would return. But many became increasingly disillusioned after 1955, when a second election victory removed the excuse that it was the Conservatives' small majority that stopped them dismantling 'Socialism' with greater speed.

In 1956, seventeen critical motions were sent in by constituency associations on the topic of Government Policy and Public Relations. The one selected for debate complained:[69]

> as part of the large force which toiled vigorously to return a
> Conservative Government to power, we view with concern the
> Government's apparent inability to reverse trends resulting from
> Socialist maladministration, and we urge the use of its strong
> majority to implement more forcibly its election promises.

Speakers in the debate complained that Government performance had not matched its promises to curb inflation, promote home ownership, and raise investment; the cost of administration and the size of the bureaucracy remained at their levels under Socialism, and the middle classes were still forced to foot the bill for such things as 'sorbo rubber mattresses and press button flush lavatories' in prisoners' cells.[70] Mr Peter Emery declared[71] that there was discontent and criticism in the constituencies; The TUC was becoming the Cabinet of the country. We want more Conservatism more quickly, he said.

The motion was defeated after a soothing speech from Butler, and a vigorous intervention by Mr Goldsmith, who lambasted the People's League for the Defence of Freedom as 'fairweather Tories' and reaffirmed the One Nation strategy:[72]

79

The Conservative Party is a classless party and will not pander to any one class as the Labour party does. Of course we stand for the middle class, but we also stand for the others too, and the day that we overlook that fact is the day we cease to be a political force in this country.

But the middle class could not be laid to rest so easily, and their sense of neglect and frustration erupted still more strongly at Llandudno in 1962. Mr J. Hunt there spoke against the official motion on economic policy because, he said, it was too complacent:[73] 'It skates over those issues of economic policy which have aroused such very fierce controversy in our constituencies, and which have contributed certainly more than anything else to the sharp falling off in support for our party at recent by-elections.' He denounced the style of the Conference: 'Many Conservatives in our constituencies are heartily sick of MPs and candidates and speakers at the party conference who blindly support every aspect of Government policy,' and roundly declared:

This is not a Liberal revival, this a middle-class revolt. It is a revolt by the civil servants, by the nurses, by the shopkeepers, by the young professional men and women who feel themselves, rightly or wrongly, squeezed between the expense account directors on the one hand—who seem somehow able to contract out of hardship and sacrifice which are demanded of other sections of the community —and the strength and power of the trade unions on the other— who seem able to demand almost anything and get away with it.

These little men, the people without big unions to back them, were assumed to be predominantly Conservative voters.

Lionel Grouse analysed for *Crossbow* readers in 1962 what these middle classes 'really wanted.'[74] Too much attention by the party to the floating vote and the affluent working class had steadily alienated 'hard-core Tory support.' The party, he warned, could not 'continue to flout that section in the hope of gaining marginal transfers from its opponents.' These supporters were defecting to the Liberals and might not come back at the election unless the party went 'fundamentalist'; at present it was 'ceasing to convey that sense of sympathy and interest to the hard core of (its) natural supporters in the constituencies.' The reasons, according to Grouse, lay partly in foreign policy, but mostly in domestic affairs. Abroad, most serious had been the retreat from Empire, because the imperial ideal had remained 'one of the main pegs on which the political loyalty of middle-class Conservatives hung.' At home it was above all the failure to reduce inflation and cut taxes, combined with the economic muddle and the absence of measures to reform the unions. To regain this lost support Grouse recommended policies that would 'feed the prejudices' of the middle class, including tax reliefs, 'economic rents' for council houses, cuts in NHS facilities for foreigners:[75] 'It is a question of the image of the party in the eyes of its supporters who would like to feel that their own prejudices are shared by the leaders at Central Office.'

Grouse was criticized in the *Spectator*[76] for advocating that the party should 'stand forth bold as brass as the party of petty-bourgeois reaction. Most thoughtful Conservatives see in the development of a classless society (in roughly the American sense) the last hope for the future— certainly of their country and perhaps even of their party . . . the struggle for the centre is not to be won by retiring smartly to the right flank.' Grouse's counsel 'makes no kind of sense to those of us who are waiting to see the Tories seize the chance of leading Britain into modernity.'

5 CRIME AND PUNISHMENT

After inflation and government spending, the domestic issues that caused most anxiety and resentment among the Tory rank and file in the early 1960s were crime and immigration. Both came to a head at the 1961 conference, but while party opinion forced a new policy on immigration, on its penal policy the Government stood firm. The controversy over flogging illustrates very well many of the difficulties the Conservative leaders sometimes encountered in reconciling their supporters to the new electoral perspective and the post-war state, and resisting electoral ideologies.

Crime and punishment was a major issue at the 1958, 1960, and 1961 conferences. In 1958, thirty motions were sent in, although both in that year and in 1960 it was a neutral motion that was selected for debate, and in no way represented the content of most of the speeches, which were filled with demands for the return of the birch. In 1960, ten of the resolutions on law and order explicitly advocated the reintroduction of corporal punishment. The pressure became so intense, that in 1961 the Government was obliged to confront the issue directly. A motion was selected for debate that called for a return to corporal punishment and to full capital punishment.[77] The leadership inspired an amendment that sought to remove any mention of either.

The leadership's quandary was that while they could tolerate and defuse any amount of complaining about the growth of crime, they wanted to avoid being tied down to any very specific measures to deal with it. Yet crime and punishment was a subject about which most Conservatives felt that they had at least as much understanding as their leaders. The mysteries of the money supply and the financing of the state might baffle them, but an appeal by the Government to expertise and the complexities of penal administration to justify their policy on crime was not likely to move their supporters in the same way. Most ordinary Conservatives believed that the formation of good character depended on the application of discipline in the family and the school. The growth of crime amongst the young meant that the primary social institutions, and particularly the family, were breaking down. Simple, tough, and effective measures were required to deal with it, in order to provide young criminals with the 'discipline' they had so obviously escaped in their families. Murderers were a different problem. They were beyond remedial help. Mr Beaman from Crewe expressed the traditional Tory attitude on hanging well:[78] 'If you have a gangrenous limb you cut it off. . . . I do not believe that we hang murderers because of the "eye for an eye" doctrine; I do not believe that we do it because of vengeance. I believe we hang them because they are not fit to live.'

For many Tory delegates, the most important purpose of punishment was to deter. By deterring, punishment reinforced the traditional moral code. Mr Lyte had argued at Blackpool in 1958 that the Tory party had not normally been afraid of deterrents. In foreign affairs the party was prepared to use the H-bomb to 'uphold the freedom of mankind.' So why, he asked,[79] did many in the party not want the 'cat' introduced as a deterrent to 'heinous crimes of violence.'

The power of such analogies lay in their appeal to conservative common sense and in their ability to relate the problems of government to a few sound ideological principles. They thus expressed the controlled longing of many of the delegates to subordinate the politics of power to the politics of support. Their enthusiasm for deterrents was only matched by their fear of ungovernable violence spreading through society. 'Corporal punishment must be brought back,' said one delegate, Mrs Tilney, in 1958,[80] 'otherwise we shall find ourselves in a society dominated by young toughs who violate our girls and frighten or savagely attack the older people.' The conference of Conservative women voted in 1958 to bring back the cat for sexual offences.

The opponents of the birchers did not believe that juvenile crime could be repressed by savage deterrents. Like the Home Office, they placed great trust in penal reform, scientific research, and the recruitment of a new army of secondary agents of social control—including social workers, probation officers, and psychiatrists—to supplement the efforts of the police and the magistrates. The controversy became a clash between the prescriptions of a traditional moral code and the requirements of efficient social control in an industrialized society.

The supporters of the latter always emphasized the need for ever greater research, so as to avoid 'ill-founded judgements or misconceived solutions (which) will be put forward and will find a ready audience.' Scientific knowledge, not traditional morality, was the best guide to rational social control, and in the opinion of *Crossbow*,[81] the bulk of the party's attitudes on this question was well-meaning, but misguided.

The demands for flogging and hanging, it argued,[82] 'are only the out-ward and visible signs of inward yet often inarticulate concern over the problems of crime and punishment as a whole, and of the natural desire of the individual to have some say in determining solutions.' This patronizing attitude was a common response by the Right Progressives in this period of their ascendancy to awkward demands from the 'back-ward' sections of the party.

The battle between a powerful section of the rank and file and the leadership became much more intense after Butler became Home Secretary in 1957. Butler regarded his appointment as an opportunity for bringing into the work of the Home Office a 'spirit of reform and zeal for progress.'[83] He was keen on sponsoring research to increase understanding about the causes of crime and to make treatment more effective. In his memoirs,[84] he defended himself against his critics in the party who had thought him 'soft in standing out against the reintro-duction of corporal punishment,' and boasted that he had brought in comprehensive legislation on penal policy 'in line with the best modern thought.'

The climax of the controversy came in 1961—Butler's last conference as Home Secretary. On a motion that was at last satisfactory to the campaigners for corporal punishment a full debate took place. The resolution called for the speedy return of both corporal and capital punishment. Geoffrey Howe, acting for the leadership, proposed an amendment which deleted both specific recommendations. The argu-ments of the supporters of the motion poured out the accumulated resentment and bitterness of many in the party who thought their views were being suppressed. Mr Lucas set the tone when he declared:[85] 'It is time the Government listened to the will of the people.' He proposed that hanging be extended to cover all premeditated murders, and that graded corporal punishment should be applied to fit the nature of the crime and the age of the criminal. These hooligans, he argued, 'can easily escape a thrashing by not committing the crime.' The implication, however, was that they would still be hooligans at heart, and would drift into crime if given the opportunity. Mr Lucas was uncompro-mising: 'The only way to deter potential criminals,' he said, 'is to get them through their skin. Toughness must be answered by tough-ness.' Mr Butler, he declared, was a humanitarian, and not tough enough.

The advocates of flogging wished the Government to declare war against criminals and vandals. Their sense of urgency was manifest. As Mr Ian Paley from Manchester put it:[86] 'We are becoming desperately anxious to stop this nation from becoming so morally corrupt that criminals will rule the roost, and the way crime is increasing, that day is getting ever nearer.' He favoured flogging gang leaders in order to 'belittle' them, a policy he supported with an argument characteristic of his side: 'I believe that sore backsides, not psychiatrists will cure big heads.'

Mr Ronald Hall likewise advised the conference not to consider the views of intellectuals, but the views of magistrates. He drew a rather bizarre parallel between the present situation in Britain and Christ's onslaught on the moneylenders in the Temple:[87] 'Those robbers and thieves of that day are the spivs and Teddy boys of today, and in my opinion they can only react to the same treatment.'

Many delegates were bitterly hostile to the platform. Councillor David Toleman for instance thought that the amendment to the motion had been inspired by Central Office to stop the Government being defeated. Mr C. F. H. Walters complained that the amendment was not a true amendment, whilst Mr John Cheshire castigated the leadership:[88] 'We are being treated as a democratic representation to a continuation of the Socialist principle that the man from Whitehall knows best . . . the opponents of drastic action against the enemies of society will use any specious argument to defeat us.' Crime was beginning to pay, he said. Even if it could not be eliminated, its growth could be stopped 'by the ruthless elimination of the criminal tendency.' This could be done, he thought, by sterilizing the 'socially unfit.' Meanwhile, Mrs O. Roberts from Pudsey emphasized again that violence could only be curbed by violence:[89]

> We are told that we shall be going back a hundred years if we reintroduce the birch for sexual offences. Do you not think the country has already gone back a hundred years when these crimes are allowed to be committed every day. . . . I feel that the Government should find a deterrent to put the fear of death into these thugs.

The debate, however, differed from earlier ones because the leadership had decided to confront its critics. Instead of providing merely the usual conciliatory speech by the Minister to wind up the debate, a powerful group of speakers was assembled to support Geoffrey Howe's amendment. Two main arguments were advanced against bringing back corporal punishment; firstly, that it was against the 'great Tory tradition of penal reform', and secondly, that birching was in fact ineffective as a deterrent when ordered by the courts.

The first argument was put forward by Howe when he proposed his amendment, and was reiterated by Butler at the end of the debate. But it was put most sharply by Norman St John Stevas. He told the conference[90] that the motion was 'totally unacceptable' to those, like himself, who had joined the party 'back in the dark days of 1945', when it had then seemed 'the embodiment of progressive Conservatism.' He was reminding the conference that it was the electoral perspective of the

Right Progressives that had restored the party to government, and not the ideology of the Die-Hards.

The second argument was deployed by two members of the Home Office Advisory Committee, which had recently produced a report on methods of punishment for the Home Secretary. What they stressed was the practical ineffectiveness of corporal punishment to achieve what its supporters expected. Lady Elliott of Harewood felt obliged to inform the conference that of all the people whom the Committee had interviewed, not one who was closely involved in dealing with young people and delinquents had advocated the reintroduction of corporal punishment. This point was put still more strongly by Sir John Hobson, QC, MP, (a future Attorney-General). He pointed out that it was incorrect to suggest that under existing law magistrates' hands were tied in regard to the sentences they could impose:[91]

> The only question which we have to decide is whether we ought to put back into the hands of the courts a power that they never used when they had it and which has never been shown to have the slightest effect on offences generally or crimes of violence.

He reminded the conference that flogging and whipping were removed from the criminal system by the Derby-Disraeli ministry of 1861. If corporal punishment, he claimed, 'does not reform the criminal, and . . . does not reduce crime, it can only be justified on the basis that you want an eye for an eye and a tooth for a tooth.' In other words, he implied, if birching was no deterrent to violent crime, much of the case for corporal punishment collapsed.

In his speech, Howe was careful to draw a distinction between the different situations in which such punishment was applied. It was quite all right, he assured the conference,[92] when used at home and at school but 'ineffective and unjustifiable when imposed by the courts.' He was supported in this line by Butler, who offered the conference in place of their revengeful instincts his own instalment of the Tory tradition of penal reform, which included a strengthening of the police, greater strictness in the courts, adequate prisons and detention centres, and revised legislation on such matters as betting, gaming, and prostitution.

None of this really satisfied the lobby for tougher deterrents, which wanted, as Hobson correctly perceived, not merely an effective policy to fight crime, but a symbolic one; one that reaffirmed the traditional order of England by drawing a sharp line between those within and those who stepped outside. They demanded a return to the simple truths of a morally unified society. To these, Butler gave little comfort. He told them that the decision not to reintroduce corporal punishment was not his own personal decision that might be reversed if another Home Secretary were appointed. It was rather a collective decision of the Government.

The leadership did not hope to convince their disgruntled supporters that they were wrong. Their strategy was firstly to emphasize to them the electoral risks of adopting a savage penal policy—the possible loss of support in the middle ground if the party forfeited its 'humanitarian image'; secondly, to show that realism, based on experience and expert advice, contradicted the promptings of ideology; finally, to make it clear that the Government fully supported the policy and would not be deflected from it. These three arguments persuaded sufficient delegates to remember the tradition of their party as the party of government, and Howe's amendment was carried. It was a remarkable demonstration of the leadership's skill in negotiating the politics of support in the party. The issue had been fully ventilated, a majority in the party would almost certainly have welcomed a change in policy, yet party unity was maintained on the leadership's terms. But there were to be greater difficulties ahead.

Chapter 5
THE CHALLENGE TO THE CONSENSUS: OPPOSITION 1964–70

A Conservative's Principles
I find it very hard to state
What principles we follow
The old are mostly out of date,
The new too tough to swallow
But if we haven't quite the nerve
To sack the little bl——der
Conservatives had best conserve
If Nothing else, their leader.
                    Christopher Hollis[1]

1 THE CRISIS OF THE LEADERSHIP

The Tories' second spell of opposition since 1945 plunged the party into a ferment. The ideological convulsions were much greater than after 1945, and the leadership was much less securely in control. The combination of a deepening domestic crisis with defeat at the polls exploded or threw into question many of the assumptions of the New Conservatism of the 1950s. What was novel about the challenge to the leadership was that it came not so much from the old diehard elements in the party —Whigs and Imperialists—although these did rouse themselves, as from the forces of a new right tendency, whose leaders were often the New Conservatives and Right Progressives of the past. Progress for them now pointed in another direction.[2]

The leadership was particularly weak to meet the challenge during this period, because the Leader himself did not command his usual authority, a state of affairs which began with Macmillan's retirement in 1963 and did not properly end until the Conservative election victory of 1970.

Strong, able, and occasionally charismatic leaders had always been an essential ingredient in the Tories' One Nation strategy. The party had offered good government, not detailed programmes, men not measures, the authority of a traditional governing class rather than tribunes of the popular will. The party leaders since 1945, Churchill, Eden, and Macmillan, were all firmly within this tradition, closely identified with the aristocracy and the upper-class establishment of England. Macmillan's retirement in 1963, however, through ill-health, created a serious difficulty over the succession. The new professional Tories, the leaders of the Right Progressives, who had staffed Macmillan's cabinets, naturally wanted a modern Tory to become Leader of the party; either Butler himself, or Macleod, or Maudling were the favoured candidates. Macmillan, however, was determined to prevent Butler succeeding him, because he doubted that Butler could unite and rouse the party behind him to the pitch necessary to win the election. Macmillan's choice was Lord Hailsham, formerly Quintin Hogg, who was both one of the founders of the Right Progressives and very popular in the party, especially with the constituency associations, a reputation he acquired during his period as party chairman before the 1959 General Election.

What upset Macmillan's calculations was that his retirement coincided with the 1963 party conference and before any clear successor had 'emerged.' Since there were no definite procedures for electing the next Leader, it was inevitable that the conference should have taken on something of the atmosphere of an American primary election, and been transformed into a jousting match for the leadership. Urged on by some of Macmillan's associates, Randolph Churchill and Julian Amery among them, Hogg made the error of trying to take the conference by storm. His stage-managed appearances elicited huge ovations, and he renounced his peerage in flamboyant style. Presumably he thought that he could establish an impregnable position as the candidate of the rank and file. If he could demonstrate his appeal to the electorate and to the party, he could appear as the leader with the best chance of winning the election for the Tories. In fact, however, his conduct swung many powerful groups in the parliamentary party and in the leadership against him. In their eyes he showed lack of judgment by seeming to canvass support in the rank and file. That was not how leadership was conferred in the Tory party.

Yet the conference still played an important role. It could not determine who became the next Leader, but the poor performances by Butler and Maudling certainly weakened their claims, while the impressive speech by Home, and his rapturous reception strengthened his. Once he realized that Hogg could not become Leader, Macmillan switched his support to Home. In different circumstances, no doubt, he would have backed either Macleod or Heath, but he recognized that the former was viewed with too much suspicion in the party through his handling of decolonization, whilst Heath was too inexperienced. In this situation, Home was the only candidate who could stop Butler, and in his favour was his undoubted popularity, and the absence of strong feelings against him in any section of the party. Macmillan knew that Home was no ideologue of either the Whigs or the Imperialists. Under his leadership, the dominance of the Right Progressives in the leadership would be safe, yet at the same time the party in parliament and in the country would feel reassured by Home's reputation for honesty and straight-dealing, and his traditional image.

The canvassing conducted in the parliamentary party, amongst the

peers and the constituency associations, all reported majorities for Home
and a consensus that he was the Leader most likely to unite the party.
Only in the Cabinet was there serious disquiet. Seven or eight Ministers
were strongly opposed to him, and right at the end, Hogg, Maudling,
and Macleod came together to press Butler's candidature. They were
unsuccessful, however; Home was appointed Prime Minister. Butler
agreed to serve. Macmillan had his way. Even a united Cabinet it
seemed could not prevail against the power of a modern Prime
Minister, certainly not one so skilful as Macmillan. Macleod and
Powell, however, refused to serve, and Macleod subsequently denounced Home's selection as a victory for the 'magic circle' in the
party. He claimed (quite erroneously) that the party for the first time
since Bonar Law was being led from right of centre. His resignation and
this broadside effectively put him out of the running for the leadership
in 1965, although he still remained the best politician amongst the Right
Progressives, and their best potential Leader of the party.[3] Macmillan
no doubt enjoyed the irony that after his Premiership during which he
had steered his party towards a new realism about Britain's place in the
world market, his successor should be so much in the image of the
traditional Conservative. At the 1964 General Election the Conservatives thus possessed both a detailed programme of modernization, which
fully reflected the ideology of growth, and a leader whose personality
and social status seemed capable of reassuring the party's traditional
supporters after the buffeting they had received.[4]

The mixture, however, could not survive a defeat at the polls.
Enormous pressure built up for a change of leader, so that the party
could present a completely 'modern' image. Sir Alec, since he was not
the spokesman for any anti-Progressive faction within the party, con-
nived unwittingly at the undermining of his own position, for he gave
his assent to reforms that strengthened the influence and dominance of
the Progressives within the party.

The organizational shake-up of the party was not so far-reaching as
after 1945, but it further confirmed the growing power of the professional bureaucracy in the party. The major developments were these:

1 A new procedure for electing a Leader. This followed a strong
campaign by Humphrey Berkeley and others, and was accepted by the
Conservatives to avoid a repetition of the disorderly scramble for the
succession at Blackpool in 1963. It brought the party into line with the
Labour party, and reduced the opportunities for control of the leadership by a small clique.[5]

2 A reorganization of Central Office. This involved the integration
of the CPC and CRD, and the appointment of new officials. In particular, David Howell, a former editor of *Crossbow*, became Director of
the CPC, Edward Du Cann became Party Chairman (in January 1965),
and Sir Michael Fraser, who had been Head of the CRD since 1951,

became the deputy Chairman, a newly-created post. All this meant a much closer relation of the party's research effort to their electoral strategy. In addition, Du Cann's business experience was expected to be of use in introducing modern business ideas about market research, publicity and recruitment, and the raising of finance into the management of Central Office.

3 A big expansion in the polling of the electorate carried out or commissioned by Central Office. After the 1964 election the pollsters were back in favour at Central Office. ORC was commissioned to conduct the most extensive electoral surveys ever undertaken in Britain. Five and a half million target voters were identified.[6]

4 A reform of the selection procedure for parliamentary candidates. Although the Maxwell Fyfe committee had abolished the financial contribution candidates made to their own election expenses, they had left a good deal of power in the hands of the local selection committees for choosing who should be their candidate. Maxwell Fyfe had later regretted that this had meant the 'hindering of talent' but still believed complete Central Office control to be undesirable.[7] Now a new attempt was made to change the balance of the Conservative intake into Parliament by reducing the number of peers and landowners, as well as business men and retired army officers. This followed long agitation from the Right Progressives.[8] A new list of parliamentary candidates was drawn up, partly on the basis of an interview of prospective candidates by management consultants.[9]

5 Finally, and most important, a major policy review was undertaken. Straight after the election, on 24 October 1964, Heath was made chairman of the Advisory Committee on Policy, in succession to Butler. He had soon set up twenty different policy groups which rose to thirty-six by the spring of 1965. These groups, each with eight to twelve members, were instructed to make detailed practical studies of particular areas of policy. It was exactly what the Bow Group had for so long been calling. Out of the labours of the groups came a new policy document, *Putting Britain Right Ahead*.[10]

The vigour of the Progressives, coupled with the feeble performance of the Conservative Front Bench against the Labour Government despite the latter's slender parliamentary majority, all sabotaged Home's leadership. His weakness was his inability to appear fully committed to the modernization of Britain. At the same time, however, he had no electoral perspective other than the Progressive to put forward. So his position was undermined on all sides.[11]

The election that followed his resignation in July 1965 was the first held in accordance with the new rules. There were only three candidates —Heath, Maudling and Powell. Heath appeared to have risen from nowhere as he had not been a contender two years previously. Since then, however, he had stood out as the leading modernizer in the party, firstly in the Cabinet as Secretary of State for Trade, Industry and Regional Development, when he forced through the bill to end Resale Price Maintenance against violent opposition, and secondly after 1964, as the Chairman of the Advisory Committee on Policy. Apart therefore from doubts about Maudling's energy and alertness, Heath appeared as the natural successor in 1965, the man to benefit from the quiet transformation of the party conducted by Macmillan and an earlier generation of Right Progressives. The succession had been denied to Butler in 1963, but now the logic of the party's development asserted itself. A modern Conservative was chosen to lead the Tories.

The great surprise therefore was that after Heath's triumph, the Conservative's Leadership crisis did not abate. This was partly due no doubt to Heath's personality, and his failure to get across to the electorate,[12] a failure aggravated by his handicap of being the first Conservative since Austen Chamberlain in 1921 to become Leader when not already Prime Minister.

But the main reason must be sought elsewhere. It lay in the growing exhaustion of the New Conservatism which Heath had inherited. The concentration on the politics of technique, which was Heath's hallmark, might not have mattered if the party had been in power, but was inadequate for negotiating the politics of support in Opposition. He has been judged by some to see Opposition 'more in an administrative than a political light', and to lack any definite political philosophy.[13]

Heath's abiding commitment was to the ideology of growth. Like the Bow Group it was the heart of his political perspective, the triumph of pragmatic, problem-solving, non-ideological politics. In the circumstances of the late 1960s, however, it had other implications also. It meant that the leadership was politically vulnerable in a way it had not been before. The Right Progressives of 1945 had had a very clear electoral perspective which specified not only a programme for the politics of power, but also how that programme could be used to rebuild Conservative support in the electorate, by restoring the party's One Nation image. Heath's accession to the Leadership came at a time when that electoral perspective was run down, but he made no attempt to forge another. As a result, he was sometimes at the mercy of electoral ideologies. The very politics of technique which Heath prized so much drew a blank political map for the party in Opposition.[14] The new electioneering techniques could not, by themselves, fill it in.

The crisis of leadership in these years was thus at the same time a crisis of ideology. The electoral perspective of the Conservative leaders no longer seemed able to straddle the politics of power and the politics of support. The New Conservatism needed recasting, but the Conservatives chose as their Leader a man who was supremely ill-equipped to do this. Heath offered a detailed analysis of Britain's economic problems and a list of appropriate remedies, but he had little conception of how this programme could be presented to secure the support and enthusiasm of his followers in the party and in the country. The result was that Heath's Conservatism appeared to many little different from the Socialism it sought to replace. This was a serious handicap for a party in Opposition.

Heath's concentration on the politics of power did not mean that the politics of support were ignored in the party. On the contrary, a great jumble of electoral ideologies appeared, in part stimulated by the vacuum created by the leadership, in part a natural response to the evident and growing troubles of the British economy and British society. These new currents created a new tendency of opinion in the party—the New Right. But it lacked real unity. There was no single theme like Imperial Preference or Home Rule which could orchestrate all the dissident forces in the party, as happened before 1914, and no well-defined economic interests that the New Right represented.

What occurred therefore was not a 'right wing' takeover of the party, or even a concerted 'right wing' challenge. Heath and his supporters stayed firmly in control. But the electoral perspective they espoused underwent substantial change as a result of the constant ideological pressure from the Right. By a curious irony the neglect of the politics of support by Heath meant that the interpretation and to a lesser extent the substance of his programme for government was altered and shaped by other groups in the party.

2 THE COMPETITION POLICY

Heath's programme for government became known as the 'competition policy.' Its purpose was to make economic growth and modernization reality, and its origin lay in ideas put forward over a long period by the One Nation Group and the Bow Group,[15] but which only acquired real force in the economic crisis of 1961-2. The defeat at the polls in 1964 meant the triumph of the competition policy, its acceptance as official party policy. It went through several reformulations, but its basic elements stayed fairly constant. In 'Putting Britain Right Ahead' there were, according to Heath himself, five major policy changes:[16]

1 A shift to the high wage, low cost, productivity agreement economy.
2 A new legislative framework for industrial relations.
3 The implementation of the levy system in agriculture.
4 Selectivity in place of universalism in the social services.
5 A war on waste in government expenditure.

The first two of these proposals were aimed primarily at increasing investment and profits in productive industry; the last three all involved the level of government expenditure. But they were designed mainly to contain the growth of government expenditure rather than to reduce its overall level.

The slogans of the competition policy were efficiency and modernization, and Heath had given a practical demonstration of what these might mean and whose interests they favoured, when he forced through his bill to end Resale Price Maintenance (RPM) in 1964 against considerable opposition in his own party.[17] The interests and the needs of the large public companies were to be paramount. His experience of this bill had no doubt convinced him that the obstacles to a competition policy could and should be broken down. At the 1965 conference, his first as Leader, he spoke in the debate on Conservative Policy, and declared:[18]

> If there is one thing which I regret about the thirteen years of
> Conservative achievement, it is that we were unable sufficiently to
> change the mood and attitude of people in this country. There is
> still so much more to be done. The Labour party, of course, has
> pushed it further into the past. They have become static and
> unwilling to face change.

Three themes ran through the party's new policy document, he said: 'the central place of private enterprise in the economic reform which we want to bring about'; the transformation of the Welfare State to meet 'our needs' today; and Britain's new place in the world, in particular her developing relationship with the EEC. So much of Heath's political perspective and his whole programme for the politics of power turned on the eventual entry of Britain into the Common Market. It was the framework of the competition policy:[19]

> The world has changed . . . we have travelled a long and honour-
> able road from Empire to Commonwealth with independent
> countries . . . we have had to face, and are still facing—and the
> way is going to be hard—the problems of economic change, as some
> of our industries decline and we move over to the new ones. But
> that path is now nearly over. We are at the point where we can
> start a new advance and it is for that advance that the people of our
> country are crying out today.

They did not cry out loudly enough in either 1964 or 1966, but in the meantime, a gale of modernization and efficiency swept through the party. The Right Progressives thought they understood only too well the causes of the party's defeat in 1964 and what it needed in order to recover. In a *Crossbow* symposium on the election[20] Timothy Raison and Iain Macleod set out their analysis. Raison argued that there were two main reasons for the defeat. Firstly, 'we did not pursue moderniza-tion with sufficient gusto', which alienated the young technicians and executives; secondly, the existence of a 'disgruntled and depressed middle class element', which had been hit by the Pay Pause and other

Tory policies, had lost the party many votes. This suggested, said Raison, a contradictory strategy; either more Conservatism or more dynamic change. Macleod accepted this analysis in broad terms, but put more emphasis on the new working class rather than the new middle class. The defeat, he said,[21] was the outcome of two opposing movements. There had been 'a movement of the burdened middle class away from us' and at the same time, 'a movement of the comfortable working class towards us.' The middle class defections, according to Macleod, had been caused by the burden of mortgage repayments and rising commuting fares, as well as fury at the power of the trade unions. But he regarded the future as hopeful provided that: 'we can recover the lost ground in the centre represented by the first movement, without losing the natural expansion of the Tory party represented by the second.' His confidence rested on the fundamental tenet of the Right Progressives' electoral strategy: 'Politics is always about the centre because the wings have nowhere else to go.'

With that perspective both he and Raison rated modernization much more highly than the appeasement of traditional supporters. Macleod typically called for concentrated 'work' on policy at all levels of the party and quoted approvingly David Howell's definition of modernization: the giving of 'supreme priority to managerial efficiency in all sections of the government and industry.' Raison too advocated a more professional approach to research in the party, and an overhaul of the party machinery for formulating policy and generating ideas, and put forward five basic problems which he claimed should form the basis of Tory rethinking: how to establish a dynamic economy; how to reform the social services; how to respond to the egalitarian movement in education; how to fit the new technological industries into the 'politico-industrial structure'; and how to deal with new social problems like crime and illegitimacy.

The reform of the party organization gave the Right Progressives a powerful platform in the party. Their ideas poured out of Heath's policy groups and were paraded in CPC pamphlets. Two important series were published in 1965, 'New Tasks', and 'New Techniques'. The new competition policy and the electoral perspective it embraced were clearly set out.[22] At the same time, a new emphasis in right progressive thinking was evident.

In *The New Competitors* Eldon Griffiths answered the question 'why did we lose the last election?' by arguing that the Tories had lost control of the centre. To regain power the party had to ask three important questions: who are the centre people? what do they want? what Conservative policies have to be changed or strengthened to regain the loyalty of the centre people and retain it?

The centre people turned out to have many names—the technocrats, the new model bourgeoisie, the salariat, but what defined them were their education and their occupational role as the 'gearbox of an increasingly technical society.' Like Curran,[23] Griffiths assumed many of them had risen out of the working class but had no links left with it, nor any common identity. Instead they had a quite different culture, were attracted by ideas of self help, and had no time for working class solidarity or for equality. At the same time their hostility to unions was combined with hostility to social snobbery.

The precise wishes of the centre people, however, who were, by definition, unorganized, were difficult to ascertain, and the connection of what the Conservatives thought necessary to reinvigorate the British economy by providing a favourable climate for the operations of the big firms, to what the voters were believed to want was a difficult task. This was why these two functions became increasingly specialized. The research on policy could continue largely independently of the research into voters' intentions, and attitudes.[24] The state and the political market were organized in different ways, so different kinds of expertise were appropriate for planning the management of the former and securing a majority of the nation in the latter.

In another 'New Task' pamphlet, *Conflict and Conservatism*, Timothy Raison set out quite clearly some of the implications of a competition policy for industrial relations. Raison complained that the Conservatives always tried to operate a 'largely capitalist economy without a capitalist ideology.' Such an ideology was, however, to hand; the neutral, technical, practical ideology of growth. It was the neutrality that Raison most disliked:[25]

> We should regard the Conservative party in the economic context
> as the management party, prepared to take the initiative in achieving
> efficiency and tackling abuses on the union side (and elsewhere) with
> a determination which we have not hitherto shown. In the process,
> we must accept that there *are* two sides in industry.

Raison's argument was framed inside a general discussion about the merits of conflict versus adjustment in social life. His realism about the role of the state was pronounced. For while he proclaimed that the 'achievement of an efficient economy today *is* the national interest', he argued that national interest had to be defined in terms of the objectives of one section of the nation—the managers. This would entail a refusal to pursue conciliation at all costs and a readiness to accept strikes. An anti-union bias had to be developed, he wrote.

This was the new One Nation perspective of the Right Progressives. Raison criticized the One Nation perspective of Monckton and, by implication, that of the right progressive tendency in the past, because it strove to adjust conflicting interests, and suppressed dynamism, ruthlessness and audacity. The creative tension of the class struggle meant

an efficient capitalism, by encouraging a more rapid growth in productivity. Raison's first concern, therefore, was for measures that would
revive the class war, although, as one would expect from someone
familiar with social science, he was anxious to limit it to the work roles
of managers and workers, lest it got out of hand. To this end, he
advocated on the one hand anti-union legislation to curb strikes, the
forced contraction of inefficient industries, and the ending of incomes
policies, which inhibited the competition policy by preventing proper
incentives being paid. On the other hand, he wanted more action to
ensure freedom of choice for the working class, and positive discrimination in favour of the deprived.

Raison's views received support in another 'New Task' pamphlet,
Efficiency and Beyond, written by David Howell, at that time Director
of the CPC. The unvarnished character of the new utopia was again on
full view. America was held up by Howell as the ideal to which Britain
should aspire. It was not a 'materialist, ulcer-ridden hell', as many in the
Labour party believed. On the contrary, its very materialist achievement
had made possible the 'reassertion of individualism' and a new awareness of social problems:[26] 'The most powerful engine of capitalism has
also become the most powerful engine of social advance and reform.'
Howell argued that only a rapidly expanding economy could guarantee
rising standards of welfare. The post-war settlement in Britain had
established a high level of welfare, but had helped to slow down the
rate of growth of the economy, which meant that Britain had now
actually fallen behind many other countries in her spending on welfare.
Apart from supporting a limited reopening of the class war, however,
Howell's solutions were not very radical. For at this time, like all the
ideologists of growth, he believed that greater efficiency and dynamism
could come if the government pursued the right policies, the correct
interventionist strategy. This would leave the overall size of the state
sector in relation to productive industry unchanged.

Accordingly, Howell put forward three main aims of a future
Conservative economic policy. It should ensure, he wrote,[27] a cadre of
highest quality management, a competitive climate in which it could
operate, and a 'sensibly organized, flexible, co-operative and highly
trained supply of labour, operating in a socially secure environment.'
It was obvious that it was the third of these that would be the most
difficult to achieve, in order to make the comprehensive competition
policy a reality. Better management could be taken care of by better
incentives and training, i.e. more pay and less tax. The competitive
climate could be achieved primarily through lower tariffs (which meant
entry to the EEC) and stricter anti-monopoly laws to allow the big
firms to operate more freely. It was the reform of industrial relations,
however, that required most attention. Management, he thought, must
be better equipped to 'push and pull a reluctant labour force into the

new age.' This meant they must be re-educated in how to fight the unions, for as Howell pointed out, the workers' 'short-term interests, if not their long-term needs, must necessarily conflict from time to time with those of the managers.' Strikes had a positive function. If there were none, it meant that industry was probably being run inefficiently:[28]

> Strikes do at least indicate that toughness is being shown on the management side in face of unreasonable demands. . . . The absence of strikes may well be evidence of a tacit conspiracy between management and work people to do nothing new and disturbing, to give in to all wage demands swiftly and in general to preserve a cosy climate of inefficiency.

The responsibility of the new state itself for this cosy climate of inefficiency quite passed Howell by. He argued that it was more important to ensure that both sides of industry were working towards higher productivity, than to maintain industrial peace. If productivity was rising, he implied, the way income was distributed would not create uncontrollable conflicts.

Russell Lewis was another of the growthmen who shared this analysis. In one of the 'New Techniques' pamphlets, *A Bonfire of Restrictions*, he congratulated Mr Heath on being free of the 'One Nation psychosis', which had plagued the Tories since the war. He denounced incomes policy as a 'turning down a blind alley.' The Conservatives had adopted the idea, he thought, only as a result of their anxiety to avoid strikes and their willingness to concede inflationary settlements. Lewis justified the competition policy and its provisions for anti-union legislation by the ideology of growth. He saw it as a piece of social engineering which would satisfy the long term needs of the people, however much it might be against their short-term interests. It is not surprising, therefore, to find him praising that supreme social engineer, Jeremy Bentham, who up to then had not figured overmuch in the Tory intellectual tradition. Bentham, wrote Lewis,[29]

> violently attacked outdated customs and laws under which his fellow-Englishmen lived. He subjected social arrangements to the simple test of whether they contributed to the greatest happiness of the greatest number and, if he found them wanting, sought their abolition. With all its crudity, it is an approach we could certainly use today.

The greatest happiness of the greatest number meant the highest possible rate of economic growth, but the initiative had to come from productive capital and not the state. The role of the state was to arrange the 'creative destruction of brakes on our national energies', but no more. Competition policy was a policy for private enterprise, not a recipe for state planning. It rested, said Lewis, on two assumptions; that the initiative of individuals is the mainspring of economic advance, and that voluntary effort is always preferable to compulsion. Given the existing organization of most branches of industry, it was obvious what 'individuals' meant—the giant corporations—whilst compulsion was evidently to be outlawed only for them. It was to be positively encouraged in dealing with the unions.

The second defeat in 1966 did not trouble the supporters of the competition policy who generally thought the election had come too soon for the new policy and the new Leader to get across to the electorate, and for the image of the Tories' last years in office to be dispelled. An editorial in *Impact* summed up this view:[30] 'People did not vote against us in 1964 and 1966 because they thought we were not leftwing enough, they voted Labour because they wanted a new dynamic society—they thought we had exhausted ourselves.'

With this perspective time was clearly on the side of the growthmen. For they thought it axiomatic that Labour could not produce a dynamic society, and consequently the lost votes of the salariat would come scurrying back. In a scathing review of the Labour party's mid-term policy document published in 1968, two Bow Groupers put the issue concisely:[31]

> For Socialists change is desirable because the whole structure of society and its institutions is considered morally wrong. For others change is primarily necessary for ensuring greater efficiency and thereby encouraging economic growth.

The Labour party was thus diverted by its ideology from identifying and solving the real problems facing the accumulation of capital. The Tory growthmen were resolved that ideology should not deflect them from this primary task. As Nigel Lawson put it in a CPC pamphlet, the party political debate had become irrelevant:[32] 'the party lines do not coincide with the real problems that have to be solved.' Lawson argued that there was now like a British foreign policy, a British economic policy 'which can be implemented with greater or lesser skill and efficiency.' The central question of this economic policy was the role of the state in the economy—Manchester School liberalism was out of date because it no longer fitted the facts of modern industry. But, whereas the Socialists put a different value on various kinds of growth:[33]

> By contrast, the Tories should insist that for them it is economic growth and economic growth alone that is the overriding objective of long term state intervention in the economy, and that consumer choice expressed through the market rather than paternalist planning should determine the actual shape of the economy.

David Howell, in the same pamphlet, was even more explicit:[34]

The pursuit of a national economic growth policy demands the state as an active partner, particularly in the export field, where the state's bargaining power can be decisive in backing up individual export enterprise. The state has to serve free enterprise.

These Tories accepted the state sector and the commanding role of the state in the economy, and wished to use it so as to aid productive capital in accumulating and investing in Britain rather than maintaining a broad immobile national consensus, or pursuing egalitarian ends. It is not surprising therefore that Lawson quoted Leo Amery with approval:[35] 'The total expansion of our productive activities is the real test of the success of economic policy and the basis alike of national strength and national welfare.' What the growthmen offered was a reinterpretation of Amery's political perspective—state intervention in the economy to aid accumulation of industrial capital—except that the framework was now different. The Empire had been replaced by Europe as the most important external market, and a floating exchange rate was now considered a better solution to balance of payments deficits than import controls.

The question remained, however, how this new programme for government could be linked to electoral success. Who would replace the legions of sober deferential working men and the solid, patriotic, middle classes, united in defence of Crown and Empire? A year after the election *Crossbow* suggested:[36]

> The two questions we really have to settle are intimately related.
> Who are our future supporters going to be? And what kind of
> society are we going to offer them? . . . At the moment we are in
> danger of becoming a rootless party and a boring party. A political
> party is a collection of interest groups, and if it loses the support of
> some of the old interest groups it can only survive by winning over
> new ones. It is therefore a false sense of political daring which
> allows us to face the alienation of some of our traditional supporters
> with complacent equanimity.

This editorial also warned, rather sensibly: 'We should . . . remember that the number of people attracted by strident calls for technology, dogmatic claims for pure economic liberalism and even heartfelt appeals to the spirit of individualism is severely limited.' The conclusions, however, were rather ordinary. *Crossbow* advised the party to be loyal to those who had been loyal to it in the past, the solid middle classes, whilst at the same time putting itself at the head of the active elements in society, of all classes. How the two were compatible *Crossbow* did not say. Iain Macleod was more aware than many of the advocates of the competition policy of its electoral risks. He had pointed out some of them at the CPC Summer School in 1965. He asked whether the party was ready to follow the logic of its words into action. It was easy to proclaim efficiency, he said,[37] but it was less easy to say that the inefficient must fail, because 'the inefficient too have votes, and in some industries they are formidable in numbers.' He wondered too if the party was ready to put a reduction in surtax to increase incentives for managers above a rise in pensions, and whether it was really prepared to legislate on the trade unions.

The situation was complicated by other considerations. As Mark Schreiber from the CRD pointed out,[38] the image of the Tory party which was at large in the electorate was of a party,

> of privilege, of 'big business' interests, lacking in integrity, opposing change and failing to understand the new techniques, run by tired old men, lacking in understanding and sympathy for the problems and aspirations of ordinary men and women, opposed to the working class and unrepresentative of the country as a whole.

The difficulty with the competition policy was that it was likely to confirm much of this image. At the same time the new image of the Labour Government might take away votes as well.

Crossbow noted the popularity of the Labour Government's wage freeze among the middle classes and warned that the Tories might no longer be able to rely on their support. The struggle over Resale Price Maintenance, it suggested,[39] was another sign that the values of competition and individualism were no longer so dear to the professional and small business classes who formed the bedrock of Tory support. Since *Crossbow* had taken to seeing ICI and Shell as the embodiment of economic individualism, this was perhaps not too surprising. In the end, however, the only electoral strategy the supporters of competition policy had was to push ahead regardless and try to attract the new salariat and the affluent working class by a policy of rapid economic growth. The new competitors, the Centre people, were still believed to be out there, waiting for the correct lead. But there was a new uncertainty about the electorate. David Howell noted that one third of all voters changed their voting behaviour between 1964 and 1966 and commented:[40] 'That over eleven million people should have cast themselves afloat in the electoral sea is a staggering commentary on the public mood with dangerous implications.' He put it down to the frustration of people's expectations of a rising standard of living. In the end economic growth and electoral success were treated as synonymous, and the priority which the Bow Groupers gave to competition policy also indicated the direction in which the party should look for support. As James Lemkin argued in *Crossbow*, there were two large disenchanted groups in Britain in 1967, the salariat and the 'nonconformist right.' Which the Tories decided to appeal to, he said, would decide their status as a national party.[41] Only an appeal to the centre could keep the One Nation strategy intact.

The growing ideological offensive of the New Right in the party in the late 1960s, therefore, was unsettling for the progressive wing of the party. Whereas the New Right in the main directed their appeal firmly at the party's traditional support and other solid elements in the country, the progressive tendency was trying to attract the support of new groups whose precise existence and attitudes were a little vague. The New Right imperilled its electoral strategy, and threatened the leadership's interpretation of the competition policy as well.

Crossbow noted in 1968[42] the increasing activity of the 'Right' in the party, but believed that the 'Left' still had important weapons. Although it lacked the big 'constituency battalions', it still had 'the sympathy of much of the leadership of the party', and 'an understanding that a visible lurch to the Right was hardly a recipe for electoral victory.' What *Crossbow* had in mind, no doubt, was that a lurch to the right, on immigration for example, might alienate many of the new salariat. Whether this would cost the party electoral victory was another question. *Crossbow* opposed making any further concessions to the Right—their demands were insatiable, it claimed. Its advice was not heeded. Six months later in a further editorial, 'The Swing to the Right or Back in Trouble', the journal complained[43] that on two politically crucial issues, immigration and law and order, 'gratuitous concessions have been made to the party's reactionary wing.' This threatened, said *Crossbow*, the whole electoral strategy the leadership had followed since 1966. After the defeat of that year there was talk of the need to retrench, but Heath had decided, rightly in *Crossbow*'s view, that 'appealing to those who did not vote for us was more important than simply appeasing those who did.' In *Crossbow*'s view it was the middle ground, the floating vote, that was always what was most important. The shift to the right on immigration and crime threatened the appeal to the centre, and with it the competition policy:[44]

There is now a real danger that, while on issues such as these, the leadership rushes to the backwoods to put on the woad the whole laboriously constructed fabric of *new* Conservative policies will collapse from neglect. . . . After the last election, a tremendous amount of work on policy was set in hand. The hope was that this would come to fruition about now and pave the way for a definitive, and above all forward-looking, restatement of modern Conservative belief in time for the next election. . . . Most of this work has now been completed. Yet somehow nothing seems to be happening.

The New Right offensive was seen by *Crossbow* as a return to 'ideology', a retreat from modernity:[45]

It is just not good enough for a modern Conservative party to
return to the well worn fields of race, law and order, and Marshallian
economics, make emotional speeches and pretend this is going to win
back the voters who left us for Harold Wilson in 1966. The country
is faced with new and different issues from those of ten or even
five years ago. The party has perfectly adequate intellectual equip-
ment to produce and present the policies for which these issues call.

Support for this position came from the Young Conservatives. Under
an editorial headed 'The old and hoary right wing' *Impact* called on all
'left and centre' Conservatives to unite against the danger from the
right. It was the inflexibility of right wing attitudes, it claimed,[46] that
drove so many people away from the Conservatives. The achievement
of Butler and the group around him after 1945 had been to develop
'contemporary relevant and democratic policies.' There was need for
such rejuvenation again.

There was a general failure on the part of the Progressives to understand the new strength of the Right and the sources of that strength,
and the fact that the challenge of the Right was not simply on 'liberal'
issues but on the whole question of the post-war consensus.

3 THE HYDRA OF THE RIGHT

For this old and hoary right wing was, in some respects not old and
hoary at all, and certainly not unified. The *Spectator* stated bluntly in
July 1968:[47] 'The notion of a coherent body of right wing opinion
trying to make a takeover bid for the Conservative party is palpably
false.' This editorial distinguished three different 'rights' in the party—
on foreign policy, on economic policy, and on home policy—but
emphasized that no single Conservative of any importance could be
found in all three.

This was on the whole correct,[48] but then the real challenge of the
right lay elsewhere, not so much on particular items of policy, as in its
ability to articulate electoral ideologies that drew wide support in the
party and undermined the electoral perspective of the leadership. The
weakness of the modern wing of the party was its slender grasp of
the requirements of the politics of support in Opposition. Instead it concentrated on its programme for the revival of British capitalism, the
competition policy. By contrast the new right was overwhelmingly
involved in the politics of support, in the questions of the meaning of
Conservatism and the identity of the Conservative party. The Right
grasped what the modern wing did not, that a competition policy,
however necessary, could not be recommended to the electorate and to
the party on technical grounds alone, but had to become part of a much
more general political and ideological offensive. The competition policy

and the appeal to the centre would not carry British capitalism through its deepening crisis. The New Right wanted a new approach to the nation, based on the fundamental principles of the One Nation strategy —strong national leadership, a new national consensus, and avoiding the drift towards politics being seen in class or interest group terms. This was their general message, expressed in many different ways and by many different spokesmen.

Peregrine Worsthorne put it clearly:[49]

> The economic arguments for capitalism have never by themselves . . . been enough to elicit a national response, which is why the Tory party has seldom really been at ease with itself, or with the country, except when it has been able to define its purpose in much broader terms, both as the custodian of individual liberty and the instrument of social order and stability.

Worsthorne regarded the abiding aim of the Tory party to be the creation of a governing class, a class skilled in the art of negotiating the politics of support and power. If the party ignored this central problem of social leadership, how it could be achieved and maintained, then it was doomed:[50]

> [the Tory party's] whole purpose is to make it possible for a governing class to get on with the job of governing, within the context of universal franchise; to relate the practical requirements of good government to the contemporary circumstances of majority rule, to translate the idea of aristocratic rule into terms which make sense in a democracy, which means organizing mass support for what is basically an elitist or paternalist system of government.

Worsthorne was therefore very critical of the whole strategy of Heath's new Tories. The competition policy was so framed that it could only appeal to the innovators and the pacesetters. The majority had to be left outside. But it was of crucial importance, insisted Worsthorne, if the Tories were to secure popular endorsement, that the successful achieved success in a way which encouraged the rest of society to try and keep up.

In the meantime, he argued,[51] continued Labour rule would bring three dangers: economic stagnation through assaults on private wealth, political dictation through the disruption of market disciplines, and social disintegration through the undermining of the existing basis of social authority and leadership. Although Worsthorne saw the economic question as the root of all these threats, he did not view the situation in narrow economic terms. Instead he argued that a fundamental reappraisal of Tory policy since the war was now possible. The Tories had been on the defensive too long and had been content to put the case for private enterprise in terms of 'economic efficiency' rather than 'social desirability'. Now the economic crisis, the growing power of the state, and the undermining of social leadership all combined to make an overturning of the post-war settlement and the reversal of the 'trend towards egalitarianism' essential: 'The doctrines of Enoch Powell cease to be merely fanciful; they become politically practicable as well as economically right.'

That Worsthorne's words were something more than the ramblings of an eccentric Tory romantic is shown by the many new growths in Conservative thought that began sprouting in this period. Angus Maude was one of the most coherent spokesmen for the New Right. He lost his place in the Shadow Cabinet in 1966 after contributing a gloomy piece to the *Spectator* entitled 'Winter of Tory Discontent.' He had argued that the party had lost the political initiative and was divided and deeply worried. To the electorate at large it had become a 'meaningless irrelevance.' In the past, he wrote, the party had survived in a crisis not by rallying to its leader, but by trusting in its 'ability to discern in doubtful situations what the people of this country really want', and then choosing a leader to project this instinct into action.

This was one of the first public criticisms of Heath's leadership. The early years of the leadership of both Baldwin and Macmillan, wrote Maude, had seen solid achievement:[52] 'In each there was achieved a national consensus in favour of certain necessary but potentially divisive social changes.' Maude clearly felt that similar leadership to guide the Conservatives and the country was no longer forthcoming. Implicitly, it was Heath's grasp of the politics of support that he attacked. Yet he admitted it was difficult to know the instincts and attitudes of the electorate, because of the speed of technological change and the size of organizations. Tradition too had 'almost ceased to be a helpful guide.' But he was sure of one thing: 'for the Tories simply to talk like technocrats will get them nowhere.'

In the years that followed he began to develop answers to these questions. In his 1967 CPC Lecture, *The Consuming Society*, he directed his attack against the ideology of growth on the one hand, and Conservative empiricism on the other. He called for a return to a politics based on principle:[53] 'Every political party needs some solid ground of philosophy to stand on—otherwise it is apt to be swept away by the tides of passing fashion and fancy.' British Conservatism he found a ragbag of borrowings—Locke's theory of property, Adam Smith's economics, militant imperialism, social justice, collectivism, the Welfare State. According to Maude, the content of a Conservative philosophy was not a matter of academic interest—the lack of philosophy was at the root of the current Conservative malaise. Philosophy would tell the Conservatives what it was they wanted to conserve.

In other words, Maude wanted the search for new policies to be conducted in terms of a discussion of identity, in terms of the politics of support rather than the politics of power. The Progressives were not interested in that kind of discussion, and Maude, like Worsthorne, criticized them for concentrating on how the active, the clever, and the strong could rise to the top, without bothering about what happened to the rest. Maude proposed the Tories throw out Locke's theory of property because it justified large accumulations of property and an unlimited right of acquisition. Instead Tories should recognize that full and complete citizenship was impossible without the possession of property:[54]

> It is the only thing that gives an individual or a family a special private place in the world, confers the necessary degree of independence and a recognisable status, and brings him into a meaningful relationship with his environment.

The property owning democracy must become a priority, declared Maude. 'We say we believe in small businesses . . . but we adopt policies that achieve the opposite.'

Maude was still more caustic about the central idol of the Tory growthmen—economic growth itself, a fetish he called it; that produced 'a sterile cycle of increasing production for increasing consumption of increasingly trivial things.' The Tories adherence to the Liberal theory meant that they could not question the verdict of consumers expressed through the market, even though many of the things produced and consumed were not 'spontaneous consumer "wants" at all, but gimmicks thought up by producers and foisted on the public by massive advertising.'

The onslaught on the consensus by the New Right led naturally to the adoption of the 'silent majority' perspective, the idea of a growing gulf between the decision-makers and opinion formers at the centre and the great mass of 'ordinary' people. It was to be exploited most dramatically by Powell. Many in the party thought that his eruption over immigration in 1968 had a significance beyond the issue of immigration itself. Maude, for instance, in an article headed 'The end of consensus?' wrote that Powell's speech allowed many other issues to be debated, including the permissive society, education, and 'international standardisation..' There was a gap between 'opinion at the grass roots' and 'current political dialogue in Parliament and the Press':[55]

> There are those in all three political parties who have accepted, in a kind of left-wing package deal, the objective of a society which seems permissive almost to the point of anarchy. . . . There is a reaction, increasingly finding expression in open protest, against the trend towards size, centralization and uniformity.

Maude supplied a critique of the ideology of growth, and how it reflected the interests of the big companies. He related it to the social malaise and disenchantment with politics, but he remained rather scornful and patronizing about what he called the 'reactionaries' in the party. Their prescriptions, he wrote, are 'normally hopelessly unrealistic and they do not understand the root causes of the symptoms that trouble them.' Some of these reactionaries, however, thought Maude's prescriptions equally unrealistic, especially his commitment to work within the Tory party to try and persuade the leaders to adopt different policies, and even his support for Powell. A review of his book *The Common Problem* in *Monday World* acknowledged that it gave 'uncommon answers', but questioned the practicability of Maude's attempt to make Labour the party of technical progress and the Conservatives the champions of human values:[56]

> Can one really see Heath and the Left and Centre of the party (i.e. at present the most powerful part) as the champions of anti-materialism? And as for Powell (who in most people's minds, however mistakenly, is the main alternative to Heath) nothing could be further from his brand of dynamic super capitalism.

The articulate 'reactionaries' within the Conservative party were concentrated most heavily in the Monday Club.[57] The Club had been formed in 1961 by a group of younger Conservatives to oppose the Government's Africa policy. After 1964 it became a focus for many right wing dissidents in the party and the main institutional expression of the new right tendency. It attracted a mass membership and organized as a faction to change Conservative policy by applying pressure through parliament, constituency associations and the annual conference. By 1970 it claimed to have ten thousand members and thirty branches. The number of MPs who were enrolled increased after the 1970 election from sixteen to twenty-seven. In addition, six members of the new Government were members of the Monday Club, including Geoffrey Rippon, Julian Amery, and John Peyton. The Club rarely spoke with one voice, but through its publications and its journal it helped to advance what became a fairly general new right critique of post-war Conservatism. The Monday Club claimed that it had replaced the Bow Group as the most important pressure group in the Conservative party by 1970, but in truth their roles were very different. The Monday Club was oriented overwhelmingly to the politics of support within the party, and sought to develop an electoral ideology that could challenge the leadership's addiction to the consensus. The Bow Group, by contrast, functioned as a research group for the leadership, and worked within its electoral perspective. It was in general far more concerned with the problems of government policy than with electoral ideologies.

In the new right critique of the electoral perspective of the leadership, the break up of the existing national consensus was treated as a priority. John Biggs-Davison, MP, had all the arguments. In a pamphlet

The Centre cannot hold or *Mao, Marcuse, and all that Marx*, quite as rambling as its title suggests, one message came over clearly:[58]

> Post-war Conservative Administrations wonderfully increased the wealth and welfare of the people; yet they were also content to accept with modifications the Socialism they inherited. Thus each succeeding Labour Government has carried us further towards the Total State whereas Conservatives put back the clock of doom only a few minutes. The next Conservative Government, while seeking the widest support for its measures, must end consensus politics. . . . . Under the creeping socialism of a generation we have been stripped well-nigh naked of our monetary, military and moral defences. The threat to our kinsfolk and partners overseas, is matched by the threat to domestic economy and social order.

The Conservative party, in Biggs-Davison's view, faced 'an almost superhuman labour of national rescue and revival.' Unfortunately the party itself had not been immune from 'degeneracy and materialism.' In the past it had compromised with sectional interests and the 'Whiggish or Liberal or Socialist spirit of the age.' There had been a long battle between the 'truly Tory' and the 'narrowly and selfishly Conservative.' Thus like those before him who sought to change the direction of the Conservative party, Biggs-Davison appealed to the Tory tradition to rescue the Conservative Nation. The Right Progressives were consigned to the bin of anti-national Whiggish elements. In this task of purifying the party, the Monday Club, like the Tory Reform Committee before it, had a special role:[59]

> The Monday Club has done a special service to Conservatism and to Britain. It has given new hope to many who had begun to despair of both. It has rescued Toryism from tepidness, from trimming and from toadying to an intellectual, cultural and political establishment that is pink and permissive. . . . Conservatism in Britain has lost the people and gone down to deserved defeat when it has followed the fashionable fallacies of the age, gone wandering in search of that mythical 'middle ground of politics' and allowed itself to be blown hither and thither by winds of change.

The New Right made the 'middle ground' the opposite of the silent majority. Instead of it holding the great bulk of moderate opinion as the Progressives imagined, the New Right saw the middle ground being occupied only by the Progressives themselves. The Progressives used their power to suppress discussion of certain issues and justified their policies by saying the middle ground, the centre, supported them. Their chief agent was the mass media. As *Monday World* commented[60] after the Surbiton affair in 1969, in which a Monday Club caucus had attempted to get rid of their MP, Nigel Fisher, because of his liberal views on immigration,

> The treatment of the Surbiton affair by the mass media is sympto-
> matic of consensus politics and the national crisis of will. We are
> probably moving into a decade of unprecedented political insta-
> bility, uncertainty and change. Unless the Conservative party and its
> individual members of Parliament are able both to recognize and
> to meet the challenge of the changing times we could be in for a
> period of civil disturbance unparalleled since Chartist agitation over
> one hundred years ago.

The remedy was plain; a policy of 'genuine Conservatism' which would overturn the consensus:[61]

> The 'opinion formers' and the politicians can no longer ignore the
> increasing demands of the people. They are calling for stricter
> control of immigration to protect standards of education and
> housing; they are seeking sterner penalties for criminals in the face
> of the phenomenal increase in crime: they are demanding a return
> to discipline in the universities.

Two other influential spokesmen for the New Right echoed this view, Rhodes Boyson and Richard Law. Both attacked the post-war consensus and the electoral strategy and perspective of the Right Progressives. Like many others on the New Right they emphasized the importance of principles to guide political practice.

Boyson pointed to the increasing swings in public opinion as evidence that politics was becoming less and less about fundamental moral concerns and more and more about material benefits. Unlike the growthmen and social engineers he took no delight in this development. For it meant the emasculation of the Conservative party. In the 1930s, he argued,[62] both parties made moral appeals. The Conservative appeal was based on patriotism, 'pride in King, country and empire.' Since the war, however, while the Labour party still made a moral appeal,

> the Conservatives offered no alternative morality of politics but
> attempted and still appear to the general public to attempt to win
> popularity and even esteem by outbidding the Labour party in
> social welfare. With the exception of the early years of the 1951
> Conservative Government under Winston Churchill, the country
> continued to advance step by step to socialism, more government
> control, more egalitarianism, and to a reduced-choice, heavily
> taxed economy.

Richard Law argued likewise[63] that there was 'a tendency of the modern Conservative government to reflect passing fashion rather than any coherent principle of government.' The opportunity of 1951 had been lost; instead socialist policies had been continued and extended. By 1964 he claimed, half of Labour's programme had been realized and most of its plans already endorsed, by its predecessor. The party had been captured by the doctrinaires of progress who rejected Conservatism as a political philosophy and argued that a Conservative party, to be an effective political force, had to turn its back on the past and become a party of progress. It would no longer differ from the Labour party by its outlook or aims, but only in the means which it used to reach them. This had now reached its climax and ultimate absurdity, according to Law, in the goal of modernization:[64]

> A Conservative party which makes an idol of modernization,
> which sees itself as dragging Britain, an unruly child, kicking and
> screaming into the twentieth century, is abrogating its most
> important function: that is, to test the new idea against experience.

The pursuit of modernization within a 'socialist' framework had meant a steady debasement of politics. The New Right intensely disliked the new 'scientific' techniques of electioneering. For Boyson[65] the situation was approaching when 'the electorate chooses between the parties as if between rival supermarkets selling the same goods but with varying prices and special offers to attract the consumer. This would be the end of our hopes for a mature democratic society.' Furthermore, wrote Law,[66] the parties assumed that they had to win the support of the floating vote by pursuing policies of the centre. Floating voters were imagined to be progressive and anti-conservative. The result was that 'policies which in themselves command wide backing, or which at the least ought to be the subject of public debate, have to be suppressed for fear of repelling a minority on whose support office is thought to depend.' The examples Law gave included immigration and the social reforms of the 1960s. He agreed with Boyson:[67] 'Electioneering is at least as much a moral as it is a political exercise.' Both were agreed also that unless the Conservative party renewed its moral appeal and broke with the consensus it could only hope to win power through the mistakes and incompetence of its political opponents, and would itself be ineffective in power. At bottom they discerned a failure of leadership. The Conservatives, said Law, had done nothing to form the climate of opinion. They had only learned how to live with it:[68] 'Those who set the trend, not those who reflect it, have the real power.' His opinions, isolated in the 1940s, now received increasing attention.

What the Monday Club and the spokesmen of the New Right provided was not an alternative to the competition policy so much as a new framework in which it could be discussed. They expressed and helped to mobilize a growing body of opinion in the party, and their strength was recognized by the leadership who made concessions to them. In the contest between the perspective of the middle ground and the perspective of the silent majority, the latter had many advantages, not least that its support was at least visible, and not very silent.

4 LIBERTYVILLE

Much of the New Right critique, however, during the years of opposition dwelled not only on the blanket fog of welfare and the creeping 'socialism' of the consensus, but also on a more general cultural malady that was afflicting Britain. A tide of permissiveness was seeping forward as the old traditional order was relaxed. It threatened the Conservative Nation at its roots for it attacked many of the fundamental institutions and attitudes that Conservatives regarded as the source of nourishment for the whole social and economic order. Not only the family was in danger, but all established authority, including 'the moral props against surrender to avarice, envy, and lust.'[69] Such props included church attendance, patriotism, middle class codes of behaviour, pride in work, and a stable class system. Norman St John Stevas defined the permissive society as[70] 'a society where law in relation to morals, and especially sexual morals, plays a minimum role.' But the meaning of the phrase to many Conservatives is much better caught by E. Rhys Williams, writing in *Monday World*:[71]

> The Permissive Society is what we call the world we see approaching, the system with no justice and no escape. This is Libertyville, where the law won't protect you and the angels won't help you; and the saints won't welcome you here.

Permissiveness was associated in the first place with the various measures of social reform—capital punishment, abortion, divorce, and homosexuality—that the Labour Government allowed to pass through Parliament as private members bills. But increasingly it was identified with other trends in the 1960s, over which legislation had little or no control; the increasing use of drugs other than alcohol and nicotine, the spread of venereal disease, vandalism of all kinds, violent demonstrations and student unrest.

The Labour Government could hardly be blamed directly for such varied and deepseated ills. Yet it was held responsible for the climate in which such things could flourish. Edward Taylor, MP, told the 1968 conference that the only thing that was booming under Labour was crime. Yet it was not Labour's policy to make it boom. This was a difference from the first post-war period of opposition. In those years, the Labour Government had been attacked for weakening the national character by taking away incentives for hard work and thrift, and by removing opportunities for enterprise and self-reliance. But few Conservatives thought the mischief permanent. The community was under attack from the alien and misguided policies of the Government. But the attack came from outside, and so, like the German Luftwaffe, it could be met and repulsed by a united people, provided the Nation's spirit stayed strong and its heart sound. Permissiveness was not launched directly by any Government, so could not be resisted by political means only. A mere change of Government would not reverse its progress. It was thus more like a cancer than an enemy invasion, and it ate away from within at the heart of the Nation—the institutions of established authority.

In each year of opposition the Conservative conference debated some aspect of permissiveness; in 1965, crime; in 1966, law and order; in 1967, drugs; in 1968, law and order, and student unrest; in 1969, law and order yet again. What worried many Conservatives increasingly, in all parts of the party, was that the very affluence which Conservatives had fostered and claimed as their own, now seemed to be engendering unsuspected monsters. There were conflicting interpretations as to why this should be so. Reginald Maudling was wont to ascribe these social evils to fundamental changes in human societies, in which he included the scale of war, economic growth, and the application of science to human behaviour:[72]

> All these things are shaking our society to its very roots. The old disciplines have disappeared or are disappearing. The old discipline of mass unemployment and grinding poverty has largely been eliminated. Family ties and family discipline are loosening. The influence of religion on social behaviour seems to be fading. The sense of personal obligation to society has been dimmed and dulled in a world that is changing so fast and in a society grown so complex that the individual feels helpless to influence his own destiny.

A general sense of unease pervaded the party. But many on the New Right tried to blame what had gone wrong on the post-war settlement. It was the politics of power and the new state, which both parties had been happy to man since 1945, that had unleashed these evils. Mr Clive Howson put this argument in its most extreme form when he declared at the Brighton conference in 1969 that the real crimes were not homicide, assault or battery, but the 'violence' of dope peddling, abortion, easy divorce, pornography and homosexuality, immigration, town planning and euthanasia. All these crimes had one source[73]— 'violence against a parent's self-respect, committed by the Socialist state apparatus crushing self help and a parent's natural desire to work, to save and to insure and to educate his children independently.' These themes were echoed by many on the New Right. The secret of national regeneration, therefore, not just for the economy, but for the whole society, lay in a radical new course that broke with the post-war settlement.

The dilemma for the Tories, however, was acute. Opposition to permissiveness lived uneasily alongside economic individualism. In the 1950s, a strong lobby had waged a successful campaign for the introduction of commercial broadcasting. Its supporters urged that any monopoly was totalitarian, and that to leave broadcasting in state hands was to pass a vote of censure on the British public, and to accept the principle that the state knew better than the citizen what was good for him. The opposition to commercial broadcasting had stressed that the high standards of the BBC would be endangered if competition were allowed, and that broadcasting was not an industry like any other. There was only one British way of life and one moral code. Its communication had to be safeguarded. A single broadcasting authority was the best way of ensuring that the new medium was not abused.

Here was a real dilemma, which surfaced again in the 1960s. Were there areas in society which should be protected from the ideology of the free market? The Right Progressives and the supporters of the competition policy had no doubts. As Eldon Griffiths, MP, declared in 1966:[74] 'Higher standards in broadcasting as in most other things cannot be legislated; they can only be achieved by increased competition and by widening the area of choice.' This argument was widely accepted in the party and commercial radio was voted for by Conservative conferences in 1966 and 1969. But if it was accepted that the state had no business in controlling the content of broadcasting because the only arbiter could be the individual himself, then ought not the state to withdraw from upholding and enforcing standards in all areas of social life?

This was a very relevant question for many of the social reforms of the permissive society, such as abortion, divorce, and homosexuality. It was also true of such matters as the use of drugs. At the 1967 conference the motion on drugs strongly disapproved of any move towards a more permissive attitude to soft drugs. But one speaker, Mr Martin, although shouted down several times, pointed out the illogicality of the conference's attitude, especially since the theme of individual freedom had been so prominent in so many other debates. He openly advocated the legalization of marijuana, because, he argued,[75] 'we must not identify ourselves with the school which tells the individual what is best for him. This is a paternal and dangerous attitude which is nearer to socialism than to the true beliefs of this party.'

Martin was only using the arguments that Eldon Griffiths and all the other supporters of free broadcasting had used. Standards and rules of conduct should not be imposed on the individual by the state; they could only be truly established if individuals were allowed to choose from a variety of alternatives, and that meant allowing competition—in the economic sphere between different commodities, and in the social sphere between different ways of life.

But this most Tories were far from ready to accept. Quintin Hogg informed the conference in 1969[76] that cannabis smoking had been associated for 2,500 years 'in precise degree to the way in which men and women become dependent on it with physical weakness, mental weakness, mental instability, violence, and crime.' The man in Conservative Central Office still knew best and the people had to be protected. T. E. Utley was profoundly disturbed as well. The spread of pot smoking, he wrote,[77] was part of a movement of cultural protest which no-one 'concerned to maintain any kind of social cohesion' could contemplate 'without horror and abhorrence.'

Free choice was one thing when applied to the economy. It was an important principle that could justify the enlargement of the sphere of private enterprise. But few Conservatives believed that liberal individualism could be allowed to flourish in the social sphere. The forces of the alternative society might be small, but Conservatives had no trouble in recognizing them as a threat to the British way of life and the British state because they undermined the elaborate ideological defences and institutions of social control that protected the interests of property. It was with relief that many Conservatives found they could still contemplate and celebrate the British way in their electoral stronghold—the countryside. As Sir Cyril Osborne explained in 1967:[78]

> Village life still retains much of England's traditional virtues—
> self reliance and self respect, and a willingness to work. Our big
> cities are breeding a tiny but growing minority of spongers, whose
> ideal is to thumb a lift through life, and who, lacking roots, are
> not ashamed to eat the bread of idleness . . . you country people
> have a natural gentility, dignity, and decency, which contrasts vividly
> with the dirty, scrappy, long-haired, and weirdly attired minority of
> city-bred exhibitionists.

A special danger was that permissiveness might undermine the will to work and, together with full employment, might release the workers from the discipline imposed by unemployment, poverty, and the schooling of many generations in the ways of industrial society. Conservatives detected increasing signs of dissatisfaction among people in their work. Some put this down to the youth culture which had helped to break up family ties and the controls of the school, the church and the community, by making young people more independent both financially and culturally. Encouraged to believe in success, they identified with the successful, 'the hairy idols of the entertainment world', in one MP's words,[79] with the result that 'many failures in the lower streams of life, and of school life in particular, identify themselves with these idols, and their values become anti-social, anti-moral, anti-work.' Here was another drawback of affluence.

Violent crime was still a major preoccupation of the Conservative rank and file, and was firmly linked in their minds to the spread of permissiveness. Little was heard, however, after 1961, about bringing back the birch. Instead attention switched to the rope. Following the bill to end capital punishment in 1965, a very strong campaign was mounted in the party to get the Conservatives committed to bringing it back. In 1966, William Deedes and Duncan Sandys, both former ministers, moved an amendment to the resolution on law and order, calling for the reimposition of the death penalty for the murder of policemen and prison officers. It failed, partly because Hogg, the Shadow Home Secretary, appealed for it to be thrown out, and partly because a majority in the party wanted all murderers to be hanged, not just those who happened to murder policemen and prison officers. In 1969, however, an amendment to the law and order resolution, pledging the party to restore full capital punishment was forced to a vote, one of the first ever held at a Conservative conference. It was carried by 1,117 votes to 958, a majority of 159. Its proposer, Patrick Jenkin Jones, attacked the leadership for not making hanging an election issue.

The conference, however, did not get its way, even though it had openly defied the leadership in a way it had not done over corporal punishment. This vote and the extent of party feeling on violent crime certainly influenced the leadership in making law and order an election issue, but Heath himself would not commit the party to any pledge to bring back hanging. All he promised was a free vote in the House of Commons, which everyone knew would mean an abolitionist majority.

Violence was certainly the aspect of permissiveness which Conservatives feared the most, for many seemed to think that increasing violence was inevitable if traditional standards and controls were relaxed. It was not so much that they believed in a past age of order and obedience which had never existed, as that they felt the power of 'society' to defend itself had been gravely weakened. This kind of feeling was put very clearly by Edward Taylor, MP, in one of the debates:[80] 'The vast majority of decent people in Glasgow and other great cities are living in fear and terror, afraid to open their doors at night.'

Apart from violent crime and vandalism, however, Conservatives became perturbed in the late Sixties that 'violence' was spreading to the universities and the trade unions. Violence was not in fact very precisely defined, and increasingly what it meant to Conservatives, and especially the New Right, was not physical assault, but any actions that challenged established authority and established procedures. Thus student demonstrations and sit-ins which in England were remarkably non-violent, were still considered violent by many Conservatives because they existed at all. Conservatives realized that the great expansion of university education their Government had launched in the early Sixties as part of their programme of modernization and speeding economic growth, had a negative side. It did not mean simply a new army of technologists and professional workers to staff the new middle class and middle income society of which the Right Progressives were dreaming. The universities might also provide new seedbeds for the forces of disruption and subversion, all ready for planting by groups of 'professional agitators, riff-raff from various parts of the world.'[81]

Thus, uncomfortably for Heath's new Tories, most of the evils of permissiveness were identified with affluence, economic growth, and modernization. It further narrowed support in the party for the electoral perspective that was bound up with the competition policy, and strengthened feeling in the party against the post-war settlement and the consensus and defensive Toryism that had followed it. Yet this mood in the party did not add up to a real challenge to the leadership. That was to come from another quarter.

5 ENOCH POWELL

> The greatest task of the statesman . . . is to offer his people good myths and to save them from harmful myths. (Enoch Powell)[82]

> I am just going to cast my vote for Conservative . . . but Sir I am voting for the Rt Hon Enoch Powell. I have always voted Labour; but with such a great man (A REALIST) in the opposition, it leaves me no choice. (an elector from Bootle)[83]

> Don't shout at me. I'm not a foreigner. (Enoch Powell—attributed)

The most articulate and controversial spokesman for the New Right was Enoch Powell. But his significance is often misunderstood. His economic policies for instance were widely described as 'laissez-faire' and economically illiterate by the press,[84] and his speeches on immigration have been seen as an opportunist bid for the leadership of the Tory party.[85] There is, however, a great deal more to Powell than this. It is true to say that his ideological offensive in the 1960s was the only comprehensive assault on the dominance of the Right Progressives in the whole of the post-war period. Powell fed from the same trough as the New Right, but he went far beyond them. Powellism, as it unfolded, came to offer not merely a new politics of power to reorganize the state and a new politics of support to win the assent of the nation, but also an alternative leadership to carry them through. It offered in effect a new national strategy to the Tories. To achieve this meant that Powell himself had to accept political isolation with no immediate or certain prospect of eventually returning to power. But such politicians are important because by putting forward clearcut alternatives they are available in a political crisis to replace the leaders and the policies that have failed. In the meantime they gather support as best they may outside the existing political machine.[86]

The other interesting fact about Powellism was its ideological strength inside the Tory party. Many of Powell's ideas could be brushed aside by the leadership when the Tories were in power, but it was hard to resist them ideologically, especially during Opposition. This is one reason why the party had swung so much towards Powell's point of view, especially on such questions as prices and income policy and government intervention in industry by the time the 1970 election took place. The interests that supported Powell in the Midlands and elsewhere were mostly drawn from the middle class of small businessmen and shopkeepers. This was a group strongly represented in the constituency associations.

For a long while Powell's political thinking was concerned overwhelmingly with economic questions—the superiority of the market to state planning.[87] He acquired therefore the reputation of being a particularly rigorous economic liberal who accepted absolutely that the free play of forces of supply and demand in a market would establish an equilibrium between them at full employment of resources.[88] He advocated therefore applying this rule to every problem and institution where economic criteria were relevant. He has constantly proclaimed:[89]

> The Conservative party, being a capitalist party and a party of free
> enterprise, accepts the market as the arbiter of measurable material
> benefit, and rejects the state. Hence the necessity of eliminating
> state decisions or intervention wherever economic benefit is
> accepted as the touchstone.

The areas where Powell advocated the reintroduction of market forces and the withdrawal of the state included housing, social services, trade unions, nationalized industries, and exchange rates.[90]

The central distinction throughout Powell's thinking is thus between the free society and the Socialist state.[91] He spelt out the electoral ideology behind this position in characteristically stark terms in May 1964:[92]

> Whatever else the Conservative party stands for, unless it is the party
> of free choice, free competition, and free enterprise, unless—I am
> not afraid of the word—it is the party of capitalism, then it has no
> function in the contemporary world, then it has nothing to say
> to modern Britain.

For Powell, the free society, the reign of the market, meant that decision making was dispersed as widely as possible. It offered the best way of guaranteeing both economic efficiency and economic independence. It was also the natural counterpart of a democratic political system.[93]

A community of sturdy individualists, standing on their own feet and taking responsibility for themselves and their families was not however an ideal that put Powell outside the Tory party. Similarly, his emphasis on competition and market forces to speed economic growth and create prosperity rather than state intervention were widely supported by Conservatives. Powell also found himself in strong agreement with the Bow Group, especially on the question of applying the free market to the social services.[94] Big differences, however, began to emerge between them over the question of the state and the competition policy. Most of the Bow Group favoured using the government to intervene to make the economy more competitive and efficient and to ensure the operation of market forces. This reflected the interests of the big companies and their importance to the economy. Powell's stand against all forms of state intervention in the name of the principles of liberal economics made him more and more the spokesman for small capital.

What really began to separate Powell from the bulk of the Tory leadership was thus his hostility to the new role of the state in the economy. This first became clear at the time of his resignation from the Government with Thorneycroft and Birch in 1958, after Thorneycroft was overruled in the Cabinet over the question of holding down government expenditure.[95] Subsequently Powell argued that 1958 was a turning point. Before then government expenditure as a proportion of national income had fallen in every year from 1951. After 1958 it rose each year, until by 1964 it was back to the level that had been inherited from Labour.[96]

In the following years, except for a brief interlude as Minister of Health,[97] Powell became the foremost critic of the new interventionist state that the Conservatives developed to help restructure capital and contain wages, and which was taken over and extended by the new Labour Government.[98]

The growing economic crisis during the 1960s, however, and the association of 'planning' with Labour lent Powell's onslaught on the expansion of state intervention extra force. His critique ranged over many topics, but in essence it was about inflation and the causes of inflation. Inflation, he argued, was always either caused or permitted by the government.[99] The explanation of it which governments favoured was a blind alley, a ruse by which politicians sought to 'escape from responsibility for the consequences of their own policies.'[100] They tried to blame inflation on rising costs, and in particular on rising wages, which they claimed were forced up by the monopoly power of trade unions in the labour market.

Powell argued, however, that trade unions had at most only a marginal effect on wage levels.[101] Indeed he claimed that the effect of unions was often to hold wages down below what they might be if there were no collective price fixing in the labour market.[102] The real cause of inflation in Powell's view had been government expenditure, which since 1958 had risen faster each year than national income. Since private savings had not risen sufficiently to bridge the gap, the government's borrowing requirement had been covered by creating money—by selling government securities to the money market and giving the money market the cash to purchase them.[103] Powell noted that the inflation since 1945 had been unique. Formerly the price level had fluctuated, but only since the war had there been a continuing depreciation in the value of money.[104]

Powell put the blame on the new role of the state in the economy and the new size of the state sector, and therefore called into question the whole basis of the post-war settlement. He saw inflation not just as an economic problem, but as a means by which Socialists hoped to extend the control of the state over the economy. For if the responsibility of the state for inflation were not recognized, then the government had an excuse to control prices and wages, which involved a colossal distortion of the price system and an attempt to establish a kind of corporatism, by managing individual workers and firms through the organizations, the trade unions and employers federations, which were supposed to represent them.[105] Powell saw very clearly from the outset that no voluntary policy would ever work for long, and that the government would increasingly be obliged to step in to control wages and prices at source, by regulating the forces of supply and demand at the level of local bargains and contracts.[106]

Powell's solution to the inflation crisis was fairly simple. Public expenditure had to be drastically reduced and the exchange rate for sterling floated. The aim behind both was the same:[107]

> Only give us a money system which will tell us the truth about the consequences of our choices and decisions, about the true cost of importing, the true profit of export, the true return upon investment; give us this and we can do the rest ourselves.

For he emphasized:[108] 'Upon the sound working of [the] money system, and above all upon the stability and honesty of the currency, depend not only the operations of industry and commerce, but . . . the structure of society itself.' Powell thus attacked the prevailing politics of power for making wages the scapegoat for inflation, because it rested on the mistaken need to maintain the existing parity of sterling,[109] and because it did not touch the real cause of inflation, the level of government expenditure. As a result the policies that were adopted to curb rising prices and wages extended the state sector and threatened the 'free society.'

The consequences of this in Powell's view were calamitous. For inflation was still not halted, and this eroded the value of savings, the life blood of his free enterprise economy.[110] At the same time, the whole price system was upset by government controls and interventions and this meant that for 'too long too much of British industry has ceased to be orientated to profit and therefore to real demand at home and overseas.'[111] He was a fierce critic of all CBI and business collaboration with the government, because he argued that businessmen running the IRC, the little Neddies, and so forth, did not increase economic efficiency, but only cut 'the umbilical cord of self interest which attached them to the nourishing forces of profit and competition.'[112] Big business, he recognized, was only too happy to cooperate with the new interventionist state which was intervening in its interests. Inflation too did not threaten it in the way that it threatened small business.

But perhaps the most serious consequence he discerned from the way in which the prevailing politics of power explained and handled inflation was the impact on political stability. For it brought the government into the front line of the battle of wages. In Powell's view this fatally undermined collective bargaining:[113]

> The whole structure of collective bargaining, and its chance of
> operating freely within a framework of stable money values,
> depends on the fact that the ability of the customer to pay is not
> unlimited. The trouble is that with a public corporation, such as the
> Post Office, no less than with an actual department of government,
> everybody knows that this assumption does not hold good.

Powell therefore advocated that government spending should be drastically cut, the nationalized industries returned to private enterprise, and income tax halved.[114] The government would cease to intervene directly in the economy, would stop investment grants and regional subsidies of all kinds, and would concentrate on maintaining a stable currency.

Powell's ideas caused apoplexy amongst many professional economists and were often dismissed as absurd, or as only reflecting the views of disgruntled small businessmen. The technical questions, however,— whether for instance private savings would rise enough to finance public sector investment if this was no longer raised by taxation and channelled through the government's account—do not concern us here. Besides they are not the most important questions. For Powellism is not simply a set of economic proposals. After the 1964 election Powell's thinking broadened into other fields as well. His economic ideas do not appear in a vacuum but as one element in a new politics of the Nation, a new electoral ideology which in embryo could furnish a new electoral perspective.

The new areas into which Powell ventured included Britain's defences and her place in the world market; immigration, the EEC; and Ulster. Underlying all of them was a concern for defining a new national identity. All these were questions which, as far as Powell was concerned, had to be considered from the political not the economic standpoint,[115] and that meant from the standpoint of the nation. For as he recognized,[116] 'Nationhood, with all that word implies, is what the Tory party is ultimately about.' He stressed the importance of patriotism and the need for 'a realistic appraisal of the true stature of a nation, neither exaggerated, nor underestimated.'[117] He therefore saw his role as helping to make that appraisal, by sweeping away the myths that guided policy and substituting better myths, and by alerting the nation to its true identity and the enemies that threatened it. Once an ardent imperialist he now rejected the Empire ideology totally.[118] His enduring purpose was to forge a new conception of the relationship of the nation to the state.

The two myths he saw as most pervasive and most in need of replacement were the beliefs that Britain was once an imperial power,[119] and the workshop of the world.[120] The abandonment of Empire and Britain's poor economic performance compared to her main rivals meant that most people in Britain had felt the post-war years to be a period of national decline. Powell argued that a new feeling of national strength and a new patriotism could be fostered if the vital relationship between geography and military power[121] were again made the basis of Britain's foreign policy. He therefore advocated that Britain should concentrate her military strength in the place 'where she lived', Europe and the eastern Atlantic. He strongly opposed the attempt to maintain a military presence overseas to put out 'brush fires', because he thought it ineffective, unnecessary, and a heavy cost to be borne by the balance of payments.[122] He also opposed all foreign aid. What was not economic to produce in these countries should not be produced at all. The way forward for the Third World was to follow the path of the West: 'The secret of aid to the developing countries is not capital itself: it is capitalism.'[123]

A new national identity also required, however, a feeling of what sort of people the British were, which meant defining what sort of people they were not. The language of identity always talks in terms of those who belong and those who do not; often it will go further and point out the enemies and the dangers that threaten the existence of the identity it seeks to protect. In this period Powell took up two such threats to his nation, immigration and the EEC.[124]

In both these issues the political question of national identity far outweighed for Powell the 'economic' and technical aspects. Common Market entry, for instance, which he had once supported on orthodox 'laissez-faire' grounds, he now utterly opposed. It was the new and fragile sense of national purpose that was at stake:[125]

> I do not understand how a nation which is in the throes of rescuing
> its identity from the delusions and the deceits of a vanished Empire
> and Commonwealth can at the same time undertake to merge that
> identity again in half the continent of Europe.

Powell identified the English national tradition most strongly with the history of the British Constitution and its two key institutions—Crown and Parliament.[126] It was these the Common Market threatened to subvert. He argued that to the extent that the EEC was more than a mere trading agreement, it meant that certain centrally approved policies would be imposed throughout the Community. The Common Agricultural Policy (CAP) was only the first of these. Most serious he thought were the moves towards the establishment of a common currency. If one were eventually set up, then 'practically the whole of economic decision-making would have been removed from West-minster—and from the United Kingdom.'[127] That might benefit the multinational companies, but not Powell's closest supporters.

Immigration was the issue which marked Powell's break with the Tory leadership. The significance of his 1968 speech, however,[128] was not in what he said but the manner in which he said it. As T. E. Utley has written:[129] 'In its handling of the statistics, in the telescoped and emotive form of much of the argument, it appears as a political act rather than a contribution to debate.' There is little doubt that Powell intended it as such.[130] What he advocated on immigration was no different from current Tory policy; it was his attempt to stigmatize immigrants as strangers, an object of justifiable fear and hatred, and a source of future division in the nation that broke new ground.[131] His speech was an attempt to search out a new constituency, by breaking with the restrictions placed on the politics of support by what was practicable for the politics of power. He achieved a remarkable success. He received 105,000 letters of congratulation within a few days of the speech,[132] together with some threats of assassination. There were demonstrations by dockers and meat porters in his support. The Gallup poll revealed that in May 1968, 74 per cent of those questioned 'agreed' with the speech; 69 per cent thought Heath was wrong to sack Powell from the Shadow Cabinet; while 24 per cent now wanted him to be Leader of the Conservatives if Heath went. This made him overnight the most popular Conservative politician; in April only 1 per cent had selected him.[133]

Powell was seen by his admirers in the New Right as breaking down consensus politics and establishing the basis for a new popular Conserva-tism.[134] He had achieved that most difficult feat for a Conservative politician—winning substantial personal support in the working class. He was described in *Monday World* as the inheritor of the Sorelian tradition in politics. This involved[135] 'emphasizing those aspects of one's programme which are least popular with middle ground opinion. Rather than repressing them in favour of mild deviations from orthodox opinion, the Sorelian politician will flaunt his most extreme policies to emphasize the revolutionary nature of the movement he represents.' This side of 'Powellism' was therefore concentrated overwhelmingly on winning support, and on reflecting views and interests that were not represented in the consensus politics of the two main parties. The normal process of political debate had been suspended, he argued. Debate and conflict between the two parties on most important questions was conspicuous by its non-existence.[136] A 'deep and dangerous gulf' had opened in the nation between 'the overwhelming majority of the people on the one side, and on the other side, a tiny minority, with almost a monopoly hold upon the channels of communication who seem determined not to know the facts and not to face the realities, and who will resort to any device or extremity to blind both themselves and others.'[137]

It was paradoxically Powell's success in winning a new constituency outside the electoral territory of the two main parties that gave his economic programme a new relevance. For a politics of power is only viable so long as it can ensure political stability. The apparent inability of consensus politics to solve Britain's economic crisis in the late 1960s, the growing signs of estrangement and unrest amongst parts of the electorate, enhanced Powell's political importance as an alternative Leader in a future major political upheaval. Powell's great asset was that his politics of the nation appeared to cut across class conflict and mobilize support from all classes.[138] The particular One Nation strategy of the Right Progressives and consensus politics seemed to be dividing the community more and more openly on class lines through the clash between the government and the organized working class over incomes policies. In assessing Powellism, therefore, it is not enough to point out the irrelevance of his economic theories. For in certain circumstances they might become relevant. It is clear that Powell's description of the market economy bears no relation to the economy that actually exists, which is one dominated in most sectors by a few giant corporations.[139] These corporations have a vested interest in the role of the state in the economy, but they have an even greater interest in political stability. In a real crisis they would not oppose Powell if he emerged as leader of the Conservatives. In power Powellism, like every other electoral ideology, would have to come to terms with their other interests. Powell's Nation would have to compromise with the state.

6 CONCLUSION

The second post-war period of Opposition was very different from the first because of the vigour of the electoral ideologies that challenged the electoral perspective of the leadership.

The new right tendency was feeling its way towards a new Conservatism based on moral principles, that would enlist the active enthusiasm of electors and party members. It gained in strength because of a growing belief in the party that it was not enough to put forward just a competition policy. A far more comprehensive programme was needed designed to remedy all the manifold ills of British society, break with the existing consensus politics, and build a new national coalition. The Progressives still believed they could modernize the British economy and restructure British capital without altering their basic electoral strategy and the kind of consensus which had existed since the war. In the end they did not seek to disturb the political and social arrangements that already existed, because they did not wish to alter the essential role of the state in the economy. The competition policy had a quite different meaning depending on the size of the state sector that was to be maintained. The organization of the state was the heart of the consensus, reflecting as it did a balance between the interests of the dominant sections of capital and the claims of the Labour movement. Far more than issues like crime and immigration, it was the main area of disagreement between the Right Progressives and the New Right. It was here too that the New Right had most influence. They strengthened those Right Progressives who wanted to have done with the 'One Nation psychosis' of the 1950s and make the competition policy much tougher than the leadership had originally intended. The Selsdon Park conference[140] of the Conservative leadership held in early 1970 to plan the strategy for the election showed the extent to which the competition policy had been hardened. Selsdon Man's face was not wreathed in smiles. The main themes of the conference indicated abrasive measures to shake up the British economy, curb the power of the trade unions, and restore law and order. The kind of intervention practised by Labour was to be abandoned. Market forces would rule instead—in industrial relations, in housing, in welfare, in the distribution of income. The inefficient would not be propped up and the unprofitable would not be subsidized. The leadership believed that such policies could succeed, where Labour's had failed, in maintaining the state. It was noticeable, however, that no details were given of the promised tax reforms, or of how expenditure could be reduced when the party planned to increase spending on defence in order to keep forces east of Suez. Heath continued to believe that a more efficient administration of the state—a new style of government—could rescue it. He retreated before the pressure from his party until the leadership had accepted an interpretation of many items in the competition policy that seemed to commit the party to a course of collision with several priorities of the prevailing politics of power, and confrontation with the Labour movement. Yet he continued to reject the radical 'ideological' measures to reorganize the state that alone could free any future Tory government from the constraints of the existing one. He did not seek to overturn the prevailing politics of power but to make government more effective and more purposeful in certain directions. He was to suffer a rude awakening.

Chapter 6
THE ROOTS OF INFLATION

An extraordinary feature of Conservative economic performance is that it
grew worse rather than better as time went on.

(Samuel Brittan)[1]

1 THE SETTING: THE STATE SECTOR AND PRODUCTIVE INDUSTRY

After the 1945 election, the Conservatives accepted the new role of the
state, in particular the new level of government spending on social
services, and the new responsibility of the government for managing
the overall level of demand. But the party fought very hard to prevent
the state being extended any further. So nationalization and the level of
public expenditure were the Labour policies that drew most fire. Above
all, Conservatives were anxious to establish a frontier between the state
and the productive sector which would give the greatest possible
freedom to the latter. For they believed that prosperity and growth
depended overwhelmingly on providing the right opportunities for
private capital.

The world boom of the 1950s provided such opportunities, and the
productive sector flourished.[2] The Conservative faith in the market
appeared justified, the more so as Labour's regime of controls and
intervention[3] had coincided with the period of postwar reconstruction.
During the 1950s therefore the Conservatives celebrated the central
importance of the market, and stressed that the government must dis-
charge its responsibility to maintain full employment by acting on the
overall level of demand—i.e. by monetary policy—rather than by direct
intervention.[4] Most Tories at this time shared Enoch Powell's view of
further government intervention:[5]

The Conservative in principle denies, in practice minimizes,
Government intervention in the economic field. Of non-economic
decisions he rejects those which are particular in character and tend
to abolish the economic field, and is critical of those which are
general in character and tend to limit it.

124

The 'economic field' meant activities in which the pursuit and accumulation of profits for private capital was the overriding objective. The Conservative economic policy after they returned to power was aimed at setting enterprise 'free', by restoring competition, reducing taxation, and restricting the state. Yet in practice, Conservative freedom turned out to mean little more than speeding the removal of war-time controls. Under Churchill, the Conservatives had been careful not to commit themselves to any detailed policy statements whilst they were in opposition. When they regained power, Churchill surprised the party by making Butler, and not Oliver Lyttleton, Chancellor of the Exchequer. This was a strong clue as to how far the Government would set the nation free.[6]

Butler continued to dismantle the physical controls on the economy as the Labour Government had done before him. In 1954, food rationing was finally ended. He placed great emphasis on controlling the economy by monetary and budgetary policies. Accordingly, the policy of cheap money was ended, and Bank Rate was moved up and down in a bid to give the Government control of domestic credit and to attract foreign capital into London. When they took office, the Conservatives faced a serious balance of payments crisis, following a £400 million deficit in the wake of the Korean War. In 1952, however, British trade went back into surplus, largely due to an abrupt change in the terms of trade in Britain's favour, and the imposition of import controls. After 1952, the economy began expanding strongly, and Butler was able to assist the boom by cutting taxes. Britain suddenly appeared to have burst out of post-war austerity, and the Conservatives naturally claimed the credit, although in reality the real cause was the boom in the world economy in which Britain shared. Butler confidently predicted in 1954 that the standard of living would double in twenty-five years.

In these years of boom, economic management aimed through budgetary and monetary policy to keep the economy on a course of expansion, and to moderate fluctuations. The Government had to assess whether demand was rising or falling, and then take measures to stabilize it. The effect of such policies was greatly to moderate the old business cycle. Yet it did not do away with it entirely. Economic activity still fluctuated; but it was noticeable, especially in these early years, that it was output rather than employment that varied.[7]

If full employment was one central aim of demand management, the other was balance of payments equilibrium. Unfortunately, however, this second aim did not always square with the first. Neither were technical policies that could be pursued independently of the real world. They reflected the balances and compromises of the prevailing politics of power.

Full employment, for instance was one of the main planks of the post-war settlement, and one of its effects was greatly to strengthen the bargaining power of organized labour in the labour market.[8] Keeping Britain's trade in balance was greatly complicated because governments still sought to maintain two of the chief buttresses of Britain's old role in the world market—the status of sterling as an international currency, and a high level of overseas military spending.[9] (It rose from £12 million in 1952 to £313 million in 1966).

The countries that grew fastest in the post-war years were not burdened by such policies. The strength of their working classes was weak, so wages were held down in the early years of expansion, and they had no pretensions to financial or military independence of the Americans. The British economy grew more slowly at the tail end of the boom. As a result, profits, measured both as a return upon capital and as a proportion of national income began to fall.[10] This further depressed investment, and made British industrial capital increasingly uncompetitive compared with its main rivals.

The basic cause of Britain's slow growth was that the requirements for defending sterling more and more took priority over expanding national output. In the sterling crises of 1955, 1957, and 1961, this became very clear. Conservative Chancellors proved ready to cut back home demand through fiscal and monetary means in order to protect the pound and retain the confidence of international finance. Full employment was not harmed; neither was the export of capital. It was domestic industrial investment that suffered most. Conservative economic management led to a new cycle of economic activity—Stop-Go —that was determined by the actions of the government. Bursts of expansion were always terminated by a balance of payments crisis as imports of raw materials and manufactures rose to feed the boom. Governments acted to deflate the economy to protect the reserves and defend the existing parity of sterling. These crises grew steadily more severe. A chief underlying cause of the deficits, however, was the burden on the balance of payments caused by capital outflows, particularly overseas military spending. This policy was combined with keeping intact the Sterling Area and upholding the status of sterling as an international currency, both as a medium for international trade, and a haven for surplus world capital. Between them they shackled governments to the Stop-Go cycle. Fortunately for the Conservatives, they found they could align it with the electoral cycle. The periods of expansion coincided with general elections.[11]

Stagnating investment, which was the chief result of this policy made the impact of inflation very much worse in Britain than elsewhere. Inflation was not peculiar to Britain, nor was the size of her state sector. It was the rate of growth of her economy that was so low. As a result, Britain's share of world trade began declining, and more seriously, so did her international competitiveness. In this situation cost inflation began to erode profit margins.

The underlying cause of the permanent inflation which was suffered by all the industrialized states and which grew steadily worse, was not faulty demand management by the government, but the size of the state sector itself and the policies that were required to maintain it. The formal condition for inflation to exist is an expanding supply of money. The government allows the money supply to grow in response to demand, rather than reduce its own expenditure or cut back private credit. As a result, the price level is no longer tied to a gold standard, but to a labour standard;[12] there is no external mechanism to keep prices in check by holding the money supply steady, and they therefore rise as costs rise. The accumulation of private debt and the maintenance of the level of government spending (rather than actual budget deficits) ensures that prosperity and full employment are secured.[13]

For a time, a relatively modest inflation was held by some economists to be an unavoidable, but not too costly consequence of a policy of full employment. Optimism gradually evaporated, however, during the 1950s and 1960s, until inflation came to be seen as the most serious economic problem which governments had to tackle. There were several reasons for this in Britain. First, because productivity was rising more slowly than in other countries, the price index of exports rose faster than the international average. This in turn made the balance of payments situation worse, and reduced still further the kind of investment that raised productivity.[14] Second, inflation undermined the world monetary system. Once there was no longer any 'objective' standard, such as gold, and no sound substitute like the dollar or the pound, to regulate exchanges between countries, the basis for exchange, on which continued expansion of world trade depended, appeared increasingly arbitrary. It seemed likely to collapse if countries inflated their currencies at different speeds, and could not agree on how trade deficits were to be financed.[15]

Third, whenever inflation has appeared, it rots the social order of capitalism. It erodes the value of savings and thus blights one major source of new capital and new capitalists. It also makes capital values rather than earnings the source of real wealth, thus encouraging a boom in speculation. It can therefore alienate large sections of the middle classes and those on fixed incomes from the state. At the same time, it breaks the relationship between effort and reward. The idea that there is a just exchange for labour power, and that the market prices the different services of the various factors of production fairly, is a fundamental one for the justification of capitalist institutions. It is naturally undermined when the real value of money is changing so quickly. Inflation thus fuels a new aggressive wage militancy.[16]

The final, and most important, reason why the British state had to resist inflation was the impact on profits. The overall effect in Britain of inflation was falling profit margins and a falling share of profits in national income, because the economy was stagnating in comparison with the world economy. Stagnation in the 1930s had not harmed profits because unemployment had kept down costs. In the post-war period, however, investment stagnated, while prosperity and full employment were maintained by the state. The new state made permanent inflation possible, and so unleashed forces that, in Britain, because of the low rate of growth of productivity, threatened the profitability of the private sector. Governments were therefore obliged to step in to restore that profitability, by confronting the pressure for wage increases directly, by redistributing income to profits through the tax system, and by attempting to modernize and rationalize British industry. This was the course on which the politics of power embarked in the 1960s.[17]

The impact of inflation revealed conflicts between the interests balanced in the state. On the one hand, finance capital and multinational companies actually profited from inflation. Higher interest rates, the ability to choose sites for investment, the switching of funds between different national centres, the reduction in historical investment costs, and the staggering boom in capital values all benefited these sections of capital. Their mobility and liquidity, which reflected their dominant position in the economy, made inflation a source of opportunity rather than despair. What suffered from inflation were the interests of small business, the trade unions, and the national economy. Small business struggled to cover its costs and maintain its cash flow, the unions suffered cuts in the real wages of their members as fast and sometimes faster than they could negotiate wage increases, and the national economy was harmed by the erosion of profit margins in productive industry. Governments felt obliged to intervene because they had to maintain the national economy as a site for profitable investment in productive industry for international capital and for their own industrial firms. Employment and prosperity depended upon it. If the rate of inflation was higher than the international average so that investment and productivity stagnated, Britain's trade and eventually her living standards would decline. No national government could permit that, so long as it remained responsible to the nation through the political market. Capital could move elsewhere, outside a particular nation-state, but a government could not.

Inflation thus gradually transformed the postwar state into a confrontation between the government, acting as the representative of the national economy, and the unions. Governments singlemindedly chose to put the main blame for inflation on the unions, and sought to dramatize the conflict as one between the greedy workers on one side and the powerless consumers and pensioners on the other. Capital was presented as being merely a passive intermediary, passing on higher costs in higher prices. The unions on the other hand came to see the issue more and more as a question of the distribution of income between property and labour. The progress of inflation thus took the covers off the fragile balance of power between the main interests in the state that had been established in the post-war settlement. The government's claim to be a neutral arbiter of the affairs of the state became more and more hollow. The cry for wage control was countered by a cry for price control, and control of land speculation, and the profits of the banks. The whole nature of the 'social contract' which was supposed to underlie the state began to enter political debate once more, and all the assumptions on which it was based came into question.

Within the Conservative party during the 1950s, there was a strong campaign to reduce government expenditure, so that inflation might be held down, and the personal incentives, that were believed so necessary to encourage investors and entrepeneurs to take risks, increased. The electoral ideology behind this campaign was to protect the interests and consolidate the support of the solid middle class—small businessmen, shopkeepers, professional people, farmers—who found themselves particularly affected by inflation and high taxes, and particularly affronted by the prosperity of organized labour.

Yet, although the state did not expand under the Conservatives at first, neither did it contract very far. State expenditure fell as a proportion of GNP until 1958, but not by a great deal, and certainly not by enough to satisfy the clamour for tax cuts, or to threaten the post-war settlement. The nationalized industries were left mostly intact, so were the social services. The Conservative Government recognized the strength of the organized working class and the new importance of the unions in the running of the state, and sought to conciliate them. There were sound electoral reasons also. The middle classes were vocal, but not particularly numerous. A delegate at the 1952 conference undoubtedly echoed the view of the leadership when he argued that the party should pursue a vigorous national policy 'to establish economic stability, social security, and to dispel the fear of war, unemployment and want.' He reminded the conference that the country was evenly divided politically:[18] 'Those who call for a more full-blooded Conservative policy must also fully appreciate the position and show forbearance.' The national appeal of the Conservatives could not be sacrificed.

The difficulty was that a policy of forbearance led to a rising share of wages and salaries in the national income, and stagnating investment. The distribution of real income did not change more only because of inflation and the level of taxation.[19] In the opinion of many Conservatives, it was the reduction in inequality and the redistribution of income, represented by the great expansion of the state, and the attack on the 'profit ethos' that were hindering faster accumulation in Britain. Conservatives were alarmed that if wealth was redistributed any further, the

THE ROOTS OF INFLATION

future of economic growth would be put at risk, because capital would no longer be accumulated in sufficient amounts to justify further investment.[20] All available funds would be diverted overseas or into property speculation.

Before the end of the 1950s, therefore, Conservative leaders were becoming more and more preoccupied with the problem of inflation. Their dilemma was highlighted by Thorneycroft's brief reign as Chancellor of the Exchequer from 1957 to 1958. Thorneycroft became obsessed with two problems, inflation and the defence of sterling. When a sterling crisis arose in the autumn of 1957, not this time due to a balance of payments deficit but to other external international factors, he had no hesitation in deflating the economy still further. His other main priority was to keep the price level stable. This could not be done if workers kept demanding pay increases to keep up with the rising cost of living. For that would lead to further price increases, and a further decline in the competitiveness of British manufactures, while investment and productivity remained stagnant during the period of deflation. Thorneycroft proposed, therefore, that the Government should cease to finance inflation, by holding the supply of money steady. This would mean that any increases in costs and prices would lead to rising unemployment, by causing the bankruptcy of those companies whose credit became over-stretched. Companies would have a new and powerful motive for resisting wage demands. Thorneycroft, and his two Economic Secretaries, Enoch Powell and Nigel Birch, showed themselves ready to sacrifice full employment in the interests of price stability and the value of sterling. Instead of the Government taking responsibility for ensuring full employment, they proposed to shift the 'responsibility' back to the unions. If the unions wished to avoid unemployment, they would have to moderate their wage claims, which meant being prepared to accept wage cuts whenever the economic situation and the plight of capital demanded it.

To be effective, such a policy demanded the closing of the main avenue for increasing the supply of money—government borrowing to finance its own expenditure. Thorneycroft therefore proposed that government expenditure be cut back, and the budget balanced. Such a thorough-going repudiation of the basic features of the post-war settlement was unacceptable to Macmillan and the Right Progressives in the Cabinet. Thorneycroft, accompanied by Powell and Birch, resigned on the issue of increasing Government expenditure. The amount in question was small, but the principle was all-important. Macmillan for his part was not prepared to sabotage the post-war settlement, nor to give up the great electoral boon of inflationary budgets that encouraged the upward swing in the managed Stop-Go cycle to occur just before general elections.[21]

The problems of reconciling full employment, a stable price level, economic growth, and the defence of sterling, in the context of the new state did, however, stir the Right Progressives and Macmillan's Ministers to some fresh thoughts after the 1959 election. The catalyst was undoubtedly the economic troubles in 1960 and 1961. A new awareness about the condition of the British economy brought a determination to find new solutions within the framework of the prevailing politics of power. Rather than dismantle the state sector and all it represented these solutions revolved around giving a far more positive role to the government in order to create the structural conditions for faster growth. In other words, the government itself had to step in to redress the harmful effects which its own level of expenditure and its management of demand were creating.[22]

This produced three major new policies—modernization, rationalization, and incomes policy. The instrument of modernization was new, large-scale government spending programmes, aimed at capital investment in the social services, education, and the regions. Rationalization was pursued chiefly through the NEDC, set up by Selwyn Lloyd, after considerable pressure from business. The NEDC inaugurated indicative planning in Britain, and settled on a 4 per cent growth target. Other signs of rationalization were the Resale Price Maintenance Bill pushed through the Commons by Heath in 1964, and the white paper on the nationalized industries in 1961, which led directly to the Beeching plan for the railways and an accelerated programme of pit closures.[23] Finally, incomes policy was launched in 1962 with the idea of setting a norm for wage increases of 2-2½ per cent. It was later formalized in the National Incomes Commission. Little progress was made, however, in securing the unions' cooperation, mainly because the proposal was made in the shadow of Selwyn Lloyd's Pay Pause.

Alongside these new policies, the Government made its bid to enter the Common Market. But despite all the rethinking and the new directions, certain priorities stayed unchanged. Indeed the background for the new policies was another enactment of the Stop-Go cycle. The balance of payments crisis of 1960 was followed by a sterling crisis in 1961. The economy, which was moving into recession, was helped on its way by Selwyn Lloyd. Private credit and government spending were cut back, bank rate was raised to 7 per cent, the new consumer tax regulator was raised by 10 per cent, and wages were frozen. The Treasury and the Bank of England were urging still sterner measures. Expansion was resumed in 1963 with Maudling as Chancellor, in time for the 1964 election. Another balance of payments deficit loomed, for the pound was now seriously over-valued and ten years of stagnating investment were taking their toll, but Maudling was reported to be ready to use import controls or devaluation, rather than deflation, to counter it. He never had the opportunity because the Tories lost the election, so whether he would have been politically strong enough to change a major priority of the prevailing politics of power and abandon sterling, was never tested.

The electoral perspective that accompanied the Conservatives' economic policies started from the existence of the new state. It accordingly placed enormous emphasis on economic growth, because the new state only seemed workable if governments could ensure prosperity and a rising national income. Only through growth could the social services be expanded, higher living standards achieved, and the Conservatives' place in the political market protected. Right Progressives believed that if Conservative governments could successfully manage the new state, then the party could secure broad working class support and destroy the link between belonging to the working class and voting Labour.[24]

The way events unfolded, however, posed serious problems for Conservative ideology and policy, especially when a Labour Government inherited the new planning institutions and the new policies in 1964. The interventionist policies which Conservatives had viewed as an instrument for creating the conditions for more profitable and more competitive business, now seemed more threatening, encroaching on the productive sector. Most Conservatives were convinced that Socialists had no real appreciation of how industry worked, and so, whatever their intentions, were bound to harm the economy and endanger profitability and prosperity. The dominance of the needs of capital in the state was expressed in a different manner under Labour, and Conservatives began to fear that the interests of the Conservative Nation were at risk.

Conservatives for instance saw very clearly a direct link between inequality and a healthy productive sector. Substantial personal material incentives were the counterpart of high returns for productive enterprise, and also one source of new capital.[25] Labour in power threatened this relationship by its huge tax burdens and its discrimination in favour of undistributed profits. In addition it favoured the large corporations, penalized small business, and greatly enlarged government handouts to the big firms. Small business was being squeezed out by taxation (especially new taxes like the Selective Employment Tax (SET)), while the monopolistic and oligopolistic tendencies of big business were being reinforced by government intervention to 'rationalize' industry (for example through the Industrial Reorganization Corporation (IRC)). Furthermore they were being turned into clients of the government as more and more of their post tax profits resulted directly from government concessions, and as the government took over more and more responsibility for regulating wages in the private sector. As one conference delegate put it:[26] 'We see the ignominious and dismal spectacle of industries and firms queuing up for Government handouts of assistance like paupers at a Victorian soup kitchen.'

The reaction in the party to Labour policies showed the extent to which the electoral ideology of private enterprise and the free market was interpreted by the bulk of the party to mean the interests of small business. These interests were indeed heavily represented in the Conservative party at constituency level, and to a decreasing extent in the parliamentary party. The party leadership, however, was far more attuned to the interests of the big public corporations, the banks, and the multi-national companies. These now dominated the economy and exercised enormous influence over the state. The actual implementation of the competition policy could be expected to favour their interests far more than it helped small business. The abolition of Resale Price Maintenance was a foretaste. Yet the interpretation of the competition policy whilst the party was in opposition emphasized the needs and the plight of small business in deference to the pressure from the rank and file. The electoral ideologies of the Conservative Nation (and Powellism only reinforced this pattern) were not ideologies of big capital. They expressed the interests of small firms and small shopkeepers. The interests of the leading sections of capital—finance capital, the multi-nationals, the big industrial firms—were represented far more directly in the state through both direct and institutional channels.

There existed therefore a real tension between the existing state which on the whole under both Labour and the Conservatives served the interests of big capital in finance and industry, and the bulk of the private sector, which contained the multitude of small firms. In its electoral ideologies the Conservative party opposed the private sector to the state; in office, it did little to redress the balance between them. The party leadership had made no real attempt, when the Conservatives were in office, to keep the British a nation of shopkeepers and family businesses. It too had encouraged a nation of supermarkets and giant public companies.

The Labour Government's interventionist measures to reorganize the British economy and speed growth were based on the same fundamental reappraisal of Britain's economic performance that had been triggered off by the events of 1960–61. Like the Conservatives, Labour now sought to administer the new state created by the post-war settlement in a much more positive way to compensate for the shortcomings of the private sector.[27] Indicative planning and the commitment to faster economic growth were formalized in George Brown's National Plan, unveiled in 1965. An Industrial Reorganization Corporation was established to restructure some industries into larger units. Steel was nationalized. A Ministry of Technology was set up to speed the dissemination of scientific research and new technology. Lavish incentives to boost investment and exports were paid out. Finally, an ambitious prices and incomes policy, policed by the Prices and Incomes Board under Aubrey Jones, was launched to contain wage inflation. Labour faithfully followed Conservative precedents, even accepting the case for Europe and applying to join the EEC in 1967.

Labour's commitment to the same politics of power as their electoral opponents, however, received even more startling confirmation. For despite the rhetoric of expansion—on which Labour's whole programme of social reforms, such as it was, depended—Labour in practice remained firmly committed to the defence of sterling. This produced several years of stagnation, a growing burden of taxation to maintain the state sector, and a wage freeze, imposed just after the 1966 election.[28] In such a climate, the chances of building a national consensus to restrain inflation, as Labour intended, were slim. It was not surprising that Labour Ministers were soon attracted by the idea of compulsory legislation to get an incomes policy.

Devaluation, however, when it was finally forced on the Government in 1967, did free British governments from one major constraint on their economic policy. Unlike the 1949 devaluation, it occurred in a world where the international monetary system established after the war, was breaking up. Fixed parities for currencies were being jettisoned and many currencies were floated in the late 1960s and early 1970s. Labour finished its term of office with a large balance of payments surplus. But the National Plan, the prices and incomes policy, economic growth, and the EEC initiative, had all fallen by the wayside. The state sector, however, was larger than ever. It accounted for over 50 per cent of GDP. Inflation, meanwhile, appeared to be accelerating, even though unemployment was rising.

The failure of Labour's interventionist strategy to lift Britain out of economic crisis and slow growth caused Conservative economic policy to harden towards the new state. The framework of the competition policy remained as Heath had formulated it at the 1966 conference:[29]

> It is the job of the Government to help industry to overcome [its] problems and to help modern capitalism to work . . . our task is to remove the obstructions which exist, wherever they may be, to enterprise and competition in our business world.

But the government's direct role in the competition policy was steadily limited. Under pressure from Powell and opinion in the New Right, the party turned against intervention. Instead much greater emphasis was placed on competition. As it happened, this fitted in with the views of several of the younger Right Progressives. A partnership between 'Industry' and 'Government' was increasingly thought unrealistic. So the party began to reject 'planning', in particular National Plans and the IRC, and prices and incomes policies. A motion passed at the 1968 conference declared that 'attempts to control prices and incomes by statute are at complete variance with the basic Conservative principle of free enterprise.' Although a move to delete the words 'by statute' was defeated, this was a clear victory for Powell's position, which he had had to defend three years earlier against strong advocates of incomes policies in the Shadow Cabinet, including Maudling and Macleod.

The field for legitimate intervention by the government was whittled down by Conservatives until it covered only very limited projects which met needs acknowledged by industrialists and which could be entrusted to them to carry through. Conservatives proclaimed that economic problems, including inflation, could best be met by free market solutions. The task of the government was to ensure a competitive climate in which productive industry could grow. To achieve that meant that the government had to change the way it ran the state —by altering the tax system to give greater incentives and encourage cost efficiency; by reforming trade union law; by introducing new management techniques into the handling of government expenditure and the running of the nationalized industries.[30]

One aspect of this was a much tougher line on trade unions. The Conservative proposals for trade union reform were understood in the party as a weapon of confrontation which would redress the balance between employers and unions. This was necessary if the government were to withdraw from its responsibilities for wages outside the public sector. On government spending too the Conservatives promised reductions and big cuts in taxation, including the abolition of SET and the introduction of a value-added tax. The reductions were mainly to come from 'pruning' and from greater 'selectivity' in the social services. The commitment of the party to selectivity in welfare became complete after 1965, following the long agitation by the Bow Group, the One Nation Group, and the economists of the Institute of Economic Affairs. Schemes were devised for allowing all social services, including education, to be purchased rather than provided free. The leadership kept more limited aims in view, namely the holding back of the rate of growth of spending on social services and the restoration of personal incentives.[31] The Conservative plans for welfare were pushed with such vigour because they offered the main chance for cutting government spending, although the Conservatives were already pledged to higher expenditure on defence.[32] The other area for savings was government subsidies of all kinds to industry.

On these three issues—unions, taxation, and welfare—the leadership did move while in Opposition in response to pressures from its supporters. But on certain key questions they remained silent. They did not advocate any major cuts in public spending such as Powell did in his Morecambe Budget; they made no mention of denationalizing public enterprises wholesale, even steel; and most important, they gave no undertaking that they would refuse to finance inflation. These omissions were sufficient to raise a big doubt over the likelihood of a new Conservative Government escaping from many of the constraints of the politics of power that determined the course of policy (in particular over wages and government intervention) under the Labour Government. But at least their intentions were clear. The economic crisis they blamed on the *kind* of role the 'Socialist' State was playing in the economy. The solution was to re-establish the strength and the independence of the productive sector.

In an important speech which portrayed this new, although in retrospect short-lived policy, John Davies, the new Conservative Minister for Trade and Industry and former Director-General of the CBI, told the 1970 Conservative Victory Conference:[33]

> self-reliance and initiative have been undermined by intervention
> and the pursuit of false objectives—production without profit,
> restructuring without resources, consultation without confidence,
> advice without answerability.

He reaffirmed that profitability was the priority for the productive sector. Labour had failed to make it so in its interventionist strategy:[34]

> Industrial management has been cajoled and coerced into believing
> that it should pursue other ends but the success of the enterprise.
> Of course, profits are not the be-all or end-all of all industrial
> management, but they are its primary objective and without them
> all the social purposes, all the regional policies, the export perform
> ance, the reduction of unemployment and the pursuit of research
> will go by default.

In the cause of profitability Davies pledged that the Government would not 'bolster or bail out' companies for which there seemed no prospect of profitability being restored. Capital was to stand on its own feet again.

2 TAXATION AND EXPENDITURE

The traditional nineteenth century view of finance and expenditure was expressed by Lord Hugh Cecil:[35] 'Expenditure ought never to be considered apart from the taxes which will be required to meet it.' It is precisely this link which the modern state has broken. The Conservatives' acceptance of the post-war political settlement committed them to a new view of finance. Government expenditure was now, in T. E. Utley's words[36] 'an instrument of the social purposes upon which the community was resolved.' The consequences of ensuring full employment were thus, according to him, an economic structure characterized by 'a powerful trade union movement and a perpetual scarcity of labour', and therefore by inflation.

Some Conservatives welcomed the new level of expenditure without reservation. Leo Amery, for instance, celebrated it as a victory for the ideological opponents of laissez-faire, and more particularly for industrial capital over finance capital. Previously, he wrote,[37] the keeping down of expenditure as such was regarded as the most important function of administration. Today, when expenditure on a vast scale is not only unavoidable for such purposes as defence, but regarded as desirable in itself for social purposes, the supreme object must be the encouragement of the productive energies by which alone that expenditure can be sustained . . . we cannot afford a repetition of the disastrous policy of deflation pursued after 1919 in order to screw sterling up to the old gold parity . . . the Treasury should not be the master but the faithful steward of the productive departments.

There was obviously a dilemma here, a fact noted by Lord Woolton,[38] because the Conservatives were obliged both to supervise the new enormous budget and to put forward an economic policy 'based on the competence of capitalism to provide the essential wealth of the country.' This required that government expenditure be held constant or reduced. Yet precisely the opposite occurred during Conservative rule after 1958. The basic elements of the policy of the Socialists, said Butler in 1959,[39] are 'extended nationalization, excessive taxation and extravagant spending . . . an infallible recipe for inflation.' The Conservative Government, however, had its own recipe. It was ready to adopt the same policy. No serious attempt was made to hold back the accelerating trend of public spending in the 1960s. When Powell as Minister of Health, asked for economies in the health service, including cuts in welfare milk and higher prescription charges, he was opposed by Macmillan at a Cabinet in 1960:[40] 'I do not like this regressive taxation very much— nor do some of my colleagues. . . . But the enormous increase in the Estimates makes one feel that something must be done.'

The spending plans of government departments dictated the pace in the 1960s. Ever more ambitious plans were unveiled, especially for education, roads and health. In 1964 the Conservatives fought the election on a programme to modernize Britain with the necessary public spending. As Geoffrey Smith noted at the time in *Crossbow*:[41]

One of the most interesting political developments of recent months has been the extent to which the Government has become committed to a continuing high level of public expenditure. The Tories will be going into this election not as the latter day apostles of Gladstonian economic principles but as the party which can best use the nation's resources to modernize the country.

The White Paper on Public Expenditure in December 1963 showed that public expenditure was back to the level of the early 1950s—40 per cent of GNP in 1963 compared to 41 per cent then. In 1951 it had been swollen by higher defence spending during the Korean War and rearmament. Subsequently it had declined to 36 per cent of GNP in

1958, but had risen ever since, and the White Paper predicted that it would rise further to 41·5 per cent by 1967-8.

The dyke had burst and several influential Conservatives predicted calamity.[42] They argued that an expanding state sector taking a greater and greater share of national income by increasing taxation in one form or another was not only inefficient, but would create first an amoral then an immoral society by undermining economic independence and self-reliance. This failure of the Conservatives to control public expenditure whilst they were in office was clearly linked to their willingness to appease the unions. Both were pragmatic policies of acceptance of the priorities of the post-war settlement. Yet there was an implicit tension between them, which became more marked as time went on. The cause was inflation; the new kind of permanent, creeping inflation suffered by all the advanced capitalist states after 1945.

Conservatives explained inflation, as did professional economists, by pointing to 'demand pull' or 'cost push' factors.[43] Either inflation was due to excess demand in the economy which had to be eliminated by monetary policy, or it arose from the excessive market power of the unions which allowed them to loot the economy so long as full employment was maintained. The debate, however, was always far more than a technical one. For if the new state itself created the structural conditions for inflation, then monetary policy could only work if the state sector were drastically reduced and the old business cycle restored, or if governments could establish direct control over cost inflation. An important White Paper in 1956—the Economic Implications of Full Employment—argued that all the excess demand in the economy caused by the war and reconstruction had been eliminated. Since inflation still persisted, its source must be rising costs, so new institutional arrangements were advocated to curb the rise of wages. It followed that the government would be forced to extend control over wage bargaining if inflation was to be reduced. The alternative was to cut back the state sector to at least its pre-war size, and restore the old relationship between the state and the economy, and the old business cycle.

During their first period of opposition, Conservatives generally saw nationalization and the extension of state control as the greatest dangers to their Nation. The real issue of the next General Election, Sir Anthony Eden told the 1949 conference at London, was[44] 'whether we are to suffer more Socialism with its rigid and bureaucratic methods which are so unsuited to the economy of our country and so alien to the whole spirit of our people or whether we will build again on the sound foundations of an enlightened free enterprise.' Inflation and the high level of taxation were put down to the amount of expenditure Labour required to finance its schemes of nationalization. Mr Godber, proposing

a motion on the cost of living and taxation at the 1950 Conference, said
that the answer to inflation lay[45]

> in a more honest approach by the Government in thinking more of
> the Nation and less of nationalization. The Labour Party's insistence
> on carrying out these costly, wasteful schemes of nationalization,
> coupled with their inept and extravagant administration and their
> incompetent stewardship of the social services have had the effect of
> forcing a continuance of taxation at a crippling level.

This was a general cry. Two years earlier, Mr Peter Black had opened
a similar debate by declaring:[46] 'At the moment I believe that the British
working man and industry are rather like Sinbad the Sailor, with the
old man of the sea round their necks in the form of gigantic taxation
and the carrying of a useless, non-earning and non-productive bureaucracy.' All were agreed on the evils of inflation. Mr Nigel Birch, MP,
quoted Lenin, that favourite Conservative authority, on how to subvert
a regime by debauching its currency. He continued:[47]

> If you do get your currency debauched, if people do not reap what
> they have sown, then you get a breakup of all accepted values, and
> you get a continual and progressive decline in morality, and you get
> a continual decline in confidence in any country.

The remedy according to Birch was plain: government spending must
be reduced. This was the prime cause of inflation.

The question of reducing expenditure, however, was never much
discussed at conferences. Most delegates no doubt assumed that it
would be a priority of any future Conservative Government. There
was some unease in the party, however. Lord Hinchingbrooke pointed
out that taxation could only be reduced if the people were prepared
to pay directly for the services they used. Yet all the statements of
policy that were flooding out of Central Office to be greeted enthusiastically by the rank and file, seemed to commit the party to increased
rather than reduced public expenditure.

During the debate on the *Right Road for Britain*, Sir Waldron Smithers
intervened to point this out. The crisis faced by Britain and the world,
he said,[48] was

> neither a financial, economic or dollar crisis; it is a spiritual and moral
> crisis and it cannot be solved by promising a materialistic utopia
> ... the pledges in 'The Right Road' ... are irreconcilable with the
> reduction of public expenditure. We cannot hope for national recov-
> ery while public expenditure continues unabated. . . . It is futile to
> compete with the Socialists in promising a Welfare State.

In reply Quintin Hogg trotted out what was to become the familiar
refrain of all parties. The proposals, he said, would not cost too much.

They would be paid for largely by increased production. Butler, winding up the debate, defended the policy statement in rather different terms:[49]

It is as I see it a policy of humanity and commonsense—humanity because it associates the Conservative party with the spiritual, human and physical needs of our large population, and commonsense because it uses the instrument of change where change is in the national interest, and accepts economic facts where these are unanswerable and ineluctable.

This committed the party firmly to the Welfare State and to government intervention to secure full employment. Together they meant that the Conservatives would maintain the state sector.

They did not disappoint. Churchill had condemned Labour's four years in office as 'a Rake's progress of unbridled expenditure', but the Conservatives did not pull the reins in hard, and it was not long before protests were voiced. In 1952, one of the resolutions on the economy that was debated read: 'In the opinion of this Conference, public expenditure has increased, is increasing and ought to be drastically diminished.' Richard Law took the rostrum to urge that the party could not afford to be timid on this question:[50] 'If the electorate is faced with a choice between two parties, each of which is going to give it high expenditure and heavy taxation, the electorate will go for that party that believes in high expenditure and heavy taxation.' In 1955, conference pledged its support to the Government 'in the exercise of the strictest economy and all measures designed to eliminate the dangers of inflation.' The next year there was a still stronger resolution for debate:[51] 'the weight of taxation in the UK upon industry, commerce and private individuals is excessive and ought to be reduced; this conference therefore urges the Government to take all possible action to restrict public expenditure and thereby make possible substantial reductions in taxation.'

The conference had to be satisfied with crumbs. In 1953 Butler promised that government expenditure would be 'pruned' and that there would be a drive against waste, but he felt obliged to tell the conference[52] that 'the real truth about expenditure is that there are certain levels which it is almost impossible readily to cut.' He gave defence as an example, no doubt because it was expenditure most likely to find favour with Conservatives, but what he said applied to all the major items of government expenditure. This would have been unpalatable, so Butler contented himself with observing that taxation was not going to be reduced just by cutting expenses, but by improving the strength of the economy and increasing savings. In 1957 it was ironically Enoch Powell, then Financial Secretary to the Treasury, who was chosen to reply to the debate on taxation. He delivered a very correct Govern-

ment speech, pointing out[53] that 'all government expenditure is a pay-
ment to somebody. In every branch of government expenditure there
is a vested interest.' He rammed home this argument by claiming that
there were eighty motions on the order paper calling for an increase
in some item of government spending.

Such arguments made little impact on the critics. Mr Kershaw from
Cheadle declared at the 1955 Conference that the post-war prosperity
was false prosperity so long as there was inflation. The 'so-called' high
level of employment, he said,[54] was only created and maintained by
'the insatiable demands and profligate spending of government departments and nationalized industries.' In the same debate, another delegate, Mrs de la Motte, wondered why there was no abatement of wage
claims, now that the working class was so prosperous. On the other
side of the street, she said,[55] were 'millions of thrifty, hard-working,
people living on fixed incomes and pensions, trotting many of them
to pawnshops.' At the same time she wished to blame government
spending as well as the unions for inflation: 'We are taxed too high
and we are producing too little still. . . . It is no use maintaining the
Welfare State here if it means we are going to price ourselves out of the
world markets.'

The dire predictions of electoral disaster if inflation were not checked
and the loyalty of the middle classes regained, were soundly contradicted by the 1959 election victory. But this did not still the critics. In
1956 Mr Winston-Jones had called inflation legalized robbery:[56] 'It is
not an act of God', he said, 'it is an act of government itself.' In 1960
Mr Wadsworth revealed that it was not the act of a Conservative
government either:[57]

> In this country, Conservatives have for the last eight or nine years
> been putting into practice policies which would not have been
> dreamed of by a Conservative party before the Socialists had had
> their six years of office.

Almost every speaker in this debate condemned the high level of
taxation. 'Income tax', said Ted Leather,[58] 'is a tax on work; and the
harder you work the more you are penalized.' Mrs H. Brickhill was
of the opinion[59] that the 'operation of surtax is opposed to the principle
that the labourer is worthy of his hire.' A rare exception to the general
trend of opinion was Mr D. Chapman, who thought that priority
should not be given to the reduction of taxation if it meant reducing
spending on social programmes. He justified this eccentric view by
declaring:[60] 'We must carry forward the great Tory tradition of social
legislation.' It was never a popular line at a Conservative conference,
even though it represented more and more the practice of the leadership. Macmillan boasted to the end of conference rally that year:[61] 'We

have the biggest social programme in our history and we are spending on it a bigger proportion of our wealth than ever before.'

The resolutions on taxation at the 1965–9[62] conferences trod a well-worn path. They called for reforms of the present tax structure 'in order to give realistic incentives for the encouragement of harder work' (1966); so that taxation should be 'simple, sensible, and encourage effort, thrift and enterprise' (1967); the way cleared for economic growth by making taxation a 'charge on spending' instead of a 'penalty on earnings' (1968). Mr Campion summed up the spirit of rank and file views on taxation when he told the 1966 Conference:[63] 'there is only one Conservative policy on taxation necessary; it can be summed up in a four letter word—D–O–W–N.' With a Labour Government again in office, high taxation, high government spending, and the extension of controls over the economy were all generally seen as different manifestations of the same menace. As Peter Walker put it:[64]

> Socialism and high taxation have always been synonymous—synonymous because Socialism is often linked with squandering, and because the Labour party bears a basic malice towards the enterprising and successful that provokes in their taxation thinking a constant desire to penalize the successful.

The greatest evils of high taxation were on the one hand its destruction of incentives, and on the other its erosion of individual responsibility. Both evils derived from the overall level of taxation, but the first could be somewhat mitigated by altering the distribution of taxation between direct and indirect taxes. This solution, which had been followed to a small extent by Conservative governments, was not sufficient for many of their critics in the party. Clive Elliott expressed their view at the 1968 conference. He complained that the problem was not at all the balance of direct and indirect taxation, but the overall amount:[65]

> The Conservatives are supposed to believe in freedom. One of the greatest freedoms that any individual has is the freedom to spend his money as he sees fit. 40 per cent of our earnings are taken away from us in one way or another, so we are only 60 per cent free.

He returned to the same theme the next year. We must not be seen to be reducing direct taxation by increasing indirect taxation, he said:[66] 'Our cuts in indirect taxation must be financed from reductions in government expenditure and from incentives to saving.'

But it was cuts in direct taxation that were demanded most, because it was expected that they would make a dramatic impact on productivity and enterprise. As Councillor Trixie Gardner expressed it:[67]

> Too many people have learnt that under the present penal taxation the rewards for extra work are far too little for the effort involved.

Too many of the wealthy have been reluctantly forced to live abroad. That cannot help our economy.

Cyril Osborne, MP, two years earlier had been less concerned with the plight of those whose wealth forced them into exile than with the effect of taxation on the working class:[68] 'We pay the worker too little and workshy too much through the Welfare State. The present savage taxation is the chief cause of the Socialists shockingly poor industrial record.' Osborne correctly saw that the real burden of very high taxation was borne by the wage earner and not by those with high incomes, who found it only too easy to find ways round the tax system. Six years earlier, during Selwyn Lloyd's Pay Pause, Osborne had set out his ideas to the conference on a new social contract between Labour and the state as the only solution to the problems of the British economy, and in particular to inflation. He argued that only by a united effort in which all sections of the community made sacrifices could the country's economic difficulties be overcome and inflation contained. He pointed out that the key to the whole economic problem (profitability) was wages, since they comprised 62 per cent of total industrial costs, and that therefore the crisis could only be overcome if the government could 'carry' organized labour with it. In a classic early statement of the political case for an incomes policy, he claimed[69] that the British working man would 'do anything, provided he is well led and is convinced that what is proposed to him is fair all round.'

This meant a bargain. In return for taxes on capital such as a two-year statutory dividend limitation, a capital gains tax, stricter control of expense accounts, and the postponement of surtax concessions, labour would agree to a two-year wage freeze, the ending of restrictive practices, a free transfer of labour from inefficient to efficient industries and financial penalties for unofficial strikers; a remarkable package, expecially in the light of the various attempts to construct incomes policies that followed under Conservative and Labour administrations. Osborne had recognized that successful economic management under the constraints laid down after 1945 required a bargain with the unions. If an incomes policy was to work the cooperation of the unions was essential. But in the development of Conservative policy towards the unions the politics of support and power sometimes pulled in opposite directions.

3 THE CONSERVATIVES AND THE UNIONS

Conservative party relations with the trade unions have never been easy. On the one hand it has not been possible for Conservatives to ignore the unions and they have had to be accepted as one of the most powerful interests in the state; whilst on the other, the unions are identified with political forces hostile to Conservatism and to private capital.

Conservative dealings with the unions have therefore had one over-riding aim: it is to separate unionism as a political and as an economic force, and to squeeze the life out of the former. But the means for achieving this have varied according to the changing requirements of national economic policy and the changing fortunes of the class struggle. Conservative strategy for the trade unions has therefore varied as these have changed.

Trade unions had to struggle long and hard to be recognized as a legitimate interest within the state. In their early years, they were held to be conspiracies against property and prosperity, a view shared by believers in economic individualism and by more paternalist employers alike. The former could find no 'economic' justification for trade unionism because it harmed both efficiency and justice by its monstrous interference with the freedom of contracts; whilst the latter, though they emphasized the duties as well as the rights of ownership, could not stomach negotiation about wages and conditions that was initiated by the labourers themselves.

A number of developments in the second half of the nineteenth century, including the increasing size of factories and scale of industry, and the growing risk of uncontrollable strikes, compelled legal recognition of the unions in the 1870s.[70] The unions, however, had not been accepted into the state. Their main dealings were with private employers and they were still vulnerable to attack through the courts. What transformed the situation was the steady growth of the activities of the state and the increasing adherence of the unions to a socialist ideology and to the support of the Labour party.[71]

The revolutionary period that followed the end of the Great War saw an open struggle between Conservatism and political trade unionism, that eventually ended in the defeat of the militant sections of the working class and a strengthening of the power and legitimacy of both the Labour party and the trade union leaders. This victory, which was won most dramatically in the 1926 General Strike, was consolidated by the 1927 Trade Disputes Act that followed. It outlawed sympathy strikes; reversed the rules governing the unions' political levy to the Labour party under which individual trade unionists had to contract out if they wished to avoid paying it; and drastically restricted picketing. This policy went hand in hand with attempts to encourage class collaboration, on the employers' terms. The 1929 Conservative Election Manifesto loudly trumpeted the Conservative triumph in passing the Trade Disputes Act, through which, it claimed,[72]

the trade unions were protected against the misuse of the strike weapon for political and revolutionary ends, and the trade unionist has been secured against intimidation and coercion in the free exercise of his industrial and political rights. The threat of the Socialist Government to repeal this Act is in itself a ground for asking the support of the workers for the present Government.

The lesser form of political trade unionism, however—the close connection of the unions with the Labour party—remained. The victory of the Labour party in the 1945 Election was regarded as a victory for this form of political unionism. The Conservative response in Opposition was twofold. The Right Progressives saw the unions playing a leading role in the new order, but at the same time there was a strong desire in the party to separate the unions from Labour. Corporatist thought emphasized how the unions should be recognized as an important estate of the realm, playing a major role in maintaining social stability by regulating the demands and aspirations of their members and putting compromise and negotiation in the place of class war.[73] But it was hard for Conservatives to become completely reconciled to the unions as a major and valuable national institution, so long as they were still pledged to the electoral support of the Labour party.

The attitudes of the party towards the unions after 1945 reflected this ambivalence. The Right Progressives treated the unions as an indispensable support of the post-war settlement; at the same time they wished to neutralize them politically. Now that the unions' claims to represent working people had been met and a Welfare State created, the unions ought to have no more general political aims, but should be content to confine themselves to detailed bargaining about the administration of the economy and the distribution of welfare.

The balance of forces had altered in Britain after 1945 and one sign of it was this new readiness of the Conservatives to accept the unions. In part it reflected the new role of the state in the economy, in part it stemmed from electoral calculation. During their first period of Opposition the Conservatives had to combat the idea, spread assiduously by the Labour party, that there would be an open war between the unions and the government and the deliberate creation of unemployment, if the Conservatives were returned to power. The Right Progressives took great pains therefore to stress that the Conservatives were strong believers in the principle of trade unionism and quite ready to cooperate with the TUC in government. As a result the Conservatives offered little opposition to the repeal of their Trade Disputes Act by the Labour Government in 1946, and concentrated instead on a policy of conciliation. Its monument was the Industrial Charter (1947).

According to the Charter:[74] 'If the sum of human happiness and welfare is to be increased in this country, it will only be through fostering a sense of united purpose among all those engaged in industry whatever their position.' It argued that industry should provide certain rights to all workers, including security of employment, the incentive to do the job well and get a better one, and status as an individual 'however big the firm or mechanized the job.'

The Right Progressives believed that the class war was now over. Indeed, it had been a mistake, an unfortunate state of affairs brought about by doctrinaire Liberalism which had turned labour into a commodity and driven a rift between employers and workers which had been further widened by the rise of trade unions as fighting organizations. Lord Salisbury spoke in the same vein:[75]

> In days happily gone by, labour was universally regarded as a commodity, which the employer bought. . . . And so there grew up in the public mind an idea that the interests of capital and labour were inevitably opposed. This has been the cause of many of our troubles.

Conservatives' faith in their ability to suspend the laws of capitalist economics by a magical infusion of goodwill and cooperation into industrial relations led them naturally to the belief that they rather than the Socialists were the best protectors of trade unionism under the new political order. The Right Progressives hoped that the unions would realize that they no longer needed the Labour party to represent their interests in the political system, because they could now gain direct access to the government. This in turn might break the links between trade unions and Socialism, because, Conservatives held, the new state threatened the independence and essential interests and economic aims of the unions more when it was controlled by the Labour party than when the Tories were in office.[76] In the debates on industrial relations and trade unions at the annual conferences during this period of Opposition these two themes were prominent.

Anthony Barber, for instance, proposing the motion at the 1949 Conference emphasized[77] that the effective working of British trade unions was 'absolutely essential' to the political and industrial stability of the country. David Maxwell-Fyfe, replying to the motion, claimed that Conservatives had brought trade unionism into existence in order to counter laissez-faire in industrial relations. Now, he said,[78] it was the duty of the Conservative party to 'deliver trade unionism from the paralysis of Socialist collectivism.' But he stressed that there would be no 'head-on clash' with the unions when the Tories got back to power. He repeated this pledge the next year:[79] 'The maintaining of the value, responsibility, and independence of British trade unionism is one of the main tasks of Conservatism and Tory Democracy.'

But the unions' affiliation to the Labour party remained to irk the Tories. It was condemned in every conference debate on industrial relations during the years of opposition. The 1946 resolution, whilst affirming the Conservatives' traditional support for trade unionism, condemned what it called the current tendency for trade union leaders to concentrate on political issues 'to the detriment of their primary function.' In 1947 the resolution regretted the continued intrusion of party politics into trade union affairs and deplored[80] 'the subservience of the present Socialist Government to the TUC', and expressed 'its lack of confidence in the Government's ability to safeguard the interests of the nation as a whole.'

But the growing strain between the unions and the Labour Government gave the Conservatives hope. In 1950 Boyd-Carpenter confidently proclaimed[81] that what Conservatives thought would happen only in the distant future was about to happen in the near future, namely 'the divorce between the trade union movement and the Socialist party.' Socialists, he said, had good cause to be afraid. By this time the hope of detaching the unions from the Labour party by accepting them as full partners in the state and industry as outlined in the Industrial Charter, seemed less promising than stressing the opportunities for free collective bargaining in an expanding economy. This was partly due to the relative eclipse of the kind of thinking enshrined in the Industrial Charter by the new wave of liberal ideas that developed after 1947. Partly too it was due to the ideological and electoral advantage to be won from emphasizing how the Conservatives differed from the Labour Government. An expanding capitalism meant that Conservatives needed no longer to be on the defensive. Capitalism itself would solve the problem of the unions. As in the United States, the unions might be won to a policy of speeding growth rather than fighting to redistribute the existing wealth. Conservatives now argued that the experience of the Labour Government showed free trade unionism to be incompatible with Socialism.

As Mr Anthony Fell announced at the 1949 conference:[82] 'We should tell trade unionists throughout this country that their only interest lies in a strengthened system of free competitive capitalism.' David Gammans, MP, told delegates that the unions must be won over to schemes of co-partnership in industry:[83] 'Our job is to point out that under private enterprise there is a fuller, richer and freer life.' A great opportunity existed, he said, now that nationalization had proved such a flop, by not giving the workers the security and control which they wanted, and he pointed to the success of American business in selling to their workers a belief in free enterprise. In 1950 it was Ted Leather's turn. Where there is a real competitive system, he claimed, the wage earners benefit most:[84] 'For fifty years [American] trade unions have devoted themselves to the development of a great industrial movement and have refused to dabble in politics.' In a socialist economy, by contrast, the only job for the unions was to discipline the workers.

The revival of confidence in capitalism as an economic system, however, did not cause any return to old attitudes to the unions when the

Conservatives returned to power in 1951. The state sector bequeathed by the war and the Labour Government was still in being, and the new ministers took no steps to dismantle it. TUC representation on Government committees was maintained; there was no move to reintroduce the Trade Disputes Act or any other anti-union legislation. The Government did not waver on the policy of maintaining full employment and the existing level of social services.

The new Conservative labour policy was symbolized by the appointment of Walter Monckton as Churchill's first Minister of Labour. According to Butler,[85] Churchill 'with unhappy memories of the General Strike to live down, was determined to pursue a policy of industrial appeasement.' Monckton had served in the Coalition Government during the war, but was not a professional Conservative but a professional conciliator. He was therefore about as 'neutral' a Minister in party political terms as could be arranged.[86] Sir Vincent Tewson, General Secretary of the TUC from 1946 to 1959, testified later[87] that 'both sides of industry had greater confidence in Walter Monckton than in any other Minister of Labour.' Monckton himself described his brief from Churchill as follows:[88] 'Winston's riding orders to me were that the Labour party had foretold grave industrial troubles if the Conservatives were elected, and he looked to me to do my best to preserve industrial peace.'

The policy was described at the time and still more during the Conservative second period of opposition as appeasement. Sir Lincoln Evans, at that time General Secretary of the steelworkers union, later wrote that industrial relations had deteriorated since the war. He blamed the Tory Government elected in 1951, which had been so anxious, he thought,[89] to wipe out what it imagined was its anti-trade union image, even though this had only been created by 'decades of propaganda.' The result had been that the Tories 'made a habit of surrendering too easily on issues that called for firmness.'

The policy of appeasement, however, followed naturally enough from the electoral perspective of the Right Progressives. The need to rebuild the Conservatives' national coalition and to secure the unions' cooperation in managing the economy seemed more important than a confrontation over pay. So long as the economy was expanding, the problems of strikes and inflation seemed relatively minor. Conservatives continued to believe that the industrial problem was one of human relations. If human relations could be improved by removing frustration, all other problems such as raising productivity and maintaining profits could be solved.[90] This was reflected in the tone of many speeches at conference.

Charles Curran, MP, told the 1954 conference at Blackpool that the Tories had disproved the lie spread by the Socialists that a vote for the Tories was a vote for the dole. The Tories record on full employment since 1951, he said, had re-established the credit of the Tory party with the working class. Socialism had nothing to offer the workers except a return to rationing and financial crisis. But what he asked should the Tories do now?

Harold Watkinson, in his reply for the platform, answered him. What the Conservatives were trying to do, he said,[91] and the Ministry of Labour in particular, was to bring a new climate into British industry, 'a new sense of working together for the efficiency, the well-being of the nation as a whole.' The aim of Conservative policy, he stated, was to give practical implementation to the idea behind the Industrial Charter, namely that the nation could only earn its living in a 'tough and competitive world' if it got its human relations and industrial relations right. Watkinson thought the industrial problem to be getting better communication. If the Tories could not get through to the men at the shop floor, he warned, then the agitator at the gate would, and who would be more likely to tell the truth? The proof that conciliation was the right policy, he claimed, lay in the statistics for strikes: there were fewer than under Labour. Tory policy, he suggested, was causing strikes to wither away.

This judgment proved premature. Tory policy had not yet really been tested. The first deflation, forced on the Government after the 1955 General Election, brought a more open clash with the unions. There was a sharp increase in strikes. In 1957 more than three times as many days were lost through strikes than in any year since the war. The number of stoppages rose too, and there were some major strikes in the engineering and shipbuilding industries and a London bus strike. Macmillan reacted to the wave of unrest with some distaste. He discounted the notion, however, that there was a political plot between Communist and extremist union leaders and the Labour party to bring down the Government, and preferred to believe[92] that because 'the unions have got their own way for so long (since 1939) . . . they cannot imagine that there is any point at which they can meet firm resistance.' He gloomily confided to his diary in March 1957:[93] 'The truth is that we are now paying the price for the Churchill-Monckton regime—industrial appeasement with continual inflation.'

In the midst of this growing labour unrest, however, Conservative policy remained unchanged.[94] The role of the Minister of Labour was still that of a conciliator, whose job was to minimize the number of strikes and improve the human relations of industry by personal intervention. The new Minister of Labour, Macleod, despite his tough line in the bus strike, loudly proclaimed this policy to successive conferences:[95]

The true conception of industry is not that of boss and man, nor of master and servant, not is it, as Karl Marx once said, a battlefield of

class, of industrial, or of political warfare . . . we have heard the
voices of schism raised again this autumn. But it is those people in
other parties who preach conflict who are the reactionaries . . .
[they] fail to see the immense social and human force in the industrial
relationship, because the link must be that of partners and not of
opponents.

In 1957 in the midst of the labour troubles of that year, he announced
that he was not in favour of either a wage freeze or a national wages
and incomes policy to cope with the situation, because neither was
practical politics. The reason he gave was that the Government was
not at war with the unions but with inflation. This would sound a
strange distinction to later Conservatives, but Macleod stuck to it. In
Blackpool in 1958 he claimed that the refusal of the TUC to extend the
bus strike showed that the forces of sanity were stronger than the forces
of schism. The Tories, he said,[96] still favoured independent voluntary
arbitration to settle disputes, coupled with clear statements from Ministers on the 'economic facts' of the country. This, he insisted, was the
right policy because the only hope for good sound industrial relations
was a partnership, 'independent of politics', between the government,
the trade unions, and the employers.

Thus throughout the first ten years of their rule, the Conservatives
favoured a loose form of cooperation between the government, the
employers, and the unions. They rejected plans to make this into a
more formal, corporatist arrangement by adopting a wages policy, and
relied instead on persuasion and an expanding economy to keep the
compact in being and wage increases in bounds. The old concern with
the affiliation of the unions to the Labour party faded away during the
1950s, partly because it showed no signs of disappearing, and partly
because the unions proved ready to cooperate with a Conservative
Government as a non-political interest group.[97]

But a new trend had become evident in Conservative thinking during
the 1950s, which although only an undercurrent then, was to dominate
the party's discussion of the unions and industrial relations during the
1960s. It concerned the whole question of the responsibility for inflation. Having saved trade unionists from the dragon of collectivism
and preserved their right to bargain collectively and freely, Conservatives became increasingly alarmed by the gusto with which trade
unionists exercised this freedom. What complicated the issue for them
was that often it was not the union leaders who were calling the strikes
and bringing 'anarchy' into industrial relations, but shop stewards acting
unofficially.

This was a dilemma for Conservatives, because they had traditionally
supported the 'rights' of the individual worker against the power of the
union bureaucracy. After 1945, there were frequent statements of sup-

port at conference for ordinary trade unionists who were being persecuted or not properly represented by their leaders.[98] Even unofficial strikes received sympathy as protests against centralization under Socialism.

There was not much sympathy, however, when the *trend* of unofficial strikes, far from abating, continued to grow after the Conservatives returned to office. Conservative leaders whose industrial relations strategy depended on the cooperation of the trade union leaders were no longer eager to castigate these same leaders for being affiliated to the Labour party. This and the problem of the political levy seemed minor matters now compared to the potential help the unions might provide in controlling their members, so as to reduce strikes and the rate of inflation of labour costs. Attention began to shift to the activities of subversive minorities of militants within the unions.

The party leaders were singularly deaf, therefore, to the passionate appeal of Councillor Broadbent, a self confessed Tory working man, at the Margate conference in 1953, when he called for action against the political levy and the closed shop:[99]

> Let us be firm and strong, no dilly dallying, and live up to full tradition, the fullest meaning and the very fundamentalism of what Conservatism stands for . . . do something concrete, not just empty words, to restore trade unions to a semblance of sanity. Or is the Conservative party afraid to do it?

The leaders were apparently too afraid and continued to dilly dally over industrial relations. Harold Watkinson told the 1954 conference[100] that the Government had not passed legislation because it had tried to be 'impartial and fair.' Monckton himself repeated this view the next year. What was needed in industrial relations, he said,[101] was not legislation but 'an upsurge of a feeling of responsibility towards our people as a whole.'

This line was continued by Monckton's successor, Macleod, who however was a far sharper party politician, and not blind to the electoral handicap which a close association with the unions imposed on a constitutional Labour party. He therefore kept the policy of ignoring questions like the closed shop and the political levy, and concentrated instead on fostering a moderate and responsible union leadership, which in practice was prepared to separate industrial and political questions in its dealings with the government. Such a policy fitted well with the politics of power to which the Conservatives were by this time committed. But it suited the politics of support less well. Macleod was obliged to defend his policy against calls for action against the unions.

At the 1956 conference for instance he had to reply to a motion which expressed concern at the damage caused by industrial disputes and demanded a secret ballot of the members of a union before a strike was called. Macleod replied that there was no objection in principle to a secret ballot. But would it contribute to industrial peace? The experience of other countries showed that it would not. Besides, he said,[102] underlying the motion was the idea that 'workers are less militant than their leaders. All I can tell you, speaking quite frankly, is that this is not my experience, nor is it the experience of any Minister of Labour.' Ballots, he argued, would actually increase strikes. Macleod had no faith in the theory that the great mass of wage earners was fundamentally sound and sober, but at times led astray by cunning leaders. He held it more likely that setting the people free in the sort of world the post-war settlement had produced could threaten the survival of the capitalist industrial system by forcing employers to resort to inflation to maintain their share of national income. The union leaders were a valuable bulwark against this threat to property.

Meanwhile unrest in the party over the state of industrial relations was growing. In 1961 at the Brighton conference, the motion on industrial relations called for an enquiry into the unions, and reforming legislation. It was defeated, but it was noticeable that in the debate new anxieties appeared alongside the old demands. The proposer of the motion, Mr T. Wray, told the conference that Britain had entered a very new era of history, and there was a need for a broad enquiry into the unions because of the concern about restrictive practices, unofficial strikes, the conduct of union elections—highlighted by ballot rigging in the ETU—and the political levy. Councillor Jeffrey Tillett denounced unofficial strikers:[103] 'Do they not realize that by their folly they simply play into the hands of our foreign competitors, and that they are digging one vast grave for themselves in the long run'. Councillor W. H. Smith warned that wages must be geared to production, and not to the cost of living index, whilst Miss Joan Hall said that although the Government had always said it was up to the TUC to put its own house in order, it was now time for the Government itself to 'grasp the nettle of trade union reform'. She was echoed by John Peyton, MP:[104]

> If the unions prove unable to stop the activities of unofficial strikers and remove from the industrial scene . . . agitators who deprive others of the means of earning a livelihood without interruption, then the responsibility lies firmly and squarely . . . on the shoulders of the Government themselves.

Such views, however, did not go unchallenged, and indeed the motion was defeated after the intervention of the Minister of Labour, John Hare. From the floor it received a battering from several of the party's trade unionists. Mr Culleton, a member of the trade union NAC, explained to the Conference that the motion should be thrown out because it would undermine the 'tremendous amount of work' done by Tory trade unionists; it would destroy 'the immeasurable fund of goodwill built up during the last ten years by successive Tory Ministers of Labour;' and it would tie the hands of the present Tory Minister. Councillor Sir Edward Brown, a trade unionist and a member of the National Union's executive committee, said:[105]

> If King Street, the Communist party Headquarters, wanted to put a resolution on the order paper which would destroy the fraternity which exists between trade unions and the Tory party, they could not have made a better job of it.

He contradicted John Peyton who thought that the unions were not above the law and should not claim to be so, by saying that it was impossible to bring the law into industrial relations: 'No Government could operate a law forbidding unofficial strikes, closed shops or restrictive practices for the simple reason that there is no sanction which the Government could apply against them if the men refused to accept it.' Councillor Brown was supported by George Fox, a shop steward, who predicted stiff resistance by all trade unionists to government interference and argued that it would do more harm than good to the Conservative party and its industrial relations. Communist infiltration he thought should be dealt with by trade unionists themselves.

The decisive speech came from John Hare, and it is noteworthy as one of the last major statements of the policy which the Conservatives had pursued since the Industrial Charter, and was so shortly to be abandoned. Hare argued that[106] 'Legislation of the kind that is suggested would play slap into the hands of the extremists in the unions—the people who long to claim that the Tories are a class party and cannot wait to sabotage the rights of the working man.' He said that the record of unofficial strikes was not as bad as some claimed, and that some of the blame in any case attached to the employer: 'Those of us who were in the army during the war will remember that a bad unit very often was caused by bad officers and NCOs.' He thus emphasized again that industrial relations was essentially a human problem, a problem of communication and understanding, a problem of leadership. For this reason he declared:[107] 'In general I am against legislation . . . the legislative answers . . . can well lead to the sanction of sending thousands of men to gaol if they refuse to obey the law.' He finished with this grave warning to the conference:

> If this policy on which we have embarked fails, then . . . legislation may well be the only answer. But, in my opinion, this would be a tragic day that would divide and weaken our free society, and I pray that it does not come.

This policy was not abandoned during the thirteen years of Conservative rule. But it was essentially a policy of containment, sprung in part from the Conservatives' wish to avoid confrontation with the unions and prove their commitment to the post-war settlement. In part too no other policy was necessary; the problems of British capitalism did not warrant it. The Conservatives drifted with the current they found flowing. As Enoch Powell put it:[108] 'The party came into office . . . without any specific commitment on trade union law and practice, and it faithfully carried that non-commitment out for thirteen years.'

Conservative leaders opposed legislation because they knew it would be interpreted as anti-union, and because the 'human relations' approach to industrial relations seemed appropriate for the relations between the government and the unions. There were also wider electoral risks to be run, if concessions were made to opinion in the party that wanted action against the unions.

This was a matter highlighted by Charles Curran, who warned[109] that any surrender by the leadership to calls for secret ballots and other examples of 'inverted Marxism' would only imperil the post-war settlement and the great purpose of post-war Toryism—'to assimilate into the free society the ex-proletarian mass that has been lifted from poverty to abundance.' He reminded his leaders that it might be electorally lethal, since three million trade unionists on his reckoning now voted Tory. Still worse, it would mean the formal abandonment of the One Nation strategy and the image of the Conservative party as a party of all classes.

What caused the reversal of Conservative policy was the growing seriousness of Britain's economic difficulties and the Conservative defeat in 1964. It had by then become apparent that the post-war settlement had created certain problems on which neither the human relations approach nor the expanding economy were having much effect. Indeed they were growing worse. Chief among them were inflation, unofficial strikes and restrictive practices. What they meant for capital was falling profits.

In government the Conservatives reacted to the second and more serious economic crisis of 1961-2 by launching a Pay Pause—the Battle of Wages as Macmillan termed it[110]—and then the first formal incomes policy in Britain, with a guiding light for wage increases of $2\frac{1}{2}$ per cent. At the same time new planning agencies were set up, among them the NEDC. The view of the Government remained that the TUC itself should be invited to eliminate 'abuses' such as restrictive practices and unofficial strikes. But many Conservatives became increasingly doubtful about the ability of the TUC to do this. Their image of the TUC as a rather slow, uncoordinated carthorse, a giant octopus that had lost control of its tentacles, grew during these years.

The Pay Pause in fact collapsed. The Battle of Wages was lost.[111] The Conservatives were saved from the consequences of this by an easing of the economic situation, but the election still went against them, for all their manipulation of the electoral cycle, and there followed a major rethinking of the party's trade union policy.

The main stimulus for this rethinking came from the recent experience of government and the apparent failure of Conservative policy. Just before the Pay Pause Macmillan bemoaned[112]

the *utter irresponsibility* of labour in some of the *new* industries (motor cars, aviation and the like) and the *hopeless conservatism* of labour in some of the *old* industries (shipbuilding etc.). So what with 'wildcat' strikes in one and 'restrictive practices' in the other group, our poor economy suffers grievously.

The phenomenon which Macmillan noted was what made control of wages so difficult. For the wages of workers in high productivity, capital-intensive industries were bid up by the employers themselves, often faster than the unions could negotiate rises. Workers in the labour intensive industries, many of which were now in the public sector, did not benefit from such 'wage drift', yet demanded that their wages be raised in line with wages in these other industries in order to retain 'comparability'. Such increases could rarely be justified on productivity groups since the scope for increases in productivity in such industries was by definition small. The mechanism of collective bargaining institutionalized a steady increase of money wages, so long as the government maintained full employment.[113] Companies protected themselves by raising prices.

Incomes policy was originally designed as a solution to this problem. It was intended to nationalize the annual increase in productivity and spread it around 'fairly' between different groups of workers. By this means social justice, profit margins, and the share of national income going to property could all be protected. The increasingly unstable edifice of wage rates which straddled the public and the private sectors would be replaced by a wages edifice based on 'socially just' differentials. In this way the stability of the post-war state would be maintained. The difficulty was that an incomes policy always threatened to apply only to wages in the public sector. To be effective, it needed to take over completely from private industry the responsibility for determining wage rates and differentials. How this was to be reconciled with economic efficiency and free enterprise capitalism, let alone the existing distribution of income between property and labour, was not easy to say.[114] This solution, adopted naturally by Labour, seemed to many Conservatives tainted with the wrong ideology, and in opposition there was a strong movement within the party towards a second alternative. This was a new legislative framework for trade unions. One of its sources was a pamphlet published in 1958 by the Inns of Court Conservative Association entitled:[115] 'A Giant's strength: some thoughts on the constitutional and legal position of trade unions in England.' This pamphlet provided an historical and economic analysis of the British economy and the trade unions and made detailed suggestions for reform. It stressed Britain's precarious financial and economic situation:[116]

> No longer have we those great foreign assets which for many years provided a large part of the national income. No longer are we able to cushion the effects of bad times by drawing on the accumulated wealth of the past. We have spent all in the defence of liberty and in the creation of the Welfare State.

These Conservative lawyers then suggested that since Britain now had to face the full force of international competition, the state could no longer afford to maintain the legal privileges of the unions,[117] especially as the unions now tended to abuse their powers.

There were two aspects of trade union power; from the point of view of the economy as a whole, and from the point of view of the individual worker. One set of their recommendations therefore aimed at reducing strikes and restrictive practices, whilst another sought to weaken the power of militants within the unions. As the pamphlet delicately put it:[118] 'the problem is . . . how to retain the right to strike while limiting its scope to the minimum necessary to give the worker sufficient countervailing power against his employer.' Among the most important proposals were the outlawing of political strikes; the registering of unions with the Registrar of Friendly Societies; the banning of strikes in breach of union rules; the holding of an inquiry by an independent tribunal into any strike to be followed by a fourteen day cooling off period; the imposing of standard rules on the unions which would outlaw for example the closed shop; and the setting up of special courts to pronounce on restrictive practices.

Underlying the whole exercise was the faintly comic notion that the unions were the new feudal barons, overmighty subjects whose powers must be curbed and brought under law, just as previous estates had been before. The unions were in good company. The list included the barons (Magna Carta), the Church (the Act of Supremacy), the King (the Bill of Rights), the squirearchy (the Reform Act), and the middle class (the Parliament Act). Such a grotesque historical theory, however, —Magna Carta after all was supposed to be the foundation of British liberties—did not detract from the ideological persuasiveness of the case that these lawyers put forward.

It was taken up by the Bow Group and the advocates of competition policy, and by the forces of the New Right. It promised both a technique for making the economy more dynamic and efficient by allowing 'controlled' class war, and a clear commitment by the party to take action against a clearly defined enemy of the Nation—the subversives and extremists within the trade union movement. Its weakness, as Aubrey Jones has clearly seen,[119] was that it treated the unions as economic monopolies, whose power had to be curbed for the market in labour to function properly again, and thereby encouraged the belief that legislation on the trade unions was an alternative policy to incomes policy for curbing inflation.

This concept of trade union reform became incorporated in the competition policy from the beginning, but the party leaders were still a little anxious about the possible handle they were giving to their political enemies. So Edward Heath, in presenting the new policy during the debate on party policy in 1965 tried to show how it was not a reversal but a continuation of the Conservatives' previous policy. He insisted that the proposals were fair:[120]

> Anyone who suggests they are aimed at creating conflict in our society is, in fact, himself resorting to the old slogans of the class war and dividing unions from management. No-one can accuse the Conservative party of being anti-union. Those who look back on the record of Walter Monckton, Iain Macleod, John Hare, Joe Godber, cannot possibly hold that belief for one moment. I was Minister of Labour myself.

The motion at that conference called for comprehensive reform of of the trade union movement. Many of the old battle cries were heard —for dissolving the political links between the trade unions and the Labour party and ending the present form of the political levy,—but the main demand was for action against unofficial strikes. One speaker, Mr W. Lott, accused unofficial strikers of being 'foreign-powered.' They believed, he asserted, in a foreign government and deliberately fomented strikes to damage the economy. Aidan Crawley, MP, put the issue bluntly:[121]

> Let us stop pretending . . . the fundamental reason why we must have an Industrial Relations Act is that a few trade unions and a much larger number of trade unionists are abusing their powers.

The second defeat in 1966 and the Labour Government's groping after an incomes policy only strengthened the party's commitment to trade union reform and their hostility to any further direct government involvement in labour relations. Their proposals were published in Fair Deal at Work (1967). Its main proposals were the setting up of an Industrial Relations Court; the granting of power to the government to order a pre-strike ballot; the outlawing of the closed shop; a Registrar for the trade unions to fix, approve, and supervise their rules; greater control of shop stewards by union officials; new provisions for calling national emergencies; the banning of strikes in breach of contract; and a code of fair industrial practice.

The Labour Government's own plans for union legislation—'In Place of Strife'—were abandoned after a major revolt in the Labour party and the Cabinet. The Conservatives attacked Labour's proposals as being too 'coercive', by which they meant that Labour was relying too much on direct intervention by the government, instead of using another arm of the state—the courts. Both parties had become convinced by the late 1960s that drastic action against the organized working class was necessary in order to protect the state and maintain the viability of the prevailing politics of power. The Conservatives, however, had become committed to the view that strikes and inflation were caused by the excessive monopoly power of the unions. Legislation was therefore necessary to reduce this power. A prices and incomes policy was not. If the balance of power between employers and workers was redressed in favour of the employers, free collective bargaining would keep wages down and militants could be dismissed.[122] The Tories proposed to use the judicial arm of the state rather than the governmental arm to find a solution to inflation.

It was not then appreciated that such legislation could only be effective when the power of the unions was already broken, not before, and that therefore a Conservative government would either have to follow Powell's strategy to its conclusion, or reintroduce some kind of wages policy. Robert Carr insisted that this was not the case:[123]

> For the trade unions as for the rest of us, the alternative in the modern world to State intervention in the details of our life and work is the acceptance of a just framework of rules which lays down duties as well as rights but within the limits of these rules leaves us free from interference and compulsion.

Events were to prove that this was no alternative for the Conservatives.

Chapter 7
THE SEARCH FOR SECURITY: NATION AND STATE IN THE WORLD MARKET

1 INTRODUCTION

The guiding principle of Conservative foreign policy has been to advance the interests of the nation-state overseas, safeguard its security, and maintain its strength. The interests of the nation and the interests of the state are assumed to be identical. For Conservatives, Britain has no permanent allies and no permanent enemies. Practical economic interests come before the realization of international ideals, and Conservatives point with scorn to Liberals and Socialists who believe foreign policy to be an instrument for achieving moral ends and universal principles, and are prepared to sacrifice vital interests of the established nation-state to realize them.

It would be strange indeed if the Conservatives managed to realize their conception of foreign policy, for it would mean that they had discovered a way of separating interest from ideology, and escaping from the dilemma of being involved in both the politics of power and the politics of support at the same time. When we look at actual Conservative foreign policy, we find the usual fierce disagreements between different tendencies of opinion resulting from different perspectives and ideologies. There was a marked lack of clarity in the party during the post-war period about the real interests of Britain, mainly because the interests of the Conservative Nation clashed more and more openly with the interests of the state. The union of the two in the past had contributed to the enormous cohesion and electoral strength of the party. Keeping the two together became a major task for Conservative leaders after 1945.

Nevertheless, the Conservatives own conception of what foreign policy should be about has reflected certain patterns in their thinking on international issues. One has been their automatic distrust of the Labour party's ability and commitment to maintain Britain's defences and security. Another has been their overwhelming identification of foreign policy with Britain's place in the world market. For most Conservatives the two have never been distinct. Britain's trading strength and overseas investments were a central aspect of her defence and security.

The treachery of Liberals and Socialists lay in their temperamental readiness to subordinate Britain's practical interests as a trading nation and one of the leading centres of finance capital to such nebulous entities of international liberalism as the United Nations. This could mean the boycott or neglect of important markets and potential allies, such as South Africa and Spain, on 'moral' grounds because of the kind of government established there. In addition, it could mean that the defence of Britain and of British investments overseas were sacrificed to more spending on social services and the like. As Lt-Colonel W. Reeve told the 1969 Conference, the switch of resources from defence to social services was indeed the right priority for a Socialist government, but 'it is not the right one for a British government.'[1] This was a basic view in the party. Only a Conservative government could properly defend the nation-state.

The electoral ideologies of the Conservative party in the past had been organized around the idea of national greatness and Labour was therefore defined from the start as an anti-national party which did not fully accept the essential symbols of British power and history.[2] This was intensified by Labour's internationalism, in particular the association of Labour, however tenuous it might be in reality, with the international Labour movement and international Communism. Labour was pictured as a fifth column, a trojan horse, or at best an unwitting staging post for communism. Although Ernest Bevin's record as a cold warrior was hard to assail, the attacks on the Labour Party did not abate whilst he was Foreign Secretary. Above all, it was Labour's record on rearmament in the 1930s and its predilection for collective security, as well as its moral disapproval of colonialism, that Conservatives found threatening.

The politics of power in the post-war period quickly established two major priorities for Britain's foreign policy—the acceptance of membership in a world economic and political system dominated by the United States and organized to contain communism; and the consequent withdrawal from the Empire and the beginning of a search for a new role and a new security for the British state in the world market. This latter had enormous significance for all the electoral ideologies of the Conservative Nation and for the electoral perspective of the Conservative leadership. It involved not merely an adjustment to Britain's declining strength, but the abandonment of both the colonial Empire and the Commonwealth as economic bases for Britain's power, and a commitment instead to join the European Common Market. This required the greatest ideological transformation in the party's history, for it meant accepting that Britain's material interests could no longer be secured in an international bloc which she dominated. The whole concept of national sovereignty and national greatness, based on the world-wide Empire, was thereby undermined, and with it withered the particular appeal to the electorate that the Conservatives were accustomed to make. The application to enter the EEC and the Conservatives' growing commitment to Europe during the 1960s threatened for the first time in the history of the national democracy to make the Conservatives and not their electoral rivals the anti-national party. It was a striking confirmation that the Conservatives subordinate the politics of support to the politics of power. The interests of the Conservative Nation were sacrificed to the interests of the British State. But it was only accomplished after a long period of hesitation, anguish, and controversy.

2 THE CONTAINMENT OF COMMUNISM

The Cold War is often presented as predominantly an ideological struggle; democracy versus totalitarianism. This seriously mistakes its real character. It is true that the ideologies on both sides were particularly virulent and uncompromising, (a nice irony in an age celebrating the end of ideology), and that this led especially in America to a foreign policy guided in part by 'ideological' rather than 'practical' considerations. But the cold war cannot be satisfactorily explained simply as a struggle between two competing ideologies. It was also a struggle for political influence, markets, and economic resources, between two imperialist states which divided up the world between them.[3] Some of the same irrationality appeared that had been evident in the scramble for Africa in the 1880s and 1890s;[4] the seizure by both sides of as much territory as possible, often regardless of real importance or possible material returns.

What was new about the situation after 1945 was that there were initially only two imperialist powers, one of which was far stronger than the other. America's global strategy was at first to incorporate all the other industrial states, including Russia, into a unified world order under its leadership. When this broke down, America moved swiftly to a policy of containment, both military and economic, which sealed Russia off from the world market. The Russians responded by trying to make their position secure in Europe. The European countries assigned to them at Yalta were rapidly transformed into buffer states. A world wide contest began for the allegiance or neutralization of all other countries in the world. Control was sometimes exercised directly, but more usually through client governments. The states of western Europe, including Britain, were welded into an Atlantic Alliance to stand firm against the imminent Communist advance they all expected.

How little the cold war had to do with defending democracy and freedom across the world, and how much with securing spheres of influence and markets to allow the free movement of capital, goods and raw materials, can be seen by the kind of Governments throughout the world that the Americans backed and the kind they overthrew.[5] Similarly, the Soviet Union's interest in spreading socialism to other countries may be judged from the character of the regimes it established and maintained in its satellites, and by the foreign policy it pursued, aimed at extending its own sphere of influence and consolidating the power of its state. America rebuilt the shattered European economies through Marshall Aid, but on her terms. Accordingly, the post-war years saw the realization of what had been a major aim of America's policy since the 1930s and during the war—the elimination of the British, French, and Dutch colonial Empires. As Julian Amery has written:[6] 'Roosevelt planned to build "One World", and it was to be a world safe for American exports.' This was why America sought to lower tariffs, abolish discrimination and preferences, and why it supported the 'self-determination' of colonial peoples.

Britain played a subordinate role in the Atlantic Alliance. Although nominally still a great power, her freedom of action was small. Her economic revival was directly underpinned by American loans, and thereafter her economic independence was exercised only within the American orbit, in part owing to America's domination of the international monetary system. This meant that Britain accepted GATT, rearmament, participation in Korea, and a start on the dismantling of her Empire. The limits of her independence were clearly seen at Suez, when America strongly opposed the British and French action and helped to force Eden to call the invasion off, at the moment of success, by refusing to lend support to sterling. America also pressed Britain continually to speed up the process of dismantling her Empire, in order to break down one of the last important spheres of influence that remained in the 'free' world.

For the most part, the Conservatives both in opposition and in government accepted the dominant role of America in the alliance and the consequent restriction on Britain's freedom of action. Suez and GATT provoked the strongest outbursts of anti-American feeling in the party. On the general strategy of the cold war, however, the party loyally supported the Americans. There was no questioning of the American belief that international communism was monolithic and malevolent, seeking by every means in its power to flood across the world. Conservative spokesmen repeated all the fallacies on which the policy of containment was based. Quintin Hogg described Russia as a 'tiger on a leash' while Stalin was alive:[7] 'Only the fear of American reprisal by the atomic weapon prevented him, I am sure, from over-running Europe.' It was an attitude strongly reflected in the publications of Central Office:[8] 'There can now be few who still doubt that the campaign of International Communism throughout the world against the free system of democracy is indivisible.'

The less hectic pace of confrontation in the late 1950s did not change Conservatives' views of international communism. In Home's words:[9] 'The theory of peaceful coexistence . . . is tactical, a mask to disguise the absence of concession on principle, a means to achieve the *ultimate* victory of the Communists over the capitalists.' A strong front against Communism was the priority of British foreign policy throughout this period, and successive British governments willingly accepted inclusion in the 'West' and the consequent limitation on the special interests of British capital in the cause of resisting the spread of Communism. Such a united international outlook would have done credit to the world socialist movement. Conservatives talked freely about the 'West' and its competition with the Soviet system. This competition between the blocs was seen at first predominantly in military and defence terms, but when the situation stabilized in the 1950s, economic competition was emphasized. As David Eccles wrote:[10]

> The supreme need in the West is a continually expanding economy out of which, in conditions of free enterprise, savings can be generated and investments made on a scale that will keep us ahead of the Sino-Soviet bloc.

Only if the West could accumulate faster than the Soviet bloc, he argued, could the allegiance of the Third World be won and maintained. This was why Russian feats like the launching of the Sputnik in 1957 and the very high Russian growth rate during the 1950s caused such alarm and despondency.

During the 1960s, however, the Americans' cold war strategy began to break up. On the one hand the growing rift between Russia and China, dating officially from 1961, made the idea of a unified international communist conspiracy still more preposterous than it had been previously as a guide to foreign policy. On the other hand, America found it increasingly difficult to maintain her leadership of the West. The open defiance of France, the rise of Japan, and the moves for a new united Europe, signified the return to the familiar pattern of rivalry between the great industrial states. This trend was accelerated by the collapse of the dollar as the main underpinning for the international monetary system, and by the Vietnam war, the final cruel absurdity of the policy of containment.

As a result British foreign policy began to veer onto a new course. Conservatives rediscovered their old concept of the balance of power. The cold war ideology was not of course overthrown. It had struck too deep roots for that. Besides, it still served functions, and Russia and China remained two world powers. But the weakening of American hegemony allowed much more discussion of what policy Britain should follow to secure her interests. The Conservatives in the end overwhelmingly chose adherence to Europe. The acceptance of American leadership and the new pattern of world trade made the preservation of the colonial Empire both difficult and irrelevant.

The acceptance of Europe by the Conservative leadership meant a fundamental reorientation of Conservative attitudes and ideas. But at the same time it meant endorsement of a still more basic principle that lay at the root of Conservative politics. Military strength, an independent foreign policy, and a secure place in the world market required a strong economic base. Britain's colonial Empire and Commonwealth could no longer ensure such a base for Britain. But in association with Europe Britain might once again be part of a bloc that could rival the other industrial powers.

An essential preparation for this new orientation of policy was therefore to cut short Britain's overseas military commitments which were ruinously expensive to the balance of payments and were more related to Britain's fading Empire than to any real commercial advantage.[11] With Heath's approval, therefore, Powell as Shadow Minister of Defence launched a major attack at the 1965 conference on the defence policy of British governments since the war. He first reminded the conference that[12] 'to defend this nation's existence and its continuity is the one object which a Tory places unconditionally above all others.' In addition there were secondary national interests, such as trade and access to raw materials, and the containment of Communism, which might at times require the commitment of British troops overseas. But Powell stressed that circumstances changed, and they could not be considered a permanent part of Britain's defence. Indeed he argued:[13] 'A military presence has more than once proved rather an obstacle than a safeguard to the development of trade, and hindered instead of promoting that recognition of mutual material interest which is the only sure basis of all trade.'

Furthermore, the containment of Communism Powell redefined to mean the containment of the Russian and Chinese *Empires,* and argued that the limits to their expansion would be set by a balance of forces created by that expansion: 'Western military intervention may hinder the attainment of this balance.' That being so, Britain's role east of Suez had no real importance for the defence of Britain, contrary to what was so often claimed. A new frank assessment of Britain's defence needs, based firmly upon her regained status as an island off the coast of Europe in the eastern Atlantic was urgently required. This also entailed a rejection of the 1957 White Paper with its emphasis on nuclear weapons as the main prop of Britain's defence. The strength of Britain's conventional forces was to be the new priority.

Powell's logic, however, based on his complete escape from the imperial ideology[14] was not digested by the imperialist wing of the party. Heath discovered he could not proceed as fast as he wished with the development of the new foreign policy. East of Suez was a mighty slogan, for it implied that Britain was still a power with world wide responsibilities. It was patriotic therefore to continue to support a British military presence overseas, and the Labour Government's increasingly evident anxiety to wind it up seemed to prove it. The leadership bowed to this view. After Powell's departure from the Shadow Cabinet in 1968, the motion on defence at the conference put forward three planks for a Conservative defence policy: a substantial military presence in Europe; a network of land bases in areas where Britain still bore responsibility to participate in 'regional defence'; a small and efficient mobile force for use in 'trouble spots'. An addendum was tacked on welcoming[15] 'a pledge given by the Leader of the party that the next Conservative Government will maintain a British military presence east of Suez.'

The speeches in this debate stressed the intimate link between Britain's defence commitments and her commercial interests. Communism threatened 'political stability', hence the maintenance of British trade and investment. A new danger also was arising alongside Communism —the rivalry of other industrial states. As Patrick Wall asked in the 1969 defence debate:[16]

> Do you know that Japan is winning economic control over the area she won and lost in World War II and that both Japan and the Soviet Union plan to have the largest merchant fleet in the world during the next decade? Do you realize that once we have completely withdrawn from East of Suez there will be no going back and our investments, trade and influence will all be at risk.

Christopher Gent from Dulwich complained that the motion was 'a sentimental looking back to defence needs which are basically irrelevant in this modern era of total destruction of nuclear warfare.' But he was alone. Geoffrey Rippon replied to the motion and pledged the next Conservative government to restore Britain's position in the South Atlantic, the Indian Ocean and East of Suez: 'It is hard to exaggerate', he said,[17] 'the damage which the Labour Government have done by weakening our defences and undermining our national interests and commitments throughout the world.' For the moment the relics of the old Empire strategy were to stay.

3 IMPERIAL PREFERENCE: THE LAST PHASE

Empire has occupied such a special place in Conservative ideology because although imperialist sentiment lasted but a short time, it coincided with the period when the Conservatives were first making an appeal to a mass electorate. For almost all Conservatives, therefore, the Conservative Nation has been a Nation with an imperial destiny, and the British state has been a great power with world wide interests. This may account for the fact that some Conservative MPs have barely recognized that a domestic politics existed at all. Disraeli first discerned the possible advantages of making the Conservative party the party of the Empire, despite his private judgment that the colonies were 'millstones around our necks.'

He laid out the now familiar contrast between Great Britain and Little England:[18]

> The issue is not a mean one. It is, whether you will be content with a comfortable England modelled and moulded upon Continental principles and meeting in due course an inevitable fate. Or whether you will be a great country—an Imperial country—a country where your sons when they rise, rise to paramount positions and obtain not merely the esteem of their countrymen, but command the respect of the world.

This struck deep roots in the party. For most Conservatives the Empire became their most important ideological symbol. Leo Amery spoke for many when he wrote[19] that the starting point of his political thinking was 'the British Empire or Commonwealth conceived as a unit and as the final object of patriotic emotion and action.'

For a long while the Empire was the cornerstone of both the politics of power and the politics of support. It guaranteed Britain's economic independence in an age of increasing inter-imperialist rivalry, both before and after the First World War, and at the same time it offered a way of strengthening the authority and increasing the acceptance of British institutions by identifying the Conservative party as the party of national greatness, and their opponents therefore as the anti-national party. This underlay the great onslaught on Free Trade and the Liberal party in the years before 1914, and it governed the main Conservative political strategy for fighting the class war and containing Socialism. For Amery, one of the great merits of the long campaign for tariff reform and imperial preference was that it cut across class lines:[20]

> The one thing I dreaded then, as I have ever since, has been a political cleavage based on class, on the desire for the material gain of one class of the community at the expense of others and of the banding together of those others in defence of their possessions. If my long political life has had any meaning it has lain in my constant struggle to keep the Tory Party true to a policy of Imperial Greatness and social progress, linked with a definite economic creed of its own, and to prevent it drifting into becoming the party of a mere negative laissez-faire anti-Socialism.

The Empire thus became one of the pillars of the Conservative Nation. It gave Britain a place in the world and a base line for all thinking on relationships with other countries. As a conference delegate, Major Ian Fraser put it;[21] 'We are not ourselves exclusively a nation of Europe, but a people of the world.' Britain did not therefore look inward to herself or to the group of nations in western Europe, but acted and thought in world terms. The guarantee that Britain was a world power was the colonial Empire. The notion that Britain's essential interests were bound up with the maintenance of her position as the centre of a world-wide community of nation was enormously strong in the Party. It figured in all the official literature:[22]

> The Conservative Party by long tradition and settled belief is the party of the Empire. We are proud of its past. We see it as the surest hope in our own day. We proclaim our abiding faith in its destiny. We shall strive to promote its unity, its strength, and its progress.

Yet it was precisely this tradition that was so swiftly undermined after 1951. Successive Conservative leaders were obliged to lead the party away from its imperial faith.

The strength of this faith is manifest in the conference debates during the first period of opposition. In 1948 Mr J. Campbell, proposing the motion, declared:[23]

> Although not all members of the Conservative Party, sad to say are Imperialists, it is true to say that all Imperialists have been, and still are, Conservatives, either initially or by the process of gravitation.

He was echoed by Bernard Braine:[24] 'Let me proclaim the faith that every man and woman in this hall shares. We are an imperial power or we are nothing' (applause). He derided the Socialists for neglecting Britain's imperial commitments. The result of their policy was that now the very heartland of the Empire was bankrupt:[25] 'Under a spiritless Socialism, which has succeeded only in dampening down the fires of our native genius, we have become dependent for our very existence upon foreign aid.'

This was the main charge levelled by Conservatives at the Labour Government in these years. Labour had failed to understand how important the Empire was to Britain, and had succumbed to American pressure. There was strong opposition to the conditions attached to the Washington Loan Agreements which the Government signed after the war. The Loan was negotiated to replace Lend-Lease which the Americans terminated abruptly a week after the ending of the Japanese war. The financial terms of the Agreements were good; the Americans could indeed afford to be generous. But attached to it were political conditions—first that sterling should be made convertible by 15 July

1947, and second that Britain should join an international trade organization pledged to work against all forms of trade discrimination. This was the origin of GATT—the general agreement on trade and tariffs—and it effectively ruled out any move by Britain to restore or extend the tariffs and imperial preferences in her Empire. If Britain was to be prosperous, it would only be in a world market dominated by American exports and the dollar. Many Conservatives, therefore, unhesitatingly attacked Britain's participation in GATT because it limited Britain's freedom of action.[26] The party leaders pledged the party to renegotiate the terms of the agreement.

Withdrawal from colonies did not cause much dispute in this period; the main instance of it, the granting of independence to India and Pakistan, was supported by the Conservative leadership and was the conclusion of the policy of both the pre-war Conservative Government and the wartime coalition.[27] The majority of Conservatives acquiesced quietly enough, but the warm reception given to a speech by Mr Andrew Fountaine at the 1947 Conference, indicates the feelings of a substantial minority of the party. Fountaine fulminated against 'the ever increasing subversive influence within our own country and the Dominions overseas' which had finally produced[28]

a full Socialist Government in this country with all its attendant foulness. Look what they have done. India! The finest jewel in the British Crown it was called. It has now been cast like pearls before swine, and not because the Indians wanted it, but because of a small minority who had been got at by Communist influence. (applause.)

But the main charge against the Labour Government was not the suspicion that it was scheming to give up the Empire, but the anxiety that it was neglecting the opportunities for imperial development. Anthony Nutting, MP, chairman of the Young Conservatives, told the 1949 conference[29] that there was 'no will in the Socialist Party to develop the British Empire.' Julian Amery was still more emphatic. He accused the Government of betraying the achievements of the Ottawa Conference and weakening imperial preference:[30]

Instead of developing new wealth and new resources in the Empire the Socialists have preferred to import borrowed goods which we could not possibly earn and to pay for them with borrowed money which we could not possibly repay. The result is that we find ourselves today on the verge of bankruptcy.

Conservatives, he said, had warned of the consequences of abandoning an Empire economic policy, and had foreseen that the dollar gap could not be bridged merely by increasing exports. He called for a new version of Joseph Chamberlain's policy which could simultaneously strengthen the economy and win electoral support. At the General Election, he said, the Conservatives would have a strong case in their support of free enterprise against nationalization. But the effect of the war meant that a Conservative government would still have to ask the people to make sacrifices. In order to do this successfully it would have to hold out to them hope and a vision of the future. Amery at least was in no doubt as to what this should be:[31]

> Surely we can find no better than the ancient faith that it is the mission of the British people to develop the resources of their Empire, to bring forward its backward peoples, and so to strengthen the whole combination of the Commonwealth, that we can give to the world that moral leadership which it so sorely needs.

This idea had long had great appeal to Conservatives, because it made a strong national economic policy the basis for national greatness; it united domestic and imperial policy; and it supplied a concrete programme on which to win support from all classes of the community. For many Conservatives the slogan of imperial preference was far more than just another economic policy that might or might not be appropriate depending on circumstances. It was the means by which the Nation could regain control of its future and be re-united with the state. Free Trade meant that the country was largely at the mercy of economic forces it could not control. The Government could only adjust to them as best it might, but adjustment might mean economic slump and three million unemployed as in the 1930s, or the dismemberment of the Empire, or even the loss of Britain's sovereignty.

One student of the Conservatives' colonial policy has written that[32] 'the imperialism of most Conservatives existed chiefly as an emotion (that of pride), and bore no necessary relation to the specific policy objective of unification.' But this was only because the leadership put forward no programme for unification. There can be little doubt of the enthusiasm for such a programme, regardless of its practicality, if one had been announced. Those who did advocate such a course saw correctly that the heart of it would have to be an economic union, the welding of the disparate Empire into an economic bloc with a common tariff and preferences which would give it common interests in opposition to the rest of the world. But the refusal of the leadership to be drawn on this meant that the grand vision of imperial unity was cut loose from any solid foundation and floated off into dreams about a common citizenship based on nothing more tangible than common sentiment and historical connection. According to David Gammans:[33]

> Our real problem, surely, is that we have to create a sense of Empire citizenship, so that a man from Nigeria will talk about his status as a British subject permanently and with pride, just as a man would who was born in Yorkshire.

169

He was echoed by Lt-Cmdr L. R. Ramseyer at the 1950 Conference:[34] 'I look forward to the day, and I trust we shall all live to see it, when Britons all over the world will call out to the skies again "Civis Britannicus sum".' Such attitudes were put to the test by Commonwealth immigration to Britain during the 1950s and 1960s.

Far from yielding to the pressure for imperial preference, the Shadow Cabinet began to lead the party away from its commitment to the Empire. A strong lobby, led by Macmillan and David Maxwell-Fyfe favoured a European policy, and the Conservative party through them became a more eager participant in the post-war Strasbourg Conference than did Labour. The Conservative spokesman for the colonies was Oliver Stanley, who was in general agreement with the Labour Colonial Secretary, Arthur Creech-Jones, on the need to prepare for the orderly winding up of the Empire. But he was forced to tread warily, due to the strength of feeling in the party. Replying to the debate in 1948 he stressed:[35] 'There is no subject on our agenda more important for the future of our country than the one with which we are now dealing.' In 1949, faced by Julian Amery's call for a new bid to implement imperial preference, Stanley made use of the Imperialists' own demand that the Empire as a whole should decide policy. Britain, he said, could not dictate to the Empire. The Empire itself had to decide questions, and for this to mean anything, Britain must sometimes accept things to which Conservatives were opposed. He cited the British Nationality Act of 1948.[36]

Time of course was with the leadership, for the longer no plan for imperial economic union was agreed or put forward, the more obstacles appeared in its path. The Empire began to disintegrate as an economic bloc in the wake of the new trading patterns which grew up after 1945. Shadow Ministers were therefore prepared to ride out the pressure for imperial preference whilst they were in opposition, by giving merely verbal reassurances of their faith in Empire economic union. When they took office the problem re-appeared, since they were in no doubt of the feeling of the party on the subject. At the same time they had inherited the involvement with GATT, and could see no way of abandoning it. Apart from the very real immediate advantages it conferred, it was unthinkable to Conservative leaders to risk shaking the anti-communist Western alliance so soon after the Korean War.

In 1952 the Imperialists returned to the attack with a motion that demanded new moves to develop the Commonwealth through imperial preference, and urged a revision of GATT. L. S. Amery himself spoke, declaring 'the two policies of Empire and of GATT are irreconcilable.' Oliver Lyttleton, the new Colonial Secretary, accepted the motion for the platform and promised that Government would seek to renegotiate GATT.

At the 1953 Conference, since no progress whatsoever had been made in this direction, the platform faced a hostile motion moved by Lord Balfour of Inchrye. Leo Amery again spoke in the debate and complained that there had been no lead from the Government on GATT. In view of the pledge he had given the previous year, Lyttleton did not reply to this part of the debate. Instead Thorneycroft, the President of the Board of Trade was brought in to answer the amendment on GATT. Lyttleton spoke only to the original motion on colonial affairs. The decision had been made to face the Conference squarely on the issue. Thorneycroft was uncompromising in his support for GATT. This, he said,[37] was not the whim of an individual minister; it was 'the united policy of the whole of Her Majesty's Government.' In addition, it was the policy of the Commonwealth.

A last stand was made by the diehards at the Blackpool Conference in 1954. The last part of the motion chosen for debate read: '[Conference] . . . emphasizes the need to maintain traditional ties of trade and culture if need be by revisions of GATT.' The imperialists moved an amendment to delete the words after culture and substitute: 'by such revision of GATT as will restore freedom of action in respect of Imperial Preference.' Leo Amery, appearing for the last time at a Conservative conference, made a final plea for the policy for which he had struggled all his life:[38]

> This amendment today asks for no new or strange departure in policy. It has been affirmed by every Conference since the war, accepted by Ministers on every occasion, embodied in every official manifesto or declaration of the party. What is perhaps strange is that this Conservative Government in three precious years has done nothing whatever either to advance their declared policy or even to make sure of keeping it alive.

The reply again came from Thorneycroft, who moved not at all from his earlier position. All speakers, he said, had stressed the importance of having a sound and sensible commercial policy to underlie Britain's approach to the Commonwealth and Empire. The object of this policy must be to secure wider trade, and at its centre therefore were two great organizations—the IMF and GATT. We remain in GATT, Thorneycroft told the conference, because it pays us to be in it. In addition, he said, all the independent countries of the Commonwealth were in favour of GATT and opposed to imperial preference. The amendment was lost.

This defeat underlined some of the features of the post-war state and the interests it represented. In the past the battle between imperial preference and free trade could in part be understood as a battle between industrial and finance capital. In the 1930s with the collapse of free trade and the abandonment of the gold standard, imperial preference had gathered still more support from industrial capital. Its main focus was the Empire Industries Association founded by Leo Amery, Neville Chamberlain, and Lord Lloyd in 1923. Two hundred Conservative MPs were members. A policy of protected markets in the Empire and the reduction of foreign competition was greatly favoured by many sections of industry, especially during the slump.

There was no such support, however, from industry after 1945. This was partly because of the changing organization of British capital, and the creation of new concentrations of finance and industrial capital. This meant that there was much less disagreement and conflict between the two. The new links enabled many of the top British companies to become multi-national by expanding abroad. The renewed boom in foreign investment in the 1950s and 1960s (Britain's stake abroad rose from £3,300 million in 1945 to £9,300 million in 1957 and to £11,800 million in 1961) was largely undertaken by these new consortia of banks and large industrial firms, whilst domestic investment languished. Before 1914, export of capital had been predominantly the purchase of foreign government bonds by individual investors and City firms.

The other reason, however, was that the short-term interests of British industry always favoured an expanding world market as opposed to a protected Empire market. After 1945, moreover, a new pattern of trade was evident. World trade grew fastest between countries that were exchanging sophisticated manufactures, rather than between those that were exchanging manufactures and primary products. GATT and the IMF were thus the guarantee of prosperity for most sections of industry. Only the declining industries such as cotton, and shipbuilding were hit hard by the new era of freer trade.

This helps to explain why the interests of finance capital have generally been so dominant in the British state. Its interests are represented institutionally through the Bank of England and the Treasury, but that would not by itself be sufficient to account for the sway it has exercised over governments of all parties. The basic reason is that finance capital has been very successful in aligning its interests with the needs of the national economy in the world market. The main need as Britain's industries became ever more specialized and dependent on imports of raw materials and food to fuel its production and feed its workers, was for an expanding world market and stable trade, so that British exports could keep pace. That is why the particular policies that advance the interests of finance capital—particularly the defence of sterling and the export of capital—have so often seemed to governments what the national economy also required. The rise of the multi-national companies whose interests fit easily with those of finance capital has further reinforced this pattern.

The imperialist tendency in the party therefore proved weak in its campaign for imperial preference after 1945 because it lacked any real support from capital. Its support was ideological, rooted in the most potent electoral ideology the party had fashioned. But it increasingly lacked real force.

4 THE SUEZ EXPEDITION

The steady crumbling of the electoral ideology of the Imperialists in the party was highlighted by the events at Suez in 1956. The decision to take military action against Egypt was probably the most popular decision among Conservatives of any decision made by the Conservative Government. The failure of the expedition did much to explode the old certainty of the imperial ideology, for it brought into question Britain's ability to act as a great power. The episode showed how strong was the identification of the party with national greatness, and how necessary therefore it was to their politics of support that the Conservative party remained the party of Great Britain. Eden, whose reputation and popularity had collapsed after the 1955 election, found himself riding an unprecedented wave of support. If party popularity had been the only goal of Conservative policy, the task of Conservative politicians would have been simple in these years.

The pressure for military action to assert Britain's interests reached a climax in the party at the 1956 Llandudno Conference. Foreign affairs was the first subject on the agenda, and the motion read:

> Conference strongly endorses the Government's resolute policy throughout the Suez crisis; in defending the sanctity of international contracts; in upholding the rights set out in the 1888 Convention; in condemning Egypt's act of seizure; in calling together the nations principally concerned, and in seeking a peaceful solution according to the principles of the UN charter. It deplores the Opposition's attitude, which cannot but divide the nation, at a time of grave national emergency and pledges its support to the Government in reaching a just solution.

Members of the Suez group,[39] a parliamentary alliance in the imperialist wing of the party, led the strong support for vigorous action. Captain Waterhouse declared:[40] 'At all costs and by all means Nasser's aggression must be resisted and defeated. For let us have no doubt at all, that at this moment Britain is at a vital crossroads in her history.' Julian Amery attacked the Opposition:[41]

> I am sure our party will not be moved by the defeatists in the Press and in the Socialist party whose vapourings we have seen only too much of in the last few weeks. I do not believe the Socialist leaders speak for England or even for the majority of their electors.

Suez was a symbol not merely of an attack upon a British interest but of the whole global political strategy which British governments had followed for so long, a strategy in which British national greatness was at one with her commercial interests. Nasser's seizure of the canal threatened not merely Britain's main trade route, but the viability of Britain's world role itself. The supporters of Empire and the Commonwealth therefore regarded the seizure of the canal as a mortal blow to what remained of the imperial strategy. As Peter Walker declared in the debate:[42]

> Let us keep one factor clearly in mind—that Suez is basic and vital to the economic survival of our nation and the nations of the Commonwealth. It would surely be unthinkable for a Tory Government to take any other action than a resolute stand against a dictator threatening the very life line of British trade and commerce.

In the view of several Conservative leaders afterwards, the invasion failed because the Government was trying to pursue two purposes at once, which could and did become contradictory—the removal of Nasser and the occupation of Egypt on the one hand, securing the 'international' status of the canal by stopping the fighting between Israel and Egypt on the other.[43] The result was that neither was achieved, and the canal blocked into the bargain, but the second aim at least gave the Government an excuse for calling off the operation.[44]

What is quite clear amidst the fog of speculation about collaboration, Cabinet splits and intrigue, is the enormous success the Suez invasion achieved in terms of the politics of support within the party. For a time it entirely restored Eden's position as leader, which had been gravely undermined since the election.[45] Charles Curran wrote that Eden's 'tumbril had turned into a bandwagon',[46] and that his authority was now 'greater by far than it has ever been before.' In the Gallup poll of 1 November, 76 per cent of Conservative voters approved Eden's policy. A week later it had risen to 89 per cent, while Labour voters opposed to the invasion had fallen from 72 per cent to 63 per cent. Opposition to Eden in the parliamentary party was estimated at between twenty-five and fifty—there were eight abstentions in the debate on 8 November.[47]

The more serious problem of support, however, occurred when the invasion was halted, and the decision to withdraw was made. Eden's position was utterly destroyed. A typical judgment was Angus Maude's:[48] 'Perhaps the most frightening failure', he wrote, 'has been the failure to take advantage of the warmth of support for the Government in the country, and to use it for the benefit of the nation.' One political commentator reported[48] that Eden had lost the confidence even of the stolid centre of the party. He reckoned that Eden now had no section of the party to which he could turn for unqualified support. One hundred and twenty-seven Conservative MPs signed an Early Day Motion in late November 1956, which stated that the attitude of the Americans on Suez was 'gravely endangering' the Atlantic alliance.

The Imperialists went further. Fifteen abstained in December 1956 over the withdrawal from the canal zone, and fourteen abstained in May 1957 over the British Government's advice to shipowners to start using the canal again on Nasser's terms.

What was certain for the future was that no Conservative would again be able to celebrate the canal zone as 'the Clapham Junction of the Commonwealth, the hinge of our Imperial strength.'[50] As with India and imperial preference, another prop of Britain's imperial mission had gone forever.

5 THE LIBERATION OF THE COLONIES

The collapse of imperial preference and the failure of its supporters to revive it, knocked away one of the main pillars of the electoral ideology of the imperialists; the liberation of the colonies, the experience of Commonwealth immigration, and the commitment to enter the Common Market were to complete the process. The Empire which for so long had been the idea which organized Conservative thinking about both the politics of power and the politics of support was no more.

What is surprising in retrospect is the speed with which decolonization took place. The confident predictions of Conservative colonial ministers in the 1950s that Britain would stay in Africa for at least a generation[51] provoked an outburst of rejoicing among white settlers in Kenya and elsewhere when the result of the 1959 Election was known. This did not last for long. Having rebuilt the American alliance, Macmillan was preparing to withdraw from the colonial Empire in Africa, and redirect British energies towards Europe.

From the standpoint of the real interests of the national economy the winding up of Britain's overseas colonies was already overdue by 1960. A booming economy based on expanding trade between the industrialized states, the rise of nationalist movements that threatened civil disturbances and armed uprisings, and the acceptance of the world leadership and cold war strategy of the USA weakened the case for staying on.[52] Once the economic and political arguments for retaining the colonies had lost some of their strength, the ideology of the imperial mission, of providing good government in the colonies to help the native peoples climb up the ladder of civilization, grew weaker too.

There were three basic kinds of colonies in the British Empire— native colonies, settler colonies, and fortress colonies.[53] The function of the fortress colonies such as Cyprus and Aden was strictly to safeguard the lines of communication within the Empire. They could therefore be disposed of easily enough when there was nothing left to safeguard. The native colonies no longer needed direct political control and could be freed as soon as a 'responsible' local elite had been formed. The real problem lay with the settler colonies. Many of these—like Australia,

Canada, and South Africa—had already seceded from the Empire although they remained members of the Commonwealth. They had succeeded in winning not just political independence from Britain, but economic independence as well. The settler colonies that remained threatened secession in this double sense, while the native colonies did not. What really sabotaged the schemes for Empire Union was the existence of such settler states within the Empire which refused to subordinate their economic interests to those of England. So paradoxically the countries in the Empire which had the greatest cultural links with England were also those whose interests were most opposed, whilst the native colonies, although often adopting an anti-British and anti-imperialist ideology, proved usually just as subservient to British capital after independence as before.[54]

From the standpoint of the politics of support in the party, however, a policy of decolonization was highly risky, especially when it touched the interests of the settlers, because of the widespread identification of many in the party with these settlers. It was well known that the settlers and their British supporters would oppose any move to independence that weakened their control of the economy. Every western government therefore that had resolved on decolonizing a settler colony normally acted with precipitate haste in order to forestall any attempt at unilateral secession by the settlers.[55]

The same calculations governed British strategy. The ideology of trusteeship proved an admirable smokescreen behind which the new policy could be prepared and implemented. This ideology was a familiar one within the party. A typical expression of it was Home's speech to the CPC Summer Conference in 1955:[56]

> This colonial administration which we have undertaken so successfully for so many years is in the nature of a trust for the people who live there, and to hand over these people to incompetence or corruption or social chaos would be nothing less than to abandon our responsibility. While we will always consult the local people on the pace of change, nevertheless the pace must be largely for us to lay down.

In the CPC pamphlet *Wind of Change*, published in 1960, a group of Conservative MPs spelled out the policy that their Government was about to discard:[57]

> The moment at which a viable dependent territory should become sovereign should be determined primarily by the political maturity of its inhabitants and, in the case of multi-racial territories, by the disappearance of race differences as the predominant feature of politics.

The new policy which Macmillan appointed Macleod to carry through, made the main condition for independence the existence of an organized elite which could command popular support and was ready to take over. Very little indication was given in advance of the change in policy for it would have been much more difficult to carry through the constitutional changes in the African colonies if the leaders of the white settlers and Tory backbenchers had known that the pace of withdrawal was to be speeded up. At the same time Macmillan made his Wind of Change speech to inaugurate the new policy, he was busy privately reassuring white leaders in Africa and his own backbenchers that no change was intended.

His precautions did not prevent the formation of the Monday Club to commemorate Black Monday, on which the speech was delivered. In general, however, the Government's plans were well laid and de-colonization proceeded smoothly.[58] The Rhodesian Federation was dissolved, and independence granted or promised for all the states of east and central Africa. The party was shaken, but the issue never emerged at the party conference which continued to pass resolutions welcoming the steady advance of the colonies to independence. The fiercest opponents of the withdrawal were the League of Empire Loyalists, but they were most active during the 1950s, and had already been discredited in the party before the Wind of Change era by the savagery of their assault on Macmillan for pulling out of Cyprus. Their attempts to disrupt the 1958 Conference were suppressed by Conservative stewards with considerable violence. The League was subsequently to merge with other extreme right wing organizations to form the National Front.[59]

6 RHODESIA

Two issues were to arise, however, during the 1960s, which showed the decomposition of the imperial ideology and aroused considerable controversy in the party. They were Southern Rhodesia and immigration. Rhodesia was the one failure of the policy of disengagement which the Macmillan Government had carried through so well. It proved the most difficult colony in Africa to relinquish because, far more than Kenya, it was a colony of settlers. Once the Conservatives had made up their minds to give independence to the African colonies, it was inevitable that the Federation of Southern Rhodesia, Northern Rhodesia, and Nyasaland, set up in 1954, the last great experiment in Empire building, would break up. The problem for the British Government was that the bulk of the white settlers were concentrated in Southern Rhodesia, which had enjoyed self-government since the 1920s. This white minority numbering some two hundred thousand was firmly entrenched and cohesive, and consequently it was much more difficult to dispossess it and pass power to the Africans, the majority of the population, as had been done successfully in Kenya.

Under their leaders, and alerted by the dissolution of the Federation, the white settlers resolved to fight the British and obstruct the handover. Negotiations were protracted, and eventually broke down, leading to a unilateral declaration of independence by the white Rhodesians in 1965. This created a most difficult situation for the Conservative leadership, since they naturally supported the continuation of their colonial policy by the Labour Government and were forced to condemn UDI. Yet it had always been the settler colonies which stirred the strongest feeling and drew the greatest support among Tory backbenchers and party members. The white Rhodesians appeared to a majority in the party as the last representatives of that fine breed of Englishmen who had set out to start a new life across the seas and to spread the values, habits, and arrangements of capitalist civilization around the world. They were kith and kin not just by descent, but ideologically as well. White Rhodesia was the property-owning democracy in motion, a Christian outpost of the Victorian middle class, devout in its respect for property, prizing hard work, responsibility, initiative, independence, yet at the same time paternalistic and protective of its subject black population. All branches of the Conservative Nation were represented. Coming at the end of Britain's imperial period, the Rhodesian dispute illustrated the powerful hold on the party's imagination and loyalties which the imperial ideology had exercised.

The leadership did their best to smother the issue because of the deep splits it caused within the parliamentary party. Many Right Progressives and supporters of entry into Europe had no patience with the sentimental attachment to the cause of the Rhodesian whites displayed by a large section of the party. In the debate in Parliament over whether to impose oil sanctions on the rebel regime, the party split three ways.[60] The party leaders found themselves tied down by an electoral ideology that had once been part of their electoral perspective, but which now belonged to an earlier period of the nation-state. The pressure on them was accentuated because the party was in opposition, which meant that the leaders could not take any real initiative in policy, yet had to show their supporters how their position differed from that of the Government. A majority of their supporters in Parliament and in the constituencies wanted the party to give full backing to the rebel regime, and cordially detested the Labour Government.

The ideological strength of the white settlers in the Tory party was fully displayed at the 1965 conference, which was held just before UDI was declared, but at a time when most people regarded it as inevitable. Lord Salisbury emerged from his enforced retirement to become their spokesman. He had protested before about the direction of the foreign policy of the consensus, both over Cyprus and over the earlier withdrawal from the other African colonies.[61] Now the party was in opposition, however, he commanded immeasurably greater influence.

At Brighton, he moved an amendment to the official emergency resolution on Rhodesia, deploring any imposition or threat of imposition of
sanctions against Rhodesia, whether economic or military, if she declared UDI. He told the conference[62] that the Rhodesian crisis raised
'the whole issue of what our party stands for, whether it stands for
anything at all before this country and the world.' One of the great
principles of the Tory party, he stated, had always been, 'to spread the
British idea of liberty and justice among the more primitive peoples of
the world, and educate them up to formal self-government in accordance with those ideas. But of late it must seem at any rate to a great
many of us that there has been a sad change. There has been a sad
confusion in the minds of our leaders . . . between liberty and independence.'

There had been a determined effort, he claimed, to get rid of Britain's
responsibilities, and the Rhodesian situation was the final degradation.
The Labour Government, he said, was asking the British people not
only to 'abandon' friends and kinsfolk, but also to tell them to abandon
their wives and children to 'the tender mercies of men who . . . are
as yet totally unfitted to conduct any free form of government at all.'
The pace of advance towards African rule could only be determined by
those 'on the spot', who could not possibly be regarded as traitors.

Salisbury's defence of the white Rhodesians, echoed by many other
speakers at this and at later conferences, was not easy for the leadership
to handle. Lacking the authority and the protection of power, they
could hardly declare as did Henry Clark, MP, at Brighton that the shouts
for UDI were not shouts for independence but shouts for white domination. They could hardly disown one of the central ideological traditions
of the party, in which all Conservatives had been nurtured. Yet at the
same time they were reluctant to allow this fading electoral ideology
to triumph and force their hand. So they attempted to hold an un-
comfortable position in the middle. They deplored UDI and they
deplored sanctions. As a result they tried to get the parliamentary party
to abstain in the vote on sanctions in the House of Commons. It was an
inconsistent policy, as they no doubt knew. There was little practical
point in opposing UDI, unless the party was prepared to impose
sanctions. Yet this compromise, coupled with the vague promise to
reopen negotiations, became the leadership's policy and reflected their
deep embarrassment. It did, however, succeed in preventing the party's
programme for government on this issue from being dictated by ideological pressure from their supporters. It proved virtually the last stand
of the imperialist wing in the party.[63]

7 IMMIGRATION

The other issue which turned the party's imperial traditions and ideals sour was immigration. A common citizenship for all countries in the Empire that shared a common allegiance to the British crown was a fundamental part of the Conservative conception of Empire. The most important privilege that Empire citizenship bestowed was free movement within its boundaries. By a strange historical irony, the British who had so indefatigably spread themselves across the world in the course of four centuries, expropriating, enslaving, and sometimes eliminating the native population in the process, found themselves hosts to a great army of immigrant workers from the new Commonwealth in the 1960s. Formerly, it had been expected that only citizens of the white Dominions would want to use their Empire citizenship to return to the Mother country, but the labour shortage in Britain after 1945, which was shared by other countries in Western Europe, meant that employers began to bring in workers from those countries of the Commonwealth where unemployment was very high.[64]

The British exercised much less control over their immigrant work force than did West Germany or France. Because these immigrants were Commonwealth citizens, they were also British citizens, and could not be sent back when there was no longer any need or welcome for them. It is a measure of the strength of the imperial ideology and of the inertia it induced that no steps were taken to control Commonwealth immigration until 1961, by which time there were an estimated three hundred and fifty thousand immigrants in the country.

Under the Empire, there had been no legal boundary between British and non-British. All were British subjects by virtue of the common allegiance of all imperial territories to the British Crown. The granting of independence to colonies and the resulting extension of the Commonwealth created new problems, because some of the new Commonwealth states wished to remain within the Commonwealth, but as republics. This clearly made legal nonsense of the criterion for a common imperial citizenship, and led to the British Nationality Act[65] of 1948, which distinguished between two classes of British subjects— the separate citizenships of the independent Commonwealth countries and the citizenship of the United Kingdom and her remaining colonies. This formula permitted Commonwealth states to define their own citizenship and to control immigration into their countries. They were no longer formally bound to admit all British subjects. Britain, however, took no further steps to control the entry of Commonwealth citizens. The open door policy was considered one of the most important and tangible links between members of the Commonwealth.

The Conservative party strongly attacked the 1948 Act because it infringed this right to free entry. David Maxwell-Fyfe declared in the House of Commons:[66] 'There would be no point in these new "categories" of the right honourable gentleman unless to drop the old idea of the common status and our proud boast of the open door.' The

Conservative Government after 1951 made no moves towards a stricter definition of British nationality. Yet it passed in 1953 a Royal Titles Bill which recognized that the basis of the new Commonwealth was not allegiance to the Crown, and devised a new title for the Queen—Head of the Commonwealth. This too aroused considerable opposition and misgiving in the party. Most Conservatives continued to ignore the changing character of the Commonwealth and behaved as though the Empire was still in being. Alan Lennox-Boyd, then Colonial Secretary, impressed on the 1955 conference that there was a need to help all members of the imperial family including[67] 'coloured immigrants, who are just as much citizens of the UK, as their passports will show you, as are you and I.'

But there were other elements in the party, more conscious of grass roots feeling in some constituencies, who saw fairly early the explosive possibilities of a large coloured population, and began to campaign to get the government to impose control on immigration. In Parliament this was led by Cyril Osborne and Norman Pannell, but they received little support or sympathy from the bulk of Conservative MPs. Their efforts in the National Union were more successful. At the 1958 conference a motion proposed by Pannell was debated. It was one of the two resolutions chosen by ballot of the delegates, and talked about the grave social problems arising from 'unrestricted immigration' from the Commonwealth and colonial countries.

In the light of what was to come, its terms were moderate, but its meaning for the party was still clear. It was calling for the subordination of one of the main planks of the imperial ideology—the idea of common citizenship and the open door—to the interests of the nation more narrowly defined. Immigration thus presented the Tories with one of their cruellest ideological dilemmas. The Empire had always been seen as an extension of Britain, an area where British enterprise, British institutions and British traditions flourished. Although the rhetoric of the Commonwealth emphasized that its members were equal partners, a free association of sovereign nations, with common interests, links, and traditions, many Conservatives continued to think of the Commonwealth as the *British* Commonwealth. In that way the imperial ideology was least affected. The real test of this new Commonwealth came, however, when the ideal of Commonwealth brotherhood manifested itself as large black communities in the main cities of Britain, and when the Commonwealth Prime Ministers Conference pursued policies that clashed with the interests of the British state. The expulsion of South Africa from the Commonwealth in 1961, one of Britain's largest markets and sites for investment, was the first major example of this.

The campaign to restrict immigration gathered support at a great rate in the 1960s. At the 1961 conference, by which time the Government was having to consider legislation, forty motions on immigration were sent in by the constituencies. Thirty-nine called for stricter control. The motion chosen for debate was blunt: 'Conference expresses its concern at the very serious problems being created by the uncontrolled number of immigrants flowing into the United Kingdom. It asks her Majesty's Government to take action quickly on this matter.' The debate was a bitter one and aroused sharp controversy, but the liberals in the party were clearly a small minority. The supporters of restriction used several arguments, ranging from the administrative to the outright racialist. A strong body of opinion in the party was represented by Toby Jessel, who argued that 'the policy of uncontrolled immigration leads to conditions which cause colour prejudice.' He mentioned the low standard of hygiene among immigrants, educational problems and housing. Before him, Councillor Clarke who proposed the motion, talked of the overcrowding created by immigrants especially from the West Indies and Ireland, and put forward four controls which would limit numbers. Every immigrant, he said, should be obliged to have adequate accommodation available, a clean bill of health, a job to go to, and no criminal record.

Norman Pannell spoke again in this debate, and while he framed his speech around these same social problems, he pushed the argument a little further. First he berated the leadership. Nothing had been done, he said, since the conference passed a similar resolution three years before:[68] 'The clearly expressed view of the conference has been treated with casual disregard.' In the meantime, he warned, the situation had got incomparably worse. Britain could not be expected to keep an open door for the unemployed of the Commonwealth, which had a population, he reminded delegates, of 600 million (all of whom might be unemployed sometime). He listed the reasons for control as housing, the danger to health and morals, unwanted children, the drain on public funds, and (significantly), the fact that coloured immigrants 'though they may not be inferior are different in background, tradition, and habits.'

In this way, straightforward racialism began to gain a hearing in the party. One delegate, Mr Taylor from Moss Side, declared that the threat from immigration stemmed from the shortage of houses, the increase of disease (leprosy he claimed was up 150 per cent), and immigrant spongers:[69] 'You and I are keeping him and his wife and about six delightful little piccaninnies round his knees.' Yet even this delegate still clung to the imperial ideology, however ambivalent he now found it. What, he asked, if economic winter comes? 'We want to preserve our Commonwealth institutions to the utmost, but we want a fair crack of the whip.'

Against these arguments, those who opposed restriction battled in vain. They concentrated on emphasizing the damage to the Commonwealth of limiting immigration, for as Nigel Fisher, MP, pointed out, the principle of free entry was one of the few positive Commonwealth ties that still remained. He urged the Conference:[70] 'We preach partner-ship in Africa, let us practise it in Britain.' Mr Barr from Yorkshire wondered if the conference wanted Britain to remain the central focal point of the Commonwealth, and stressed that Britain needed immi-grant labour and that accepting immigrants was one of the most useful forms of aid Britain could give the developing countries.

The leadership, however, had decided to side with those who wanted restriction. Ministers were alarmed about the explosion of anti-immi-grant feeling in the party, and the absence of any administrative control over the situation. They evidently hoped that the imposition of a measure of control would cause the anti-immigrant agitation to subside. In fact, it only led to demands for more controls in an escalating cycle throughout the 1960s. Controls on immigration and the size of the immigrant community already in Britain became election issues at the 1964 election, particularly in some Midlands constituencies such as Smethwick. 'If you want a nigger neighbour, vote Labour' was a typical slogan, and helped win that seat for the Conservatives, but its prediction proved inaccurate. The Labour Government, despite its earlier opposition to controls, soon added them to its consensus with the Conservatives, and the parties kept trying to outbid one another on which could introduce or promise the strictest controls. Powell's intervention in 1968 pushed the Conservative leadership still further to the right on this issue,[71] and the party entered the 1970 election pledged to introduce a new Immigration Bill that would make all Common-wealth citizens subject to the same controls as aliens. The fact that the party at the same time was happily preparing to end immigration restrictions on all citizens of Common Market countries once Britain's application was successful, did not seem inconsistent. Colour rather than numbers was of the essence of the problem.

8 THE APPROACH TO EUROPE

As the withdrawal from Empire gathered pace, so another new policy was launched. The translation of the Conservative party from the party of Empire to the party of Europe was one of the greatest changes in its short modern history. It required a major reorientation of the electoral perspective of the leadership and of the electoral ideologies of the party for it involved a fundamental change in the conception of the Con-servative Nation and in the role of the British state. Macmillan himself thought the decision to apply for membership[72] 'perhaps the most fateful and forward-looking policy decision in our peace time history.'

But the transformation was a slow one. An opportunity existed for a new Europe to be built immediately after the Second World War. Many expected Churchill to take the lead in calling for a strong united

Europe. There was a vocal, if small, European lobby within the Conservative party which believed that Britain's post-war problems could best be handled in cooperation with other European states, and participated eagerly in the new European institutions that began springing up.[73]

Despite however the expression of goodwill and friendship, practical steps towards cooperation proved more difficult to arrange. The Labour Government under Ernest Bevin's direction was committed to the American alliance and looked suspiciously at steps towards unity in Europe. This became increasingly true of the Conservatives. They came to believe there was a clear choice between trying to rebuild Britain's strength in association with the Commonwealth or in association with Europe. Once the issue was posed in those terms there was not much doubt on which side Conservatives would line up. As Julian Amery explained:[74]

> The ideal of a United Europe does not evoke the same response in
> Britain as it does in most countries on the Continent. This is natural
> enough. For one thing we have not experienced occupation and the
> consequent loss of confidence in our ability to solve our problems
> at the national level. For another, our aspirations towards a wider
> patriotism already find their fulfilment in the Commonwealth and
> Empire.

The preoccupations of the leadership at this time were rather different. On the one hand, much greater European co-operation seemed both necessary and desirable, both for reasons of defence and economic recovery. Churchill before the war had advocated European Union, although not the integration of Britain in Europe, and he was looked to as a strong supporter of the European movement. On the other hand, he was now also leader of the Conservative party and in opposition. Some attention to the politics of support in his own party was therefore necessary. There was little enthusiasm for the European movement inside the Conservative party, as distinct from the Conservative leadership. Macmillan analysed Churchill's dilemma shrewdly:[75]

> As a party leader he could not fail to recognize that a considerable
> portion of the Conservative party were doubtful and even anxious
> about this new movement. They feared, and not unnaturally, that
> in one way or another, both on the political and economic side,
> Britain's position as head of the Empire and Commonwealth might
> be prejudiced.

Churchill was also aware of the new importance of the American alliance, both as a source of economic aid and as the foundation for an offensive strategy against Communism. He therefore developed his famous formula that Britain stood at the point where three great circles touched: the circles of America, of Europe, and of the Commonwealth. This was a masterly ideological mystification that satisfied all sections of his party by making it appear that no choice had to be made between the three. John Grigg was later to contrast Churchill's reluctance to commit Britain to Europe at this time with De Gaulle's decision. De Gaulle saw, he wrote,[76] that France had to choose

> between being a technically sovereign but second class power, and pooling some of her sovereignty in order to wield authority in the world. Churchill and his successors have failed to make the choice for Britain, because they have refused to admit its necessity.

The failure of successive British governments to make a positive choice in favour of either a new Empire union or a European Common Market meant that Britain was forced ever more closely into the American orbit. A capitalist state that seeks an independent foreign policy must first establish relative economic independence of the leading world power. Britain's position was clearly shown by her acceptance of GATT and the premature attempt to make sterling convertible, following American pressure. This effectively precluded any attempt to rebuild an Empire Union. At the same time British Governments chose not to join in the various schemes for European cooperation that began sprouting.

In the early years after 1945, debates within the party were fairly one-sided, since the Europeans could not challenge the supremacy of the Empire and Commonwealth. The first motion on the subject, at the London Conference in 1949, welcomed the Council of Europe and closer European unity, but added the proviso that it should be consistent with the unity of the Empire and with collaboration with the USA. Duncan Sandys, its proposer, put forward two main arguments for a united Europe: it would turn the tide of Communism and it would give Britain a new market:[77] 'Our economic future does not lie in trying to undercut the Americans in their own home market, but rather in creating another market equally large, secure and prosperous of our own.' David Eccles, a leading spokesman for the New Conservatism, told the conference about the advantages of the European market, and was echoed by Harold Macmillan:[78] 'Let us find a place to be rich in, not a place to be poor in.'

Plans for European unity at this stage had two aims; a new economic association to secure prosperity, and a political association to resist Communism. Supporters of Europe naturally tried to link, even to confuse the two, whilst supporters of the Empire argued that Britain's participation in any European union should be confined to the second. Leo Amery was quick to exploit the ambivalence of the 1949 resolution. He explained to the party that the resolution meant:[79]

'this Conference would not approve of our going inside a customs union from which the rest of the Commonwealth were excluded to their disadvantage.' Still less, he argued, should the party approve of Britain

> entering as a subordinate unit, a state or province, some rigid
> Federation of Europe from which the dominions kept aloof: enter
> into a constitutional system which would in any way sidetrack or
> degrade the status of that ancient common Crown, which is the
> symbol of our Imperial unity.

Having shown how unattractive an electoral ideology the European case was, he could afford to be as European as any. The Communist threat, he said, made 'the unity and independence of Europe . . . essential to the development and security of our own unity in the British Empire.' Since he was used to thinking in political economic terms about Britain's Empire and alliances, Amery was the first to see in the new conception of Europe a threat to Empire Union. At this time all the ideological arguments and sentiments were on his side; and Britain's material interests were ambivalent. There was no certainty that Europe's economy would revive. But the undoubted success of the imperialists in these early years in blocking the European alternative was matched by their failure to force on the leadership their Empire policy. Since Britain shrank away from the two positive policies open to her, it is hardly surprising that her dependence on the strongest world power should have grown.

Conservatives entered office in 1951 with definite pledges on Britain's role in the world. The 1949 *Imperial Charter* had stated:[80] 'We believe that if the British Empire were to break up Britain would become a third-class power unable to feed or defend herself.' Although there was already an influential European lobby in the party leadership by 1950 Britain's residual Imperial interests guided the policy of the new Government. Eden was the leading spokesman for this point of view within the Cabinet. In a speech at Filey in June 1950 on the question of Britain joining in European cooperation he had declared:[81]

> In any conflict of interest or friendship the British Commonwealth
> and Empire come first . . . because we know that it is as the heart
> and centre of the Commonwealth family that we can make our
> fullest contribution to promote our own prosperity and the peace
> of the world.

Eden did not change his views when he became Foreign Secretary, and indeed he helped to frustrate early attempts that were made to involve Britain in the moves towards a European common market. Eden was in general control of foreign policy in the new Conservative

Government and had no particular enthusiasm for Europe. His negative policy led Macmillan at one point to contemplate resignation.[82] Eden stated his attitude towards the developing Common Market in 1952.[83] It was clear, he said, that the six nations were moving towards a complete federation. 'There is no dispute', he maintained, that Britain could not join such a federation. He was echoed the following year by Charles Longbottom who proposed the motion on foreign policy and defence:[84] 'We cannot enter any federation which would bind us closer to foreigners, however friendly, than to our kinsmen and companions of the Commonwealth and Empire.'

The consequence of Eden's policy was that Britain continued to play the part of a great power. This involved a high defence budget, a substantial military presence overseas to protect markets and sea routes, and a close alliance with America to share the policing of the free world. The advantage of this posture was that it continued the traditional policy and image of Britain overseas. Its drawback was that it increasingly ran counter to important interests in the British state, as far as the national economy was concerned. The export of capital flourished, but domestic investment languished.

Other Conservative leaders had a sharper sense of reality than did Eden, unbalanced perhaps by his single-minded concentration on foreign affairs during his political career. Of these Macmillan was the most prominent. He had been closely associated with the European movement when in opposition. He did not lose touch with it when he became Minister of Housing in 1951. In 1953 he received a memorandum from Lady Rhys Williams[85] which stated that there were only three possible courses for Britain—to attempt to remain a power in her own right; to choose isolationism and independence like Sweden; or to become another state of the United States. In her view the only way of ensuring the first way was to cooperate fully with Europe. She argued[86] that Britain could not possibly remain a world power on the present basis—the Commonwealth was 'non-existent except as a Coronation pageant.' Britain's traditional markets and spheres of influence—the Middle East, Africa, India—were no longer secure, whilst Europe itself was settling down into 'an anti-British mould, the main hope of whose statesmen will be to pillage British trade, while claiming her contribution to the defence of their own frontiers against Russia.'

Macmillan evidently agreed with the diagnosis, although he appreciated the political difficulties of acting upon it. What was to swing things his way, both by presenting him with the Leadership[87] and by severely discrediting the old British policy was the Suez episode. Macmillan had not contributed as much as Butler to the development of the party's new One Nation programme since 1945. But this was not a handicap to him, because of the importance that Conservatives still placed on the quality of the leaders that implemented the One Nation strategy. Butler's apparent equivocation during the Suez crisis raised doubts about his political soundness and his capacity for national leadership. This was especially damaging to him because Conservatives judged national leadership by war-time leadership, and Suez was close to being a war situation. Macmillan's vigorous backing of strong action against Egypt during the early days of the invasion won him the confidence of the party. It was, however, ironic that Macmillan should 'emerge' as Leader in 1957 because he was thought more resolute in defending Britain's national interests. For he held more radical views than Butler about how to overturn all the policies and postures on which the Suez invasion had been based. His main interest during his Premiership was foreign affairs, and he worked towards the fulfilment of a Grand Design. This was aimed firstly at rebuilding the alliance with America which had been damaged somewhat by Britain's independent action at Suez. Macmillan clearly intended to submit to the world leadership of the United States, and to reassure the Americans that there would be no more independent moves, in return for the American nuclear protection and a privileged place in the councils of the western alliance.[88] The second stage was to wind up the colonial Empire, in particular in Africa, whose mounting cost now far outran the economic advantages of protected markets for trade and investment. The third stage was to negotiate entry into the European Common Market, where Britain's trade was growing fastest.

This Grand Design was never presented as a whole to the Conservative party to be accepted or rejected. It appeared in small pieces, each justified by its own compelling circumstances. Macmillan knew the political difficulties of getting such a shift in policy accepted by his party and he did not hurry the pace.[89] In the end, however, only stage three was not accomplished, and even there the decisive groundwork had been done.

9 THE FIRST APPLICATION: THE PARTY DEBATE

There were three critical party conferences for stage three—1960, 1961, and 1962. In 1960 at Scarborough, before any application had been made to join the Six, the resolution chosen for debate appeared fairly neutral, but had wider implications, and was obviously intended to test the party's mood:

> Conference believes that if Western Europe can work together economically, the gain both for world peace and prosperity will be enormous, also that the results, if Western Europe were to become increasingly divided into rival blocs, would be correspondingly grave; and therefore urges the Government to take positive steps to bring the Six and Seven into still closer economic cooperation.

The motion received the expected broadside from the diehards, yet it was a sign of their new defensiveness that they had to concede what made a European policy so urgent, the changing pattern of trade. They might complain as did Mr Paul, that the party was tending to think too much about Europe and too little about the Commonwealth and Empire. But he himself supplied the reason,[90] 'World trade is expanding now in every country in every direction, but only between this country and the Commonwealth and Empire is the proportion declining.' He ascribed this to the diversion of Britain's interests and ruefully reflected that the biggest portion of the decline in Commonwealth trade had taken place in the last ten years under a Conservative Government.'

But the resolution also displeased the convinced Europeans in the party, and one of them, Gordon Pears—a leading member of the Bow Group—pointed to the fallacy in the motion as it stood:[91] 'The only realistic way of bringing the Six and Seven together is by the entry of the United Kingdom and anyone else in the Outer Seven into membership of the Common Market, on acceptable terms.' This was undoubtedly what most Ministers thought too by this time, but they were not quite ready to say so. Heath, however, in his new role as Lord Privy Seal with special responsibility for Europe, showed where Government thinking was moving in his reply to the debate. He gave the usual disclaimer that Britain did not have to choose between Europe and the Commonwealth. If she had, he said, then there could be absolutely no doubt about the answer. But his actual speech was entirely devoted to the economic and political advantages of belonging to the EEC. The former included a market of 150–200 millions 'on our doorstep'; the attraction of risk capital and investment which might otherwise move away from Britain and America and towards the Market countries; competition abroad in international markets; and avoiding the exclusion of Commonwealth trade from the EEC. Moreover, the political advantages, according to Heath were even more weighty: the release from the danger of political disunity and the threat that economic blocks (in Europe) could lead to political blocs.

Heath painted an entirely favourable picture of the EEC. He told the conference that it had given new interest and purpose to its member countries and had banished ancient political rivalries. In coming to terms with this new Europe, however, Britain could not pretend she had no commitments or traditions. We face the EEC, said Heath,[92] 'with our Commonwealth, with our agriculture, with our well-known Parliamentary system and our known attitude to supra-national institutions.' The dilemma for Britain, as Heath stated it, was that this most attractive and successful international club would ask Britain whether she was prepared to share in the 'new dynamic outlook' they were creating. Heath of course did not spell out what this meant, or even what a 'dynamic' outlook might be. He was putting forward a negotiating position, but how he intended Britain's basic commitments to be weighed against the new 'dynamic outlook' was left vague.

The bulk of the enthusiasts for the EEC at this stage belonged to the right progressive tendency in the party. The Bow Group and the Young Conservatives, for instance, were prominent in their support for entry.[93] The Europeans wanted Britain to become a member of the Community partly because it seemed the most sensible course from the standpoint of the British state, and partly because it was part of their programme for modernizing Britain. David Howell, for instance, bemoaned Britain's failure in the 1950s to enter Europe:[94]

Had the realities of the trade patterns developing between Europe and the Commonwealth and Britain been more closely considered, instead of being set aside in favour of less reasoned appeals to imperial sentiment, the commercial arrangement which we seek today . . . might now be ours.

The politics of power, he implied, required greater scientific precision and more careful separation from the politics of support. William Rees-Mogg supported this point of view at the 1962 CPC Summer School on Europe, and argued that if Britain was to reap full benefit from Europe she needed to go in on a 'rising surge of national efficiency. This means a rising trend in investment, in productive efficiency, and a willingness to reconsider every traditional method and to remove every handicap which old-fashioned or conservative attitudes to business management might still leave.'

The following year, on 10 August 1961, Britain made its first application to join the EEC.[95] The significance of the event was not lost on Julian Critchley:[96]

Only a party of the Right could have presided over the liquidation of the British Empire. What is the more surprising is that it now seems that the same party, with its empirical tradition and freedom from closely defined doctrine, will be the one to take the nation into the next stage of its history. . . . The majority of Tory MPs have now come to see Europe not simply as a political concept, exciting in itself, but as essential to our long-term economic well-being.

The next two conferences took place under the shadow of this decision and started a vigorous controversy in the party about Europe and the Commonwealth. The leadership trod warily and were successful in winning a substantial majority of the party for their new course, although their efforts were temporarily to be set at nought by the French veto.

At Brighton in 1961, the resolution was moved by two of the younger Conservatives, Andrew Bowden and David Lane. Its wording was calculated to arouse the minimum of dissent:

Conference notes the strong political and economic links being forged between the six countries of the EEC, believes that it is in the interests of Britain that we should lose no time in negotiating a form of closer association with the Six compatible with our Commonwealth and EFTA responsibilities, economic and political, and our pledges to British agriculture.

The strategy of the Leadership at this stage was to present the Common Market policy not as a new course, but as a natural development of Britain's existing commitments and policies. The opposition to the Market[97] was of course hardly deceived. They tried to outflank the Government's persuasive presentation of the 'national interest' by demanding certain pledges which would not be negotiable at Brussels. They thus attacked the leadership through the politics of support rather than through an alternative programme for government. Their amendment to the Brighton resolution was moved by Sir Derek Walker-Smith and proposed to delete all the words after EEC, to make the resolution read:

Conference notes the strong political and economic links being forged between the six countries of the EEC, and the U.K.'s application under Article 237 of the Treaty of Rome to become a member of the Community. Animated by goodwill to the countries of the Community but mindful of Britain's special position and unique Commonwealth connection and of the views expressed at the Conference of the Commonwealth Finance Ministers and the Commonwealth Parliamentary Association, it calls on the Government to declare its clear resolve not to approve any proposals which involve surrender of British sovereignty, or are inconsistent with pledges to British agriculture and horticulture or with the continuance by the United Kingdom of its traditional role in the Commonwealth and world affairs.

Against this celebration of Britain's traditional role the supporters of Europe again stressed Britain's vital interests in joining the Six. The threat from Communism was again uppermost: 'If the free world is to unite,' said Andrew Bowden,[98] 'then it must unite politically, militarily and economically.' David Lane echoed him:[99] 'We are engaged in a struggle with international Communism, certainly for years, probably for decades, and our way of life will not prevail except through the maximum unity of the entire free world.' John Biffen told the Conference[100] that Britain must enter Europe 'in the determination to lead and to form and to shape the policies of a really strong West.' Heath himself, one of two Cabinet Ministers who spoke in the debate played down the economic arguments. The objects of the EEC, he said,[101] were threefold: a rapprochement between France and Germany; an improvement in the standard of living of its peoples so that they would not be 'attracted to the Communist way of life' but would be prepared to 'defend their own free way and their own independence'; and an increase in the cohesion, power and force of the European countries.

In reply, the supporters of the amendment tried to turn the debate onto the sacrifices Britain would have to make if she entered Europe. The keynotes, said Sir Derek Walker-Smith, were sovereignty and the Commonwealth. He emphasized that hanging over any participation in the institutions of the Market was the threat of political union. Joining the EEC would therefore in his view[102] lead eventually to the 'loss or impairment of our prized national institutions, the sovereignty of Parliament and the common law.' As if this were not serious enough, there was the effect on the Commonwealth: 'What would be the cumulative effect on the Commonwealth connection [of negotiations]? It must be damaging and it could even be disastrous.' This was a general refrain throughout the debate, and was expressed with particular force by Mr R. Moate and Lord Hinchingbrooke. Moate asked:[103] 'Surely any Amendment so fundamentally Conservative, so essentially founded in true Tory principles, will be accepted by the Government this morning?' Its fundamental Conservatism lay in its desire to preserve the vital factors in British life—sovereignty, independence, and Commonwealth. The EEC was not just a trading agreement. If Britain joined she must subscribe to the 'European idea.' Hinchingbrooke, like the leadership, had drawn lessons from the Suez expedition, but they were different ones. The question he told the conference was this:[104]

> Do we ally ourselves with our history and all that we have done to
> make and maintain this enormous Commonwealth . . . or do we
> put obstacles in its progress, at the behest of the USA for the sake
> of a purely commercial and ideological connection with a corner of
> Europe?

But the weakness of the case for the Commonwealth and of all the anti-Common Market groups remained the lack of any alternative political economic strategy that was viable. It was hardly necessary for Duncan Sandys, winding up for the platform, to point out that however advantageous Empire Free Trade might be for Britain, it was not wanted by the rest of the Commonwealth. The realism behind the Government's move commanded wide support in the party. Nigel Birch, for instance, opposed the amendment on the grounds that entry was vital for the *continuance* of the Commonwealth:[105] 'The Commonwealth has been held together in the past and is held together now by the strength of this country, by our industrial strength, our financial strength, our ability to lend, invest and give money away.' Only in the EEC, he said, could Britain now find the large market she needed.

After another year of negotiations, the Government clearly felt it had weathered the anti-Europe storm in the party, and chose a more positive motion for the debate at Llandudno in 1962:

> Conference welcomes the progress being made in the Brussels negotiations in working towards solutions of our problems of entry to the EEC: expresses confidence in the Government's determination to find adequate safeguards for our special interests and those of our partners in the Commonwealth and EFTA; and stresses the importance of a successful outcome to the negotiations for the strength and unity of the free world and the future prosperity of the UK, the Commonwealth, and Western Europe.

The economic arguments were far more prominent in this debate, which was again given top priority by allotting it extra time, and by arranging for two Cabinet Ministers to speak in it. The first of these was Butler, who made the economic case crucial, and declared yet again that the choice was not one between Europe and the Commonwealth. Instead, he described the EEC as 'the greatest adventure of our time.' To support this claim, and referring to Gaitskell's speech the week before, Butler managed a complete reversal of the normal Conservative standpoint:[106] 'The Socialists have decided to look backwards and to leave the future to us. For them 1,000 years of history books, for us the future.' Such positive enthusiasm for a new course, oriented to the future rather than to national traditions and historical identities, might be thought an unlikely success at a Conservative conference. But it did answer a mood in certain sections of the party whose voices were not silent at this conference. John Selwyn Gummer told delegates that FUCUA was six to one in favour of the Government. He thus attempted to line up youth and its special arguments behind the platform, whilst Aidan Crawley, MP, a refugee from Socialism, began a general celebration of change. The main obstacle to the spread of Communism in Europe, he said,[107] was no longer the United States, but 'the emergence in Western Europe, near the heart of the Soviet Union, of a new and thriving civilization based on free enterprise.' That was why Britain must take part, he concluded: 'The future lies with this great party, and with all its traditions and its name, it has to become the party of change. It is leading the changes that will lead to greater changes.' G. Lloyd, MP for Sutton Coldfield, announced that an overwhelming majority of Birmingham industrialists favoured entry to Europe, whilst Patrick Jenkin, after describing Commonwealth Free Trade as moonshine, again asked what alternative Britain had:[108] 'Those who oppose our joining Europe would indeed condemn Britain to a grim struggle for existence.'

For Butler too this was the decisive consideration. The vital economic reason for going in, he argued, was the need for a wider home market.

Only if Britain were economically strong could she help the Common-wealth:[109]

> Modern progressive industry must have a Continental-sized market into which it can sell its products absolutely freely. If Britain does not fit herself into one of the larger markets which are inevitably forming themselves, we shall have too narrow an industrial base for our technological industries.

These arguments did not impress the anti-Marketeers. Both sides recognized that this Conference was likely to be the last before the negotiations for entry were completed. The anti-Market amendment, therefore did not equivocate. Strictly speaking, it was not even an amendment, but a completely new resolution, since it proposed to delete the whole of the motion on the order paper, and put instead:

> Conference, recalling the pledges given that Britain will not join the EEC unless the terms are satisfactory to British agriculture, to our EFTA partners, and to Commonwealth interests, considers that, unless these pledges are fulfilled, it cannot commit itself to support Britain's signing the Treaty of Rome, and calls upon HM's Government to make it clear that it is neither their wish nor their intention to become absorbed in any form of European political or federal union that would result in loss of sovereignty of Parliament or in irreparable damage to the Commonwealth system.

It was moved by Robin Turton and David Clarke. Turton contented himself with the fairly safe observation that the terms Britain was likely to obtain would not allow the pledges mentioned in the amendment to be fulfilled. On the whole the anti-Marketeers were rather quiet. John Paul tried to remind his Leaders that they won a majority in 1959 on the pledge of no Common Market. He warned that the interests of Europe and the Commonwealth were irreconcilable, and hinted at incipient totalitarianism in the Six, spearheaded by the nine faceless men of Brussels (The EEC Commission). Derek Walker-Smith returned to the rostrum to declare that the economic case had not been made out and that only now the real political reasons for entry were emerging. But he did not think that the political case could outweigh the sacrifice of the Commonwealth and the surrender of sovereignty. Besides he reminded the Conference, had they forgotten that the British heritage did not belong to the present generation to do with as they pleased; they only held it in trust for the generations to come.

The character of the opposition to the Market is clearly revealed by the fact that the economic case for entry was hardly ever attacked—except as regards agriculture. Much of the debate indeed centred around 'political questions'—defence, sovereignty, and the like. The economic case seemed generally accepted by all. It was its political and ideological cost that the anti-marketeers opposed. The only exception at this conference was a speech by Harmar Nicholls, MP, who deftly paid tribute[110] to Macmillan's great judgment and his capacity for taking full account 'of our views, of our moods, and our instincts in the rank and file support of the Party . . . before committing the nation to any major policy decision.' He still stressed, however, the need to insist on pledges and safeguards from the party Leaders. He mentioned the farmers and their opposition to entry, and then commented on the effects of opening the British market:

> The PM said that this would give British industry a cold douche and liven them up. But a hard, well-known manufacturer I know said that it might give us a cold douche which would result in pneumonia and put us on our backs.

Such a viewpoint, that a larger home market, freer movement of labour and capital and more competition, might not necessarily guarantee prosperity for all the people, was seldom aired in the debates. Two important sections of Conservative supporters—the farmers and small businessmen—stood to lose by entry. The Prime Minister himself brushed such doubts aside. At the conclusion of the conference he told the delegates that the EEC was one of the facts of the modern world and there was danger for Britain if she delayed going in, because she would lose her chance of influencing events. Entry was to be the first step in a fundamental reshaping of the framework of world trade. The party endorsed the policy of their Government.

10 THE EEC AND THE COMPETITION POLICY

The collapse of the negotiations in 1963 took Europe out of the issues of the 1964 election, but this was clearly not the result of the strength of the anti-Market group. Heath's election as Leader in 1965 confirmed that a European policy would be among the party's long-term aims. Indeed a commitment to Europe was an essential part of the competition policy and the electoral perspective that went with it. Anticipating the breakdown of negotiations in 1963 the *Spectator* had warned the party that it must stay committed to Europe:[111]

> by abandoning its European design the Conservative Party would be robbing itself of its appeal to the young, to intellectuals, to all that growing class of technicians and white collar workers who desire a modern and efficient Britain. It would be pinning its faith on elements in our society which are moribund, to emotional chauvinism and sickly nostalgia. It would go into battle with its face resolutely turned to the past. Whatever happens in Brussels Mr Macmillan and his Government must not renounce their intention of entering the European Community.

The 1966 Manifesto was silent on Europe, but following their second defeat, and the prospect of at least a full term in opposition, the Leadership decided that entry into Europe should be one of the main planks of a revitalized Conservative programme. Accordingly a resolution moved by Sir Anthony Meyer was chosen for the External Affairs Debate at the 1966 Conference. After calling on the party to make a 'fundamental reappraisal of Britain's role in the world', which would include a recognition of the 'limitations' of the United Nations and an assessment of the 'real value to British interests of present commitments east of Suez' the motion demanded that 'a proper priority' should be given to the construction of a United Europe as 'equal partners of the United States.'

This motion clearly marked a break with previous resolutions on the subject. For the first time the real nature of the political economic choice was debated—the rivalry with America openly admitted, and questions about the value of overseas military spending to maintain British interests that belonged to an older pattern of trade and markets at least raised. The Labour Government now too accepted the realism of the case for entry and applied to join in 1967. Its application was also rebuffed.

During its second spell of opposition the Conservative party went a long way towards ridding itself of the ideological encumbrance of the Commonwealth. There was a growing recognition throughout the party that a strategy to secure Britain's place in the world market based on the Commonwealth connection was no longer viable. As Quintin Hogg wrote in 1965, the Commonwealth was still important to Britain, but it had become certain that [112]

> it can never provide, now or at any time in the future, a substitute for the realities of a balanced economic, military, social or diplomatic policy based solidly on the position of Britain in the world independent of her role as centre of the Commonwealth.

The attack on the Commonwealth and barrenness of the three circles conception was pressed especially hard by Young Conservatives. John Selwyn Gummer argued at the 1965 Conference that: [113]

> We must be clear what our priorities in foreign affairs are . . . if we are to have a strong Commonwealth and an Atlantic Alliance, we must make sure that we have a strong and prosperous Britain; and we do not get that by talking about the Commonwealth in the same sense as we talk about Europe. Once upon a time the Commonwealth was an Empire and the source of our strength. Today it is a Commonwealth which claims our responsibility and if we are to carry out our responsibilities east or west of Suez, we must be a strong nation, and we cannot be that unless we are part of a united Europe.

The following year another Young Conservative, Eric Chalker, informed the delegates:[114]

> We are desperate for a United Europe—a politically united Europe, united carefully, but united soon. We know that 75 per cent of our generation, seven million young people, are with us when we say that we want to concentrate all our power, all our influence and strength, on creating for Britain a new, modern, active and positive role in the world through Europe.

Which of Britain's vital interests were today represented by the Commonwealth he asked?—not trade, not development, not the Sterling Area, not democratic government, not the ideal of free speech, not racial harmony, not peace, not national security, and not the security of the West.

A Conservative Conference had not been treated to so wide ranging an attack on the Commonwealth before. That it was heard without protest showed the disillusion in the party with the new Commonwealth, created above all by the experience of immigration and the loss of Rhodesia, and the steady build-up of support for Europe. As Chalker put it:[115]

> How much is our freedom of action to protect and advance our interests hampered and hindered by the Commonwealth, especially in Europe? Is Britain perhaps an old woman who now lives in a shoe and has so many children she just does not know what to do? Many of these children seem to have power without responsibility, influence without experience, meddling without money.

Any thought, however, that the debate on Europe within the party was now over proved to be premature, There was to be a last convulsion, a final conflict over the right political and economic strategy for the British state abroad. But the option of a trade link with the Commonwealth now looked decidedly faded. So the opposition concentrated still more on the affront the EEC represented to the traditions of the Conservative Nation. This was unlikely to win majority support in a party that prided itself on its feel for the politics of power and was confidently preparing itself for another spell of office. There is no doubt that an anti-Market leadership, even at this stage, would have received overwhelming endorsement from Conservative conferences, because they could have presented their argument in terms of the old electoral ideology, and played on all the attitudes and sentiments most dear to the rank and file supporters. Yet historically the party leaders have always placed the requirements of the politics of power above the promptings of the politics of support. At conferences they have sought majorities for whatever policies they deem are necessary for a viable politics of power, one which best advances the needs of the state and which therefore reflects the balance of interests that the state represents. So it was beside the point when a delegate pointed out at the 1969 conference that of the 35 motions on the agenda dealing with the EEC, only seven were in favour of entry, and 28 were either against or wanted the party to look again. The motion that was chosen for debate was one of those seven, proclaiming that 'joining the EEC would make a major contribution to the security and prosperity of Britain.' The nation was not to be allowed to override the state.

In this debate the supporters of entry clearly no longer felt inhibited in their arguments. Eldon Griffiths told the conference that Europe would be the 'anchor' of the foreign policy of the next Conservative Government. D. Atkinson, a member of the Young Conservative NAC declared:[116]

> I am convinced that young people today are prepared to support the same courage and determination of Edward Heath that Britain should share the prosperity and opportunities currently enjoyed by the Six and with it the competition and responsibilities which will force upon us more efficient management, modern technology and responsible unions.

In 1970 at Blackpool, Norman St John Stevas tried to claim that entry to the EEC far from being a new course, was merely the fulfil-ment of Britain's old one:[117] 'In joining, in building, a European union, Britain, far from being false to her history, is fulfilling it, and the Tory party, far from abandoning its traditional principles is applying them . . . in the contemporary world.' The British Empire, said St John Stevas, 'the greatest civilizing force' of all time, was gone, but the idea behind it, that of 'Great Britain' was still with us. For this idea to find new fulfilment Britain had to join Europe. Time was pressing: 'Today while the European nations dither and bicker, the barbarians are massing outside the walls—and some of them are even within the gates of the city.'

All this was news to the opponents of entry. David Mudd for instance warned the Conference in 1969[118] that with the departure of General de Gaulle there was taking place

> the very thing we have twice fought to prevent in Europe—the economic, industrial, political and military leadership going auto-matically to Germany . . . let us remember that twice in 50 years the talons of the German eagle have failed to savage the British lion. Let us not through this Motion and its sentiments be lured to rape on a bridal bed watched by those unhappy bridesmaids of the EEC.

Similarly, Nicholas Winterton evidently thought that joining Europe was the last thing that would keep the barbarians away. He listed at some length the achievements of the Conservative Nation—twice in the last sixty years Britain had saved the world from tyranny; during the Industrial Revolution Britain had been in the vanguard of world development; the British parliamentary system was unique; and Britain had built up the largest and finest Empire that the world had ever known or would know. It was therefore with some amazement that Mr Winterton contemplated the efforts of the new Conservative Government to place Britain in Europe:[119]

> in the face of overwhelming public opposition, for no good proven reason, we bow and scrape to be allowed to join the unholy alliance of Europe, to shackle ourselves to a hotbed of disruption, insecurity and costly uncertainty, in the process sacrificing our most treasured possession—our independence.

Sovereignty was now the key issue for the anti-Marketeers, the issue of Britain's national independence. As such it was a particularly weak one, for it was not enough to assert national sovereignty and independence—there had to be some evidence for it. The history of the post-war years, which had seen the long retreat from Empire with its attendant fiascos from Suez to Rhodesia, was not happy in this respect. The advocates of Empire Union had never held the view that Britain could develop or even survive within her own borders. They emphasized that Britain must carve out a place for herself in the world market with the aid of her Empire, so as to be in a position to stand off the other great powers. This question of basic national security was what swung many previous supporters of Britain's traditional role to the European camp.

These Tories were less interested in the modernization of the British economy and the attraction of the new salariat to the Conservative ranks as in maintaining conditions under which Britain could stay a great power. They believed that if national greatness could be restored electoral success would also be achieved. The interests of the British state and the Conservative Nation would be in harmony once again. The primary requirement for this 'greatness' was economic strength, and it was here that the case of the anti-Marketeers was weakest. This accounts for the considerable support to be found for Britain joining the EEC among some Conservatives normally classed in the new right tendency.[120] Europe offered a solution to Britain's economic problems that would at the same time permit a British government to pursue a foreign policy that was independent of the Americans. This was a point emphasized by Heath. European unity, he wrote,[121] offered Britain three things; an end to wars in Europe, a voice for Europe in world affairs, and a single market which would allow European industry to match Soviet and American. Sir Alec Douglas-Home, a more conservative spokesman, paid less attention to the economic case for entry and concentrated instead on the contribution that a united Europe could make to Britain's defence and security. He told the 1969 Conference[122] that there were major 'political' arguments for entry: 'Within the European councils, sitting with our major allies, Britain can exercise considerable authority, perhaps at times decisive authority, on the side of political stability and of peace.' At the same time he assured delegates that Britain's national identity would be protected, and that Britain could not be 'cajoled' into a federal structure against her will, since constitutional changes had to be unanimous.

In 1970 after the election the case of the anti-Marketeers was answered still more strongly. One delegate told the conference that he preferred a realistic definition of sovereignty based on power rather than on abstract national independence:[123]

> the power to take decisions affecting our own country and our own people. The extent of a country's sovereignty can be measured by the range of alternative options open to it in any situation.

This point was taken up forcibly by Geoffrey Rippon, the Minister responsible for the new negotiations in Brussels, in his closing speech. Complete national independence, he declared, was a myth in the modern world. The only question therefore he implied, was which alliance, which shelter, would give Britain greater protection and greater prosperity in the world market:[124]

> I regard the effort to try to join the Community as an act of strength. To try and stand aside, believe me, would be a gesture of weakness and despair. In any event, let us and the British people understand this: there is no soft option open to us in this country today. We face increasing competition whether we are inside or whether we are outside.

No ballot was needed. Entering the Common Market was a major priority of the new Government and this time the application was to be successful.

As with imperial preference the opposition had not been greater partly because there were no major economic interests campaigning against entry. Finance and big industrial capital fully supported the applications. The former coveted the prize of becoming the principal money market in the Community, the latter wanted the opportunities of the wider market and expanded scale of production it promised. The fears of the farmers and the small businessmen were voiced by politicians like Lord Hinchingbrooke and increasingly by Enoch Powell, but they made little headway. The destruction of the imperialist ideology had left the party with an earnest desire to find something to replace it. Then there was the political skill of the leadership in persuading the party to see itself as the party of Europe, and to see Europe as the only possible solution to many of the problems of the British state at home and abroad. The Conservative Nation embarked without much enthusiasm but with its customary obedience on the new and uncertain course charted by its leaders.

Chapter 8
CONCLUSION AND POSTSCRIPT: THE TRADE UNION OF THE NATION AND THE CRISIS OF THE STATE

'We are the trade union of the nation as a whole.'

Edward Heath, 20 February 1974

1 THE CONSERVATIVE ELECTORATE

The historical achievement of the Conservative party was to find sufficient support in the new political nation to make it the normal party of government, and yet to do this in a political market dominated after 1867 by the votes of propertyless manual workers. Its image has always been the party of property—led by men of property, financed by property, responsive to the changing interests of property. It has protected privilege, justified inequality, and defended the established order of society. Why then have so many of the propertyless voted for it? The question is familiar, but the usual answers are far too restricted. What is really required is to understand how the facts of the political market and the nature of the state are yoked together through the organization and electoral strategies of the political parties.

The Conservative electorate divides conveniently into two halves. Since 1945 the party has drawn roughly half its votes from the middle class and half from the working class. The evolution of Conservative support has followed the two major alignments that have dominated the political market. The first took shape in the 1860s when the mass parties began to be formed.[1] Party organization, however, only coordinated what already existed—two camps of common sentiment and opinion that divided the nation. The basic line of political cleavage in the political market for the middle classes, and for the newly enfranchised workers as well, was religion. The Tory middle classes defined themselves in opposition to the Liberal middle classes primarily on the basis of the Church they belonged to. Dissent became associated with Liberalism, the Established Anglican Church with Toryism. This was true too for the working class. The pattern was not uniform; in Lancashire, for instance, the Tories captured the Orange anti-Catholic vote. But it does seem to have been the dominant pattern. Membership of a religious community tied men to a particular party, and made them responsive to different sets of political attitudes and ideas. Party affiliation from the beginning was more a consequence of social identity than of rational deliberation. This fact, confirmed by the great bulk of modern research into how people vote, is of enormous importance in understanding electoral behaviour in a political market.

Social identity is not, however, dependent upon the preferences and values of the sovereign individual. On the contrary, it determines them. Different social identities arise from the way in which the structure of society distributes men into groups, classes, and communities, and determines the framework of their opportunities and experiences. The opposition between Liberalism and Conservatism in the political market was a contest in which each party drew on different sections of the nation for support. The party struggle reflected objective consequences of the social structure. The Conservative party was firmly identified with the traditional institutions of the state system—the monarchy, the aristocracy, the Established Church, the army, the Law, the old universities,—while the Liberals were identified more with the institutions of capitalism and the nonconformist churches. Both parties commanded part of the press. The varied impact of these institutions on the experience and consciousness of different social groups created the social cleavages and social identities that different political alignments and voting loyalties then expressed. The new urban areas were the constituencies where Conservatism had least impact, whereas Liberalism made little appeal to such important groups as household servants who comprised one third of the employed population in the nineteenth century.

The Tory middle classes as they emerged were drawn from all the typical branches of the middle class, old and new. They included farmers, professional men, shopkeepers, manufacturers, teachers and clerks. In terms of voting behaviour, there was at this time no sharp divide between the middle classes and the working class. Occupational class was not the criterion of social status that divided men politically, even though it divided them in other ways. The Conservative Nation, even in the days of Tory Democracy, has rarely been conceived by Conservatives as a coalition of interests, still less of classes. Far more often it has been viewed as a united body of patriotic opinion and sentiment in the nation. Such an image first arose in the early days of the political market.

The electoral ideologies of the Conservative Nation in its period of formation were ideologies of the Empire and the established order of England. This separated them sharply from the Radicals in the Liberal coalition, who disliked the cult of national greatness and were estranged from the main institutions of the state, which still reflected the culture and ethos of the aristocracy. It further consolidated the alignment of patriotic opinion with the Conservative party. The notion that Conservative support, especially among working class voters arises from feelings of deference to a governing elite of superior social status only describes attitudes associated with a social identity which is determined by other factors. Electoral ideologies can reinforce an existing social identity and help to make it politically significant, by assisting the organization of mass political parties with particular political images.

Yet Conservative leaders were always uneasily aware how frail was the raft they were riding, how uncertain were the moods and the changes in the electorate. The history of the modern party has thus seen a succession of leaders who have tried to widen the basis of Conservative electoral support by appealing to groups outside the existing Conservative Nation. In Chapter 2, Joseph Chamberlain's efforts to win wider electoral support for the Unionist cause amongst the working class by appealing to their material interests were briefly described. His campaign followed earlier, more half-hearted and short-lived attempts by Disraeli and Lord Randolph Churchill to develop a popular Toryism in the new industrial towns, which championed the interests of the working classes, and attacked the selfishness of the Liberal manufacturers.

Chamberlain's move was timely, for it foreshadowed the major realignment of political forces that was to take place in the 1920s. In place of religion, social class defined by occupational status became the principal dividing line which determined how the electorate voted. Many observers have been puzzled how the new pattern left any future for the Conservative party, since manual workers have more than two thirds of the votes at general elections. The answer lies in the nature of this class alignment. If all manual workers had interpreted politics as a battleground of opposing class interests, the Conservative party could not have survived as a competitor in the market politics of liberal democracy. But this is not how most workers have seen politics hitherto. Other dimensions of class consciousness have been more important in explaining class voting, particularly the perception by manual workers of themselves as a group with common status and a common culture, not in conflict with other groups but different from them. In other words, class has become the major basis of alignment in the political market because occupational status has become the basis on which social identity is most often defined, and not because democratic politics is widely seen as a class struggle between the owners of property and the propertyless, capital and labour. Class consciousness has generally meant consciousness of common status rather than consciousness of common interests.

The middle classes likewise redefined their social identity in opposition to the working class during the 1920s and 1930s. Status criteria of income, occupation, education, and life-style were what counted now for electoral behaviour. The result was that the bulk of the Liberal middle classes forsook their old allegiance and began to vote for the Conservatives. Since that time the voting of the middle classes for the Conservatives has always been much more solid than the working class vote for Labour. In the post-war period, 85 per cent of the solid middle class has normally voted Conservative, and 70 per cent of the lower middle class.[2] This accounts regularly for about half of the Conservatives' thirteen million votes.

The Conservative appeal to the middle classes after the emergence of the Labour party as a serious electoral competitor is not hard to understand. As David Butler and Donald Stokes have argued: 'The Conservatives' appeal as a "national party", the governing agent of an integrated if stratified social order, has helped keep the middle class strongly Conservative since the rise of the Labour party.'[3] Voting Conservative was a way of affirming differences in status. For members of the constituency parties, loyalty was further strengthened by the party's electoral ideologies—in particular the ideologies of imperialism and the free market. To the celebration of the Empire and established institutions of the country, the Conservatives now added the defence of the free market and private enterprise. This consolidated the support of all sections of the business community, particularly small business, behind them.

What needs to be explained is why one third of working class votes were still going to the Conservatives in the 1950s, if the class alignment was so pervasive. It is normally put down to the survival of attitudes of deference among some working men and the rising affluence of others.[4] Such theories, however, investigate the attitudes of electors rather than the structure of the political market. If the former are treated as derivative of the latter, then attention is directed to the different impact Labour's image as the party of the working class has on different sections of the working class. This impact depends to a great extent on the varied social organization and social structure of the class.[5] For a large part of the electorate, (Butler and Stokes put it as high as 25 per cent), there is no association between social class measured by occupational criteria and party allegiance. For manual workers in particular, where there exist important cross pressures, the association between class status and Labour voting is not maintained. Labour's class image and consequent electoral appeal to manual workers is greatly reinforced for those workers who belong to a trade union, live in working class communities, and are employed in large factories. Where these are absent, the disposition to vote Labour will be correspondingly weaker, and religious and regional identity can be expected to play a bigger part.[6]

The mass of evidence that is now accumulating about the electorate allows us to locate far more precisely the sources of working class support for the Conservatives. With the decline of the Liberals, Conservative acquired a remarkable and undisputed degree of legitimacy. The party was associated with all the dominant institutions and values of British society. To the traditional institutions of the state system it now added the institutions of industrial property and private capital. It also enjoyed almost total support from the press, ownership of which was concentrated in increasingly few hands. Against the all pervasive influence which these institutions, associated so strongly now with Conservatism, exerted, Labour's appeal was far narrower, confined mainly to trade unionists, strong working class communities and small groups of intellectuals. Former Tory and Liberal working men were more likely to vote Conservative than Labour if they had little contact with the organized working class movement and did not live in communities whose composition and ethos was predominantly working class.[7]

For those workers who were not exposed to the counter culture of the Labour movement, the Conservative party naturally appeared to them as the party most likely to provide good government. In this way, substantial sections of working class voters were welded into the Conservative Nation. The electoral ideology of imperialism and patriotism clearly made an appeal to some of them, but what is sometimes less emphasized is that the small contact many of these workers had with the trade unions reflected not only the backwardness of certain parts of the economy, but also the opportunities that still existed for self-help, social mobility, and, above all, for the setting up of small businesses in various regions of the country and in various types of employment, such as the service sector. This gave constant recruits to the middle class and a quite different perception of the relationship between class membership and voting.

After 1945 Conservative leaders naturally endeavoured to maintain their hold on the loyalty of their traditional supporters in the nation. Yet so precarious has been the electoral balance that they were obliged to seek out new possible bases of support. Two such were identified by the leadership—affluent workers and the mobile middle class.[8] In the first case, the appeal was frankly secular—'Conservatives give you a better standard of living—don't let Labour ruin it,' 'you've never had it so good', and so forth. The Conservatives presented themselves as the best possible managers of the post-war state. But Tory strategists also shared the hopes of many political scientists that these affluent workers would detach themselves from the working class and seek to acquire middle class status, and thereby a much more permanent attachment to Conservatism. All the electoral surveys showed that workers who considered themselves middle class were very likely to vote Conservative to prove it.

The mobile middle class, the salariat, was another group which the Conservatives believed they could attract. This group was defined mainly by the extent of its education and its possession of expertise. It seemed to fit perfectly with the notion of a property owning democracy, although the spread of white collar unionism in its ranks appeared paradoxical. Yet it was clearly an expanding sector of the population. The proportion of the workforce engaged in manual occupations fell by five per cent from 1950 to 1965, and much of the increase was registered by the new salariat.

The dilemma for the Conservative leaders was that they needed to expand the base of the party's support, yet the existing Conservative Nation was firmly entrenched in the constituency associations and the parliamentary party. In its politics of support the party had to satisfy two main groups—the rank and file, and the wider electorate. The situation, however, was still more complex. For the politics of support had to be reconciled with the politics of power, and the government of the state.

2 CONSENSUS AND THE STATE

The state, I have argued, is often conceived far too narrowly. Either it is identified with the government or with a specific set of institutions. But that gives us no understanding of what the state is. It neglects what is most important—the objective basis on which the state rests and the consequent balance of power between social classes and political forces that it expresses. This means identifying the established priorities in the prevailing politics of power, and how they are related to the interests and the classes that rule in the economy. If this is not done, government can be represented as no more than technical administration on the one hand, or as the exercise of power by dominant elites on the other. The technical exigencies of government policy and the recruitment, social background, and interaction of elites, are necessary parts of any thorough analysis of the state. But it is only possible to grasp the dynamics of the state—what it stands for, whose state it is, and what role it plays in the economy, and what relationship it has to the political system, by analysing its relationship to private property and private ownership of the means of production. No other source of power compares in importance to this.

This is because any given state must express and uphold the dominant organization of private property. That is what it exists for. At the same time, property is never monolithic; the interests of its different branches are disparate and sometimes conflicting. That is why a politics of power exists at all. If it were the case that the interests of a ruling class were never in doubt and never ambiguous, then government could be their direct expression. The term ruling class, however, refers not to the elites that man the government and the other institutions of the state, but to the class that wields economic power through the concentration of wealth and ownership of property in its hands. The essence of property is not merely legal ownership but the control of economic power. The figures for Britain are worth recalling. Seven per cent of the population still own 84 per cent of the wealth; 1 per cent own 81 per cent of privately owned company shares, while the top 150 manufacturing companies in 1961-3 had 70 per cent of all company net assets and 57 per cent of gross company income.[9]

The role of political parties in the state is different from their role in the political market. In the politics of support their function is to mobilize electoral support and to represent various sections of the electorate. In the politics of power the function of parties is to be an instrument of government, and thereby to reconcile their supporters in the political nation to the existing state. Parties in government and often in opposition formulate a conception of the national interest. Despite its name, this invariably reflects not the interests of the nation (which has no interests), but the interests of the state, the consensus of established policies and priorities, the framework of a viable politics of power.

Since the middle of the nineteenth century there have been three such periods of consensus—the free trade consensus, (up to 1914); the retrenchment consensus, (1918-40); and the welfare consensus, (since 1945). Each of these reflected a balance of dominant economic interests and political forces—sometimes expressed through Parliament, sometimes outside it. The essential priorities of these periods of consensus were endorsed by the practice, if not always in the rhetoric, of party leaders, and reflected this balance of power in the state, rather than any mythical concord in the nation.

Competition between the parties meant of course that no consensus was ever immutable, and it also provided a means whereby virtually the whole of the political nation could be harnessed through their parties to the state and made to feel part of it. Each consensus gave scope for different interpretations of the priorities, and therefore for different policies. Interests and classes have sought to influence policy both through direct contact with government and through political parties. But although the Conservative party has always been a party of property, it has never been the mouthpiece for business interests in the way that it was once the mouthpiece for landed interests.[10] Since Disraeli, the Tories have realized that they needed a national strategy, a national leadership, and a national image in order to compete effectively in the political market. The Conservative leadership has normally organized its One Nation perspective around the established consensus, the prevailing priorities of the politics of power. It has then appealed for support on the basis of national, not class issues, its capacity to provide national leadership, and its identification with national institutions.

The great electoral success the party has enjoyed however, conceals the uncertain and hazardous nature of the leadership's task. The uncertainty is derived from the need to reconcile the various dimensions of the politics of support and power with one another. Divisions within the ruling class for example, have affected not only the state but the political parties, for they have often given rise to different groups, tendencies of opinion, and ideologies within the party organization. Since 1850, there have been four major divisions which have had important repercussions on Conservative politics.

During the early nineteenth century there was the conflict between industrial and landed property. 1846 saw the decisive and irreversible defeat of the latter. With the progress of the economy industrial property became overwhelmingly dominant by the end of the nineteenth century, but its interests became fragmented. Opposition grew between capital based in manufacturing industry and capital based in finance. Furthermore, the increasing concentration of industry in some sectors, the scale of production in large plants and the rise of the joint stock company, split big business from small business. Finally the establishment of a large public sector and the acceptance by governments of overall responsibility for the national economy has brought with it a conflict between the interests of multinational companies and the interests of the national economy considered as a whole.

All these conflicts of interests have had enormous implications and consequences for Conservative politics. For the way they have been resolved has helped determine the kind of state that has developed and to which the Conservatives have been committed, as a party of government. In general, the Conservative leaders have tried to negotiate the politics of support to suit the requirements of the politics of power. Groups in the party, however, have often championed particular sections of property, and tried to force the leadership to reorganize the state in their interests.

They have been successful more often than is sometimes realized. The free trade consensus before 1914 safeguarded the ruling interests of finance capital and leading export manufacturing industries, but was challenged by other sections of industry through the Tariff Reform campaign. The retrenchment consensus after 1918 reflected the overriding concern of all sections of property to stem the advance of socialism. An attempt was made to reestablish the pre-war policies that had favoured finance capital, notably through the return to the Gold Standard. World recession in the 1930s, however, and the consequent dethronement of the City, brought a partial victory for industrial capital, and the belated establishment of imperial preference.

The welfare consensus after 1945 restored the strength of finance capital in the state, and increasingly reflected the needs and interests of multinational companies and large-scale industry. Small business and the national economy suffered most from their ascendancy, and the former through its strong representation in the rank and file of the party fought strongly for different policies. What distinguished the welfare consensus from its predecessors was the explicit recognition of the need to involve organized labour in the running of the state. Trade union leaders were given improved access to government and were integrated in the machinery of consultation and negotiation, and new priorities for government policy were accepted—notably redistributive taxation to finance social services, a larger public sector, and government management of the economy to maintain full employment and (later), rising living standards.

The acceptance of these priorities followed considerable pressure channelled through electoral institutions. They meant concessions by property in the hope of political stability. Yet the real concessions were not made by finance capital and the big industrial firms, who in general found the new state perfectly compatible with their interests once accumulation got under way again. The real burden, it slowly became apparent, was borne by small capital. They had to fight not only the competition of the big companies, but also the fiscal and interventionist policies of successive governments that favoured their larger rivals. At the same time, the new state brought permanent inflation, which they were least well placed to dodge, and which therefore squeezed their profits.

3 LEADERS AND FOLLOWERS

For the Conservative leadership, the practice of politics has always meant the pursuit of one overriding goal—maintaining intact the consensus of the state by organizing sufficient support in the nation. Studies of the social composition of the Conservative party have found it is like a pyramid—the higher you go the more exclusive it becomes. Although the Conservative electorate is fifty per cent working class, the constituency associations are dominated by the solid middle class. The parliamentary party is recruited from still further up the social scale, whilst the leadership itself tends to have been educated at the top public schools and at Oxford or Cambridge, and to be drawn disproportionately from aristocratic and upper class families. With few exceptions, Conservative leaders have been drawn, and continue to be drawn, from the wealthiest and most exclusive groups in British society.[11]

Yet certain changes are noticeable, especially in the post-war party. The number of landowners who have become Ministers has declined. There has been a rise in the representation of other occupations, especially business and professional groups. Most important, however, has been the professionalization of the political career. A growing number of Conservative leaders are professional politicians, and many of them started their careers in Central Office or worked their way up through the Young Conservatives. Almost all of them hold directorships in companies, but they usually do so on a part-time, and often honorary, basis. In the past, Conservative leaders and MPs either owned property themselves or belonged to families that did. Major landowners like Salisbury, and substantial industrialists, like Bonar Law and Baldwin, often rose to be Prime Minister. This is now much rarer.

At one time, the aristocratic origins and education of Conservative politicians imparted a certain style to their leadership.[12] They acquired a habit of authority and a preoccupation with the practical requirements of good government. So confident was this governing class in its ability and its right to govern, that it was able to adapt itself to the new political market and the new party system with remarkable ease. Much of its flexibility and political common sense derived from its relative independence from the dominant sections of property. The curious accommodation between a class of landowners who no longer wielded the decisive economic power but still dominated the established institutions of the state, and the class of industrial capitalists created an aristocratic model for political leadership that became the standard for leaders of all classes. The ability such leaders showed in electoral politics to imagine themselves custodians for the interests of the nation as a whole and to interpret politics in national terms, undoubtedly contributed to the orderly and relatively peaceful evolution of British institutions, because it made a policy of concessions respectable.

The One Nation strategy of the Conservatives consisted in identifying the consensus of the state and fostering an image of the Conservative party as the party of capable national leadership and the defender of established institutions. Its elements were altered as the political market developed. Under Disraeli and Salisbury the objects of the Conservative party were classically expressed by Disraeli himself at Crystal Palace in 1872: to maintain the institutions of the country . . . to uphold the Empire of England, . . and to elevate the condition of the people. The party was firmly reconciled to the free trade consensus and the dominance of industrial property. The electoral strategy of the leaders was to identify the party with the established institutions of the country, particularly the Crown and the Church, and with the Empire.

By this means, the party became the political expression for an important body of the middle classes and working men, who found their social identity confirmed by voting Conservative. The workings of the new political market strengthened the state, and thereby the existing consensus, because the two main parties mobilized different parts of the political nation. In the case of the Conservative leaders, one of their chief objects in government was to protect property, as they all, even the Tory Democrats among them, frequently reiterated.[13] They thus interpreted the politics of power in class terms. But they always sought to project a national image of their policies and their leadership to the electorate and to their own party, in order to prevent class becoming the basis for competition between the parties in the political market. Radicals in the Liberal party were viewed with great bitterness in Conservative ranks because Conservatives believed that the policies and appeals of the Radicals were bringing ever nearer the interpretation of politics as a struggle between classes, and thereby threatened the stability of the state. The Conservatives' One Nation strategy at this time was to defend property through the established institutions of aristocratic England. Anything which threatened these institutions threatened property. If these institutions were maintained, then property would be safe. Conservatives trusted in the traditional sources of authority—the Crown, the Church, the Law and the Land. By identifying their party so closely with them they hoped to make it the national party, the natural political expression of these essential national symbols, and Conservative leaders the national leaders. Becoming the party of Empire and the party of Union with Ireland, further strengthened this identification. The struggles over Home Rule and the Boer War were decisive in confirming the kind of national image the Tories were seeking.

Yet even by 1900 this strategy was no longer enough. The Conservatives' position in the political market was dramatically eroded by the gradual emergence of occupational class as a factor in political alignment, just as it had been so immensely strengthened by the Irish question. Chamberlain devised a strategy and an electoral ideology which he believed would satisfy many working class demands and thus retain and extend existing working class support for the Unionists. Tariff Reform, however, also involved a reorganization of the state—the replacement of a fundamental priority of the free trade consensus. The weak position of the party in the political market after 1906 allowed groups among the rank and file to challenge the electoral perspective of the leadership. The electoral ideologies of Empire and the Union dominated the party and prepared it for an open break with the state in the period before 1914.

National unity in the First World War, the realignment of political forces after 1918, and the rise of the Labour party, permitted a far-reaching reorganization of the party's One Nation strategy in the 1920s and 1930s. The identification with national institutions was reaffirmed and indeed extended, and was still the central feature of the party's image, but the leadership was back in control. The Conservative party was still the national party, but was no longer to be found gasping in the last ditch on national or Empire issues. The handling of Ireland and India showed that. The fundamental aims of the party came back into focus. Property had to be protected. National issues and national institutions were a means, and an extremely important means, for achieving this. But the management of the state was still more important. Under Baldwin, the Conservatives were a party of government again, and the electoral ideologies of the party were subordinated once more to the electoral perspective of the leaders.

Baldwin knew that the rise of the Labour party and the growing division of the political market along class lines made it essential that the Tories retained their ability to form the Government. They did so by scooping up the greater part of the old Liberal vote and presenting themselves as the national party, the party of order and sound government. Baldwin, however, seems to have been aware that the electoral advance of Labour could only be delayed, not halted or reversed. He was very concerned, therefore, to lay the foundations for a new consensus between the two parties, which might require concessions by property but would still preserve its essential interests. The retrenchment consensus was one-sided—the overwhelming strength of the Conservatives measured by seats in Parliament if not by votes in the political market meant that the ruling interests of property held unchallenged sway in the government of the state. Collectivism was contained, revolutionary trade unionism defeated, property preserved.

Yet this situation was dangerous for the Conservatives if it continued for any length of time, because it meant that an important section of the political nation was excluded from the state. Political movements outside Parliament were growing during the 1930s. A political settlement with the Labour movement had to be reached at some time if future political stability were to be assured. Baldwin himself appears to have wanted such a settlement, but, true to his political style, made no great effort to move his party. His most important achievement, however,—the reassertion of the supremacy of the leadership's electoral perspective over the electoral ideologies of the rank and file—was to be continued in the New Conservatism of the Right Progressives after 1945.

This New Conservatism and the welfare consensus have been the main subject of this book. Three major tendencies of opinion that grew up towards them in the party have been identified and described—the diehard, the right progressive, and the new right. They were the fundamental ideological orientations out of which electoral perspectives, electoral ideologies, factions and parliamentary alliances all arose. At the same time, they reflected and represented particular interests.

The diehard tendency was divided into two—Whigs and Imperialists. Whig opinion in the party was fairly mute after 1945. It disapproved of the Industrial Charter, but was on the whole skilfully mobilized by the leadership in the electoral fight against the Labour Government's regime of nationalization, physical controls, increasing taxation, social regimentation, and redistribution of income. After 1951 Whig opinion put pressure on the government over the small extent of denationalization, the level of government expenditure, and such measures as the abolition of resale price maintenance. Whig opinion and the electoral ideology of the free market and laissez-faire associated with it had expressed the interests in the past first of industrial property, and then of finance capital in Britain. After 1945, however, the interests it expressed were

213

more and more those of small business—the part of the private sector
that had least influence in the state.

The second wing of the diehard tendency, the Imperialists, campaigned for imperial preference and a vigorous imperial policy to
underpin national economic strength. The Imperialists were more influential than the Whigs because the electoral ideology of imperialism
could still galvanize the party rank and file. The Imperialists opposed
the Atlantic alliance, particularly the Washington Loan Agreements,
and GATT. They saw these policies as evidence of the imperialist
ambitions of the United States, because they ruled out any independent
initiatives by Britain herself, and so effectively sabotaged the British
Empire. The events at Suez in 1956 meant the final abandonment of
their hopes for an Empire policy. Britain's failure at Suez underlined
for the Imperialists her dependence on the Americans and the absorption
of the British state and economy within the American orbit. The
subsequent fights over decolonization, Rhodesia, and the EEC were
rearguard fights. The Imperialists in the past had represented the interests
of industrial capital, or at least certain sections of it. Their support was
strongest, both in the party and in industry during the 1930s, when 200
Conservative MPs were members of the Empire Industries Association,
organized by Leo Amery. Part of the weakness of the Imperialists'
challenge after 1945 was their lack of real support from industry.

In contrast to the Whigs and Imperialists, the right progressive
tendency was the body of opinion in the party that supported the
electoral perspective of the leadership and campaigned for the acceptance of the post-war settlement. It generated a number of reform
groups—the Tory Reform Committee, the One Nation Group, the
Bow Group, and Pressure for Economic and Social Toryism. The Right
Progressives introduced into the party, for the first time on a large scale,
rationalist and instrumental modes of approaching and solving problems.
Hearnshaw had once boasted that the Conservatives could not produce
and could never require the 'masses of verbiage' produced and required
by Socialism. Conservatives, he declared, left behind them not empty
tracts but historic monuments.

This was one tradition that did not survive the war. Empty Tory
tracts now press the walls of library vaults. The One Nation Group
succeeded the Tory Reform Committee. The CPC and CRD flourished
in Central Office. The Bow Group bustled outside. The complex
problems of administering the vast and unwieldy state sector and its
relationship with private capital made a technocratic politics almost
inevitable. Cabinet Ministers were obliged to become far more like
business executives and administrators than speakers and doers in the
public realm. The electoral perspective of the Right Progressives sought
more and more to suppress the politics of support for the better management of the politics of power. Ideology and reality were placed at

opposite poles. The more politics became a branch of piecemeal social engineering as Bow Groupers, radical Keynesians, and Growthmen all intended it should, the less room was there for ideologies that determined identity and secured participation.

The very structure of the welfare consensus, however, prevented the more extravagant dreams of the Right Progressives from being realized. It began to disintegrate under pressure from its own contradictions. In the 1950s the Conservatives had presided over the new state and made no attempt to change the prevailing politics of power. Few industries were denationalized, the social services and full employment were maintained, and most significantly, the unions were appeased. The revival of the world economy brought a time of unrivalled social peace and rising living standards. Politicians and political scientists alike spoke confidently of the new political order overcoming the old social conflicts and creating One Nation. The enlarged state sector and the new economic role for governments was believed to ensure everlasting and trouble free prosperity and growth, reflecting both the availability of new scientific knowledge to control society and the disappearance of class conflict through the incorporation of the working class into the political system. After Labour's third defeat in 1959 some spoke of Labour disappearing altogether as an electoral competitor.

The Conservative leaders were able during the 1950s to refurbish their One Nation strategy. Their appeal rested once more on presenting themselves as the party with national policies and the most capable national leadership. They appeared as the most competent managers of the system, the natural party of government, the party most likely to run affairs efficiently. On this basis they tried to attract new groups such as the salariat and the affluent workers and successfully resisted pressure from the party for different policies, particularly on the Empire and the level of government spending.

In general terms, the welfare consensus served the dominant interests in the state well. The interests of finance capital were secured by the decision to defend sterling when necessary through deflation of the domestic economy and by the encouragement given the renewed export of capital. The big industrial companies and the multinationals were favoured by the policies of modernization and rationalization pursued in the 1960s, by the encouragement of mergers, by the opportunities for exporting capital, and by the general climate of prosperity. The decision to apply for entry to the EEC in 1961 was supported by these different groups. It appeared the best long term arrangement for all of them.

1961 was thus the year in which the Tories turned away from their traditional electoral ideology the better to serve the ruling interests of the state. It was appropriate that the debate on Europe at the annual conference should take place alongside the debate on restricting Commonwealth immigration. It also proved, however, the year of the ebb tide in right progressive fortunes. Their perspective was highly dependent on the ability of government to ensure rising living standards. The Conservatives increasingly based their electoral appeal on their success in handling the national economy, and felt able as a result to discard their old electoral ideologies and discomfit their traditional supporters.

The growing professionalism of the party in the recruitment of its leaders and the organization of its secretariat spread to the techniques of electioneering. The Conservatives could be marketed like any detergent—the market thoroughly researched, the most effective selling campaign chosen, the right image projected, the wrong issues avoided. It was ironic, however, that the more the parties turned to rational electioneering as a means for overcoming the uncertainties of electoral politics the more unmanageable this politics became. The two were hardly unrelated. Just as consumers found it increasingly difficult to tell different brands of soap powder apart, so electors came to see fewer and fewer differences between the parties competing so busily for their votes.

Under the welfare consensus the way in which voters rated the ability of the parties to manage the economy became the single most important factor in determining their voting preferences.[14] The growing lack of success of the parties in government during the 1960s increased the dissatisfaction of many electors with both. The result was that opinion became alarmingly volatile, veering from one party to another in an erratic and unpredictable manner. Turnout at elections fell steadily. Another important trend was results at by-elections. It is worth recalling that no post-war government lost a by-election until 1957. The electorate seemed remarkably stable during the first ten years after the war—two great camps, strongly divided on ideology and principle; small swings at elections; and competition for a small floating vote believed to lie in between. In such circumstances rational electioneering seemed to make sense. But by the middle of the 1960s, over a third of the electorate were changing their vote between elections. In the 1970s it was to rise much higher still, to over 50 per cent. Even the safest seats could now be lost at by-elections. In the opinion polls a lead by one party of more than 20 per cent was no longer uncommon. With an electorate so unpredictable, star-gazing would have been a more reliable guide than scientific politics proved as a practical aid to politicians in their bid to win votes.

At the very moment that the polls indicated that fewer and fewer electors could tell the parties apart any longer, the economic policies of British governments met less and less success. In consequence, the electoral perspective of the Right Progressives was seriously damaged. The economic crisis of 1961, the record balance of payments deficit in 1964, and the relative worsening of Britain's economic situation under Labour through the 1960s brought a fundamental challenge to the leadership from within the Conservative party. A further tendency of opinion developed—the New Right—that was hostile to the post-war settlement and the welfare consensus that it had established. This tendency embraced what remained of the old diehard tendency—both Whig and Imperialist—but it also gathered new elements. In general the interests it expressed were the interests of small business—shop-keepers, small entrepreneurs, and family firms. Such groups were of course strongly represented in the constituency parties and were deeply resentful of many of the trends of the welfare consensus.

One reason why the New Right flourished was the growing in-adequacy of the One Nation strategy of the Right Progressives. Under a succession of Conservative leaders—Churchill, Eden, Macmillan, and Home—the Conservative Nation in the party and in the country had been harnessed to the post-war state and the welfare consensus, and brought to accept or tolerate its realities and its constraints. The political style of all these leaders, whether by nature or design, was aristocratic and traditional, and therefore reassuring to their supporters. Yet a large part of their success in negotiating the politics of support did depend also on the economic boom which gave the party the electoral success to justify the electoral perspective.

The electoral defeats of 1964 and 1966 against a background of growing economic difficulties, made this electoral perspective much less attractive. But the party no longer had as their leader a master-politician like Macmillan, whose clear grasp of the requirements of the politics of power was fully matched by his understanding of the politics of support in his party. Edward Heath brought a new kind of leadership to the Conservatives. His style was managerial and middle class. Heath's strength was his single-minded concentration on policy and the details of effective administration of the state. By 1970, the Conservatives were better prepared than any previous Opposition for assuming the govern-ment.[15] But the governmental style of opposition, the detailed pro-gramme, the comprehensive competition policy, would have been more appropriate to a Conservative administration in a period of social calm and economic advance. The years of opposition were not one of them. The outcome of the Right Progressives' electoral perspective was a leadership that ignored the politics of support. With an increasingly volatile electorate and a deteriorating economy, Heath's party still focused its appeal on the middle ground, and appeared to the electorate to offer very little that was new. The huge leads in the opinion polls registered in 1967-9 were not converted into solid and enthusiastic support for the party, and as a result the election when it came was very nearly lost.

The central weakness of Heath's style of leadership was underlined by the eruption of a new electoral ideology—Powellism—born out of the general ferment of the New Right. Like all electoral ideologies, it framed its programme for government from the standpoint of the interests of the nation rather than the state. Powell showed what a politics of support which broke away from the constraints imposed by the welfare consensus and rational electioneering could achieve. He mobilized the support of small businessmen, sections of the lower middle class, and most significantly, substantial groups of workers, by identifying new divisions and articulating new grievances in the nation, that could be made significant for political alignment. He gave his supporters the feeling of participating in politics through him, and thereby gained the loyalty and enthusiasm that the tired administrators of consensus politics in the two major parties were no longer finding it easy to arouse. Powell's success in gathering support in the party and in the country through a new One Nation strategy made his programme for government far more relevant than it had ever been when he had propounded it during the 1950s. It suddenly became a serious alternative to the welfare consensus if that consensus should ever break down irretrievably and fail to serve either the ruling interests of capital or secure political stability. Powell offered a political not a technical solution to Britain's problems—a new way of harnessing the nation to the state through a reorganization of the framework of the politics of power.

The existence of the Conservative Nation has enormously increased the stability of the British state, and thereby has protected the rights and interests of property. Yet the leaders of the Conservative party did not create the Conservative Nation out of nothing. They recognized what already existed, and their achievement was so to mobilize and organize it that their party became a major contender in the political market.

From the standpoint of its electoral perspective, the leadership has sought to use the Conservative Nation as a support to the business of government. It is hardly surprising, however, that many individual leaders and groups in the party organization have not always shared this perspective, and have valued the substance more than the functions of the Conservative Nation. Accordingly, they have taken their stand on the electoral ideologies that bind it together and express it. These electoral ideologies have proved the refuge not merely of Tory Democrats and Diehards, but of those sections of property that have sought a change in the prevailing consensus of the state. Their strength within the party has depended on the fortunes and accidents of electoral politics, and their interplay with the economic fortunes of the British state in the world market.

Aided by the structure of both the political market and the state, the Conservative leaders have generally retained the initiative and kept their supporters in line. The triumph of the new electoral perspective after 1945 appeared for a time complete. Yet its very success helped undermine the traditional landmarks that bound the Conservative Nation together. When the party faltered at the polls, and the economy deteriorated, the leadership found itself more exposed ideologically that it had ever been. It had no recipe for hard times.

4 POSTSCRIPT: THE GOVERNMENT OF EDWARD HEATH

> Over the past week or so many have described the situation which we as a nation now face as by far the gravest since the end of the war. They do not exaggerate.
>
> Anthony Barber, 17 December 1973

> The Conservatives hate Lord Randolph for divers reasons. One is that his defection from their ordered ranks deprives them of a powerful force. If he would only run in harness, giving up to party what he now wastes in isolated action, he would be an immense accession of power. If he could only be depended upon he would be welcome to take the place that has never been filled since Disraeli died. But the dream is hopeless.
>
> H. W. Lucy[16]

The 1970 election proved in one way a strange reversal of 1945. Once again the party that was expected to win comfortably was overthrown. This time it was the opinion polls, the newly enthroned oracles of the political market that got it wrong. Just as the flocks of pundits prepared to settle on the carcass of the Conservative party and announce Labour as the normal party of government, the Tories slid back into power. If they had lost they would have been rent by unprecedented internal strife. Heath's leadership would have been challenged, and the policies and the electoral perspective of the Right Progressives would have lost still more ground to the electoral ideologies of the New Right. As it was, electoral victory once more persuaded the party to see itself as a party of government and close its ranks.

Yet the experience of the previous six years could not disappear overnight. The political situation of 1970 was fundamentally different from the early 1950s. In 1951, the Conservatives had also just spent six years in opposition, but they were years in which the leadership had held the initiative throughout, and had managed to secure the party's endorsement for the post-war settlement. There was therefore a remarkable continuity of policy between the Labour and Conservative Governments. The Conservatives disappointed their critics.

By 1970, however, the priorities of the welfare consensus were obviously under some strain. All the efforts of growthmen, planners, and technocrats had not rid Britain of stagnation and inflation. Indeed inflation was accelerating, and profits were falling even faster. Moreover, the other major prop of the prevailing consensus—the Atlantic Alliance—was undermined during the late 1960s. The ending of the supremacy of the dollar threatened the international monetary system and the future growth of world trade by encouraging a flight from paper money into gold that steadily gathered pace. This coincided with the growing challenge from Europe and Japan to American domination of the world market, and the final abandonment of Britain's attempt to maintain the traditional status of sterling and the sterling area, following the forced devaluation in 1967.

Any Government elected in 1970 would therefore have needed to rethink some of the priorities of the post-war politics of power. Heath had done this before he arrived at Downing Street. The competition policy and the firm commitment to attach Britain to the EEC appeared a major attempt to adapt the priorities of the welfare consensus, although within the general constraints of the prevailing politics of power and the electoral perspective of the leadership. Under pressure from New Right opinion, it is true, the competition policy had been presented to the party in the last years of opposition as offering a radical break with the policies of the Labour Government. It was widely expected, however, that the apparent ascendancy of New Right opinion in the party would be reversed once the Conservative leaders were back in office.

There was considerable surprise, therefore, when the Conservatives were not only elected, but seemed determined to put a radical and ideological interpretation of the competition policy into effect, side by side with the new bid to join the Common Market. For the first two years, the new Government embarked quite consciously on a new course,[17] evidently designed to change the framework for the politics of power. The opportunity to do so was created by the failure of the established policies of the welfare consensus. Heath's boldness was unquestionably welcome to many circles in the City, in industry, and above all in the Conservative party. Yet this was a slender base or support on which to govern and try to alter the basis of the post-war settlement. The major weakness of Heath's electoral perspective was that the success of the competition in electoral terms depended overwhelmingly on whether it speeded economic growth. If the economy broke out of the vice of stagnation and inflation there would be greater rewards for everyone. The welfare consensus and the politics of interest group bargaining could be established on a firm basis once more. Immediately, in the short term, however, the policy meant that somehow working class living standards had to be cut.

The cost of living and strikes were the issues that influenced most electors during the 1970 election campaign, despite the high and rising level of unemployment. Inflation too was the central problem facing the new Tory Government. The outcome of previous policies to curb it had produced only a prosperity without profits, a stagnant economy in which productivity and investment had fallen so low that a continued expansion of the state had been necessary to prop up prosperity. Britain was fast becoming a rentier economy, in which the gains and returns from foreign investment and speculation in property and even simple interest generally exceeded the returns that could be expected from manufacturing industry.[18] Labour had failed to raise productivity by its interventionist policies, but instead of abandoning them it had intensified them. State spending and taxation had rocketed. By 1970 the state was responsible for over fifty per cent of GNP. The tax system was being used more and more to redistribute income from wages to profits. Net take home pay fell steadily as a proportion of national income—subsidies, grants, and state orders for private industry soared. Workers needed ever larger increases in money wages to secure even a tiny increase in real wages, given the proportion of any increase that was swallowed by taxation, fiscal drag, and inflation.

Heath's Government set itself two tasks. It was determined to secure for Britain a place in the expanding sectors of the world market—which meant less reliance on the United States and swift entry into the EEC. Secondly, it sought to revive investment and growth in the British economy by a new assault on inflation, which was equated with wage demands. Prosperity with profits was its goal. Accordingly, it prepared to end the discredited interventionist strategy of the previous decade, to close down all the boards and agencies of intervention, to reintroduce criteria of competitive efficiency into industry, to undertake a big reduction in taxation, and to introduce legislation that would reduce the bargaining strength of the trade unions.

Unfortunately for the Tories, they were embarking on their new course at the very moment that the sands of the world economy were shifting once more. At first, the main signs of this were the cracks in the international monetary system, brought about by the collapse of the dollar and the reappearance of incompatible national interests among the leading industrial powers which prevented any substantial agreement on how to reform it. Secondly there was the accelerating rise in primary commodity prices, and the belated realization that the world economy could not continue growing at its current pace without encountering serious shortages in many basic raw materials. These two components of the new international situation created growing alarm about the possibility of a new world recession. The expansion of the previous twenty-five years had greatly increased the interdependence of the national economies and had tied their prosperity still more firmly than in the 1920s to the continued expansion of world markets.

By 1970 alliance with America was clearly no longer sufficient to guarantee Britain her share of world trade, and the Empire was gone.

But the alternative, entry to the EEC, seemed already too late. The negotiations this time proved simple enough. Heath gave guarantees to the French that Britain would not seek to enter the Community while remaining a client of the United States. This assured the removal of the French veto and Britain's accession to the Treaty of Rome, but it was no great triumph of national leadership because the Labour party, a substantial minority of the Conservative party, and a majority of public opinion were opposed. Conservatives had always expected the immediate burdens, particularly the rise of food prices to be heavy, but they had argued that they were a reasonable cost for the long term benefits. The nearer the world economy approached to recession or standstill, however, the more unlikely did it seem that Britain would reap any of these benefits. The great European market was threatening to contract not to expand. In the meantime British consumers were subsidizing French peasants.

The still greater prizes that might be won as the Community moved to full union also began to recede rapidly. The chances of the European Governments agreeing to establish a common European currency, for instance, which the City of London so craved, and which would alone make a common economic policy a reality, were never very good. They quickly began to dwindle towards zero as the threat of world recession grew greater. Britain floated the pound in 1972, wound up the Sterling Area, and left the Common Market joint float. When the energy crisis came she refused to cooperate with her Market partners, and like France, negotiated independently with the Arab states. The practical value of retaining national sovereignty was demonstrated by the decisions of a Cabinet dominated by ardent Marketeers.[19]

While the fruits of entry to the EEC began to shrivel as soon as they were grasped, there were even greater disasters on the home front. Just after the election, City editors were assessing the prospects for the new economic policies of the Tories on the assumption that, as in 1951, they would enjoy a few years of calm in which to experiment. None envisaged the storm about to break. There was considerable interest in the Government's new version of the 1963 'Maudling experiment'—the policy of encouraging expansion through tax cuts and private credit, and preparing to face short term deficits on the balance of payments rather than deflate. Large tax cuts were indeed announced, and the pound was floated in 1972 when pressure built up against sterling. The Government showed it had abandoned the old priorities of policy in this field.

But on the crucial question of wage inflation the Government had no real policy. It had declared itself against the methods of government intervention practised by Labour, and these included all forms of incomes policies, voluntary and statutory. It sought to control wages and prices partly by holding down those under its control in the public sector, partly by attempting to hold down costs in the economy by attacking inefficiency and encouraging competition.

Economic management since 1945 had moderated the old business cycle, but as a result the cycle was no longer a very useful instrument for restructuring capital. The interventionist strategy designed by both Conservative and Labour Governments during the 1960s had been intended in part to remedy this. The Conservatives believed it had failed by not paying enough attention to profitability and competitive efficiency. They therefore reduced taxation on companies, withdrew subsidies, ended regional investment grants, abolished the Industrial Reorganization Corporation, and refused to prop up either the docks on Merseyside or the Upper Clyde Shipbuilders. Even Rolls Royce was allowed to go bankrupt.

Yet there was little point in getting British firms more oriented to profit if inflation were not checked. The Conservatives seemed to believe that a strong stand against workers in the public sector and the new climate of competitive efficiency, symbolized by the Industrial Relations Act, would end the inflation, especially as unemployment was still rising. The weakness of this policy was that it was still recognizably an incomes policy but a very feeble one. The Government still had a 'norm' in view, one it was prepared to enforce on luckless workers in the public sector such as the electricity workers, miners and postmen. The difference with past incomes policies was that it gave the Government no direct way of interfering in wage settlements in the private sector. The Conservatives blamed excessive wage demands on the 'monopoly power' of the unions. Their solution was to curb this power, and the Industrial Relations Act was introduced, against fierce union opposition, to do this. One of the main purposes of the Act was to increase competition in the labour market, and thus strengthen employers in their bargaining with the unions. In this way it was hoped, costs could be held down, and British industry made more profitable.

Brandishing such policies, the Conservative Ministers ignored the real causes of inflation and its roots in the state sector over which they presided. As a result they were unable to forge the new course they wanted. Conservative leaders understood well enough that the success of their growth strategy depended upon holding down wages and allowing profits to increase, so that investment would rise. Yet they had been committed by their supporters against any statutory incomes policy or wage freeze. At the same time they were not prepared to question in any radical way the size and the policies of the state sector. They merely stripped away embellishments that Labour had added. Taxation was cut, but not the level of government spending. The budget deficit was merely increased. The money supply was not controlled. Heath showed that he intended to implement his competition policy and pursue economic growth without radically altering the main creation of the post-war politics of power. Yet he believed he could do away with one of the central tools that had been developed for managing such an economy—a formal incomes policy that sought to nationalize the annual increase in productivity and distribute it between the private and public sectors, and between wages and profits.

A very curious pattern emerged. Prices and wages were held down in the public sector contrary to the Government's free market principles. But in the high productivity industries of the private sector they zoomed higher than ever. So anxious, however, was the Government to preserve its growth strategy and so deep was its aversion to statutory control of incomes that it met this accelerating cost inflation not by deflation or a wage freeze, but by adding to it. It clearly intended that whatever the level of wage demands, prices would increase still faster so that real incomes would not rise. This was achieved through the budget deficit and the floating pound. The budget deficit was allowed to grow astronomically. In addition, savings that were made in public expenditure were directed at the living standards of wage earners—these included the rise in rents under the Housing Finance Act and the increase in charges for health and school milk. The result was an enormous increase in the pressure of demand and therefore more rapid inflation at the very time that workers' living standards were being squeezed. The floating of the pound meant that there was no interruption to growth from speculation against sterling. As the pound sank downwards, however, the prices of all imports, including food and raw materials, steadily rose. By 1974 the devaluation had reached twenty per cent. British exports were competitive as never before, and inflation never faster.

The Government knew that until prosperity without profits had been turned into prosperity with profits there was no chance of investment reviving. Ministers were therefore determined to maintain prosperity and stop unemployment rising any further. Deflation would only cause the postponement of investment plans and do little to end the inflation.

The whole strategy suffered spectacular shipwreck. The Cabinet found itself obliged to choose between direct intervention to control wages, and sacrificing its hopes of economic growth. This remarkable reversal of policy was caused by the defeat of the Government in 1972 by industrial militancy, first in the mines, then on the railways, finally in the docks. The Industrial Relations Act came into force just after the miners' dispute. Rarely can any measure have been emasculated so quickly, and its inflexibility so much regretted by its sponsors.[20] While the unions boycotted this modern Star Chamber, major firms feared to resort to it.

In 1972, therefore, the Government was forced to reverse its policies on several fronts in order to keep its hopes of economic growth alive. It restored regional investment grants and gave subsidies again to unprofitable sectors. It gave in to the sit-in at UCS and announced new government aid for the yard. State spending began its upward climb again. The most significant change of all, however, was the Government's recognition that if it was going to maintain and extend the state sector as the basis of the welfare consensus, then it needed even more desperately an incomes policy. Thus the realities of the prevailing politics of power reasserted themselves. For all their election pledges, the Conservatives imposed the most far reaching and comprehensive statutory incomes policy that Britain had yet seen in peacetime.

But the change was too late. Phase I and Phase 2 of the Counter-Inflation policy were successes. Militancy was checked, profitability was raised, the economy began growing at a rapid pace.[21] The breakthrough seemed to have been achieved at last. An economic miracle for Britain and electoral triumph for the Conservatives appeared possible. Yet the recklessness with which this position had been secured raised huge questions. The balance of payments was headed for massive deficit in 1973, caused by the sinking pound and the great upsurge of imports. Domestic investment was only picking up slowly. The bulk of British funds for investment were still going abroad. In 1972, the export of capital actually doubled. With interest rates now at record levels because of the inflation and the vast boom in private credit permitted by the Government, investment in productive industry was not in any case very attractive. Firms could earn more by lending money to local authorities at going rates of interest. Most serious of all, however, the very success of the first two stages of the Counter-Inflation policy built up enormous pressure for a challenge to Phase 3. For with wages held down during 1973, prices continued to soar. The Government's insistence that the inflation was caused primarily by wage demands, always false but superficially convincing and easy to communicate to the electorate, was dramatically refuted. Trade unionists who since the late 1960s had resorted to wage militancy to defend their living standards against the ravages of taxation and inflation, were now shown by the Government itself that they were not responsible for inflation. It continued unabated when wages were held down.

By the end of 1973, therefore, the Government was already facing a very difficult winter, mainly as a result of its own policies. As under Labour, incomes policy had brought about a major confrontation with the unions in which struggles to maintain real wages were necessarily transformed into political struggles—not by the unions but by the Government. The Government had to claim that its incomes policy backed by force of law and the will of a democratically elected Parliament reflected the national interest. But that meant bringing into the determination of pay the criterion of what was fair and just—political criteria for the setting of wages had to replace economic criteria, the simple price that different kinds of labour power fetched in the market.

225

If such political criteria were used, the overall distribution of national income and wealth could not be left outside. Profits soared under the incomes policy as they were meant to. So did property values. This hardly recommended restraint to workers, who proved less and less ready to share the Government's conception of the national interest. A major onslaught on Phase 3 began, spearheaded again by the miners who were in the strongest bargaining position of any group of workers.

This challenge was for a time dwarfed by the sudden world energy crisis that was created by the Arab oil embargo and the subsequent quadrupling of crude oil prices. The effect was to plunge the British state into its worst crisis since the war. The enormous balance of payments deficit that Britain already faced was doubled. The hopes of economic growth were destroyed, and the threat of a recession in the world market became very real. At the very moment the British economy was posed for take off into expansion, the necessary export markets disappeared, and the cost of essential imports rocketed. The economic strategy of Heath's Government and with it their electoral perspective was shattered. Britain faced not rising but falling living standards in the run up to the election that had to be held by June 1975.

The Government, through its manipulation of inflation and its incomes policy, had successfully contained wages and raised profits in order to create the conditions for the expansion it had planned for. Now it found that it would have to launch a further attack on the living standards of wage earners to right the balance of payments deficit. Yet it was already engaged in a battle over the preceding phase of its counter-inflation policy, and had long since forfeited the chance of gaining the cooperation of the trade unions.

What was especially unfortunate for the Conservatives was that the oil crisis increased still further the bargaining power of the miners, and underlined the folly of the run down in the coal industry that had been government policy since the 1950s. It would however still have been open to the Cabinet when the oil crisis broke to have suspended Phase 3, paid the miners as a special case because of their new importance to the economy, and imposed a wage freeze for everyone else. The formation of a government of national unity could even have been considered.

Instead the Conservatives chose, or more probably stumbled into, a different strategy. With unpleasant memories of its defeat by the miners in 1972, the Cabinet resolved on a defence of Phase 3 at all costs. Ministers clearly hoped that a display of firmness against the miners would force all other unions in weaker bargaining positions to settle within Phase 3. The wages front at least would be held, even while everything else was collapsing around them. This thinking led them directly to the drastic step of imposing a three day week on British industry under the state of emergency regulations, as soon as the effects of the miners' overtime ban apparently began to show in dwindling coal stocks. Commentators were not slow to point out to the Government that in economic terms the cost to the national economy of paying the miners their full claim was insignificant compared to the cost and the damage wreaked by three day working. One leading industrialist called it the arithmetic of the lunatic asylum.

In political terms, however, it made much better sense. It isolated the miners, it frightened most other groups of workers into settling under Phase 3 (six million had done so by the end of February 1974), and it won strong support in the Conservative party. A policy of firmness aimed at traditional enemies of the Conservative Nation—the militants in the trade unions—was one that the rank and file had never had any difficulty in understanding. The Government had clearly abandoned its hopes of securing economic growth and was therefore determined to break trade union militancy at the start of the period of deflation and unemployment that loomed ahead.

The miners, however, had a stranglehold on the economy and there was no doubt that the Government would eventually be defeated over miners' pay. Ministers must have realized this. But the situation offered further intriguing political possibilities. The miners would have to be paid off, but in the meantime the Conservative party, having already subdued most other sectors of the trade unions, could consolidate its victory by appealing to the nation and increasing its majority at a General Election. A Conservative campaign fought on the platform of Who Governs Britain, that brought victory, could be expected to weaken the hands of militants in the trade unions, and prepare the ground for new measures to curtail still further the bargaining strength of the unions. The decision by the miners' executive to call an all-out strike in February finally persuaded Heath and the Cabinet, after some earlier hesitation, to call their election. The miners had had their ballot, and now the nation was to have theirs.

The reason given for the election was of course fraudulent, as Enoch Powell observed when he announced his decision to withdraw from Parliament (though not as it turned out from the election campaign). The Government fully intended to settle with the miners after the election. The speedy establishment of the Relativities Board, and the reference of the miners' claim to them, was intended precisely for that purpose. So the excuse for holding the election—the need to resist the overbearing exercise of union power by left-wing militants in the NUM determined to overthrow democratic government—was never very convincing, even though it awoke new enthusiasm in the Tory rank and file and was endorsed almost unanimously by the press.

The other main pretext for holding the election when the Government had still a working majority and fifteen months of its term left, was to give it fresh authority to cope with the economic crisis. It was widely suspected, however, that Conservative strategists were more anxious lest February 1974 should be the last favourable opportunity in the following fifteen months for their party to be returned with an increased majority. They certainly broke new ground in appealing for the confidence of the electorate. Ministers appeared to be arguing that because they had presided so ingloriously over Britain's lurch into economic catastrophe, they were much the best qualified to rescue the country from it.

Indeed, the Conservatives entered the election campaign with one of the least promising records any British Government had ever offered the British electorate. Their main achievements in office had been the accession to the Common Market and the Sunningdale agreement in Ulster. The Common Market was hardly mentioned at all by Conservatives during the campaign, presumably because their campaign managers had warned them of the widespread unpopularity of the EEC and its association with rising food prices. Ulster was not an issue between the parties. The Tories had continued the policy of military repression that Labour had initiated, and had supplemented it with political negotiations aimed at splitting the Ulster Unionists and the Protestant majority, and preparing the way for the eventual reunification of Ireland. The military and economic cost of securing the Protestant supremacy in Ulster, which had served the British state so well for so long, had become too great. Sunningdale was the first fruit of the new policy, and ironically it was to lose the Conservatives their solid bloc of Unionist seats in the province. The Orange card was no longer a Conservative one. Other measures of which the Conservatives were proud, including the Housing Finance Act and their tax reforms, might commend them to administrative experts, but did not win over many voters, who were more influenced by the general state of the economy. Inflation had not been brought under control—it had accelerated, to over ten per cent a year. House-building had declined dramatically, economic growth had been slight, unemployment had been high.[22]

It is not then perhaps very surprising that the Conservatives lost the election, even though the anti-union and anti-militant platform seemed such a promising one for a media election. The Conservatives had won elections before on a platform of the need for strong government, but never with such dull leaders. Men not measures had been their boast and often their programme in the past. By 1974 they had become weighed down with measures, but had never been so short of men. Heath's team of administrators obviously found it difficult to change their image from managers of economic growth. The red union dragon might be gobbling up the national cake, but the Conservatives had no champion to send against it.

Twenty-five years before, an election fought on such a platform would have polarized the political nation. In 1974 the result proved quite different. Turnout rose as predicted, but both the main parties lost votes, which were picked up by third parties, the Liberals and the Nationalists. Much ingenuity was devoted after the election in speculation about what the Electorate meant by the results, what it was trying to say, and what political arrangements would best accord with its wishes. Such fancies are of course entirely vain and meaningless, and only distract attention from the real questions.

What the election in fact showed was a further dissolution of the class alignment in the political market that developed in the 1920s and reached its full extent after 1945. This dissolution has been marked by the growing number of voters who have no strong ties to any party, and change their votes between elections. This seems largely inevitable in a political system where the parties no longer seem very distinctive to voters and compete with one another as alternative sets of executives to manage the existing state. Since both have so signally failed as competent managers, it is hardly surprising that large numbers of voters should have opted for a third party alternative. The Liberals' virtues were mainly negative—they were not either Labour or Conservative. The Nationalists identified a new basis for political alignment, regional nationalism. The switch to third parties occurred against the pull of class solidarity, which the Conservatives by intention and the Labour party by default, managed to evoke.

One of the main themes of this book has been that change and stability, and consensus and ideology in British politics, can only be understood by showing how the political market and the state are at once separate and related, giving rise to two kinds of politics. The politics of power frequently establishes a policy consensus, a set of priorities that provide the framework for government, and which express the balance of power between social classes defined not by occupation but by ownership and control of the means of production. The relationship of these classes defines the particular mode of production, the social organization of the economy, on which the whole society rests. The manner in which the economy develops has never been a simple matter of increasing investment in machinery and using more advanced technology. It has always been constrained and channelled by the opposing interests of the two classes, labour and capital, whose relationship makes possible capitalist production and the accumulation of capital. For long periods the interests of these two classes can appear reconcilable. It is at moments of crisis that it becomes clear that either one or the other has to give way for the crisis to be resolved.[23]

From this standpoint the growing failure of the welfare consensus is hardly accidental. This consensus, established at the time of the post-war settlement and based upon a greatly expanded role and size for the state, reflected the compromise between the ruling interests of capital and the demands of labour, expressed by the Labour party and the trade unions. Partly from contradictions within itself, partly from external factors, it has become unworkable in the form in which it was originally cast. Finding a new consensus is not a search for technical solutions, but political ones. At certain times, a reorganization of the state that alters the balance of power between the classes becomes necessary to make government effective once more. Only if government in Britain somehow regains its effectiveness is the present disillusion with parliamentary politics and the established parties that has produced a deadlock in the electoral system likely to be removed. Effective government in this context is government that can meet expectations and satisfy material demands.

If capitalism is to survive in Britain, then some new relationship has to be worked out with the trade unions, the organized working class. Either their power must be considerably reduced or considerably extended. In the first case the alternative appears to be further legislation to curb strikes and picketing, combined with policies long advocated by Enoch Powell. His castigation of the folly of incomes policy, his pinpointing of the role of the state in creating inflation, his reliance on control of the money supply cuts in government spending, and balanced budgets to end inflation, and his consequent acceptance of deflation and unemployment as lesser evils—all these form the framework for a really new politics of power. It means abandoning the welfare consensus and the electoral cycle, and the ideology of economic growth. Such policies, however, might well cow the unions, redress the balance of power, and protect property, with the least possible direct involvement of the political arm of the state.

The immediate alternative is an opening to the Left—a new political settlement if not a new incomes policy, though it is hard to see how one could be long avoided. Its basis would have to be a new set of concessions by property, of the kind so fiercely resisted by Heath's Government in its negotiations with the unions before it launched its Counter-Inflation policy. The unions would have to be given, in addition to new legal privileges, a virtual right of veto over many items of government policy, including rents, prices, pensions, industrial legislation, taxation, and general economic management. Wage restraint, in one form or another, would be the price. This settlement would presumably involve a further extension of public ownership into manufacturing industry, especially the unprofitable sectors, and tough controls on foreign investment and property speculation in order to ensure investment was carried out in manufacturing industry and within the national economy. In this way a trimmed but probably more profitable private sector would survive. The state of course would have expanded enormously again.

Policy is likely to veer between these two extremes for some years yet. The outcome depends on many incalculable factors, especially the course of the domestic political struggle and the development of the world economy. The present growing unpredictability of the political nation in its voting behaviour shows that it is no longer being harnessed very efficiently by the political parties to the state. Three main explanations of the current situation have been put forward. Some say it is a transient phase, and that the two main parties will soon recapture their lost supporters. Others argue that a new basis of political alignment is emerging, one that will see the end of occupational class as the dominant factor in political allegiance. Still others predict that parliamentary politics and the competitive political market will collapse, eroded by powerful movements outside Parliament.

The outcome is here too very uncertain. The old basis of political alignment is clearly losing its hold, but this is more the result of how the parties have competed and how they have governed, than of any fundamental shifts in the social composition of the electorate. The Liberals clearly offer no new basis of alignment. Comparisons with the rise of Labour in the 1920s are fanciful. The Liberals have no really new policies for the politics of power, they represent no particular social group. They would not perform in government any better than the other two parties have done. Liberal support is extraordinarily fickle and varied, and seems far more a symptom of the present disintegration of the party system than a positive replacement for it. Support for the Liberals may grow, but it will not bring back political stability.

The Conservative party faces a future of great difficulty. It failed in government, and it failed in its appeal to the nation. The Conservative Nation, in a critical election for the party, proved much smaller than expected. The One Nation strategy of the Right Progressives has broken down. The Conservatives appealed to a national consensus which did not exist. The result is that notwithstanding the fact that the Tories gained the largest share of the popular vote (38·1 per cent, compared to 37·2 per cent for Labour, and 19·6 per cent for the Liberals), and elected 296 MPs, they are probably in a weaker position in the political market than at any time since 1945.

The One Nation strategy that the Tories have followed since the 1860s has three main elements—the provision of strong, competent national leadership to govern the state, the building of support around national rather than class issues, and the identification of the party with the prevailing consensus. For a variety of reasons that have been examined in this book, the party under Heath, despite its protestations to the contrary, broke with all three principles. It failed to govern effectively and well—its overall record was disastrous in electoral terms. Moreover, through some of its policies particularly its embattled defence of the Counter-Inflation policy, the Industrial Relations Act, and the Housing Finance Act, it gave the impression of seeking confrontation with the unions. The image of the party at the election for many of its supporters as well as for many of the uncommitted voters was a class

231

image rather than a national image. This was skilfully exploited by the Liberals. Finally, this image of class conflict and class confrontation that clung to Mr Heath's administration, not least from the attitudes and behaviour of some members of his Cabinet, separated his Government from the welfare consensus. Heath was pursuing a new course but without any very great popular backing. He himself seems to have continued to interpret politics and government in predominantly technical and administrative terms. Government based on the best expert advice that Think Tanks and civil servants could make available was certainly inappropriate to the political problems the Conservatives faced after 1970.

The problem confronting the Conservatives after the 1974 election was that having narrowly lost the election, they had ceded the political initiative to their electoral competitors, a Labour party which had looked tired and defunct before and during the election campaign. Out of office, the Tory party would again be a bystander, while the Tory record in government could only become increasingly black in the memory of more and more voters. The Labour party meanwhile was given the opportunity to pose as the party of national unity, the party determined to restore consensus and defuse conflict, the party of the nation-state pledged to renegotiate the terms of accession to the unpopular Common Market. The Tories had been the party of Empire. The Empire was gone. The EEC elicited no national enthusiam except in the leader columns of the press. The Tories had been the party of the free market. In power they had introduced the most comprehensive government interference with the determination of wages and prices ever seen in Britain during peace-time. It was hardly surprising that the party should have felt disoriented in 1974. Its electoral ideologies had been trampled on; its policies in government had largely failed; and its leaders had lost an election in which they sought a mandate for strong government. The evident unity of the party leadership and the Cabinet at the helm of this sinking ship was hardly any consolation. Enoch Powell chose to leave it when he saw it was going down.

Powell still remains an alternative leader for the party, but he has never seemed further from achieving his goal. During the 1970 parliament he became increasingly isolated within the party, but continued to pursue relentlessly the issues that obsessed him—inflation, immigration, Ulster, the Common Market, and increasingly, the Conservative leadership itself. His resignation as an MP, and his public call to his supporters to vote Labour because Labour was pledged to renegotiate Common Market membership, cut him adrift from the Conservative party. His actions almost certainly caused large defections to Labour, predominantly in the West Midlands, most of them working class voters whom Powell had brought into the Conservative Nation on the issue of immigration. Just as Powell claimed to have won the 1970 election for the Conservatives, so he now could claim he lost the election for them in 1974.[24]

Apart from the feeling of the party towards him, however, it is hard to see how he could honourably return to politics as a Conservative MP, still less as Conservative Leader, so long as the party remains committed to the EEC. Powell in one sense is a very honest politician, so before he can stand again as a Conservative, it is surely necessary that the Common Market is taken out of politics, either because the Labour party withdraws Britain from it, or because it collapses from its own internal divisions. There is no political future for Powell outside the Conservative party, as he himself appears to realize, and there may well now be no future for him within it. Yet it is his policies, or variations on them, that the party seems most likely to adopt once more whether they are condemned to a long spell in Opposition or whether they are returned to power at an early election. The other part of Powellism, however, the new One Nation strategy that emphasizes issues with strong national appeal and points to new bases for political alignment, is of little use to the Conservatives without Powell himself.

Events may yet destroy the minority Labour Government and sweep the Tories back to power pledged to launch a major offensive against trade union power. But it seems more likely that despite the magnitude of the problems Labour faces, the Government will retain the political initiative and any further increase in support the Liberals gain will be at the expense of the Conservatives. Commentators always speak of the Liberals being the alternative party to Labour, as though the Conservatives have a God-given right to occupy one half of the political spectrum. Yet in the three Liberal revivals since the war their votes have always come more from the Conservatives than from Labour. In the 1974 election the Conservative percentage of the poll fell 8·3 per cent, Labour's fell 5·8 per cent, while the Liberals' rose 11·8 per cent. This was the first time support for the Liberals had grown during the election campaign itself. They finished second in 122 Conservative seats. Many of these, including such strongholds as Cheltenham and Guildford, the Conservatives won with less than 50 per cent of the vote.

The electoral task facing the Conservatives is therefore immense. They must rebuild their party and somehow wrest the initiative from Labour and resist the Liberal challenge. Nothing in their past suggests that they cannot do this. Yet it is a very long time since the electoral perspective of the leadership and the electoral ideologies of the rank and file have been in such disarray, and since the Conservatives have had such difficulty in presenting themselves as the national party and the party of good government.

The electoral struggle will be one moment in the wider struggle between capital and labour that is currently being waged to reorganize the state, and establish new priorities, a new balance of power and a new settlement.[25] Electoral politics is not determined by the class struggle, but neither is it unaffected by it. They interact on one another in surprising ways. The results of general elections can sometimes decisively influence the outcome of a struggle between classes and lead to a reorganization of the politics of power. Up to now in Britain, the workings of the political market have generally contributed to overall political stability, and therefore to the security of the state and the ruling interests of property. There are no real signs as yet that it has lost its usefulness and become dispensable, to be replaced by a more predictable political order. The Conservative Nation, however, may yet find its way to the museum of Fantastic Zoology.

Biographies

The aim of this section is to give brief biographical details of prominent Conservatives mentioned in this book.

AMERY, JULIAN   b. 1919; ed Eton and Oxford; son-in-law of Harold Macmillan; war correspondent; MP Preston N. 1950–66, Brighton (Pavilion) 1969–   ; Secretary of State for Air, 1960–2; Minister of Aviation, 1962–4; Minister of Housing, 1970–2; Minister of State, Foreign Office, 1972–4; member of the Monday Club.

AMERY, LEOPOLD STENNETT   1873–1955; ed Harrow and Oxford; Fellow of All Souls; journalist and barrister; MP, Sparkbrook (Birmingham) 1911–45; First Lord of the Admiralty, 1922–4; Secretary of State for the Colonies, 1924–9; Secretary of State for India and Burma, 1940–5.

ASTOR, WILLIAM WALDORF   1907–66; ed Eton and Oxford; director, insurance company; MP, East Fulham 1935–45, Wycombe 1951–2.

BARBER, ANTHONY PERINOTT LYSBERG   b. 1920; ed Retford G.S. and Oxford; barrister; MP, Doncaster 1961–64; Altrincham 1965–   ; Economic Secretary to the Treasury, 1959–62; Financial Secretary to the Treasury, 1962–3; Minister of Health, 1963–4; Party Chairman, 1967–70; Chancellor of the Exchequer, 1970–4.

BERKELEY, HUMPHREY JOHN   b. 1926; ed Malvern and Cambridge; writer and broadcaster; joint managing director, Investeco; Ch. CUCA, 1948; CPC, 1949–56; MP, Lancaster 1959–66; Chairman, UNA, 1966–70; joined Labour party 1970.

BEVINS, JOHN REGINALD   b. 1908; ed Dovedale Rd and Liverpool Collegiate Schools; MP, Toxteth (Liverpool) 1950–64; Postmaster General, 1959–62.

BIFFEN, WILLIAM JOHN   b. 1930; ed Dr Morgan G.S., Bridgwater and Cambridge; MP, Oswestry 1961–   ; Tube Investments Ltd, 1953–60; Economist Intelligence Unit, 1960–1; Member of YCs and Bow Group.

BIGGS-DAVISON, JOHN ALEC b. 1918; ed Clifton and Oxford; CRD, 1950–5; MP, Chigwell 1955– ; member of the Monday Club.

BIRCH, EVELYN NIGEL CHETWODE (BARON RHYL) b. 1906; ed Eton; MP, Flintshire 1945–50, West Flint 1950–70; Minister of Works, 1954–5; Economic Secretary to the Treasury, 1957–8 (resigned).

BOOTHBY, ROBERT JOHN GRAHAM b. 1900; ed Eton and Oxford; MP, East Aberdeenshire 1924–58; PPS Chancellor of the Exchequer, 1926–9; PS, Ministry of Food, 1940–1.

BOWDEN, ANDREW b. 1930; ed Ardingly; paint industry, 1955–68; director, personnel management firms, 1969– ; MP, Brighton (Kemptown) 1970– ; chairman YCs, 1960–1.

BOYD-CARPENTER, JOHN ARCHIBALD b. 1908; ed Stowe and Oxford; barrister; Chairman, Orion Insurance Co., 1969– ; MP, Kingston-upon-Thames 1945–74; Financial Secretary to the Treasury, 1951–4; Minister of Transport, 1954–5; Minister of Pensions and National Insurance, 1955–62; Chief Secretary to the Treasury and Paymaster General, 1962–4; Front bench spokesman on Housing, Local Government, and Land, 1964–6.

BOYLE, SIR EDWARD CHARLES GURNEY b. 1923; ed Eton and Oxford; MP, Handsworth (Birmingham) 1950–70; Financial Secretary to the Treasury, 1959–62; Minister of Education, 1962–4; Front bench spokesman on education, 1964–70; Director, Penguin Books, 1966– ; Vice-Chancellor, Leeds University, 1970– .

BOYSON, RHODES b. 1925; ed Haslingden G.S. and Cardiff; headmaster, Highbury Grove Comprehensive School; Chairman, National Council for Educational Standards; MP, Brent N. 1974– .

BRAINE, BERNARD RICHARD b. 1914; ed Hendon County G.S.; director, Purle Brothers Holdings Ltd; MP, Billericay 1955– .

BROOKE, HENRY b. 1903; ed Marlborough and Oxford; MP, W. Lewisham, 1938–45, Hampstead 1950–66; Financial Secretary to the Treasury, 1954–7; Minister of Housing and Local Government, 1957–61; Chief Secretary and Paymaster General, 1961–2; Home Secretary, 1962–4.

BUTLER, RICHARD AUSTEN b. 1902; ed Marlborough and Cambridge; MP, Saffron Walden 1929–65; Minister of Education, 1941–5; Chancellor of the Exchequer, 1951–5; Lord Privy Seal, 1955–9; Leader of the House, 1955–61; Home Secretary, 1957–62; Chairman of the Conservative Party, 1959–61; Foreign Secretary, 1963–4; Chairman, CRD, 1945–64; Chairman, Advisory Committee on Policy, 1950–64; Master of Trinity College, Cambridge, 1965– .

CARR, ROBERT b. 1916; ed Westminster and Cambridge; company director —John Dale Ltd, 1948–63; Metal Closures Group Ltd, 1964–70; Securicor Ltd, 1961–3, 1967–70; MP, Mitcham 1950–74, Sutton (Carshalton) 1974– ; Secretary of State for Employment, 1970–2; Home Secretary, 1972–4; member One Nation Group.

CHATAWAY, CHRISTOPHER JOHN b. 1931; ed Sherborne and Oxford; broadcaster, journalist; MP, Lewisham N. 1959–66, Chichester 1969– ;

Alderman GLC, 1967–70; Minister of Posts and Telecommunications, 1970–2; Minister of Industrial Development, 1972–4; member of the Bow Group.

CHURCHILL, RANDOLPH 1911–68; ed Eton and Oxford; journalist and author; MP, Preston 1940–5.

CHURCHILL, WINSTON SPENCER 1874–1965; ed Harrow; MP, (C) Oldham 1900–4 and (L) 1904–6, N. W. Manchester 1906–8, Dundee 1908–18 and (CL) 1918–22, (C) Epping 1924–45, Woodford 1945–64; President of the Board of Trade, 1908–10; Home Secretary, 1910–11; First Lord of the Admiralty, 1911–15; Chancellor of the Duchy of Lancaster, 1915; Minister of Munitions, 1917; Secretary of State for War, 1919–21; Secretary of State for Air and the Colonies, 1921–2; Chancellor of the Exchequer, 1924–9; Prime Minister, 1940–5 and 1951–5.

CLARK, HENRY MAITLAND b. 1929; ed Shrewsbury and Cambridge; Colonial service; company director and public relations consultant; MP, Antrim N. 1959–70.

CRAWLEY, AIDAN MERIVALE b. 1908; ed Harrow and Oxford; resigned from Labour party 1957; President of LWT, 1971– (Chairman, 1967–71); MP, West Derbyshire 1962–7.

CRITCHLEY, JULIAN MICHAEL GORDON b. 1930; ed Shrewsbury and Oxford; director of public relations firm, and journalist; MP, Rochester & Chatham 1959–64; Aldershot 1970– ; Chairman of the Bow Group, 1966–7; President of the Atlantic Association of Young Political Leaders, 1968.

CURRAN, CHARLES 1921–72; ed Cardiff High School and Stoneyhurst; journalist—sometime assistant editor of *Evening News, Evening Standard, Daily Mirror*; MP, Uxbridge 1959–66 and 1970–2.

DAVIES, JOHN EMERSON HARDING b. 1916; ed St Edward's School (Oxford); Managing Director, Shellmex and BP, 1961–5; Director-General of the CBI, 1965–9; Director, Hill Samuel Group, 1969–70; MP, Knutsford 1970– ; Minister of Technology, 1970; Secretary of State for Trade and Industry, 1970–2; Chancellor of the Duchy of Lancaster, 1972–4.

DEEDES, WILLIAM FRANCIS b. 1913; ed Harrow; MP, Ashford 1950– ; sometime parliamentary spokesman for police federation; Minister without Portfolio, 1962–4.

DOUGLAS-HOME, SIR ALEC b. 1903; ed Eton and Oxford; MP, Lanark 1931–51, Kinross 1963– ; Chairman of Junior Imperial League, 1937–9; PPS to PM, 1937–40; Secretary for Commonwealth Relations, 1955–60; Foreign Secretary, 1960–3; Prime Minister, 1963–4; resigned the leadership 1965; Foreign Secretary, 1970–4.

DU CANN, EDWARD DILLON LOTT b. 1924; ed Woodbridge and Oxford; Chairman of Keyser Ullman; founder of Unicorn group of Unit Trusts; Director of Barclays Bank; MP, Taunton 1956– ; Chairman of the Conservative party, 1965–7; Chairman of the 1922 Committee, 1970– ; former prominent Young Conservative.

ECCLES, DAVID   b. 1904; ed Winchester and Oxford; Director of Courtaulds, 1962–70; MP, Chippenham 1943–62; Minister of Works, 1951–4; Minister of Education, 1954–7 and 1959–62; President of the Board of Trade, 1957–9; Paymaster General, 1970–4.

EDEN, SIR (ROBERT) ANTHONY   b. 1897; ed Eton and Oxford; MP, Warwick, 1923–57; Foreign Secretary, 1935–8; Secretary for Dominion Affairs, 1939–40; Secretary for War, 1940; Foreign Secretary, 1940–5 and 1951–5; Prime Minister, 1955–7.

ELLIOT, WALTER   1888–1958; ed Glasgow Academy and Glasgow University; MP, Lanark 1918–23; Kelvingrove 1924–45, Scottish Universities, 1946–50; Minister of Agriculture, 1932–6; Scottish Secretary, 1936–8; Minister of Health, 1938–40.

ERSKINE-HILL, SIR ALEXANDER GALLOWAY   1894–1947; ed Rugby and Cambridge; barrister; MP, North Edinburgh 1933–45; Founder member of the Progress Trust.

FELL, ANTONY   b. 1914; ed Bedford G.S.; MP, Yarmouth 1951–66 and 1970–   . Member of the Monday Club.

FISHER, NIGEL THOMAS LOVERIDGE   b. 1913; ed Eton and Cambridge; MP, Hitchin 1950–5, Surbiton 1955–   ; Opposition spokesman for Commonwealth Affairs, 1964–6.

FRASER, SIR MICHAEL   b. 1915; ed Fettes and Cambridge; CRD, 1946– (Chairman 1970–   ); Deputy Chairman of Conservative party, 1970–   .

GAMMANS, SIR LEONARD DAVID   1895–1957; ed Portsmouth G.S. and London; Colonial service in Malaya, 1920–34; MP, Hornsey 1941–57.

GODBER, JOSEPH BRADSHAW   b. 1914; ed Bedford; MP, Grantham 1951–   ; Minister of State, Foreign Office, 1961–3; Minister of Labour, 1963–4; Opposition spokesman on agriculture, 1965–70; Minister of State, Foreign Office, 1970–2, Minister of Agriculture, 1972–4.

GOLDMAN, PETER   b. 1925; ed Cambridge; joined CRD in 1946; Director of the CPC, 1955–64; unsuccessful Conservative candidate at Orpington, 1962; Director of the Consumer Association since 1964.

GOODHART, PHILIP   b. 1925; ed Hotchkiss and Cambridge; journalist; MP, Beckenham 1957–   ; secretary 1922 Committee; founder member of the Bow Group.

GRIFFITHS, ELDON WYLIE   b. 1925; ed Aston G.S. and Cambridge; journalist—foreign editor of *Newsweek*, 1956–63; CRD, 1963–4; Parliamentary adviser to the National police federation, 1966–70; MP, Bury St Edmunds 1964–   ; Parliamentary Under Secretary, Ministry of the Environment, 1970–4.

GRIGG, JOHN EDWARD POYNDER   b. 1924; ed Eton and Oxford; editor, *National and English Review*, 1954–60.

GROUSE, LIONEL   ed Ealing G.S. and London School of Economics; Chairman of LSE Conservative Association; teacher.

GUMMER, JOHN SELWYN b. 1939; ed Kings School, Rochester and Cambridge; Chairman of CUCA, 1961 and FUCUA, 1962; editor, *Impact*, 1964–7; journalist and publisher; MP, Lewisham W. 1970–   .

HARE, JOHN HUGH (VISCOUNT BLAKENHAM) b. 1911; ed Eton; MP, Woodbridge 1945–64; Vice Chairman Conservative party, 1951–5; Minister of State, Colonial Affairs, 1955–6; Secretary of State for War, 1956–8; Minister of Agriculture, 1958–60; Minister of Labour, 1960–3; Chancellor of the Duchy of Lancaster, 1963–4; Chairman of the Conservative party, 1963–5.

HEATH, EDWARD RICHARD GEORGE b. 1916; ed Chatham House School and Oxford; administrative civil service, 1946–7; Government Chief Whip, 1955–9; Minister of Labour, 1959–60; Lord Privy Seal, 1960–3; Secretary for Trade and Industry, 1963–4; Leader of the Conservative party, 1965–   ; Prime Minister, 1970–4.

HILL, CHARLES b. 1904; ed St Olaves School and Cambridge; Chairman ITA, 1963–7; Chairman, Laporte Industries, 1967–70; Chairman of the Governors of the BBC, 1967–72; MP, Luton 1950–63; Postmaster General, 1955–7; Chancellor of the Duchy of Lancaster, 1957–61; Minister of Housing, 1961–2.

HINCHINGBROOKE, *see* MONTAGU

HOBSON, SIR JOHN GARDNER SUMNER 1912–67; ed Harrow and Oxford; barrister; MP, Warwick 1957–67; Solicitor General, 1962; Attorney General, 1962–4; member of Home Office Advisory Commission.

HOGG, QUINTIN MCGAREL (VISCOUNT HAILSHAM) b. 1907; ed Eton and Oxford; MP, Oxford 1938–50, St Marylebone 1963–70; First Lord of the Admiralty, 1956–7; Minister of Education, 1957; Lord President of the Council and Chairman of the Conservative party, 1957–9; Lord President, 1960–4; Secretary for Education and Science, 1964; Lord Chancellor, 1970–4.

HOLLIS, MAURICE CHRISTOPHER b. 1902; ed Eton and Oxford; Chairman, Hollis and Carter; MP, Devizes 1945–55.

HOWE, SIR RICHARD EDWARD GEOFFREY b. 1926; ed Winchester and Cambridge; founder-member of the Bow Group; chairman of the Bow Group, 1955; editor of *Crossbow*, 1960–2; MP, Bebington 1964–6; Reigate 1970–4, E. Surrey 1974–   ; Solicitor General, 1970–3; Minister for Trade and Consumer Affairs, 1973–4.

HOWELL, DAVID b. 1936; ed Eton and Cambridge; Economic section of the Treasury, 1959–60; leader writer, *Daily Telegraph*, 1960–4, Chairman of the Bow Group, 1961–2; editor, *Crossbow*, 1962–4; Director, CPC, 1964–6; MP, Guildford 1966–   ; Under-Secretary, Dept of Employment, 1971–2; Minister of State, Northern Ireland Office, 1972–4; Minister of State for Energy, 1974.

JENKIN, CHARLES PATRICK FLEEMING b. 1926; ed Clifton and Cambridge; barrister; MP, Wanstead and Woodford 1964–   ; Financial Secretary to the Treasury, 1972–4.

JONES, AUBREY b. 1911; ed Cyfarthfa Castle School and London School of Economics; industrialist—sometime director of Thomas Tilling, Cornhill Insurance, Stavely Industries Ltd, Guest Keen & Nettlefold, Courtaulds; MP, Hall Green (Birmingham) 1950–65; Minister of Fuel and Power, 1955–7; Minister of Supply, 1957–9; Chairman, Prices and Incomes Board, 1965–70.

JOSEPH, SIR KEITH SINJOHN b. 1918; ed Harrow and Oxford; barrister; MP, Leeds N.E. 1956– ; Deputy Chairman, Bovis Holdings Ltd, 1964–70; Minister of Housing, 1962–4; Secretary of State for Social Services, 1970–4.

LANE, DAVID b. 1922; ed Eton and Cambridge; Shell, 1959–67; MP, Cambridge 1967– ; Under-Secretary, Home Office, 1972–4.

LAW, RICHARD KIDSTON (BARON COLERAINE) b. 1901; ed Shrewsbury and Oxford; son of Andrew Bonar Law; MP, S.W. Hull 1931–45, S. Kensington 1945–50, Haltemprice 1950–4; Financial Secretary, War Office, 1940–1; Under Secretary, Foreign Office, 1941–3; Minister of State, Foreign Office, 1943–5.

LAWSON, NIGEL b. 1932; ed Westminster and Oxford; journalist—City Editor, *Sunday Telegraph*, 1961–3; editor, *Spectator*, 1966–70; Special adviser to Sir Alec Douglas-Home, 1963–4.

LEATHER, EDWIN HARTLEY CAMERON b. 1919; ed Trinity College School; MP, N. Somerset 1950–64; Director, William Baird Ltd, Hill Samuel & Co.

LENNOX-BOYD, ALAN TINDAL b. 1904; ed Sherborne and Oxford; Director, Arthur Guinness, Tate and Lyle, ICI; MP, Mid-Beds 1931–60; Minister of State, Colonial Affairs, 1951–2; Minister of Transport, 1952–4; Secretary of State for Colonies, 1954–9.

LEWIS, RUSSELL b. 1926; Chairman of the Bow Group, 1958; Director of the CPC, 1968.

LLOYD, GEOFFREY WILLIAM b. 1902; ed Harrow and Cambridge; MP, Ladywood 1931–45, Sutton Coldfield 1955–74; Minister of Fuel and Power, 1951–5; Minister of Education, 1957–9.

LLOYD, JOHN SELWYN BROOKE b. 1904; ed Fettes and Cambridge; MP, Wirral 1945– ; Minister of State, Foreign Office, 1951–4; Minister of Supply, 1954–5; Minister of Defence, 1955; Foreign Secretary, 1955–60; Chancellor of the Exchequer, 1960–2; Lord Privy Seal and Leader of the House of Commons, 1963–4; Speaker of the House of Commons, 1970– .

LONGBOTTOM, CHARLES BROOKE b. 1930; ed Uppingham; barrister; Director of numerous companies—Court Line since 1972; MP, York 1959–66; PPS to Macleod, 1961–3.

LYTTLETON, OLIVER (LORD CHANDOS) 1893–1972; ed Eton and Cambridge; company director; Chairman, Associated Electrical Industries; MP, Aldershot 1940–54; President of the Board of Trade, 1940–1; War Cabinet, 1941–2; Minister of Production, 1942–5; Secretary of State for the Colonies, 1951–4.

MACLEOD, IAIN NORMAN 1913–1970; ed Fettes and Cambridge; CRD, 1946–50; MP, Enfield 1950–70; Minister of Health, 1952–5; Minister of

Labour, 1955–9; Secretary of State for the Colonies, 1959–61; Chancellor of the Duchy of Lancaster, Leader of the House of Commons, Chairman of the Conservative party, 1961–3; Editor, *Spectator*, 1963–5; Chancellor of the Exchequer, 1970. founder member of One Nation Group.

MACMILLAN, MAURICE HAROLD b. 1894; ed Eton and Oxford; MP, Stockton-on-Tees 1924–9 and 1931–45, Bromley 1945–64; Chairman, Macmillans; Minister Resident at Allied HQ in NW Africa, 1942–5; Minister of Housing, 1951–4; Minister of Defence, 1954–5; Foreign Secretary, 1955; Chancellor of the Exchequer, 1955–7; Prime Minister, 1957–63.

MAUDE, ANGUS EDMUND UPTON b. 1912; ed Rugby and Oxford; Director, CPC, 1951–5; Editor, *Sydney Morning Herald*, 1958–61; MP, Ealing 1950–8, Stratford-on-Avon 1963–   ; resigned from Shadow Cabinet, January 1966; Member of One Nation Group and Suez Group.

MAUDLING, REGINALD b. 1917; ed Merchant Taylors' and Oxford; company director—Kleinwort Benson, AEI, Lansing Bagnall, Dunlop; Chairman, ITCS Ltd, 1966–70; First President, Real Estate Fund of America, 1969; MP, Chipping Barnet 1950–   ; Minister of Supply, 1955–7; Paymaster General, 1957–9; President of the Board of Trade, 1959–61; Colonial Secretary, 1961–2; Chancellor of the Exchequer, 1962–4; Home Secretary, 1970–2; Deputy Leader of the Conservative party, 1965–72.

MAXWELL-FYFE, DAVID PATRICK (EARL OF KILMUIR) 1900–67; ed George Watson's College (Edinburgh) and Oxford; barrister; MP, Liverpool 1935–54; Solicitor-General, 1942–5; British prosecutor at Nuremburg, 1945; Home Secretary, 1951–4; Lord Chancellor, 1954–62.

MOATE, ROGER DENIS b. 1938; ed Latymer; MP, Faversham 1970–   ; insurance broker; former YC.

MOLSON, ARTHUR HUGH ELSDALE b. 1903; ed Lancing and Oxford; MP, Doncaster 1931–5, High Peak 1939–61; Minister of Works, 1957–9; Member of the Tory Reform Committee.

MONCKTON, WALTER TURNER 1891–1965; ed Harrow and Oxford; barrister; Director Midland Bank; MP, Bristol W. 1951–7; Minister of Labour, 1951–5; Minister of Defence, 1955–6; Paymaster-General, 1956–7; Chairman, Advisory Committee on Central Africa, 1960.

MONTAGU, ALEXANDER VICTOR EDWARD PAULET (LORD HINCHING-BROOKE) b. 1906; ed Eton and Cambridge; Chairman, Tory Reform Committee, 1943–4; MP, South Dorset 1941–62; President, Anti-Common Market League, 1962; disclaimed earldom of Sandwich 1964.

MUDD, WILLIAM DAVID b. 1933; ed Truro Cathedral School; journalist and broadcaster; MP, Falmouth & Camborne 1970–   .

NICHOLLS, SIR HARMAR b. 1912; ed Queen Mary G.S., Walsall; company director; MP, Peterborough 1950–   .

NUTTING, HAROLD ANTHONY b. 1920; ed Eton and Cambridge; Chairman, Young Conservatives, 1946; MP, Melton 1945–56; Minister of State, Foreign Office, 1955–6 (resigned).

OAKESHOTT, MICHAEL JOSEPH   b. 1901; ed St George's School, Harpenden and Cambridge; Professor of Political Science at the London School of Economics, 1951–69.

OSBORNE, CYRIL   1898–1969; ed University of Nottingham; stockbroker and company director; MP, Louth 1945–69.

PANNELL, NORMAN ALFRED   b. 1901; ed Sir George Monoux G.S. and London; MP, Kirkdale 1955–64; Liverpool City Council, 1952–7 and 1967–70; Cheshire County Council, 1970– .

PEYTON, JOHN WYNNE WILLIAM   b. 1919; ed Eton and Oxford; company director; Chairman, General Electrical and Mechanical Systems, 1969–70; MP, Yeovil 1951– ; Minister of Transport, 1970–4. Member of the Monday Club.

POOLE, OLIVER BRIAN SANDERSON   b. 1911; ed Eton and Oxford; company director, S. Pearson & Sons, Chairman of Lazard Brothers; MP, Oswestry 1945–50; Chairman of the Conservative party, 1955–7 and 1963–4.

POWELL, JOHN ENOCH   b. 1912; ed King Edward's School (Birmingham) and Cambridge; Fellow of Trinity College, Cambridge, 1934–8; Professor of Greek, Sydney, 1937–9; army Brigadier, 1944; Financial Secretary to the Treasury, 1957–8 (resigned); Minister of Health, 1960–3; Member of One Nation Group; MP, Wolverhampton S.W. 1950–74.

RAISON, TIMOTHY HUGH FRANCIS   b. 1929; ed Clifton and Oxford ; journalist—editor, *New Society*, 1962–8; member of Bow Group; editor *Crossbow*, 1958–60; MP, Aylesbury 1970– ; Under Secretary, Dept of Education, 1973–4.

REES-MOGG, WILLIAM   b. 1928; ed Charterhouse and Oxford; journalist— *Financial Times*, 1952–60, *Sunday Times*, 1960–7, Editor, *The Times*, 1967– ; Conservative parliamentary candidate for Chester-le-Street, 1956 and 1959; Vice-Chairman, Conservative National Advisory Committee on Political Education, 1961–3.

RIPPON, AUBREY GEOFFREY FREDERICK   b. 1924; ed King's College, Taunton and Oxford; barrister; prominent Young Conservative; MP, Norwich 1955–64, Hexham 1966– ; Mayor of Surbiton, 1951–2; Minister of Public Building and Works, 1962–4; Chancellor of the Duchy of Lancaster, 1970–2; Secretary of State for the Environment, 1972–4; Member of the Monday Club.

ST JOHN STEVAS, NORMAN ANTHONY FRANCIS   b. 1929; ed Ratcliffe and Cambridge; author, barrister and journalist; MP, Chelmsford 1964– ; Under Secretary for Education, 1972–3; Minister of State for Education, 1973–4.

SALISBURY, 5TH MARQUESS OF (ROBERT ARTHUR JAMES GASCOYNE-CECIL)   1893–1972; ed Eton and Oxford; MP, South Dorset 1929–41; Paymaster General, 1940; Secretary for Dominion Affairs, 1940–2 and 1943–5; Leader of the House of Lords, 1943–5, 1951–7; Lord President of the Council, 1952–7 (resigned).

SANDYS, DUNCAN EDWIN   b. 1908; ed Eton and Oxford; MP, Norwood 1935–45 and Streatham 1950–74; Minister of Works, 1944–5; Minister of

Supply, 1951–4; Minister of Housing, 1954–7; Minister of Defence, 1957–9; Minister of Aviation, 1959–60; Secretary for Commonwealth Relations, 1960–4.

SCHREIBER, MARK SHULDAN   b. 1931; ed Eton and Cambridge; Fisons Ltd, 1957–63; CRD, 1963–7; Director, Conservative party public sector research unit, 1967–70; Special adviser to the Government, 1970–4.

SCOTT, NICHOLAS PAUL   b. 1933; ed Clapham College; Chairman of YCs, 1963; National President, PEST; MP, Paddington S. 1966–74.

SMITHERS, SIR WALDRON   1880–1954; ed Charterhouse; stockbroker; MP, Chislehurst 1924–45, Orpington 1945–54.

STANLEY, OLIVER FREDERICK GEORGE   1896–1950; ed Eton; MP, Westmorland 1924–45, Bristol W. 1945–50; Minister of Transport, 1933–4; Minister of Labour, 1934–5; Minister of Education, 1935–7; President of the Board of Trade, 1937–40; Minister of War, 1940; Colonial Secretary 1942–5.

TAYLOR, EDWARD MACMILLAN   b. 1937; ed Glasgow High School and Glasgow University; journalist and author; MP, Cathcart 1964–   ; Under Secretary at the Scottish Office, 1970–2 (resigned); Member of the Monday Club.

THATCHER, MARGARET HILDA   b. 1925; ed Kesteven & Grantham School and Oxford; MP, Finchley 1959–   ; member of Shadow Cabinet, 1964–70; Secretary of State for Education, 1970–4.

THORNEYCROFT, GEORGE EDWARD PETER   b. 1909; ed Eton; barrister; Chairman, Pye, Pirelli, Trust Houses Forte; Director, Securicor; MP, Stafford 1938–45, Monmouth 1945–66; President of the Board of Trade, 1951–7; Chancellor of the Exchequer, 1957–8 (resigned); Minister of Aviation, 1960–2; Minister of Defence, 1962–4.

TURTON, SIR ROBIN   b. 1903; ed Eton and Oxford; MP, Thirsk & Malton 1929–   ; Minister of Pensions, 1953–4; Minister of Health, 1955–7.

UTLEY, THOMAS EDWIN   journalist and leader writer, *Daily Telegraph.*

WALKER, PETER EDWARD   b. 1932; ed Latymer; Chairman of YCs 1958–60; company director—Deputy Chairman, Slater Walker Securities, 1964–70; MP, Worcester 1961–   ; Secretary of State for the Environment, 1970–2; Secretary of State for Trade and Industry, 1972–4.

WALKER-SMITH, SIR DEREK COLCLOUGH   b. 1910; ed Rossall and Oxford; MP, Hertfordshire E. 1955–   ; Chairman 1922 Committee, 1951–5; Minister of Health, 1957–60.

WALL, PATRICK HENRY BLIGH   b. 1916; ed Downside; MP, Haltemprice 1955–   ; Member of the Monday Club.

WATERHOUSE, CHARLES   b 1893; ed Cheltenham and Cambridge; MP, Leicester 1924–57; member of Suez Group.

WATKINSON, HAROLD ARTHUR   b 1920; ed Queen's College, Taunton, and London; Chairman, Cadbury Schweppes, 1969–   ; MP, Woking 1950–64; Parliamentary Secretary, Minister of Labour, 1952–5; Minister of Transport, 1955–9; Minister of Defence, 1959–62.

BIOGRAPHIES

WHITELAW, WILLIAM   b. 1918; ed Winchester and Cambridge; MP,
Penrith & the Borders 1955–   ; Conservative Chief Whip, 1964–70; Lord
President and Leader of the House of Commons, 1970–2; Secretary of State for
Northern Ireland, 1972–3; Secretary for Employment, 1973–4.

WOOLTON, EARL OF (FREDERICK JAMES MARQUIS)   1883–1964; ed
Manchester G.S. and Manchester University; company director (retail trade);
Minister of Food, 1940–3; Minister of Reconstruction, 1943–5; Lord President,
1945 and 1951–2; Chancellor of the Duchy of Lancaster, 1952–5; Chairman of
the Conservative party, 1946–55.

WORSTHORNE, PEREGRINE   journalist—Deputy editor, *Sunday Telegraph*.

Notes

1 Main sources: *Who's Who*, 1973; D. E. Butler and J. Freeman, *British Political
Facts*, 1900–68.
2 Abbreviations: b. : born; ed : educated.
3 By no means all the public offices and company directorships held by the
individuals listed are included. Entries do not indicate necessarily that the
individual in question still holds a particular office or directorship, or belongs
to a particular political grouping, only that he did at some time in the period
covered by this book.

Notes

1 INTRODUCTION. THE CONSERVATIVE UNIVERSE: THE POLITICAL
MARKET AND THE STATE

1 C. Hollis, 'The merits and defects of Marx', in G. Woodcock, ed., *A Hundred Years of Revolution*, London 1948, p. 87.

2 F. J. C. Hearnshaw, *Conservatism in England*, London 1933, p. 20. A less ambitious pedigree is traced by L. Lipson, 'The two-party system in British politics', *American Political Science Review*, vol. 47, no. 2, June 1953, pp. 337-58.

3 Conservative principles are discussed at length by Russell Kirk, *The Conservative Mind*, London 1954, and by Clinton Rossiter, *Conservatism in America*, New York 1962. The Tory tradition as a tradition of ideas can be studied in R. J. White, ed., *The Conservative Tradition*, London 1964, and has been analysed by Harvey Glickman, 'The Toryness of English Conservatism', *Journal of British Studies*, vol. 1, no. 1, November 1961, pp. 111-43. He makes use of Samuel Huntington's distinction between situational and doctrinal Conservatism, which Huntington presents in 'Conservatism as an Ideology', *American Political Science Review*, vol. 51, no. 2, June 1957, pp. 454-73. This distinction, however, sheds more gloom than it dispels. See M. N. Rothbard's 'Comment' in the same volume of the *Review*, pp. 784-7. It is surprising how even authors of major studies of the Conservative party, including Nigel Harris, *Competition and the Corporate Society*, London 1972, and R. T. McKenzie and A. Silver, *Angels in Marble*, London 1968, feel obliged to adopt an idealist perspective and approach their subject through a discussion of Conservative philosophy and principles, as though these were the fount from which all else sprang.

4 M. Oakeshott, 'Contemporary British politics', *Cambridge Journal*, vol. 1, no. 8, May 1948, p. 476. See also 'Conservative political thought', *Spectator*, 15.10.1954, pp. 472-4. Oakeshott's work, which has influenced a number of important Conservative politicians, journalists, and academics, (among them, T. E. Utley, Russell Lewis, Peregrine Worsthorne, and Maurice Cowling), reflects the traditions of both English scepticism and English idealism. His political theories are best studied in his collection of essays, *Rationalism in Politics*, London 1962. His philosophical standpoint can be

found in *Experience and its Modes*, London 1966, and an abridgement of his
political and philosophical theories is given by W. H. Greenleaf, *Oakeshott's
Philosophical Politics*, London 1966.

5 M. Pinto-Duschinsky, *The Political Thought of Lord Salisbury*, London 1967,
p. 59.

6 This point is argued by Ralph Miliband, *The State in Capitalist Society*,
London 1969, ch. 3.

7 This concept of nation is developed in two articles by Tom Nairn, 'British
nationalism and the EEC', *New Left Review* 69, Sept.–Oct. 1971, pp. 3–28,
and 'The Left against Europe?', *New Left Review*, 75, Sept.–Oct. 1972. The
interrelation between the formal equality of citizens in the political system
and their inequality in the social relationships of production has been
brilliantly analysed by Lucio Colletti, *From Rousseau to Lenin*, London 1972.

8 During the history of the political market four major divisions have arisen;
landed and industrial property, finance and industrial capital, big capital and
small capital, the national economy and multi-national companies. These
divisions are analysed more fully in the Conclusion.

9 J. A. Schumpeter, *Capitalism, Socialism, and Democracy*, London 1950, p. 269.
Another major influence on the theory of democratic élitism that developed
in American political science was Gaetano Mosca, *The Ruling Class*, New
York 1939. For a sharp critique of the theory see Peter Bachrach, *The Theory
of Democratic Elitism*, London 1969.

10 This is fully reflected in the precise definitions of consumer and voter
sovereignty given by Talcott Parsons and W. White, 'The mass media and
the structure of American society', *Journal of Social Issues,* vol. 16, no. 3,
1960, pp. 67–77.

11 This notion and the concept of a political market is explored most fully by
A. Downs, *The Economic Theory of Democracy*, New York 1955. See also two
important studies that build on his work: M. Levin, *The Compleat Politician*,
New York 1962, and R. Rose, *Influencing Voters*, London 1967.

12 The most important is the mode of representation which greatly influences
the kind of party system that is established. The two extremes are propor-
tional representation and representation through single member constituencies. Also important are the relationship between the executive and the
legislature, the rules governing the financing of election campaigns, and the
established procedure for calling an election. For a thorough review of the
different consequences of different party systems, see E. Lakeman, *How
Democracies Vote*, London 1970.

13 Angus Maude, 'Party palaeontology', *Spectator*, 15.3.1963, p. 319.

14 On these questions see R. Rose, op. cit. On the use of television, see J.
Trenaman and D. McQuail, *Television and the Political Image*, London 1961;
J. G. Blumler and D. McQuail, *Television in Politics*, London 1968; D.
McQuail, *Towards a Sociology of Mass Communications*, London 1969; and
Lord Windlesham, *Communication and Political Power*, London 1966. On
polls see M. Abrams, 'Public opinion polls and political parties', *Public
Opinion Quarterly*, vol. 27, no. 1, Spring 1963, pp. 9–18, and D. E. G.
Plowman, 'Public opinion and the polls', *British Journal of Sociology*, vol. 13,
no. 4, December 1962, pp. 331–49.

15 See especially W. L. Guttsman, *The British Political Elite*, London 1963, Ch.

10, and R. T. McKenzie, *British Political Parties,* London 1963, Chs 2, 3. Guttsman also analyses in great detail the social composition of the Conservative party leaders, and shows the narrow social class from which they have been drawn.

16 See the major study of backbench opinion in the party by S. E. Finer, H. Berrington and D. Bartholomew, *Backbench Opinion in the House of Commons* London 1961.

17 See N. Harris, *Competition and the Corporate Society,* London 1972, pp. 246, 255, and Angus Maude, *The Common Problem,* London 1969.

18 The best definition of faction is that of Patrick Seyd in his article 'Faction-alism within the Conservative party: the Monday Club', *Government and Opposition,* Autumn 1972, p. 465: 'A group of party members operating within the framework of the parent political party which is consciously *organized* for the purpose of replacing the politics and/or the leadership of the parent party. The group will be united in its attitudes towards a *range of issues* over a *period of time,* since the members hold a common set of political values.'

19 The notion of a tendency is discussed by Richard Rose, *Politics in England,* London 1965, pp. 152-3. The tendencies he lists, however, are far too abstract and general. In this book, tendencies are defined by the attitude they express towards the established consensus. A tendency by definition is not organized. It is a body of sentiment and opinion. Conservatives are therefore not tied to one tendency. Lord Hinchingbrooke for example was a prominent Right Progressive on the question of government intervention in the economy and the need for a political settlement with organized labour, but he remained an Imperialist on most questions of foreign policy. In the 1960s he gravitated to the New Right.

20 An additional reason for their absence is the remarkably similar social and educational background of Conservative MPs. See Guttsman, op. cit., and J. Blondel, *Voters, Parties, Leaders,* London 1963, ch. 5.

21 The contrary is the case. The greatest controversies in the party in the first half of this century were over tariff reform, Ireland, and India.

22 In accounting for Conservative success far too much attention has been paid to the character of Conservative support and British political culture, in particular the presumed existence of deferential working men, and far too little to the peculiar British electoral system, and the social structure. A fuller analysis of these questions is given in the concluding chapter.

23 David Butler and Donald Stokes have presented evidence in *Political Change in Britain,* London 1969, to show that working class Conservatism is declining, and Labour's support growing, as different age cohorts of electors pass through the political system.

24 These fears were set down by Ostrogorski, in *Democracy and the Organization of Political Parties,* London 1902. See A. Beattie, 'British coalition government revisited', *Government and Opposition,* vol. 2, no. 1, Oct. 1966–Jan. 1967, pp. 3–34, and Samuel Beer, *Modern British Politics,* London 1965, for discussion of the new conception of party introduced by universal suffrage. A major work on modern party systems is S. M. Lipset and S. Rokkan, ed., *Party Systems and Voter Alignments,* New York 1967. They distinguish between the expressive, representative, and integrative functions of modern parties.

25 See for example B. Crick, *The Reform of Parliament*, London 1967, and C. Hollis, *Can Parliament Survive?* London 1949.

26 Cf. A. Beattie, op. cit., and R. T. McKenzie, *British Political Parties*, London 1963. See also John Vincent, *The Formation of the British Liberal Party*, London 1966, especially the Introduction, and M. Cowling, *The Impact of Labour 1920–1924*, Cambridge 1971. For a detailed study of the party in Parliament see R. Butt, *The Power of Parliament*, London 1967. The history and influence of the 1922 Committee, the organization of Conservative backbenchers, can be found in McKenzie, op. cit., and P. Goodhart, *The 1922*, London 1973.

27 For the history and development of the National Union see McKenzie, op. cit, Ch. 4. The story of Lord Randolph Churchill's bid to dominate the party through control of the National Union is told by R. R. James, *Lord Randolph Churchill*, London 1959. The solid middle-class character of the Conservative party in the constituencies is shown by the analysis of constituency associations conducted by F. Bealey, J. Blondel and W. P. McCann, *Constituency Politics*, London 1965.

28 A strong criticism of this view of the Conservative party is made by M. Pinto-Duschinsky, 'Central Office and "power" in the Conservative party', *Political Studies*, vol. 20, no. 1, March 1972, pp. 1–16.

29 C. Hollis, *Spectator*, 21.10.1960, p. 586.

30 *Spectator*, 10.10.1958, p. 474.

31 A study of conference debates can give only a limited view of the ideological debate within the party. This is because very few delegates are able to speak, and it is impossible to determine how representative they are of the Conservative conference, still less of the rank and file of the party as a whole. The same is true of the resolutions that are printed in the conference agenda. What a study of the debates does offer is an understanding of the pattern of Conservative ideology and opinion—the main themes, anxieties and demands that were publicly expressed. The main subjects of debate stayed more or less constant, so the evolution of opinion on different topics can be studied over a period of time. In the analysis of trends in conference opinion that appears in some of the chapters of this book, no attempt will be made to provide a full summary of every point of view expressed in a particular debate, nor of each speaker's argument. The choice of passages is inevitably highly selective, and is based on the theoretical and historical analysis of the Conservative party, the political market, and the British state, that is set out in the first two chapters and the Conclusion. Direct quotation rather than summary has often been used, in order to give the reader an idea not merely of the content, but also of the form and style of Conservative ideas.

32 This is the definition of ideology used by Clifford Geertz, 'Ideology as a cultural system', in D. Apter, *Ideology and Discontent*, London 1964. Geertz provides a telling critique of both the interest and the strain theory of ideology. See also Murray Edelman, *The Symbolic Uses of Politics*, Urbana, 1964. A general survey of different theories of ideology is given by Nigel Harris in *Beliefs in Society*, London 1968.

33 A possibility discussed by Ulf Himmelstrand, 'A theoretical and empirical approach to depoliticization and political involvement', *Acta Sociologica*, vol. 6, no. 1–2, 1962, pp. 83–110.

2 THE CHANGING TORIES: THE ROAD TO THE POLITICAL
SETTLEMENT

1 Quoted by W. L. Burn, 'The Conservative tradition and its reformulations', in M. Ginsberg, ed., *Law and Opinion in the Twentieth Century*,
London 1959, p. 43.

2 The history of the old Tory party is lovingly described by Keith Feiling,
History of the Tory Party 1640–1714, Oxford, 1924, and *The Second Tory
Party 1714–1832*, London 1938. The conceptual framework of these books
was brought into serious question by the work of Namier and his associates.
For the party in the nineteenth century, the best general treatment is by
R. B. McDowell, *British Conservatism, 1832–1914*, London 1959.

3 See R. Blake, *The Conservative party from Peel to Churchill*, Ch. 3, and P.
Anderson, 'Origins of the present crisis', *New Left Review* 23, Jan.–Feb. 1964.

4 The best biography of Disraeli and analysis of his politics is by Robert Blake,
Disraeli, London 1969.

5 For an exhaustive account of them see M. Cowling, *1867, Disraeli, Gladstone,
and Revolution*, London 1967.

6 The key elements of a One Nation strategy are (1) the provision of strong,
able leadership (2) the building of support around national rather than class
issues and (3) the identification of the party with the prevailing consensus.
Kenneth Pickthorn has some interesting reflections on the necessity of
national politics for the Conservatives in *Principles or Prejudices*, Signpost
Books, London 1943.

7 Typical Conservative publications on these themes are *What the Conservatives
have done for the British people*, London 1963, and C. E. Bellairs, *Conservative
Social and Industrial Reform*, CPC, London 1947. Two socialist analyses of the
substance in Tory claims to be the party of One Nation are supplied by Peter
Shore, *The Real Nature of Conservatism*, London 1952, and Michael Barratt
Brown, *Who Are the Tories?* London 1959.

8 Northern Ireland has been the main exception. Otherwise the class alignment
became dominant everywhere once the earlier religious alignment began to
decline. See R. R. Alford, *Party and Society*, London 1964, and S. M. Lipset
and S. Rokkan, ed., *Party Systems and Voter Alignments*, for a comparative
perspective on the British political system. See also the discussion by D. E.
Butler and D. Stokes, *Political Change in Britain*, London 1969, part 1.

9 See H. J. Hanham, *Elections and Party Management*, London 1959.

10 Cf. E. J. Feuchtwanger, *Disraeli, Democracy, and the Tory Party*, Oxford 1968.

11 The imperial ideology is explored by A. P. Thornton, *The Imperial Idea and
its Enemies*, London 1959.

12 On Chamberlain see J. Amery, *Joseph Chamberlain and the Tariff Reform
Campaign*, London 1969. Chamberlain's importance to the Conservatives
was that he brought new sections of middle-class and working-class support
to the party. The name of the party was changed to Unionist, to emphasize
the importance of the Irish issue and the adherence of the Liberal Unionists
to the Conservative camp.

13 After the 1885 reform redrew the boundaries to give fairer representation to
the urban areas, manual workers dominated the political market. Since that
time they have never comprised less than two thirds of the total population.

By contrast, two thirds of Conservative MPs in the 1870s were still connected with the land.

14 Despite growing awareness of the existence of classes as a possible new basis of alignment, church membership had remained more important in determining how people voted, despite brief flirtations by some politicians —notably Lord Randolph Churchill—with different strategies. Much more determined attempts to attract votes on a class basis were made by both Conservative and Liberal politicians after 1900.

15 See J. R. Jones, 'England', in H. Rogger and E. Weber, eds, *The European Right*, London 1965.

16 For the history of the controversy, see Julian Amery, op. cit., and R. A. Rempel, *Unionists Divided*, London 1972.

17 See Rempel, op. cit., Chs 14, 15.

18 See A. K. Russell, *Liberal Landslide*, London 1973, Ch. 3, for an interesting analysis of the election addresses of Unionist candidates, which reveals that only 2 per cent supported a 10 per cent general tariff and a preference duty on corn. Between 55 and 60 per cent of candidates took refuge in vague evasive formulas on tariff reform. It seems clear that had the Tories remained a party of government, the leadership could have avoided a full-scale commitment to tariff reform.

19 See J. R. Jones, op. cit., for an analysis of the Right in the party.

20 Cf. H. Pelling, *A History of British Trade Unionism*, London 1971, Ch. 8.

21 The manoeuvring of the politicians is described by M. Cowling, *The Impact of Labour 1920–4*, London 1971. Labour became recognized as the main party of opposition, and social class thus became the most important basis for political alignment. The nature of this class alignment is discussed more fully in the Conclusion. Butler and Stokes, op. cit., make the important point that Labour did not simply displace the Liberals as the main alternative party and capture their electoral support. A much more complex realignment of political forces took place.

22 Cf. Michael Oakeshott, 'Contemporary British politics', *Cambridge Journal*, vol. 1, no. 8, May 1948, p. 474; P. Worsthorne, 'Democracy versus liberty?' *Encounter*, vol. 6, no. 1, January 1956, p. 6; and T. E. Utley, 'The mandate', *Cambridge Journal*, vol. 3, no. 1, October 1949, p. 17. See also L. S. Amery, *Thoughts on the Constitution*, London 1953, for an authoritative Tory view of the constitution.

23 For the organization and early history of the Labour party see H. Pelling, *Short History of the Labour Party*, London 1968, and R. T. McKenzie, *British Political Parties*, London 1963, introduction and part II.

24 The Government's Irish policy was the other main grievance of the Tory rank and file. For an account of the downfall of the Coalition by one of its leading opponents see L. S. Amery, *My Political Life*, London 1953.

25 See Julian Amery, op. cit., pp. 1003f. and Lord Beaverbrook, *Politicians and the War*, London 1959.

26 Best accounts of the General Strike are by J. T. Murphy, *Preparing For Power*, London 1970, Ch. 12, and R. P. Arnot, *The General Strike; its origin and history*, Labour Research Department, London 1926.

27 The best study of the politics of the Second Labour Government is by Robert Skidelsky, *Politicians and the Slump*, London 1967. This is a masterly

analysis of the prevailing politics of power, but note the astute criticism of its technocratic bias by Royden Harrison, 'Labour government: then and now', *Political Quarterly*, vol. 41, no. 1, Jan.–March 1970, pp. 67–82.

28 For the theory of corporatism and its influence on the Conservative party and business in the 1930s see Nigel Harris, *Competition and the Corporate Society*, London 1972. The ideas of one of its leading exponents, the 'semi-socialist' Captain Harold Macmillan can be found in *The Middle Way*, London 1938.

29 Gross trading profits slumped to £373 million in 1932, but reached £738 million in 1937.

30 For an account of the New Deal see E. W. Hawley, *The New Deal and the Problem of Monopoly*, Princeton 1966.

31 In Germany, the share of profits in National Income rose from 17·4 per cent in 1932 to 25·4 per cent in 1937. Wage rates rose 8 per cent while prices were allowed to rise 25 per cent. See E. Mandel, *Marxist Economic Theory*, London 1968, p. 537.

32 See Julian Amery, op. cit. A good general history of the interwar years is C. L. Mowat, *Britain between the Wars*, London 1955. The best economic survey of the Depression is still H. W. Arndt, *The Economic Lessons of the 1930s*, Oxford 1944.

33 J. Strachey, in A. Rogow and P. Shore, *The Labour Government and British Industry 1945–51*, Oxford 1955, p. x.

34 The war brought a shift in the balance of power between labour and capital, which was then reflected in a reorganization of the state. On the conditions for the unions' cooperation in the war effort see H. Pelling, *A History of Trade Unionism*, Ch. 11.

35 See the excellent biography of Churchill by Robert Rhodes James, *Churchill: A Study in Failure 1900–1939*, London 1970.

36 The report, published in November 1942 sold 256,000 copies, and a further 369,000 copies in an abridged version. On the report and its reception see Pauline Gregg, *The Welfare State*, London 1967.

37 The representation of interests in the new state, and the increased bargaining power conferred upon organized interest groups is analysed by Samuel Beer, *Modern British Politics*, London, 1965, using a theoretical framework drawn from Parsons and pluralism. The economic basis of the new state is brilliantly analysed by Paul Mattick, *Marx and Keynes*, London 1971. See also David Yaffe, 'The Marxian theory of crisis, capital, and the state', *Conference of Socialist Economists Bulletin*, Winter 1972, pp. 5–58. For a theoretical analysis from a different perspective see J. K. Galbraith, *The New Industrial State*, London 1967. An institutional and policy analysis of the new state as it developed in Britain and other countries is given by Andrew Shonfield, *Modern Capitalism*, London 1969. The financing of the state is the subject of A. T. Peacock and J. Wiseman, *The Growth of Public Expenditure in the U.K.*, London 1967.

38 See Michael Barratt Brown, *From Labourism to Socialism*, Nottingham 1972, p. 78, table 3.2. This book provides invaluable empirical analysis of the political economy of modern Britain.

39 Productive labour is labour that increases capital. Unproductive labour is financed out of revenue. This distinction has nothing to do with the

distinction between useful and non-useful labour or material and non-material labour. Marx's discussion of the distinction can be found in *Theories of Surplus Value*, part I, London 1969. From the standpoint of private capital most state expenditure is unproductive because it has to be financed out of revenue, however necessary it may be to the long-term interests of capital.

40 For the historical development of Britain's relationship with the world market see E. J. Hobsbawm, *Industry and Empire*, London 1969. For the modern period the most comprehensive and lucid analysis is S. Pollard, *The Development of the British Economy 1914–67*, London 1967.

41 Cf. S. Brittan, *Steering the Economy*, London 1971, and an earlier analysis by A. Shonfield, *British Economic Policy since the War*, London 1958.

42 For an analysis of the Tory Reform Committee see H. Kopsch. 'The approach of the Conservative party to social policy during World War II', Unpublished Ph. D. thesis, London 1970. In general the group supported the interests of industrial capital against finance capital.

43 Lord Hinchingbrooke, *Full Speed Ahead: Essays in Tory Reform*, London 1944, p. 38.

44 Ibid., p. 72.

45 Quintin Hogg, *One Year's Work*, London 1944, p. 77.

46 Ibid., p. 60.

47 Ibid., p. 60. The reference was to Disraeli's Crystal Palace speech of 1872.

48 Ibid., p. 44.

49 *Onlooker*, August 1944, p. 6.

50 David Eccles, *Onlooker*, November 1944, p. 7.

51 *Onlooker*, July 1944. The reviews of the books by Amery and Boothby appeared in the April 1944 issue.

52 A. G. Erskine-Hill, *Onlooker*, February 1945, p. 3.

53 Ibid., p. 3.

54 The Progress Trust is discussed by Kopsch, op. cit. It was the first expression of the whig tendency of opinion towards the post-war settlement in the party.

55 Aubrey Jones for one. See his pamphlet, *Right and Left*, Signpost Books, London 1944.

56 This was the nickname for a reform group organized in the parliamentary party during the 1920s. It was inspired by the ideas of Noel Skelton. See his *Constructive Conservatism*, London 1924. See also H. Macmillan, *Winds of Change*, London 1966.

57 Lord Woolton, *Memoirs*, London 1959, p. 257.

58 It is interesting that several of the original Tory Reform Committee, notably Lord Hinchingbrooke and David Gammans, were prominent spokesmen for the imperialist wing of the diehard tendency of opinion after 1945. In the past imperialism had always been associated with social reform in the party, but this was not to be the case after the war. Thorneycroft and Hogg were more in the mainstream of Right Progressive thinking in their support for the Atlantic alliance and the consequent surrender of an independent Empire policy.

3 REORGANIZATION AND RECOVERY: OPPOSITION 1945–51

1 Quoted by R. A. Butler, *The Art of the Possible*, London 1971, p. 130.

2 Ibid., Ch. 7.
3 Gallup predicted the result remarkably accurately, but polls were hardly noticed at that time.
4 N. Harris, *Competition and the Corporate Society*, London 1972, pp. 61, 78.
5 The Conservative party cannot be regarded as being the mere mouthpiece of business interests. The relationship is far more complex, as the discussion in the preceding chapter was intended to show. For a careful review of the problem see S. E. Finer, 'The political power of private capital', *Sociological Review*, vol. 3, no. 2, December 1955, pp. 270–94, and vol. 4, no. 1, July 1956, pp. 5–30. In this book it is argued that the real power of the different sections of private capital is shown by the established priorities of government policy. Direct business pressure is not often necessary to secure their interests. None the less, business interests are well represented in the Conservative party. The business links of Conservative MPs in the 1930s were catalogued by Simon Haxey, *Tory M.P.*, London 1939. Similar investigations for the postwar party have been conducted by W. L. Guttsman, *The British Political Elite*, London 1963, Ch. 10, esp. pp. 296–7, and Andrew Roth, *The Business Background of MPs*, London 1972. See also Michael Barratt Brown, *Who Are the Tories?* London 1959. In the past the party has been a battleground for the opposing interests of different sections of capital. Since the 1920s, however, business has been more united, although strains do periodically re-appear and are reflected in the Conservative party. In the post-war period, the split between small business and big business, and between the interests of the national economy and the new multinational companies, had important repercussions on the internal politics of the Conservative party.
6 *British Gazette* was the Government newspaper, edited by Churchill, during the General Strike. It took a hardline against the strikers and suppressed all information unfavourable to the Government, particularly the growth in the strength and militancy of the strike.
7 See R. Rhodes James, *Churchill: A Study in Failure 1900–1939*, London 1970, for an assessment of Churchill's reputation in the 1930s.
8 Cf. R. B. McCallum and A. Readman, *The British General Election of 1945*, London 1947, Ch. 2.
9 R. A. Butler, op. cit., p. 129.
10 H. Macmillan, *Tides of Fortune*, London 1969, p. 32.
11 R. A. Butler, op. cit., p. 129.
12 H. Macmillan, op. cit., p. 34.
13 Cf. J. T. Murphy, *Preparing for Power*, London 1970.
14 H. Macmillan, op. cit., p. 34.
15 Quoted in K. Young, *Sir Alec Douglas-Home*, London 1970, p. 71. Home, as Lord Dunglass, had been Chamberlain's Parliamentary Secretary. During these years of opposition he was not associated with the right progressive tendency of opinion.
16 R. A. Butler, op. cit., p. 126.
17 J. D. Hoffman argues in *The Conservative Party in Opposition*, London 1964, that the organizational changes made no contribution to restoring the Conservatives to office. But he does not consider their important role in the development of the new electoral perspective of the leadership.
18 The young Conservatives were the successors to the Junior Imperial and

Constitutional League (the Imps), founded in 1906. Between the wars the Imps claimed 250,000 members. Sir Alec Douglas-Home was their chairman from 1937–9. The membership of the Young Conservatives reached 100,000, but declined after 1960. The Imps had been firmly wedded to the imperialist ideology. The leaders of the Young Conservatives by contrast belonged to the right progressive tendency and were to become enthusiastic supporters of modernization and the competition policy. The pages of the YC magazines (*Advance*, 1946–53; *Rightway*, 1954–5; and *Impact*, 1964–8) need only be compared with those of the Imps' magazines (*Junior Imperial League Gazette*, 1920–5; *The Imp*, 1925–32; and *Torchbearer*, 1937–9), for the changed orientation of the Conservatives' youth movement to be apparent. The YC organization has been analysed by P. Abrams and A. Little, 'The young activist in British politics', *British Journal of Sociology*, vol. 16, no. 4, December 1965, pp. 315–33. The organization has served two main functions. It provided 'organized gregariousness' for the children of the suburbs, and a stage in the professional career structure of Conservative politicians. Former YC leaders include Anthony Nutting, Peter Walker, Andrew Bowden, Nicholas Scott, and John Selwyn Gummer. In 1964, one hundred and eleven Conservative parliamentary candidates were former Young Conservatives. There was naturally a conflict of aims and definitions between the bulk of the membership and the leaders, who frequently complained about the low political level of the branches. Cf. also the strictures of *Crossbow*, esp. in nos 4, 10, 13, 18, 19, 50.

19 For an account of its work see D. Maxwell-Fyfe (Lord Kilmuir), *Political Adventure*, London 1964.

20 The main source of funds remained contributions from business firms, but fundraising from the large nominal membership of the party—it reached over two million in the 1950s—was increasingly attempted. For a tribute to Woolton's work as Chairman see *CPCR 1955* p. 116, and his speech in reply.

21 The setting up of the CPC, the extension of the CRD, and the opening of Swinton College (which ran weekend courses and seminars), were all means to this end.

22 *Tory Challenge*, November 1947, p. 1.

23 Quintin Hogg, quoted in R. A. Butler, op. cit., p. 133.

24 W. W. Astor, 'The Conservative Party in Opposition', *New English Review*, vol. 12, no. 4, April 1946, pp. 344–8.

25 R. A. Butler, in *Conservatism 1945–50*, CPC, London 1950, p. 3.

26 R. A. Butler, *The Art of the Possible*, pp. 133–4.

27 The Industrial Charter (1947) and the Imperial Charter (1949) were the two main ones. The former broke more new ground than the latter. There were other charters too on agriculture and Wales.

28 N. Harris, op. cit., pp. 77, 82, 145. It also swept through the Labour party. The Labour Government's Development Councils, at first welcomed by industry, were one of the casualties of the revival of prosperity.

29 R. A. Butler, in *Conservatism 1945–50*, p. 1.

30 C. Hill, *Both Sides of the Hill*, London 1964, pp. 9–10.

31 R. A. Butler, *The Art of the Possible*, Ch. 7. The Charter sold $2\frac{1}{2}$ million copies in six months. The members of the committee that drew up the Charter were Butler (Chairman), Oliver Stanley, Oliver Lyttleton, Harold

Macmillan, David Eccles, P. F. Bennett, and David Maxwell-Fyfe.

32 *Truth*, 1.10.1948. See also the *Recorder*, which took a similar line.

33 *Truth*, 21.1.1949, p. 61.

34 *Truth*, 29.7.1949, p. 119.

35 H. Macmillan, op. cit., p. 306.

36 Ibid., p. 302. Cf. *CPCR 1947*, pp. 113–14.

37 *Truth*, 4.3.1949. An effort to defend the Tory record was M. Maybury, *The Truth about the Interwar Years. An exposure of the Socialist Myth*, CUCO, London 1949. Cf. also *Tory Challenge*, (*passim*) especially some of Illing-worth's cartoons, e.g. 'The Bad Old Days—1938; 1948—The Socialist Utopia', March 1948, p. 3.

38 Aubrey Jones, *The Pendulum of Politics*, London 1946, p. 13.

39 Ibid., p. 168.

40 Ibid., p. 166.

41 Aubrey Jones, 'Conservatism and capitalism', *Nineteenth Century and After*, June 1947, p. 271.

42 Aubrey Jones, *Industrial Order*, London 1950, p. 38.

43 Aubrey Jones, 'Conservatives in conference', *Nineteenth Century and After*, November 1947, p. 219.

44 Aubrey Jones, *Industrial Order*, p. 12.

45 See his reasons for supporting the Industrial Charter, 'Why I welcome the Industrial Charter', *Tory Challenge*, August 1947. The same theme reappears in his latest book, *The New Inflation*, London 1973.

46 *Spectator*, 28.10.1955, p. 543.

47 Michael Oakeshott, 'Contemporary British Politics', *Cambridge Journal*, vol. 1, no. 8, May 1948, p. 478.

48 Ibid., p. 488.

49 Richard Law, *Return from Utopia*, London 1950, p. 29.

50 Ibid., p. 45.

51 Cf. A. Rogow and P. Shore, *The Labour Government and British Industry*, Oxford 1955; J. C. R. Dow, *The Management of the British Economy*, Cambridge 1970, Ch. 2.; and N. Harris, op. cit., p. 123. Productive industry here refers to large-scale industry. Small business, whose interests were reflected by the whig tendency, would probably have favoured a measure of retrenchment, and a reduction in the burden of taxation.

52 For the Correspondence, see *The Times*, 3 March to 12 April 1949.

53 T. E. Utley, 'Conservative dilemma', *Spectator*, 25.3.1949, p. 388.

54 F. J. C. Hearnshaw, *Conservatism in England*, London 1933, p. 56.

55 Influential statements of the notion include H. Macmillan, *The Middle Way*, London 1938; Quintin Hogg, *The Case for Conservatism*, London 1947; and J. Boyd-Carpenter, *The Conservative Case*, London 1950.

56 J. Boyd-Carpenter, op. cit., p. 7. Maybe he had forgotten Lord Keynes's aphorism.

57 Quintin Hogg, op. cit.,

58 H. Macmillan, *Winds of Change*, London 1966, pp. 223–4. His books and pamphlets in the interwar years included *Industry and the State*, London 1927; *The Next Step*, London 1932; *Reconstruction—the plea for a national policy*, London 1933; and *The Middle Way*, London 1938.

59 Compare for instance *Right Road for Britain* with the *Industrial Charter*.

60 D. Maxwell-Fyfe, op. cit., p. 138.

61 Ibid., p. 168.

62 R. A. Butler, *The Art of the Possible*, p. 132.

63 On the average percentage vote per opposed candidate Labour also did better in 1951 than the Conservatives: 49·2 per cent, compared to 48·6 per cent for the Conservatives. The Conservatives only reversed this ratio in 1955 and 1959. See D. E. Butler and J. Freeman, *British Political Facts 1900–68*, London 1969, p. 143.

64 *Notes on Current Politics*, which is compiled and published by the Conservative Research Department, tried bravely to explain away the statistics that showed Labour had polled more votes, but finally had to admit that they had. See their issue of 26 November 1951.

65 Cf. R. Crossman, 'The Lessons of 1945' in P. Anderson and R. Blackburn, eds, *Towards Socialism*, London 1965.

66 The free enterprise campaign waged by the steel industry, and Tate and Lyle, in the shape of Mr Cube, contributed to the breakdown of Labour morale and nerve. See Rogow and Shore, op. cit. Aims of Industry, the business pressure group, was also active. Its activities and finances are analysed by R. Rose, *Influencing Voters*, London 1967.

67 Their position was well summed up by Eden: 'I would have agreed with him more, if I had not been anxious to embarrass him less.' A. Eden, *Full Circle*, London 1960, p. 5.

68 There was only token opposition. Cf. N. Harris, op. cit., Ch. 6; J. D. Hoffman, op. cit. Rogow and Shore, op. cit., note that all the early nationalization measures were based on reports prepared by Tory dominated committees during the war. Cf. Macmillan's sly comment in his memoirs: 'It has perhaps proved unfortunate from the point of view of those anxious to extend the process that so many of these industries were already declining in the immediate post-war period.' *Tides of Fortune*, London 1969, p. 74. Calls for denationalization and a roll-back of the state were raised in the party in 1947 (see N. Harris, op. cit., p. 130) by elements of the whig tendency. This feeling was manipulated by the leadership for electoral purposes, but, as it was to show in government, it had no serious intention of reversing the majority of Labour's measures.

69 H. Macmillan, *Tides of Fortune*, p. 291. Cf. A. Eden, *Notes on Current Politics*, 27.3.1950, and Lord Woolton, *Tory Challenge*, October 1949, p. 1.

70 R. A. Butler, 'Conservative policy', *Political Quarterly*, vol. 20, no. 4, Oct.–Dec. 1949, p. 318.

71 Ibid., p. 320.

72 *Tory Challenge*, November 1946, p. 6.

73 *Notes on Current Politics*, 1.2.1950, p. 8.

74 F. W. S. Craig, ed., *British General Election Manifestos, 1918–66*, Chichester 1970, pp. 113, 114.

75 Ibid., p. 120.

76 Ibid., p. 143.

77 Ibid., p. 144.

78 *Conservatism 1945–50*, CPC ,London 1950, pp. 83, 79, 102.

79 It was with some dismay therefore that the ideological champions of free enterprise contemplated the tame and in some cases only too willing surrender

of their industries by private owners and shareholders during the early years of Labour rule in return for generous compensation. For a typical Whig lament see the speech by P. J. Williams, *CPCR 1949*, p. 46.

80 *Conservatism 1945–50*, p. 106.

81 C. Hollis, 'Where should the Left be?', *Spectator*, 14.4.1950, p. 490. The leadership was noticeably reluctant to give firm pledges on denationalization. Reorganization and decentralization were stressed instead. See, for example, O. Lyttleton, *CPCR 1949*, p. 51. When the Conservatives were returned to power, considerable backbench pressure was required to get the Government to proceed even with denationalizing steel and road haulage. Cf. W. A. Robson, *Nationalized Industry and Public Ownership*, London 1962, p. 43, and R. Butt, *The Power of Parliament*, London 1967.

82 Walter Elliott, 'Why the £600-a-year man is so important', *Tory Challenge*, July 1947, p. 5. See also the debate on lower salaried and fixed income groups, *CPCR 1947*, and the debate on class warfare, *CPCR 1949*.

83 *Tory Challenge*, December 1947, p. 2.

84 *Tory Challenge*, December 1949, p. 5. Throughout the years of opposition, *Tory Challenge* ran a series on Tory workers from different industries.

85 B. Child 'Fair trade for the shopkeeper', *Crossbow*, 27, 1964, p. 19.

86 R. Carr, *CPCR 1947*, p. 80.

87 Eden revived the phrase in a speech at the 1946 conference.

88 David Eccles, *The New Conservatism*, 4 August 1951, p. 4.

89 Angus Maude, 'The Conservative party and the changing class structure', *Political Quarterly*, vol. 24, no. 2, April–June 1953, p. 141. Modern research into voting behaviour has confirmed the great importance that self-identity has in determining how people vote. See, for example, R. T. McKenzie and A. Silver, *Angels in Marble*, London 1968, Ch. 6. Angus Maude, soon to become Director of the CPC, also wrote at this time with Roy Lewis two books on the middle classes: *The English Middle Classes*, London 1950, and *Professional People*, London 1952.

4 THE STALEMATE STATE: POWER 1951–64

1 Winston Churchill, *CPCR 1954*, p. 114.

2 The term was used by *The Economist* to describe the similarity in the policies pursued by Butler and Gaitskell as Chancellors of the Exchequer.

3 P. Worsthorne, 'Class and class conflict in British foreign policy', *Foreign Affairs*, vol. 37, no. 3, April 1959, p. 431.

4 See L. A. Siedentop, 'Mr Macmillan and the Edwardian style', in V. Bogdanor and R. Skidelsky, eds, *The Age of Affluence*, London 1970, pp. 17–54; A. Sampson, *Macmillan*, London 1967; and H. Berkeley, *Crossing the Floor*, London 1972, pp. 81, 83, 86.

5 It is termed 'neo-liberalism' by J. D. Hoffman, *The Conservative Party in Opposition*, London 1964, and N. Harris, *Competition and the Corporate Society*, London 1972, pp. 73–4, 80. See C. J. Friedrich, 'The political thought of neo-Liberalism', *American Political Science Review*, vol. 49, no. 2, June 1955, pp. 509–25, for a discussion of neo-Liberal ideas and the social market economy in West Germany.

6 T. E. Utley, *Not Guilty*, London 1957, p. 10.

7 P. Worsthorne, op. cit., pp. 420–1.

8 Cf. Lord Hinchingbrooke, *CPCR 1952*, p. 72.

9 The One Nation Group, founded in the 1950 Parliament, included Macleod, Powell, Heath, Carr, Maudling and Maude. It was an informal discussion group which met weekly, and was at first firmly associated with Right Progressive opinion. Members resigned when they became Ministers. Later MPs invited to join included Lord Balneil, William Deedes, Sir Keith Joseph, Geoffrey Rippon, Christopher Chataway, and Nicholas Ridley. A surprising number of Conservative leaders thus passed through the Group, although not all remained committed to Right Progressive thinking. As an educational forum for future leaders it was unique. Its name is highly significant in this connection, reflecting concern for the fundamental requirements of Conservative electoral strategy. Heath and Powell were to interpret the precept rather differently, however. Pamphlets published by the Group were *One Nation*, 1950; *Change is our Ally*, ed. E. Powell and A. Maude, 1954; *The Responsible Society*, 1959; *One Europe*, ed. N. Ridley, 1965.

10 See the One Nation Group pamphlets and I. Macleod and E. Powell, *The Social Services: Needs and Means*, CPC, London 1952 and 1954; also G. Howe, 'Reform of the social services', in D. Howell and T. Raison eds, *Principles in Practice*, CPC, London 1961, and K. Joseph, 'Way ahead for welfare', *Crossbow* 6, 1959.

11 David Eccles, 'Popular capitalism', *Objective*, no. 20, January 1955, p. 5.

12 Ibid., p. 6. But see his later doubts in *Life and Politics*, London 1967.

13 Examples abound. See, for instance, Quintin Hogg, *CPCR 1958*, p. 153; Lord Hinchingbrooke, *CPCR 1961*, p. 56; and Iain Macleod, *CPCR 1962*, pp. 125–6. For political science, see Samuel Beer, 'Democratic one party government for Britain?' *Political Quarterly*, vol. 32, no. 2, April–June 1961, pp. 114–23, and M. Abrams and R. Rose, *Must Labour Lose?* London 1960. Their confident predictions of the Labour Party's imminent demise as a serious electoral competitor were based partly on an extrapolation of existing trends in electoral behaviour, partly on the end of ideology thesis which so bemused the minds of western liberals, and partly from the kind of analysis of western political systems put forward by Otto Kirchheimer, for example, in 'The waning of opposition in parliamentary regimes', *Social Research*, vol. 24, no. 2, Summer 1957, pp. 127–56.

14 R. A. Butler, 'Trustees of prosperity', in *Accent on Youth*, CPC SC, London 1960, p. 9.

15 Quintin Hogg, 'Introduction' in *Prospect for Capitalism*, CPC SC, London 1958, p. 8.

16 F. W. S. Craig, ed., *British General Election Manifestos 1918–66*, Chichester 1970, p. 158.

17 Ibid., p. 169.

18 Ibid., p. 189.

19 Ibid., p. 196.

20 For sociological writing on the rise of the affluent worker and its political consequences, see F. Zweig, *The Worker in an Affluent Society*, London 1961, probably the clearest expression of the 'embourgeoisement' thesis. See also M. Abrams, 'The future of the Left: new roots of working class Conservatism', *Encounter*, vol. 14, no. 5, May 1960, pp. 57–9, 'Class and politics', *Encounter*, October 1961, pp. 39–44, and 'Class distinctions in Britain', in

The Future of the Welfare State, CPC SC, London 1957; and Michel Crozier, 'Classes sans conscience, ou préfiguration de la société sans classes', *European Journal of Sociology*, vol. 1, no. 2, 1960, pp. 233–47. For critiques of the theory see J. H. Goldthorpe and D. Lockwood, 'Affluence and the British class structure', *Sociological Review*, vol. 11, no. 2, July 1963, and J. H. Goldthorpe et al., *The Affluent Worker: Political Attitudes and Behaviour*, Cambridge 1968, and *The Affluent Worker in the Class Structure*, Cambridge 1969. See also John Westergaard, 'The withering away of class', in P. Anderson and R. Blackburn, eds, *Towards Socialism*, London 1965, and a general review of the whole controversy by T. B. Bottomore, 'Class structure in Western Europe', in M. S. Archer and S. Giner, eds, *Contemporary Europe: Class, Status, and Power*, London 1971.

21 H. Macmillan, *Pointing the Way*, London 1972, p. 15.

22 The most useful source for information about British electoral behaviour since 1945 is the Nuffield election studies. See also R. S. Milne and H. C. Mackenzie, *Straight Fight*, London 1954, and *Marginal Seat*, London 1958, and for criticism of the concept of the floating vote, *Floating Voters and the Floating Vote*, Leiden 1961. The outstanding work on electoral behaviour, which shows a rare grasp of both theoretical and empirical analysis is D. E. Butler and D. Stokes, *Political Change in Britain*, London 1969.

23 A. Downs, *The Economic Theory of Democracy*, New York 1955, p. 97. Economic and sociological theories of the modern western democracies are discussed in some detail by B. Barry, *Sociologists, Economists, and Democracy*, London 1970.

24 See J. Blumler and D. McQuail, *Television in Politics*, London 1968.

25 See M. Levin, *The Compleat Politician*, New York 1962, and *The Alienated Voter*, New York 1966. For Britain the notion of a rational campaign strategy has been used by R. Rose in *Influencing Voters*, London 1967.

26 R. Rose, op. cit., p. 28.

27 M. Levin, *The Compleat Politician*, p. 141.

28 R. Samuel, 'The deference voter', *New Left Review*, 1, Jan.–Feb. 1960, pp. 9–13. See also his later article, 'Dr Abrams and the end of politics', *New Left Review*, 5, Sept.–Oct. 1960, pp. 2–9.

29 G. Dowson, 'The product—politics', *Impact*, Summer 1967, p. 9. Cf. G. Pattie, 'Marketing the Tories', *Crossbow*, 47, 1969.

30 See R. Rose, op. cit, Ch. 2.

31 On the theory and practice of the electoral cycle, see Michael Kalecki's original far-sighted article, reprinted in *Selected Essays on the Dynamics of a Capitalist Economy*, Cambridge 1971; J. Hughes, 'The British economy: crisis and structural change', *New Left Review* 21, October 1963, pp. 3–20; and M. Pinto-Ducshinsky, 'Bread and circuses? Conservatives in office, 1951–64', in V. Bogdanor and R. Skidelsky, op. cit., pp. 55–77.

32 For an analysis of modern politics along these lines see Jurgen Habermas, 'Technology and science as ideology', in *Towards a Rational Society*, London 1971. He distinguishes between a politics of practice and a politics of technique on the basis of a theory of communication and purposive rational action. He sees the politics of technique becoming increasingly dominant, and politics therefore being concerned more with the solution of technical problems than with the realization of practical goals.

33 For two accounts of the controversies from different political standpoints see Ralph Miliband, *Parliamentary Socialism*, London 1961, and Stephen Haseler, *The Gaitskellites*, London 1970.

34 This became known as the State of England literature. It was too voluminous and ephemeral to be listed here. For a summary see D. E. Butler and A. King, *The British General Election of 1964*, London 1965. For other analyses of it see J. B. Christoph, 'Consensus and cleavage in British political ideology', *American Political Science Review*, vol. 59, 1965, pp. 629–42; J. H. Grainger, *Character and Style in English Politics*, Cambridge 1969; and S. Rothman, 'Modernity and tradition in Britain', *Social Research*, vol. 28, no. 3, Autumn 1961, pp. 297–320. Two interesting and representative products of it are H. Thomas, ed. *The Establishment*, London 1959, and A. Sampson, *Anatomy of Britain*, London 1962.

35 Julian Critchley, 'The old men', *Spectator*, 27.4.1962, p. 533.

36 Ibid., p. 533.

37 *Spectator*, 20.7.1962, p. 75.

38 Henry Fairlie, *Spectator*, 20.7.1962, p. 75.

39 Angus Maude, 'Party palaeontology', *Spectator*, 15.3.1963, p. 319.

40 T. E. Utley, 'Answering Utopia', *Spectator*, 11.10.1973, p. 448.

41 T. E. Utley, 'Eleven years of Tory Rule', *Spectator*, 10.5.1963, p. 597.

42 T. E. Utley, 'Answering Utopia', p. 448.

43 For a brief analysis of the Bow Group and its role in the party see R. Rose, 'The Bow Group's role in British politics', *Western Political Quarterly*, vol. 14, no. 4, December 1961, pp. 865–78.

44 *Crossbow*, 1, 1957, p. 11.

45 Ibid., p. 11. The quotation is taken from *Edinburgh Review*, and was written before Peel's rise to the leadership.

46 *Crossbow*, 2, 1958, p. 9. Cf. M. Wolff, 'Introduction', in M. Wolff, ed., *The Conservative Opportunity*, London 1965.

47 In its early years the Bow Group was renowned for its liberalism on international issues, especially the need for giving independence to the colonies. See Maurice Cowling's complaint, 'Letter to a Bow Grouper', *Crossbow*, 10, 1960, and T. E. Utley, *Daily Telegraph*, 18.2.1960. World Refugee Year was launched by Bow Groupers, one of them Christopher Chataway.

48 *Crossbow*, 2, 1958, p. 9.

49 Gordon Pears, 'Down with Conservatism', *Crossbow*, 5, 1958. Formerly the connection between social conservatism and political Conservatism had seemed inevitable and desirable. See Lord Hugh Cecil's discussion of 'natural Conservatism' in *Conservatism*, London 1912, and Michael Oakeshott, 'On being Conservative', in *Rationalism and Politics*, London 1962.

50 *Crossbow*, 9, 1959, p. 9.

51 Ibid., p. 63.

52 Ibid., p. 66. Hogg's book was a slightly amended version of his earlier book, *The Case for Conservatism*.

53 *Crossbow*, 17, 1961, p. 5.

54 *Crossbow*, 16, 1961, p. 6.

55 Ibid., p. 6.

56 *Crossbow*, 18, 1962, p. 6.

57 *Crossbow*, 19, 1962, p. 6.

58 *Crossbow*, 23, 1963, p. 6.
59 *Crossbow*, 5, 1958, p. 7.
60 Ibid., p. 14.
61 Ibid., p. 7.
62 Crossbow, 20, 1962, p. 7. For other writing on these themes, see David Howell, 'Bow notebook', *Crossbow*, 19, 1964, p. 28, and 'Modern Conservatism in search of its principles', *Crossbow*, 24, 1963; and 'The new professionals', *Crossbow*, 26, 1964; R. Rose, 'Going up and in between', *Crossbow*, 21, 1962, and N. Scott, 'the future of Toryism', *Impact*, Spring 1964.
63 C. Curran, 'The new model bourgeoisie', *Crossbow*, 21, 1962, p. 19.
64 Ibid., p. 22.
65 When he was addressing a less sophisticated audience, Curran had another message, as well he might, given the electoral weight of the manual working class. See *CPCR 1954*, pp. 79–80.
66 Rose distinguishes between the 'solid' and the 'mobile' middle class. See 'Going up and in between', *Crossbow*, 21, 1962. In broad terms, the former comprises the established professions and traditional middle-class occupations, while the latter comprises the new white collar groups which have proliferated in the modern economy. For a general survey of the middle classes see Angus Maude and Roy Lewis, *The English Middle Classes*, London 1950 and J. Raynor, *The Middle Class*, London 1969. One very interesting early analysis of the new middle class and its political alignment is E. Lederer and J. Marschak, 'Der neue Mittlestand', *Grundriss der Sozialokonomik*, Vol. 9, no. 1, Tübingen 1926.
67 They included the People's League for the Defence of Freedom and the National Fellowship, headed by Edward Martell. This organization is investigated by G. Thayer, *The British Political Fringe*, London 1965. On the general phenomenon of middle class unrest see J. Bonham, 'The middle class revolt', *Political Quarterly*, vol. 33, 1962, pp. 238–46, and Nigel Harris, op. cit., pp. 153–4. Bonham also wrote an earlier analysis of the components of the middle class vote, *The Middle Class Vote*, London 1954.
68 *Tory Challenge*, July 1947, p. 3.
69 *CPCR 1956*, p. 45.
70 Ibid., p. 45.
71 Ibid., p. 48. See also the debate on economic policy.
72 Ibid., p. 48.
73 *CPCR 1962*, p. 14. An earlier concise statement of middle-class grievances and rank and file discontent with the leadership appeared anonymously in *Spectator*, under the title 'Conservatism—the great betrayal', 4.10.1957.
74 Lionel Grouse, 'What the middle classes want', *Crossbow*, 21, 1962, pp. 39–42.
75 Ibid., p. 42. He was echoing recurring themes in Whig opinion in the party. See H. Kerby, 'The reason why', *Spectator*, 28.2.1958, and C. Welch, 'The wrong sort of MP?', *Crossbow*, 3, 1958.
76 *Spectator*, 13.7.1962, p. 46. For Grouse's reply see *Spectator*, 20.7.1962.
77 The Homicide Act, 1957, had distinguished between capital and non-capital murder and had introduced the plea of diminished responsibility.
78 *CPCR 1956*, p. 94.
79 *CPCR 1958*, p. 98.
80 Ibid., p. 99.

81 *Crossbow*, 32, 1965, p. 5.
82 Ibid., p. 5. This whole issue was devoted to crime and punishment.
83 R. A. Butler, *The Art of the Possible*, London 1971, p. 199.
84 Ibid., p. 200.
85 *CPCR 1961*, p. 65.
86 Ibid., p. 66.
87 Ibid., p. 68.
88 Ibid., p. 70.
89 Ibid., p. 71.
90 Ibid., p. 69.
91 Ibid., p. 72.
92 Ibid., p. 66.

5 THE CHALLENGE TO THE CONSENSUS: OPPOSITION 1964–70

1 C. Hollis, *Spectator*, 24.2.1967, p. 212. The author and publishers wish to thank the *Spectator* for permission to reproduce this poem.
2 Most notable were Angus Maude, Enoch Powell, and Victor Montagu (Lord Hinchingbrooke). See e.g. V. Montagu, *The Conservative Dilemma*, Monday Club, 1970.
3 See A. Alexander and A. Watkins, *The Making of the Prime Minister 1970*, London 1970. Macleod's attack was delivered in the *Spectator*, 17.1.1964, in a review of Randolph Churchill, *The Fight for the Tory Leadership*, London 1964, which gave Macmillan's view. See also N. Fisher, *Iain Macleod*, London 1973; and H. Berkeley, *Crossing the Floor*, London 1972, Ch. 9.
4 Cf. D. E. Butler and A. King, *The British General Election of 1964*, London 1965, p. 84.
5 See Berkeley, op. cit., for his account of the reform, which he was instrumental in bringing about.
6 See R. Rose, *Influencing Voters*, London 1967; D. E. Butler and A. King, op. cit.; and D. E. Butler and M. Pinto-Duschinsky, *The British General Election of 1970*, London 1971.
7 D. Maxwell-Fyfe (Earl of Kilmuir), *Political Adventure*, London. 1964, Ch. 10.
8 A familiar theme in *Crossbow* (see e.g. no. 5, p. 12; no. 31, p. 7; and no. 33, p. 6) and in *Impact* (see e.g. Spring 1965, p. 6).
9 The scheme was implemented, but made little headway at first due to the opposition of the constituency associations. See M. Pinto-Duschinsky, 'Central Office and power in the Conservative party', *Political Studies*, vol. 20, no. 1, March 1972, pp. 1–16.
10 The organizational changes are discussed by D. E. Butler and A. King, *The British General Election of 1966*, London 1966, Ch. 3; D. E. Butler and M. Pinto-Duschinsky, op, cit.; I. Bulmer-Thomas, *The Growth of the British Party System*, London 1965, Ch. 36.
11 See D. E. Butler and A. King, op. cit. (1966), Ch. 3.
12 His personal popularity trailed far behind that of his party in the opinion polls. See D. E. Butler and M. Pinto-Duschinsky, op. cit.
13 A. Alexander and A. Watkins, op. cit. Heath cultivated a governmental style of opposition, which involved detailed criticism of the Government's

measures, and a restriction of his Front Bench colleagues to particular departments. For general surveys of Heath's background and career see A. Roth, *Heath and the Heathmen*, London 1972, and R. R. James *Ambitions and Realities*, London 1972. The concept of the politics of technique is developed by Jurgen Habermas, *Towards a Rational Society*, London 1971. The politics of technique is oriented 'toward the elimination of dysfunctions and the avoidance of risks that threaten the system; not in other words towards the realization of practical goals but toward the solution of technical problems', pp. 102–3.

14 Humphrey Berkeley has argued that Heath 'to prove his genuine Conservatism . . . wrenched the Conservative party so far to the right that it is no longer recognizable as the party which I represented in Parliament only six years ago', Berkeley, op. cit., p. 102. By 1970, many of the liberal wing of the Right Progressives—including Edward Boyle and Berkeley—had left or been forced out of the party.

15 See bibliography for a list of their most important pamphlets.

16 E. Heath, *Crossbow*, no. 42.

17 Ronald Butt has described it as 'the most bitter fight between a Minister and a section of his own party that the Conservatives had known in the post-war years.' R. Butt, *The Power of Parliament*, London 1967. The episode showed how the policies of modernization and rationalization favoured the interests of big capital, and how small business was still strongly represented in the parliamentary party.

18 Heath, *CPCR 1965*, p. 24.

19 Ibid., p. 27.

20 *Crossbow*, 30, 1965, p. 29.

21 Ibid., p. 32.

22 See bibliography for a complete list.

23 C. Curran, 'The white settlers of Britain', *Spectator*, 30.3.1962.

24 Cf. J. Biffen, 'The Conservative party today', in M. Wolff ed., *The Conservative Opportunity*, CPC, London 1965.

25 T. Raison, *Conflict and Conservatism*, CPC, London 1965, p. 7.

26 D. Howell, *Efficiency and Beyond*, CPC, London 1965, p. 5.

27 Ibid., pp. 5–6.

28 Ibid., p. 9.

29 R. Lewis, *A Bonfire of Restrictions*, CPC, London 1965, p. 3.

30 *Impact*, Winter 1966, p. 5. Cf. *Spectator*, 1.4.1966 (leading article).

31 M. Howard and N. Lamont, *Through a Glass Darkly*, Bow Group, London 1968, p. 2.

32 N. Lawson, 'The need for a national policy', in *Conservatism Today*, CPC, London 1966, p. 47.

33 Ibid., p. 53.

34 D. Howell, 'Towards stability', in *Conservatism Today*, CPC, London 1966, p. 43.

35 Lawson, op. cit., p. 55. Cf. 'A tract for the Tories', *Spectator*, 17.2.1967.

36 *Crossbow*, 41, 1967, p. 5.

37 I. Macleod, 'The target for the Tory party', in *A Fresh Approach*, CPC SC, London 1965, p. 78.

38 M. Schreiber, 'Who are our supporters to be?', *Crossbow*, 41, 1967, p. 21.

39 *Crossbow*, 38, 1967, p. 5.

40 D. Howell, op, cit., p. 37. For the best analysis of this trend see D. E. Butler and D. Stokes, *Political Change in Britain*, London 1969.

41 *Crossbow*, 39, 1967, p. 16.

42 *Crossbow*, 45, 1968, p. 5.

43 *Crossbow*, 47, 1969, p. 5.

44 Ibid., p.5.

45 Ibid., p. 5.

46 *Impact*, Spring-Summer 1968.

47 *Spectator*, 19.7.1968, p. 78.

48 The New Right expressed a mood in the party, and through its command of the party's different electoral ideologies, it secured a strong base in the constituency associations. But its leadership was fragmented, and it lacked the support of organized economic interests. The fact that the New Right had such influence in the party was more a sign of the failing leadership of the Right Progressives and the growing problems of the state, than of any particular coherence of its own.

49 P. Worsthorne, 'Priorities for capitalism', in *Conservatism Today*, CPC, London 1966, p. 25.

50 Cf. P. Worsthorne, *The Socialist Myth*, London 1971, p. 97.

51 Worsthorne, 'Priorities for Capitalism', in *Conservatism Today*, CPC, London 1966, pp. 28, 33.

52 Angus Maude, 'Winter of Tory discontent', *Spectator*, 14.1.1966, p. 39.

53 Angus Maude, *The Consuming Society*, CPC, London 1967.

54 Ibid., p. 17.

55 Angus Maude, 'The end of consensus politics', *Spectator*, 10.5.1968, p. 627. Cf. 'The road to Blackpool', *Spectator*, 7. 10.1966, p. 441.

56 G. Watson, 'Uncommon answers', *Monday World*, Winter 1969.

57 See the important article by Patrick Seyd, 'Factionalism within the Conservative party: the Monday Club', *Government and Opposition*, Autumn 1972, pp. 464–87. He gives a complete list of their pamphlets. They also published a journal, *Monday World*, and a newsletter.

58 J. Biggs-Davison, *The centre cannot hold*, Monday Club, London 1969, p. 11.

59 Ibid., p. 12. Cf. *Ireland our Cuba*, Monday Club, London 1970.

60 *Monday World*, Winter 1969, p. 2.

61 Ibid., p. 2.

62 Rhodes Boyson, ed., *Right Turn*, London 1970, p. 2.

63 Richard Law (Earl of Coleraine), *For Conservatives Only*, p. 65.

64 Ibid., p. 35.

65 Boyson, op. cit., p. 5.

66 Law, op. cit., p. 67.

67 Ibid., p. 77.

68 Ibid., p. 157.

69 E. J. Mishan, 'Not by Liberalism alone', *Crossbow*, 24, 1963, p. 31.

70 N. St John Stevas, *Swinton Journal*, Spring 1970, p. 7.

71 E. Rhys Williams, 'The machine society', *Monday World*, Autumn 1969, p. 4.

72 *CPCR 1970*, p. 73. *The Ever-changing Challenge*, CPC, London 1969.

73 *CPCR 1969*, p. 76.

74 *CPCR 1966*, p. 121.

75 *CPCR 1967*, p. 106.
76 *CPCR 1967*, p. 107. Evidently Mr Hogg had access to evidence that was not available to the Wootton Commission.
77 T. E. Utley, *What Laws May Cure*, CPC, London 1969, p. 14.
78 Quoted by Auberon Waugh, *Spectator*, 20.10.1967, p. 451.
79 *CPCR 1965*, p. 119. Other views on affluence and permissiveness can be found in G. Rippon, *Right Angle*, CPC, Monday Club, London 1969; John Braine, *A Personal Record*, Monday Club, London 1968; Esmond Wright, 'The education of a Conservative', *Political Quarterly*, vol. 41, no. 1, Jan.–March, 1970, pp. 56–66; David Eccles, *Politics and the Quality of Life*, CPC, London 1970; John Selwyn Gummer, *The Permissive Society*, London 1971.
80 *CPCR 1968*, p. 113. Cf. *Monday World*, Autumn 1969.
81 *CPCR 1968*, p. 111.
82 J. E. Powell, *Freedom and Reality*, London 1969, p. 325.
83 J. E. Powell, *Powell and the 1970 Election*, London 1970, p. 41.
84 See for instance the response of many economic journalists to Powell's Morecambe budget speech collected in J. E. Powell, *Income Tax at 4/3 in the £*, London 1970, Ch. 3.
85 Paul Foot argues this with great vigour in *The Rise of Enoch Powell*, London 1969. Biographical studies of Powell from different perspectives have been written by T. E. Utley, *Enoch Powell—The Man and his Thinking*, London 1968, and by Andrew Roth, *Enoch Powell: Tory Tribune*, London 1972. The best analysis of Powell's politics is by Tom Nairn, 'Portrait of Enoch Powell', *New Left Review*, 61, May–June 1970, pp. 3–27.
86 In a different national setting, General De Gaulle's political career also illustrates this process.
87 See the first collection of his speeches made by John Wood, *A Nation Not Afraid*, London 1965.
88 Many colleagues commented on his inflexibility and fanaticism even before he broke with the leadership. Cf. H. Macmillan, *Riding the Storm*, London 1971, pp. 368, 372, and I. Macleod, *Spectator*, 16.7.1965, p. 71.
89 J. E. Powell, *Still to Decide*, London 1972, p. 5.
90 Ibid., pp. 100-8, 135–41. Cf. J. E. Powell, 'The social services', *Spectator*, 12.6.1964, pp. 783–5, and 'Conservatives and the social services', *Political Quarterly*, vol. 24, no. 2, April–June 1953, pp. 156–66.
91 Cf. Powell, *Freedom and Reality*, p. 7.
92 Ibid., p. 18.
93 Ibid., p. 33.
94 Powell was very close to the Bow Group throughout the 1950s. He contributed articles to *Crossbow*, and was admired as a foremost exponent of the principles of neo-Liberalism.
95 For Macmillan's account of this see H. Macmillan, *Riding the Storm*, London 1971, Ch. 11.
96 J. E. Powell, *Freedom and Reality*, London 1969, p. 181. Cf. A. Maude and J. E. Powell, *Biography of a Nation*, London 1955, p. 232.
97 He was Minister from 1960–3. Utley, op. cit., Ch. 3, argues that Powell did not think it possible to challenge the concept of a free service while he was a Minister, and accordingly threw himself wholeheartedly into

administration. However, he did press in 1960 for increases in charges for welfare milk and prescriptions. Cf. Macmillan, *Pointing the Way*, London 1972, p. 366.

98 J. E. Powell, *Freedom and Reality*, Ch. 3.

99 Ibid., pp. 123, 143, 149, and J. E. Powell, *Still to Decide*, pp. 142–54.

100 J. E. Powell, *Freedom and Reality*, p. 124.

101 Ibid., pp. 201–3.

102 Ibid., pp. 207–9.

103 Ibid., pp. 177, 180–2. At one time Powell thought excess private consumption was also a factor that caused inflation. He abandoned this view. See ibid., pp. 189–90.

104 Ibid., p. 189.

105 Ibid., pp. 159–62, 164–7, and Ch. 4 *passim*. Cf. also his attack on the CBI in *Director*, February 1965.

106 Ibid., pp. 158, 36–7.

107 Ibid., p. 107.

108 Ibid., p. 188.

109 On the desirability of the floating pound see Powell, *Still to Decide*, pp. 72–4; *Freedom and Reality*, Ch. 6; and *Powell and the 1970 Election*, pp. 92–7.

110 Powell, *Freedom and Reality*, p. 182.

111 Powell, *Still to Decide*, p. 51. Cf. *Freedom and Reality*, pp. 27–8. The growing unemployment in the late 1960s he put down to unprofitability.

112 Powell, *Freedom and Reality*, p. 81.

113 Powell, *Still to Decide*, p. 90. Powell's main criticism of the Tories' plans for reforming the trade unions was directed at those proposals that would bring the government into direct confrontation with the citizen as worker and employer. See ibid., p. 87.

114 These ideas were expressed most clearly in his Morecambe Budget. See Powell, *Income Tax at 4/3 in the £*, London 1970.

115 By economic, Powell meant the relevance of market forces to particular problems and policies. He did believe at one time that the EEC was an economic question in this sense. Cf. Powell, *Still to Decide*, p. 211. Immigration, however, although theoretically desirable to ensure perfect competition in the labour market, Powell never regarded as an economic problem.

116 Powell, *Still to Decide*, p. 164.

117 Powell, *Freedom and Reality*, p. 17.

118 See Utley, op. cit., for Powell's attitudes towards India and the Royal Titles Bill of 1953.

119 Powell, *Freedom and Reality*, pp. 327–31.

120 Ibid., pp. 331–5.

121 Ibid., p. 216.

122 Ibid., pp. 240–1.

123 Ibid., p. 267.

124 The renewed outbreak of civil disorder in Ulster gave him a third after the 1970 election.

125 Powell, *Still to Decide*, p. 175. Cf. Tom Nairn's neat summary: '[for Powell] the nation is rediscovering itself, "defining itself anew",—with the aid of the coloured immigrant community— after an era of degradation. After

the long detour of Empire the English are home again, ploughing the Saxon field. The last thing they want now, evidently, is to have a lot of foreigners trampling over it.' T. Nairn, 'British nationalism and the EEC', *New Left Review*, 69, Sept.–Oct. 1971, pp. 3–28.

126 Cf. Powell, *Still to Decide*, p. 216; Powell and Maude, op. cit., and T. Nairn, 'Portrait of Enoch Powell', *New Left Review*, 61.

127 Powell, *Still to Decide*, p. 238; Powell, *The Common Market—the Case Against*, London 1971; *Powell and the 1970 Election*, pp. 112–18.

128 It was delivered on 20 April to the AGM of the West Midland Area CPC.

129 T. E. Utley, op. cit., p. 27.

130 P. Foot, op. cit., Ch. 3.

131 His main speeches in 1968 are collected in B. Smithies and P. Fiddick, *Enoch Powell on Immigration*, London 1969. See also Powell, *Powell and the 1970 Election*, pp. 97–104.

132 D. Spearman, 'Enoch Powell's postbag', *New Society*, 9.5.1968, pp. 667–9.

133 See Utley, op. cit., Ch. 1, and Smithies and Fiddick, op. cit., pp. 12–13.

134 Maurice Cowling, in *Powell and the 1970 Election*, p. 12; Angus Maude, *Spectator*, 10.5.1968. For an earlier assessment of Powell as an 'antidote to the widespread urge to take decisions out of politics', see R. Butt, 'The Importance of being Enoch', *Crossbow*, 35, 1966.

135 T. Beardson, 'Powell and Sorel', *Monday World*, Winter 1969, p. 12.

136 Powell, *Still to Decide*, p. 8.

137 Powell, *Freedom and Reality*, p. 300. Cf. M. Cowling, op. cit., pp. 9–10, 13, and Powell's speech, 'The enemies within', *Powell and the 1970 Election*, pp. 104–12.

138 Cowling, op. cit., p. 16.

139 This was pointed out by D. Howell, *Crossbow*, 33, 1965, in a review of *A Nation Not Afraid*, and by I. Gilmour, 'Enoch Powell's pipe dream', *Spectator*, 10.4.1964. See also Tom Nairn's assessment, 'Portrait of Enoch Powell', *New Left Review*, 61.

140 For the Selsdon Park Conference, see Butler and Pinto-Duschinsky, op. cit., Ch. 3.

6 THE ROOTS OF INFLATION

1 S. Brittan, *The Treasury under the Tories*, London 1964. See also his revised edition, *Steering the Economy*, London 1971, for a general account of the course of economic management in the post-war years.

2 The size of the public enterprise sector actually declined from 8·2 per cent of GDP in 1951 to 7·3 per cent in 1976. Cf. R. Pryke, *Public Enterprise in Practice*, London 1971, pp. 14–15.

3 Many of these controls had gone by 1951 in any case. See A. Rogow and P. Shore, *The Labour Government and British Industry, 1945–51*, Oxford 1955, for a general survey of the controls.

4 See e.g. One Nation Group, *Change is our Ally*, CPC, London 1954. Cf. J. C. R. Dow, *The Management of the British Economy, 1945–60*, Cambridge 1970, Ch. 3., and N. Harris, *Competition and the Corporate Society*, London 1972, pp. 232–5.

5 J. E. Powell, 'The limits of laissez-faire', *Crossbow*, 11, 1960, p. 28.

6 The Conservatives at first ran the nationalized industries as subsidized services

for the rest of the economy, and used their control over wages in these industries in their first attempts to hold down wages in the economy as a whole. The nationalized industries piled up big losses in the 1950s, and were much more inefficient than comparable firms in the private sector. In part this was due to the decentralized management the Conservatives imposed on the industries after 1951, and to their use as instruments of government economic policy. Conservative arguments against further nationalization were thus able to point to the inefficiency of those industries already nationalized. A major review of policy, however, was reflected in the 1961 White Paper, Cmnd. 1337, which argued that these industries should be run commercially, and not as services for industry or the public. During the 1960s, the overall productivity record of the nationalized industries was in fact better than the private sector. The use of these industries as an instrument in incomes policies, however, grew rather than diminished. See R. Pryke, op. cit.

7 Cf. J. C. R. Dow, op. cit. See also A. Shonfield, *British Economic Policy since the War*, London 1958.

8 The best analysis of the new strength of organized labour in the post-war labour market is V. L. Allen, *Militant Trade Unionism*, London 1966.

9 S. Pollard, *The Development of the British Economy 1914–1967*, London 1966, p. 451.

10 The evidence for this is presented in A. Glyn and R. Sutcliffe, *British Capitalism, Workers and the Profits Squeeze*, London 1972, and by C. H. Feinstein, 'Changes in the distribution of the national income in the United Kingdom since 1860', in J. Marchal and B. Ducros, eds, *The Distribution of National Income*, London 1968. The causes are in dispute.

11 The notion that Keynesian economic management replaces the business cycle by an electoral cycle was put forward by M. Kalecki, *Selected Essays on the Dynamics of a Capitalist Economy*, Cambridge 1971.

12 This concept was put forward by J. R. Hicks, 'Economic foundations of wages policy', *Economic Journal*, vol. 65, 1955, pp. 389–404.

13 For an analysis of permanent inflation see V. L. Allen, op. cit., and D. Jackson, H. A. Turner and F. Wilkinson, *Do Trade Unions cause Inflation?* Cambridge 1972. A useful collection of articles is R. J. Ball and P. Doyle, eds, *Inflation*, London 1969.

14 S. Pollard, op. cit., p. 444. He calculates that British export prices rose 14·5 per cent more than world prices between 1953 and 1963.

15 See E. Mandel, *Decline of the Dollar*, New York 1972.

16 See especially the very interesting analysis by Jackson, Turner and Wilkinson, op. cit., of the effects of the tax system on wage increases.

17 Intervention was not confined to Britain. For a comparison of several post-war states that brings out their underlying similarity, see A Shonfield, *Modern Capitalism*, London 1969.

18 *CPCR 1952*, p. 43.

19 Income was increasingly redistributed to profits through the tax system. As workers lost more of their increased earnings through 'clawback' and higher taxes, so industry was given tax concessions, subsidies, investment grants, and the rest. The state was thus financed to a growing extent by wage-earners.

20 Cf. D. Maxwell-Fyfe, in *Conservatism Today*, CPC, London 1955, p. 85.

21 See Macmillan, *Riding the Storm*, London 1971, Ch. 11. In 1962, following Selwyn Lloyd's dismissal, Birch wrote a terse letter to *The Times* on 14 July: 'For the second time the Prime Minister has got rid of a Chancellor of the Exchequer who tried to get expenditure under control. Once is more than enough.'

22 The writings of the Right Progressives on planning and modernization at this time are voluminous. See D. Howell, 'Neddy, Nicky, and the Conservatives', *Crossbow*, 21, 1962, and his enthusiasm for French planning in the 'Beau Giles' column, *Crossbow*, 17, 1961; H. Bosch, 'A new deal for industry', *Crossbow*, 26, 1964; E. Boyle, *Conservatives and Economic Planning*, CPC, London 1965; R. Lewis, 'Planning within a free economy', *Crossbow*, 28, 1964. General accounts of British planning are provided by A. Shonfield, *Modern Capitalism*, and S. Brittan, *Steering the Economy*. See also N. Harris, *Competition and the Corporate Society*, pp. 235-42, where he shows that the decisive pressure for the new planning came from big industrial companies.

23 *The Financial and Economic Obligations of the Nationalized Industries*, Cmnd. 1337, April 1961.

24 Cf. *CPCR 1963*, especially speeches by David Howell and Peter Walker, pp. 94, 96-7. It was an accurate rendering of the party's electoral task, as psephological evidence shows. The sections of the working class most likely to vote Conservative were those who did not interpret society in class terms, and were relatively immune to the Labour party's appeal as a class party. Cf. D. E. Butler and D. Stokes, *Political Change in Britain*, London 1969. They estimated that one quarter of the electorate failed to vote in line with their class identity. The Conservatives urgently needed to expand that proportion to remain electorally competitive, since 50 per cent of their votes—comprising 32 per cent of the working class—had to come from manual workers.

25 For typical writing on this theme see R. Harris, 'The morality of capitalism', in R. Boyson, *Right Turn*, London 1970; M. Ivens, ed., *The Case for Capitalism*; and K. Joseph, *Social Security*, CPC, London 1966.

26 *CPCR 1968*, p. 97.

27 A hostile review of Labour's policies is provided by F. Broadway, *State Intervention in British Industry*, London 1969.

28 See R. Pryke, *Though Cowards Flinch*, London 1967.

29 *CPCR 1966*, p. 139.

30 A typical expression of this thinking is D. Howell, *A New Style of Government*, CPC, London 1970. See also his earlier pamphlet, *Whose Government Works?* London 1968.

31 Strong arguments in favour of the principle of selectivity were presented by G. Howe, *CPCR 1966*, p. 132, and I. Macleod, ibid., p. 98.

32 Patrick Wall, MP, even argued that it should rise to 6 or 7 per cent of GNP. See *British Defence Policy in the 1970s*, Monday Club, London 1969.

33 *CPCR 1970*, p. 80.

34 Ibid., p.80.

35 H. Cecil, *Conservatism*, London 1912, p. 152. Cecil was a Unionist Free Trader. The party's conversion to tariff reform marked a break with the

liberal view of finance, which expressed predominantly the interest of finance capital. As we have seen, however, the party returned to orthodox financial policies in the 1920s.

36 T. E. Utley, 'The great soft centre', *Crossbow*, 1, 1957, p. 15.

37 L. S. Amery, *Thoughts on the Constitution*, London 1954. Amery's hopes were not to be realized. Defence of sterling continued to dominate policy until devaluation in 1967.

38 Lord Woolton, *Memoirs*, London 1959, p. 375.

39 R. A. Butler, *Tomorrow Our Responsibility*, CPC London, 1959, p. 15. Cf. I. Macleod, a few years later: 'The whole atmosphere of their appeal and manifesto will be vaster and vaster handouts.' *CPCR 1963*, p. 47.

40 H. Macmillan, *Pointing the Way*, London 1972, p. 366.

41 G. Smith, 'National equities', *Crossbow*, 27, 1964, p. 33.

42 See for example, R. Boyson, *Right Turn* (Boyson, pp. 6f, and A. Shonfield, 'Trial by Taxation').

43 For a very useful summary see R. J. Ball, *Inflation and the Theory of Money*, London 1964, and R. J. Ball and P. Doyle, eds, *Inflation*, London 1969.

44 *CPCR 1949*, p. 38.

45 *CPCR 1950*, p. 46.

46 *CPCR 1948*, p. 58.

47 Ibid., p. 62.

48 *CPCR 1949*, p. 89.

49 Ibid., p. 96.

50 *CPCR 1952*, p. 47.

51 *CPCR 1956*, p. 23. In every year from 1952 to 1956 there was a motion debated that urged the reduction of taxation.

52 *CPCR 1953*, p. 48.

53 *CPCR 1957*, p. 44.

54 *CPCR 1955*, p. 37.

55 Ibid., p. 37.

56 *CPCR 1956*, p. 69.

57 *CPCR 1960*, p. 96.

58 Ibid., p. 97.

59 Ibid., p. 92.

60 Ibid., p. 92.

61 Ibid., p. 147.

62 There were sixty-four in 1966.

63 *CPCR 1966*, p. 22.

64 *CPCR 1965*, p. 106.

65 *CPCR 1968*, p. 62.

66 *CPCR 1969*, p. 63.

67 Ibid., p. 66.

68 *CPCR 1967*, p. 73.

69 *CPCR 1961*, p. 92.

70 It was Disraeli's Government of 1874–80 that made the most important changes. See H. Pelling, *A History of British Trade Unionism*, London 1971, for a useful outline of the rise of the unions.

71 The two most important such attacks were the Taff Vale judgment of 1901, and the Osborne judgment of 1909. The former helped persuade

the union leaders to turn away from the established parties and give support to the ILP and the Labour Representation Committee. As a result the Labour party was formed in 1906. It was intended to be the political arm of the trade unions, to represent the unions in the political system. Only in 1918 did it adopt a socialist constitution and a socialist programme. Ultimately, the creation of the Labour party was to make class the most important basis of electoral alignment in Britain.

72 F. W. S. Craig, ed., *British General Election Manifestos 1918–66*, Chichester 1970, p. 48.

73 Nigel Harris gives an account of corporatist theory in *Competition and the Corporate Society*, Ch. 4.

74 *The New Conservatism* CPC, London 1955, p. 36.

75 Lord Salisbury, 22.5.1948. It was reprinted in *Conservatism 1945–50*, CPC, London 1950, p. 75.

76 Strikes were illegal under war-time regulations (Order 1305), and this was maintained by the Labour Government until 1950. Labour also made several attempts at wage restraint. Stafford Cripps achieved the greatest success. At the birth of the new state, the unions were more prepared to cooperate, than they later became.

77 *CPCR 1949*, p. 39. Cf. One Nation Group, *One Nation*, CPC, London 1950, p. 77.

78 *CPCR 1949*, p. 44.

79 Ibid., p. 55.

80 *CPCR 1947*.

81 *CPCR 1950*, p. 53.

82 *CPCR 1949*, p. 41.

83 Ibid., p. 42.

84 *CPCR 1950*, p. 53.

85 R. A. Butler, *The Art of the Possible*, London 1971, p. 164.

86 He was influenced in his views on planning and the post-war state by Sir Stafford Cripps, and supported some of the nationalization measures after the war. He had also represented unions in the courts. For his career see Lord Birkenhead, *Walter Monckton*, London 1969.

87 Birkenhead, op. cit., p. 276.

88 Ibid., p. 276.

89 Sir Lincoln Evans, 'Responsible trade unionism', in Boyson, *Right turn*, p. 139. Monckton's two biggest successes were to avert national strikes on the railways and in the engineering industries.

90 Cf. Sir Michael Fraser, *The Worker in Industry*, CPC, London, 1951. It involved seeing the workers' problem as one of status rather than of class. The link with the party's electoral strategy is obvious.

91 *CPCR 1954*, p. 83.

92 H. Macmillan, *Riding the Storm*, London 1971, p. 211.

93 Ibid., p. 346.

94 One new departure was the setting up of the Cohen Council, immediately christened 'the three wise men', whose function was to educate the public on the relationship between wages, prices, and productivity. Their reports were widely ignored.

95 *CPCR 1956*, p. 85. See also I. Macleod, *The Crisis of Confidence in*

Industrial Relations, The Industrial Copartnership Association, London
1957, p. 13.

96 *CPCR 1958*, p. 58. Macleod proved both a very tough and a very shrewd
Minister of Labour. He was the first to use the Government's control of
wages in the public sector as a weapon in the fight against inflation in the
economy. He fought the London Bus strike in 1957, which was led by Frank
Cousins, and won an important victory for the Government. It helped to
restore morale and confidence amongst the rank and file in the party. The
busmen had been selected by Macleod in preference to the railwaymen,
whose claim was settled by mediation just before it, because he judged that
the busmen were easier to beat. He broke new ground in post-war strikes by
refusing to mediate. For the story of Macleod's tenure of the Ministry of
Labour see N. Fisher, *Iain Macleod*, London 1973, Ch. 7.

97 Cf. the TUC statement of policy in 1952, H. Pelling, op. cit., p. 234. The
role of the TUC as an organized interest group in the post-war state is
described by Samuel Beer, *Modern British Politics*, London 1965, Ch. 12.

98 Typical of such speeches were J. Boyd-Carpenter, *Onlooker*, November
1946, p. 13; G. Finsburg, ibid., p. 13; and A. Barker, *CPCR 1949*, p. 39.

99 *CPCR 1953*, p. 77.

100 *CPCR 1954*, p. 83.

101 *CPCR 1955*, p. 76. Cf. One Nation Group, *The Responsible Society*, CPC,
London 1959, p. 20.

102 *CPCR 1956*, pp. 84–5.

103 *CPCR 1961*, p. 111.

104 Ibid., p. 113.

105 Ibid., p. 116.

106 Ibid., p. 116.

107 Ibid., p. 118.

108 J. E. Powell, in *Conference on Economic Policy for the 1970s*, Monday Club,
London 1968, p. 5. For other New Right views on the unions see *Economic
Affairs*, Monday Paper 3, Monday Club, London, 1966.

109 C. Curran, *Spectator*, 12.10.1956, p. 486. His approach was echoed in
The Responsible Society, and in a pamphlet by C. Fletcher-Cooke, *Trade
Unionism and Liberty*, CPC SC, London 1956.

110 H. Macmillan, *Pointing the Way*, London 1972, p. 376.

111 N. Harris, op, cit., p. 166. By May 1962, 77 industries had received increases
above the Government norm. The main victims of the Pause (disastrously
for the Government) were the nurses. The Pay Pause, however, was still
the most determined effort yet by government to use the public sector as
the front line in the battle against inflation.

112 H. Macmillan, op. cit., p. 375.

113 The way the labour market operated is described by V. L. Allen, *Militant
Trade Unionism*, London, 1966.

114 An exploration of these problems by someone with unrivalled first-hand
experience can be found in Aubrey Jones, *The New Inflation*, London 1973.

115 Inns of Court Conservative and Unionist Society, *A Giant's Strength*,
London 1958.

116 Ibid., p. 13.

117 Civil conspiracy by an individual; inducing a breach of contract by an

individual; protection of trade unions from actions in tort. The best survey of unions and the law is K. Wedderburn, *The Worker and the Law*, London 1971.

118 *A Giant's Strength*, p. 20.
119 *The New Inflation*, Ch. 8.
120 *CPCR 1956*, p. 25.
121 Ibid., p. 38. Cf. Aidan Crawley, 'Communism in the unions', in *Contemporary Communism*, CPC SC, London 1963.
122 Cf. the 'New Task' series of pamphlets, CPC, London 1965.
123 *CPCR 1968*, p. 35. He made a similar speech at the 1970 conference, *CPCR 1970*, p. 33.

7 THE SEARCH FOR SECURITY: NATION AND STATE IN THE WORLD MARKET

1 *CPCR 1969*, p. 11.
2 This theme of Conservative propaganda is examined by R. T. McKenzie and A. Silver, *Angels in Marble*, London 1968, Ch. 2, through a review of Conservative party election leaflets.
3 This interpretation of the Cold War has become known as the 'revisionist' theory. In view of the evidence it is only surprising that the 'ideological' theory was not revised much earlier. The best accounts of the Cold War from the revisionist perspective are D. F. Fleming, *The Cold War and its Origins*, London 1961; M. Barratt-Brown, *After Imperialism*, London, 1963; and D. Horowitz, *From Yalta to Vietnam*, London 1967.
4 For a Conservative account of the scramble, see *Conservatives and the Colonies*, CLC, London, 1962 (written by J. Biggs-Davison).
5 A full account is given in D. Horowitz, op. cit., part two.
6 J. Amery, *Joseph Chamberlain and the Tariff Reform Campaign*, London 1969, p. 1037.
7 Q. Hogg, *Interdependence*, CPC, London 1960, p. 20.
8 *Notes on Current Politics*, 5.6.1950, p. 6. For typical views on the communist menace, see the conference debates on communism, *CPCR 1948* and *CPCR 1950*.
9 Lord Home, 'Peaceful co-existence', in *Contemporary Communism* CPC SC, London 1963, p. 12. Such views became orthodox for the new right. Cf. D. G. Stewart-Smith, *The Handmaidens of Diplomacy*, Monday Club, London 1964.
10 David Eccles, 'The economics of competitive co-existence', in *Prospect for Capitalism*, CPC SC, London 1958, p. 75.
11 Lord Salisbury told the 1952 conference that there were more British troops overseas than ever before in British history; *CPCR 1952*, p. 34. See also Chapter 6 and S. Pollard, *The Development of the British Economy 1914–67*, London 1967, p. 451. An interesting analysis of British post-war foreign policy from this perspective is given by Robert V. Roosa, 'Where is Britain heading?', *Foreign Affairs*, vol. 46, no. 3, April 1968, pp. 503–18.
12 *CPCR 1965*, p. 62.
13 Ibid., p. 63. During the 1966 General Election, Powell condemned contingency plans to send British troops to Vietnam.
14 See the account by T. E. Utley, *Enoch Powell*, London 1968, and the three

unsigned articles in *The Times*, April, 1, 2, 3, 1964, which are generally attributed to Powell. For another 'Powellite' view see J. Bruce-Gardyne, 'Can we afford spending overseas?' *Crossbow*, 36, 1966.

15 *CPCR 1968*, p. 7.

16 *CPCR 1969*, p. 13.

17 Ibid., pp. 14, 15. This reflected the thinking of the remnants of the imperialist tendency in the New Right. See S. Hastings, *Once upon a Time*, Monday Club, London 1970, and P. Wall, *British Defence Policy in the 1970s*, Monday Club, London 1969.

18 *Conservatives and the Colonies*, CLC, London 1959, p. 6.

19 L. S. Amery, *My Political Life*, London 1953, p. 253. Two other typical statements of this kind, from men active in the imperialist movement are Henry Page Croft, *My Life of Strife*, London 1948, and W. A. S. Hewins, *The Apologia of an Imperialist*, London 1929.

20 L. S. Amery, op. cit., pp. 254–5. Cf. Croft, op. cit., p. 175.

21 *CPCR 1953*, p. 59.

22 *Britain Strong and Free*, London 1950.

23 *CPCR 1948*, p. 64.

24 Ibid., p. 67.

25 Ibid., p. 66.

26 The Conservatives had opposed GATT from its inception. Typical views from different tendencies in the party were J. Amery, *CPCR 1948* (the debate on imperial policy), and D. Eccles, *Forward from the Industrial Charter*, London 1948. For a general description of Conservative reactions to GATT see Nigel Harris, *Competition and the Corporate Society*, London 1972, pp. 129–30, 230–1.

27 For the history of the conflict in the Conservative party over India during the 1930s see W. L. Guttsman, *The British Political Elite*, London 1963, Ch. 10.

28 *CPCR 1947*, p. 69. Similar views were expressed by H. Soref, *CPCR 1953*, p. 61. The traumatic effect that the withdrawal from India had on one future Conservative leader has also been chronicled. See T. E. Utley, *Enoch Powell*, London 1968, and P. Foot, *The Rise of Enoch Powell*, London 1969.

29 *CPCR 1949*, p. 55.

30 Ibid., p. 57.

31 Ibid., p. 58. A plea repeated in the conference debate the next year.

32 D. Goldsworthy, *Colonial Issues in British Politics, 1945–61*, Oxford 1971, p. 185.

33 L. D. Gammans, quoted by Goldsworthy, op. cit., p. 177.

34 *CPCR 1950*, p. 34.

35 *CPCR 1948*, p. 60.

36 *CPCR 1949*, p. 59. The Act is discussed by N. Deakin, 'The British Nationality Act of 1948', *Race*, vol. 11, no. 1, July 1969, pp. 77–83.

37 *CPCR 1953*, p. 65.

38 *CPCR 1954*, p. 55.

39 The Suez Group was formed in 1952–3 to oppose the handover of the British military base at Suez. It grew to include 40 MPs. Twenty-five of them voted against the Government over the withdrawal from the base in

1954. Members of the Group included Julian Amery, John Biggs-Davison, Lord Hinchingbrooke, Captain Waterhouse, H. Legge-Bourke, Anthony Fell, and Angus Maude.

40 *CPCR 1956*, p. 32.

41 Ibid., p. 32.

42 Ibid., p. 30.

43 Cf. R. A. Butler, *The Art of the Possible*, London 1971, p. 89; Lord Home, quoted by K. Young, *Sir Alec Douglas-Home*, London 1970, p. 89; Angus Maude, 'Chips down in Suez', *Spectator*, 16.11.1956; and R. Skidelsky, 'Lessons of Suez', in V. Bogdanor and R. Skidelsky eds, *The Age of Affluence*, London 1970.

44 See H. Macmillan, *Riding the Storm*, London 1971, Ch. 4. Both Macmillan and Maxwell-Fyfe maintain vigorously in their memoirs that the action was stopped because Israel and Egypt were no longer fighting, and not because of American financial pressure on sterling and an IMF loan. If this were so the actions of the Cabinet are still harder to understand. It is significant that the French did not see the ceasefire between Egypt and Israel as a reason for calling off the invasion. For other judgments on this question see J. Amery, *Joseph Chamberlain and the Tariff Reform Campaign*, London 1969, ch. 122, and S. Brittan, *Steering the Economy*, London 1971.

45 Very damaging, apparently, was an article by D. McLachlan in the *Daily Telegraph*, 3.1.1956. See also D. E. Butler and R. Rose, *The British General Election of 1959*, London 1960, p. 36, and leading articles in *Spectator*, 13.1.1956 and 6.4.1956.

46 *Spectator*, 16.11.1956, p. 670.

47 L. Epstein, *British Politics in the Suez Crisis*, London 1964, Ch. 3. Israel attacked Egypt on 31 October, whereupon Britain and France delivered a twelve hour ultimatum to both sides to cease fire and withdraw ten miles on either side of the canal. This seemed rather strange to the Egyptians, since the Israelis had not even reached the canal. The ultimatum thus automatically awarded territory to the Israelis.

48 *Spectator*, 14.12.1956, p. 857.

49 *Spectator*, 21.12.1956, p. 894.

50 J. Amery, *CPCR 1953*, p. 32. The conflicts within the party at the time of Suez are described in detail by Leon Epstein. See his *British Politics in the Suez Crisis*, London 1964, and 'Cohesion of British parliamentary parties', *American Political Science Review*, vol. 50, June 1956, pp. 360–77. Other accounts are given by R. T. McKenzie, *British Political Parties*, London 1963, pp. 631–4; S. E. Finer *et al.*, *Backbench Opinion in the House of Commons*, London 1961; and H. Berrington, 'The Conservative party: revolts and Pressures 1955–61', *Political Quarterly*, vol. 32., no. 4, Oct.–Dec. 1961, pp. 363–73. Those MPs who were anti-Suez were much more severely hounded by their constituency associations than were those who belonged to the Suez Group and abstained in the votes to wind the invasion up. Nigel Nicholson's case was the most publicized. See his own account in *People and Parliament*, London 1958. Other Suez rebels were A. Nutting, E. Boyle (both of whom resigned from the Government) and Robert Boothby.

51 Cf. A. Lennox-Boyd, *CPCR 1955*, p. 32.

52 The reasons for decolonization are discussed by M. Barratt Brown, op. cit., and by P. Keatley, *The Politics of Partnership*, London 1963.

53 Cf. D. Goldsworthy, op. cit., Ch. 8. The British Empire reached its greatest extent in 1918. At that time it contained 450 million subjects and was spread over 14 million square miles, For a general survey see C. Cross, *The Fall of the British Empire*, London 1968.

54 See e.g. M. Barratt Brown, op. cit., and A. Emmanuel, 'White settler colonialism and the myth of investment imperialism', *New Left Review*, 73, May–June 1972, pp. 35–57.

55 Other examples are Algeria and the Congo.

56 Lord Home, 'The changing Commonwealth', in *World Perspectives*, CPC SC, London 1955, p. 11. Similar themes can be found in *Colonial Rule*, CPC, London 1955; *Expanding Obligation*, CPC, London 1961; *The Expanding Commonwealth*, CPC, London 1956; L. S. Amery, *Thoughts on the Constitution*, London 1953, p. 111; and R. A. Butler, *Our Way Ahead*, CPC, London 1956, pp. 17f.

57 *Wind of Change*, CPC, London, 1960, p. 61.

58 See Dan Horowitz, 'Attitudes of British Conservatives towards decolonization in Africa', *African Affairs*, vol. 69, 1970, pp. 9–26. The phrase 'wind of change' applied to British colonial policy had a long history. Macmillan had used it himself in Accra three days before and in Bedford three years before without exciting any attention. Baldwin too had used it in 1934 to defend the idea of eventual independence for India: 'There is a wind of nationalism and freedom blowing round the world and blowing as strongly in Asia as anywhere in the world', G. M. Young, *Stanley Baldwin*, London 1952, p. 188. It obviously helped Conservative leaders in recommending unwelcome policy changes to have the natural elements on their side. The policy of decolonization was strongly supported by the liberal wing of the Right Progressives. Macleod was particularly committed to the policy Macmillan entrusted to him to carry out. See especially his speech at the 1961 conference, and N. Fisher, op. cit., *passim*.

59 The policy of decolonization was opposed in the parliamentary party by a group of backbenchers led by Robin Turton. They fought particularly against the dissolution of the Rhodesia Federation. See S. E. Finer *et al.*, op. cit.

In the party in the country, the Monday Club was formed, but the most vehement opposition was organized by the League of Empire Loyalists, which eventually broke with the Conservative party completely, and was one of the organizations that combined to form the National Front. Their views are well represented by Major-General Richard Hilton, *Imperial Obituary*, Britons Publishing Company, Devon 1968. The organization is described by G. Thayer, *The British Political Fringe*, London 1965. For their violent suppression by Conservative stewards at the 1958 conference see Taper (Bernard Levin) in the *Spectator*, 17.10.1958. Hilton was also chairman of a group known as the True Tories.

60 Fifty Conservative MPs voted against the order imposing sanctions, thirty-one supported it, and the rest followed the advice of the leadership and abstained. It is notable that on this issue Macleod, only recently returned to the inner circle of the leadership, chose not to vote with his supporters in

the liberal wing against sanctions, and fostered a more orthodox image. See N. Fisher, op, cit., pp. 274–5. There is no doubt where the balance of opinion in the party lay.

61 Salisbury had been a very influential politician under Churchill and Eden, and had played a key role in the selection of Macmillan as Leader in 1957. He resigned from the Government in 1957 because of the decision to release Makarios from detention, which was an obvious prelude to granting Cyprus independence. In 1961 he had bitterly attacked Macleod in the House of Lords for his policy of very rapid decolonization, and had accused him of being 'too clever by half'. This greatly contributed to the eclipse of Macleod's reputation and prospects in the party. The policy itself was not affected.

62 Lord Salisbury, *CPCR 1965*, pp. 124–5.

63 Rodesia continued to flicker as an issue, however, In 1970, the conference debated a resolution put forward by the Monday Club through the Kensington constituency association, which called for the immediate ending of sanctions. The new Government, however, was not prepared to throw away the only bargaining counter it had.

64 The best account of the politics of immigration is by Paul Foot, *Immigration and Race in British Politics*, London 1965.

65 See N. Deakin, 'The British Nationality Act of 1948', *Race*, vol. 11, no. 1, July 1969, pp. 77–83.

66 D. Maxwell-Fyfe, quoted by N. Deakin, 'The politics of the Commonwealth Immigrants Bill', *Political Quarterly*, vol. 39, no. 1, 1968, pp. 25–45.

67 *CPCR 1955*, p. 32.

68 *CPCR 1961*, p. 30.

69 Ibid., p. 29.

70 Ibid., p. 28.

71 See especially, N. Deakin and J. Bourne, 'Powell, the minorities, and the 1970 election', *Political Quarterly*, vol. 41, no. 4, Oct.-Dec. 1970, pp. 399–415; P. Foot, *The Rise of Enoch Powell*, London 1969; and T. Nairn, 'Portrait of Enoch Powell', *New Left Review*, 61, May-June 1970, pp. 3–27.

72 H. Macmillan, *Britain, the Commonwealth, and Europe*, CUCO, London 1962.

73 They attended the Strasbourg Conference, set up to explore ways of encouraging practical European cooperation. See H. Macmillan, *Tides of Fortune*, London 1969, Chs. 6 and 8. Leading Conservatives in the European movement at this time were Macmillan, David Maxwell-Fyfe, Robert Boothby, and Duncan Sandys.

74 J. Amery, *The British Commonwealth or Western Europe*, (British Commonwealth Affairs no. 7), London 1952, p. 9.

75 H. Macmillan, *Tides of Fortune*, p. 159.

76 John Grigg, 'The politics of going into Europe', *Spectator*, 2.6.1961, p. 789.

77 *CPCR 1949*, p. 61.

78 Ibid., p. 66.

79 Ibid., p. 63.

80 *The New Conservatism*, CPC, London 1955, pp. 140–1.

81 *Notes on Current Politics*, 17.7.1950, p. 11. Eden's general views on foreign policy may be studied in two articles he wrote for *Foreign Affairs*: 'Britain

and the modern World', vol. 26, no. 1, October 1947, pp. 15–23, and 'Britain in world strategy', vol. 29, no. 3, April 1951, pp. 341–50.

82 H. Macmillan, *Tides of Fortune*, p. 472.

83 *CPCR 1952*, p. 37.

84 *CPCR 1953*, p. 29.

85 She was the Secretary of the European League for Economic Cooperation, founded May 1946. The Conservative Research Department was also conducting some long-term research on Europe at this time. See e.g. U. Branston, *Britain and European Unity*, CPC, London 1953.

86 H. Macmillan, *Riding the Storm*, p. 476.

87 For Macmillan's emergence as Leader, see A. Sampson, *Macmillan*, London 1967; R. T. McKenzie, *British Political Parties*, London 1963, pp. 587–93.

88 Cf. P. Nettl and D. Shapiro, 'Institutions versus Realities', *Journal of Common Market Studies*, vol. 2, no. 1, 1963, pp. 24–36, for an analysis of the increasing immobility of British foreign policy.

89 See D. Goldsworthy, op. cit., and Dan Horowitz, op. cit. A study of Macmillan's political style can be found in L. A. Siedentop, 'Mr Macmillan and the Edwardian style', in V. Bogdanor and R. Skidelsky, *The Age of Affluence*, London 1970, pp. 17–54. Opinion moved very slowly in the direction that Macmillan wanted it to go. As late as 1963, 'Establishment' opinion had not been converted to Europe. 67 per cent of one sample still placed the Commonwealth as the 'most valued international grouping' for Britain. See M. Abrams, 'British élite attitudes and the European Common Market', *Public Opinion Quarterly*, vol. 29, no. 2, Summer 1965, pp. 236–46.

90 *CPCR 1960*, p. 58.

91 Ibid., p. 58. EFTA was organized in 1957 as a partial counter to the new Common Market. See M. Camps, *Britain and the European Community 1955–63*, Princeton, 1964.

92 *CPCR 1960*, p. 62. Cf. E. Heath, 'Introduction', in *The New Europe*, CPC SC, London 1962.

93 Although even the Bow Group was not unanimous. For an anti-Europe view see L. Beaton *et al.*, *No Tame or Minor Role*, Bow Group, London, 1963. For pro-Europe Bow Group pamphlets, see *Britain into Europe*, CPC, London 1962; *A Smaller Stage*, Bow Group, London 1965; and L. Brittan *et al.*, *Our Future in Europe*, Bow Group, London 1970. See also D. Howell, 'Expanding prosperity', in D. Howell and T. Raison, eds, *Principles and Practice*, CPC, London 1961.

94 D. Howell, op. cit., p. 27.

95 The number of Conservative MPs who voted for the motion approving the decision to make an application was 313. Twenty-two abstained.

96 *Spectator*, 11.8.1961, p. 196.

97 Opposition to the Market was organized inside and outside Parliament. For descriptions of the opposition see J. Critchley, 'The flat-earthers', *Spectator*, 25.5.1962; H. Fairlie, 'The Earl of Sandwich's crew', *Spectator*, 3.8.1962; H. McLaren, 'Profile of a lobby', *Crossbow*, 21, 1962; and Lord Windlesham, *Communication and Political Power*, London 1966, Ch. 7. Lord Hinchingbrooke was a prominent anti-Marketeer, and when he succeeded to his earldom, his intervention in the by-election in his old

constituency—South Dorset—in support of an anti-Common Market candidate, was sufficient to lose the Tories the seat in November 1962.

98 *CPCR 1961*, p. 47.
99 Ibid., p. 47.
100 Ibid., p. 54.
101 Ibid., p. 52.
102 Ibid., p. 48. Cf. D. Walker-Smith and P. Walker, *A call to the Common-Wealth*, London 1961.
103 *CPCR 1961*, p. 50.
104 Ibid., p. 56.
105 Ibid., p. 50.
106 *CPCR 1962*, p. 53. Cf. One Nation Group, *One Europe*, CPC, London 1965, p. 20.
107 *CPCR 1962*, p. 56.
108 Ibid., p. 47.
109 Ibid., p. 53.
110 Ibid., p. 54. W. Rees-Mogg presents detailed economic arguments for entry which stress economies of scale, reflecting the interests and needs of the big industrial companies, in 'Industry and the Common Market', *The New Europe*, CPC SC, London, 1962.
111 *Spectator*, 11.1.1963, p. 31.
112 Q. Hogg, 'Britain looks forward', *Foreign Affairs*, vol. 43, no. 3, April 1965, pp. 409–25. Cf. I. Macleod, 'Reports of Britain's death', *Foreign Affairs*, vol. 45, no. 1, Oct. 1966, pp. 88–97; *Crossbow*, 31, 1965: articles by D. Howell, J. Bruce-Gardyne, H. Dykes, J. Critchley, R. Maudling, L. Reed and J. Ackers.
113 *CPCR 1965*, p. 111.
114 *CPCR 1966*, p. 116.
115 Ibid., p. 117.
116 Ibid., p. 86.
117 *CPCR 1970*, p. 58.
118 *CPCR 1969*, p. 88.
119 *CPCR 1970*, p. 58.
120 See for example J. Biggs-Davison, *Europe—Faith not Despair*, Monday Club, London 1967, and G. Rippon, *Right Angle*, CPC, London 1969.
121 E. Heath, 'Realism in British foreign policy', *Foreign Affairs*, vol. 48, no. 1, October 1969, p. 42. Cf. E. Heath, *Old World, New Horizons*, London 1970.
122 *CPCR 1969*, p. 91. Cf. Home, *Britain's Place in the World*, CPC, London 1968. See also some of his earlier conference speeches, e.g. *CPCR 1960*, p. 54, *CPCR 1963*, p. 91, and *CPCR 1965*, pp. 113–14, and the summary of his views by K. Young, *Sir Alec Douglas-Home*, London 1970, pp. 125f.
123 *CPCR 1969*, p. 57.
124 *CPCR 1970*, p. 59.

8 CONCLUSION AND POSTSCRIPT: THE TRADE UNION OF THE NATION AND THE CRISIS OF THE STATE

1 See especially J. R. Vincent, *The Formation of the British Liberal Party*,

London 1966, and H. J. Hanham, *Elections and Party Management*, London 1959.

2 See J. Blondel, *Voters, Parties, Leaders*, London 1963, p. 57.

3 D. E. Butler and D. Stokes, *Political Change in Britain*, London 1969, p. 123.

4 See especially R. T. McKenzie and A. Silver, *Angels in Marble*, London 1968; E. A. Nordlinger, *Working Class Tories*, London 1967.

5 This argument has been put most strongly by F. Parkin. See 'Working class Conservatives; a theory of political deviance', *British Journal of Sociology*, vol. 18, no. 3, Sept. 1967, pp. 278–90, and *Class Inequality and Political Order*, London 1972, Ch. 3.

6 Another important structural factor isolated by Butler and Stokes is the strong influence that parents' voting preferences have on their children. Electoral behaviour changes as different age cohorts pass through the political system. The higher proportion of old people that vote Conservative is not because old people are temperamentally Conservative, but because they formed their political identity before Labour had made a real impact as an electoral alternative in the political market.

7 Seaside resorts are notorious for their strong Conservatism, whilst mining communities are generally the most solid Labour strongholds.

8 See Chapter 4.

9 For detailed analysis of inequality in Britain, see J. Urry and J. Wakeford, eds, *Power in Britain*, London 1973.

10 See S. E. Finer, 'The political power of private capital', *Sociological Review*, vol. 3, no. 2, December 1955, pp. 279–94, and vol. 4, no. 1, July 1956, pp. 5–30. This needs to be qualified by the very close identification of certain branches of industry, such as the brewers, with the Conservative party in the past, and with evidence of the business ties that Conservative MPs tend either to possess or to acquire. See S. Haxey, *Tory MP*, London 1939; M. Barratt Brown, *Who are the Tories?* London 1959, and A. Roth, *The Business Background of MPs*, London 1972.

11 This has been thoroughly documented by W. L. Guttsman, *The British Political Elite*, London 1963.

12 See J. H. Grainger, *Character and Style in English Politics*, London 1969, and P. Anderson, 'Origins of the present Crisis', *New Left Review*, 23, Jan.–Feb. 1964.

13 Lord Randolph Churchill for instance told a supporter that the Conservative party backed progress, subject to two conditions: '(1) the maintenance of the Monarchy, the House of Lords, the Union between Great Britain and Ireland, and the connection between Church and State. (2) The careful protection and preservation of the rights of property.' Quoted by R. R. James, *Lord Randolph Churchill*, London 1959, p. 372.

14 Cf. Butler and Stokes, op. cit., Ch. 18.

15 See D. E. Butler and M. Pinto-Duschinsky, *The British General Election of 1970*, London 1971, Ch. 3.

16 H. W. Lucy, quoted by R. R. James, op. cit., p. 347.

17 The best early analysis of this new course was R. Blackburn, 'The Heath Government: a new course for British capitalism', *New Left Review*, 70, Nov.–Dec. 1971, pp. 3–26.

18 See Counter Information Services, Anti-Report Number Six, *Three Phase*

Trick; a Handbook on Inflation and Phase Three, London 1973, and *Politics and Money*, esp, 'Inflation', vol. 4, no. 1, Jan.–March 1973.

19 The support for the Commonwealth of some of the earlier anti-Market campaigners had greater realism in retrospect in the 1970s than had appeared at the time. In the 1950s and 1960s the great expansion of world trade was not between primary and secondary producers but between the advanced industrial countries, and this had been a major reason for joining the Market. Yet in the context of growing world shortages of raw materials, an economic association between secondary producers like the EEC countries began to seem less valuable than an association between primary and secondary producers like the old colonial Empires had been and like the Commonwealth might have become. The opportunity to turn back, however, had long since passed by 1974.

20 For a detailed account of the industrial struggles of the first three years of the Heath Government see A. Barnett, 'Class struggle and the Heath Government', *New Left Review*, 77, Jan.–Feb. 1973, pp. 3–41.

21 See Counter Information Services, op. cit., for an account of the impact of Phase 3.

22 See Counter Information Services, *The Unacceptable Face* (Special Report on the Conservative Government 1970–4), London 1974.

23 For a fuller analysis of the political economy of the crisis, see A. M. Gamble and P. Walton, 'The British state and the inflation crisis', Isaac Deutscher Memorial Lecture, in *Bulletin of the Conference of Socialist Economists*, Autumn 1973, pp. 1–24. See also the important new book by Michael Barratt Brown, *From Labourism to Socialism*, Spokesman Books, Nottingham 1972.

24 He in fact did so shortly after the election in a radio broadcast.

25 One direction which the class struggle could take is indicated by recent events in Italy. There, Fiat was forced in early 1974 by the threat of crippling strikes to agree to a new labour contract costing £67 million. Apart from large pay increases and subsidies for meals, the contract obliges Fiat to spend so much per employee on such things as nursery schools and public transport, and to undertake a big programme of investment in the south. This agreement is expected to become the standard for wage negotiations throughout Italian industry, and many Italian industrialists are now reported to see no future for profitable investment by private capital in Italy if the present bargaining strength of labour is maintained. Even the largest firms are becoming dependent upon the state for their solvency and and are being absorbed into the state sector. Inflation meanwhile is running at around 20 per cent a year. See 'Italian industry at the crossroads', *Financial Times*, 11 March 1974, p. 23.

Select Bibliography

The intention of the bibliography is to indicate the main sources drawn upon in the writing of this book, and at the same time to give some guide to further reading. More detailed sources are given in the Notes. In general the bibliography covers the period from 1945 to 1970.

I Primary sources

(A) THE CONSERVATIVE PARTY

Manifestos
Mr Churchill's Statement of Policy, 1945.
This is the Road, 1950.
Britain Strong and Free, 1951.
United for Peace and Progress, 1955.
The Next Five Years, 1959.
Prosperity with a Purpose, 1964.
Action not Words, 1966.
A Better Tomorrow, 1970.

Policy Documents and Charters
Industrial Charter, 1947.
The Right Road for Britain, 1949.
Imperial Policy, 1949.
Onward in Freedom, 1958.
Putting Britain Right Ahead, 1965.
Make Life Better, 1967.

National Union Annual Conference reports
1946. Report published in *Onlooker*, November 1946.
1947. 68, Brighton.
1948. 69, Llandudno.
1949. 70, London.

1950. 71, Blackpool.
1952. 72, Scarborough.
1953. 73, Margate.
1954. 74, Blackpool.
1955. 75, Bournemouth.
1956. 76, Llandudno.
1957. 77, Brighton.
1958. 78, Blackpool.
1960. 79, Scarborough.
1961. 80, Brighton.
1962. 81, Llandudno.
1963. 82, Blackpool.
1965. 83, Brighton.
1966. 84, Blackpool.
1967. 85, Brighton.
1968, 86, Blackpool.
1969. 87, Brighton.
1970. 88, Blackpool.

CPC pamphlets
Almost five hundred pamphlets were published by the *CPC* between 1945 and 1970.
CPC   'Two Way Movement of Ideas' series (1946–50).
       Conservatism, 1945–50 (no. 90, 1940).
       Conservatives and the Colonies (no. 123, 1952).
       The New Conservatism (no. 150, 1955).
       Colonial Rule. Enemies and Obligations (no. 141, 1955).
       The Expanding Commonwealth (no. 159, 1956).
       Conservative Points of View (no. 306, 1964).
       Conservatism Today (no. 350, 1966).
       The Great Divide (no. 355, 1966).
       Fair Deal at Work (no. 400, 1968).
       The Future of NATO (no. 418, 1968).
       A Presence East of Suez (no. 443, 1969).

'New Tasks' 1965
  1 E. Griffiths, *The New Competitors.*
  2 D. Howell, *Efficiency and Beyond.*
  3 G. Rippon, *Britain's World Role.*
  4 W. Rees-Mogg, *Liberty in 1984.*
  5 C. Chataway, *Education and TV.*
  6 T. Raison, *Conflict and Conservatism.*
  7 R. Hornby, *The Changing Commonwealth.*
  8 G. Howe, *In Place of Beveridge.*
  9 T. Higgins, *The Second Managerial Revolution.*
10 J. MacGregor, *Housing Ourselves.*
11 P. Goodhart, *A Nation of Customers.*

'New Techniques' 1965–6
  1 R. Freeman, *Modernizing the Rates.*

2 R. Lewis, *A Bonfire of Restrictions*.
3 F. MacCarty, *Work for Married Women*.
4 Inns of Court Conservative Association, *Let Right be Done*.
5 A. Mitton, *A Tax for our Time*.
6 H. Sewell, *Auntie*.
7 Sir Anthony Meyer, *A European Technological Community*.

CPC *Annual Lecture at Party Conference*
1953 I. Macleod, *The Welfare Society*.
1954 D. Eccles, *Popular Capitalism*.
1955 Lord Salisbury, *Conservatism and the Atomic Age*.
1956 R. A. Butler, *Our Way Ahead*.
1957 Q. Hogg, *Toryism and Tomorrow*.
1958 A. Lennox-Boyd, *Imperium et Libertas*.
1959 I. Macleod, *One World*.
1960 Lord Home, *Great Britain's Foreign Policy*.
1962 R. A. Butler, *Our New Frontier*.
1963 Q. Hogg, *National Excellence*.
1964 E. Boyle, *Conservatives and Economic Planning*.
1966 E. Marples, *No Choice but Change*.
1967 A. Maude, *The Consumer Society*.
1968 M. Thatcher, *What's Wrong with Politics*.
1969 R. Maudling, *The Ever Changing Challenge*.
1970 D. Eccles, *Politics and the Quality of Life*.

CPC *National Summer Schools*
1951 *Six Oxford Lectures—Britain in Mid-Century*.
1953 *The Good Society*.
1954 *Tradition and Change*.
1955 *World Perspectives*.
1956 *Liberty in the Modern State*.
1957 *The Future of the Welfare State*.
1958 *Prospect for Capitalism: strength and stress*.
1960 *Accent on Youth*.
1961 *Science and Society*.
1962 *The New Europe*.
1963 *Contemporary Communism*.
1965 *A Fresh Approach*.

(B) PAMPHLETS, BOOKS, AND ARTICLES BY CONSERVATIVES
AMERY, J., *The British Commonwealth and Western Europe*, Longmans, London 1952.
AMERY, L. S., *The Awakening*, Macdonald, London 1948.
——*Thoughts on the Constitution*, OUP, London 1953.
——*A Balanced Economy*, Hutchinson, London 1954.
——'Conservatism', *Chambers Encyclopaedia*, vol. 4, London 1969, pp. 28–31.
ASTOR, W. W., 'The Conservative party in opposition', *New English Review*, vol. 12, no. 4, April 1946, pp. 344–8.
——*Our Imperial Future*, Signpost, London 1944.

BELLAIRS, C. E., *Conservative Social and Industrial Reform*, CPC, London 1947.
BIFFEN, J., 'Party conference and party policy', *Political Quarterly*, vol. 32, no. 3, 1961, pp. 257–66.
BIGGS-DAVISON, J., *Europe: Faith, not Despair*, Monday Club, London 1967.
——*The Centre Cannot Hold, or Mao, Marcuse, and all that Marx*, Monday Club, London 1969.
——*Ireland our Cuba*, Monday Club?, London 1970.
BIRCH, N., *The Conservative Party*, Collins, London 1949.
BLOCK, G. D. M., *A Source Book of Conservatism*, CPC 305, London 1964.
——*About the Conservative Party*, CLC 325, London 1965.
BOYD-CARPENTER, J., *The Conservative Case*, Wingate, London 1940.
BOYSON, R. (ed.), *Right Turn*, Churchill, London 1970.
BOW GROUP, *Principles in Practice* (ed. D. Howell and T. Raison), CPC 233, London 1961.
——*Britain into Europe*, CPC 253, London 1962.
——*No Tame or Minor Role*, Bow, London 1963.
——*Milestones for the Sixties*, Bow, London 1964.
——*The Conservative Opportunity* (ed. M. Wolff), Batsford, London 1965.
——*A Smaller Stage*, Bow, London 1965.
——*Through A Glass Darkly*, Bow, London 1968.
——*Our Future in Europe* (ed. L. Brittan), Bow, London 1970.
BRAINE, J., *A Personal Record*, Monday Club, London 1968.
BRANSTON, U., *Britain and European Unity*, CPC 126, London 1953.
BUTLER, SIR GEOFFREY, *The Tory Tradition*, CPC 175, London 1957.
BUTLER, R. A., *Fundamental issues*, CUCO, London 1946.
——'Conservative policy', *Political Quarterly*, vol. 20, no. 4, Oct.–Dec. 1949, pp. 317–25.
——*Tomorrow our Responsibility*, CPC 194, London 1959.
CECIL, H., *Conservatism*, Home University Library, London 1912.
CHURCHILL, R., *The Fight for the Tory Leadership*, Heinemann, London 1964.
CLARKE, D., *The Conservative Faith in the Modern Age*, CPC, London 1947.
COOTE, C. R., *The Government we Deserve*, Eyre & Spottiswoode, London 1969.
CUTLER, H., *Rents—Chaos or Common Sense?*, Monday Club, London 1970.
DRISCOLL, J., *A National Wages Policy*, Bow, London 1955.
ECCLES, D., *Forward from the Industrial Charter*, CUCO, London 1948.
——*The New Conservatism*, 4 August 1951 (speech at Spurminster).
——*Life and Politics: a moral diagnosis*, Longmans, London 1967.
EDEN, A., 'Britain and the modern world', *Foreign Affairs*, vol. 26, no. 1, October 1946, pp. 15–23.
——'Britain in world strategy', *Foreign Affairs*, vol, 29, no. 3, April 1951, pp. 341–50.
FEILING, K., *What is Conservatism?*, Criterion Miscellany no. 14, Faber, London 1930.
——'Principles of Conservatism', *Political Quarterly*, vol. 24, no. 2, April–June, 1953, pp. 129–38.
FRASER, M., *The Worker in Industry*, CPC 65, London 1951.
GOLDMAN, P., *Some Principles of Conservatism*, CPC 161, London 1956.
GUMMER, J. S., *The Permissive Society*, Cassell, London 1971.
HASTINGS, S., *Once upon a Time*, Monday Club, London 1970.

HEARNSHAW, F. J. C., *Conservatism in England*, Macmillan, London 1944.

HEATH, E., *Parliament and People*, CPC 212, London 1960.

——'Realism in British foreign policy, *Foreign Affairs*, vol. 48, no. 1, October 1969, pp. 39–50.

——*Old World, New Horizons*, OUP, London 1970.

HILTON, R., *Imperial Obituary*, Britons Publishing Company, Devon, 1968.

HINCHINGBROOKE, LORD (VICTOR MONTAGU), *Full Speed Ahead. Essays in Tory Reform*, London 1944.

——*The Conservative Dilemma*, Monday Club, London 1970.

HOGG, Q. (LORD HAILSHAM), *One Year's Work*, Hutchinson, London 1944.

——*The Left Was Never Right*, Faber, London 1945.

——*The Case for Conservatism*, Penguin, London 1947.

——*The Conservative Case*, Penguin, London 1959.

——'Britain looks forward', *Foreign Affairs*, vol. 43, no. 3, April 1965, pp. 409–25.

HOLLIS, C., *Can Parliament Survive?*, Hollis & Carter, London 1949.

HOWE, G., *In Place of Beveridge*, CPC 316, London 1965.

HOWELL, D., *Whose Government Works?*, CPC 407, London 1968.

——*A New Style of Government*, CPC 453, London 1970.

INNS OF COURT CONSERVATIVE AND UNIONIST SOCIETY, *A Giant's Strength*, London 1958.

IVENS, M. (ed.), *The Case for Capitalism*, Michael Joseph, London 1967.

JENNER, R. V., *Will Conservativism Survive?*, London 1944.

JONES, A., *Right and Left*, Signpost, London 1944.

——*The Pendulum of Politics*, Faber, London 1946.

——'Conservatism and capitalism', *Nineteenth Century and After*, June 1947, pp. 271–86.

——'Conservatives in conference', *Nineteenth Century and After*, November 1947, pp. 219–24.

——*Industrial Order*, Falcon Press, London 1950.

——*The New Inflation*, Penguin, London 1973.

JOSEPH, SIR KEITH, *A New Strategy for Social Security*, CPC 336, London 1966.

——*Social Security: The New Priorities*, CPC 351, London 1966.

KINCHIN-SMITH, M. et al., *Forward from Victory*, Faber, London 1943.

KIRK, R., *The Conservative Mind*, Faber, London 1954.

——'Conservatism', *Encyclopaedia Britannica*, Vol. 6, pp. 371–4, London 1967.

LAW, R. (LORD COLERAINE), *Return from Utopia*, Faber, London 1950.

——*For Conservatives Only*, Stacey, London 1970.

LEWIS, R., *Growth Realities*, CPC Summer School Studies, 1967, London 1968.

——*Principles to Conserve*, CPC 417, London 1968.

LOW, SIR TOBY, *Everyman a Capitalist*, CPC 201, London 1959.

MACLEOD, I., *The Crisis of Confidence in Industrial Relations*, The Industrial Co-partnership Association, London 1957.

——'The Tory Leadership', *Spectator*, 17.1.1964, pp. 65–7.

——'Reports of Britain's death', *Foreign Affairs*, vol. 45, no. 1, Oct. 1966, pp. 88–97.

MACLEOD, I. and POWELL, J. E., *The Social Services: Needs and Means*, CPC 115, London 1952, 1954.

MACMILLAN, H., *The Middle Way*, Macmillan, London 1938.

——*Britain, the Commonwealth, and Europe*, CUCO, London 1962.

MARPLES, E., *Innovation and Revival*, CPC 383, London 1967.

MAUDE, A., 'The Conservative party and the changing class structure', *Political Quarterly*, vol. 24, no. 2, April–June 1953, pp. 139–47.

——*The Common Problem*, Constable, London 1969.

MAUDE, A. and LEWIS, R., *The English Middle Classes*, Phoenix, London 1950.

——*Professional People*, Phoenix, London 1952.

MAYBURY, M., *The Truth about the Interwar Years: An Exposure of the Socialist Myth*, CUCO, London 1949.

MOLSON, H., 'The Tory Reform Committee', *New English Review*, vol. 11, no. 3, July 1945, pp. 245–52.

MONDAY CLUB, *Wind of Change or Whirlwind?*, London 1961.

——*Bury the Hatchet*, London 1962.

——*Conservatism Lost? Conservatism Regained?* London 1963.

——*Strike out or Strike bound*, London 1965.

——*Immigration into the UK*, London 1965.

——*Monday Paper no. 2, Housing*, London 1966.

——*Monday Paper no. 3, Economic Affairs*, London 1966.

——*Monday Paper no. 5, Conservatism Tomorrow*, London 1966.

——*A Realistic Approach to Present Day Housing*, London 1967.

——*Conference on Economic Policy for the 1970s*, London 1968.

OAKESHOTT, M., 'Contemporary British politics', *Cambridge Journal*, vol. 1, no. 8, May 1948, pp. 474–90.

——*Rationalism in Politics*, Methuen, London 1962.

ONE NATION GROUP, *One Nation*, CPC, London 1950.

——*Change is our Ally* (ed. A. Maude and J. E. Powell), CPC 133, London 1954.

——*The Responsible Society*, CPC 200, London 1959.

——*One Europe* (ed. N. Ridley), CPC 314, London 1965.

PICKTHORN, K., *Principles or Prejudices*, Signpost, London 1943.

POWELL, J. E., 'Conservatives and the social services', *Political Quarterly*, vol. 24, no. 2, April–June 1953, pp. 156–66.

——*A Nation not Afraid* (ed. J. Wood), Batsford, London 1965.

——*Freedom and Reality* (ed. J. Wood), Elliott Rightway Books, Kingswood 1969.

——*Enoch Powell on Immigration* (ed. B. Smithies and P. Fiddick), Sphere, London 1969.

——*Income Tax at 4/3d in the £* (ed. A Lejeune), Stacey, London 1970.

——*Powell and the 1970 Election* (ed. J. Wood), Elliott Rightway Books, Kingswood 1970.

——*The Common Market—The Case Against*, Elliott Rightway Books, Kingswood 1971.

——*Still to Decide*, Batsford, London 1972.

POWELL, J. E. and MAUDE, A., *Biography of a Nation*, John Barker, London 1955.

PRESSURE FOR ECONOMIC AND SOCIAL TORYISM (PEST), *Will the Tories Lose?* London 1963.

——*Call an End to Feeble Opposition*, London 1965.

——*Immigration and the Commonwealth*, London 1965.

RAISON, T., *Why Conservative?*, Penguin, London 1964.

RIPPON, G., *Right Angle*, Monday Club, CPC 427, London 1969.

SELECT BIBLIOGRAPHY

SALISBURY, LORD, *Post-war Conservative Policy*, Murray, London n.d.
——'Anglo-American shibboleths', *Foreign Affairs*, vol. 36, no. 3, April 1958, pp. 401–8.
SOREF, H. and GREIG, I., *The Puppeteers*, Tandem, London 1965.
SPEARMAN, D., *Democracy in England*, Rockliff, London 1957.
STACEY, T., *A Defeatist America*, Monday Club, London 1970.
STEWART-SMITH, D. G., *The Handmaidens of Diplomacy*, Monday Club, London 1964.
UTLEY, T. E., *Essays in Conservatism*, CPC, London 1949.
——'The mandate', *Cambridge Journal*, vol. 3, no. 10, pp. 579–91, July 1950.
——*The Conservatives and the Critics*, CPC 164, London 1956.
——*Not Guilty, The Conservative Reply*, MacGibbon & Kee, London 1957.
——*What Laws may Cure*, CPC 400, London 1968.
UTLEY T. E. and UDAL J. (eds), *Wind of Change: the Challenge to the Commonwealth*, CPC 211, London 1960.
WALL, P., *British Defence Policy in the 1970s*, Monday Club, London 1969.
WALL, P. and SMITH, J., *Student Power*, Monday Club, London 1968.
WHITE, R. J. (ed.), *The Conservative Tradition*, Adam & Charles Black, London 1964.
WINDLESHAM, LORD, *Communication and Political Power*, Cape, London 1966.
WORSTHORNE, P., *Dare Democracy Disengage?*, CPC 185, London 1958.
——'Class and class conflict in British Foreign Policy', *Foreign Affairs*, vol. 37, no. 3, April 1959, pp. 419–31.
——*The Socialist Myth*, Cassell, London 1971.
WRIGHT, E., 'The future of the Conservative party', *Political Quarterly*, vol 41, no. 4, Oct.–Dec. 1970, pp. 387–98.
YOUNG, G. M., *Ourselves*, Signpost, London 1944.
YOUNG CONSERVATIVES, *The Charter of Youth*, London 1948.
——*A Changing Partnership*, CPC, London 1961.
——*The Young Idea*, CPC, London 1962.
——*Law, Liberty, and Licence*, CPC, London 1964.
——*Blueprint for Britain*, London 1965.
——*Industry in an Expanding Economy*, CLC, London 1966.
——*Social Security in the 1970s*, CPC, London 1966.
——*Challenge for Youth*, CPC, London 1969.
——*Students' Charter*, CPC, London 1969.

(C) MEMOIRS AND BIOGRAPHIES

AMERY, J., *Joseph Chamberlain and the Tariff Reform Campaign, Life of Joseph Chamberlain, Vol. 6, 1903–68*, Macmillan, London 1969.
AMERY, L. S., *My Political Life* (3 vols), Hutchinson, London 1953.
BERKELEY, H., *Crossing the Floor*, Allen & Unwin, London 1972.
BEVINS, R., *The Greasy Pole*, Hodder, London 1965.
BIRKENHEAD, LORD, *Walter Monckton*, Weidenfeld & Nicolson, London 1969.
BLAKE, R., *Disraeli*, Methuen, London 1969.
BOOTHBY, R., *My Yesterday, Your Tomorrow*, Hutchinson, London 1962.
BUTLER, R. A., *The Art of the Possible*, Hamish Hamilton, London 1971.
CROFT, SIR HENRY PAGE, *My Life of Strife*, Hutchinson, London 1948.
EDEN, A., *Memoirs: Full Circle*, Cassell, London 1960.

FISHER, N., *Iain Macleod*, André Deutsch, London 1973.

HARRIS, R., *Politics without Prejudice*, Staples Press, London 1956.

HILL, C., *Both Sides of the Hill*, Heinemann, London 1964.

HUTCHINSON, G., *Edward Heath: A Personal and Political Biography*, Longmans, London 1970.

JAMES, R. R., *Lord Randolph Churchill*, Weidenfeld & Nicolson, London 1959.

——*Churchill: A Study in Failure*, Weidenfeld & Nicolson, London 1970.

LYTTLETON, O., *The Memoirs of Lord Chandos*, Bodley Head, London 1962.

MACMILLAN, H., *I Winds of Change, 1914–39*, Macmillan, London 1966.

—— *II The Blast of War, 1939–45*, Macmillan, London 1967.

—— *III Tides of Fortune, 1945–55*, Macmillan, London 1969.

—— *IV Riding the Storm, 1956–9*, Macmillan, London 1971.

—— *V Pointing the Way, 1959–61*, Macmillan, London 1972.

—— *VI At the End of the Day, 1961–3*, Macmillan, London 1973.

MAXWELL-FYFE, D. (LORD KILMUIR), *Political Adventure*, Weidenfeld & Nicolson, London 1964.

ROTH, A., *Enoch Powell: Tory Tribune*, Macdonald, London 1972.

——*Heath and the Heathmen*, Routledge & Kegan Paul, London 1972.

SAMPSON, A., *Macmillan. A Study in Ambiguity*, Allen Lane, London 1967.

UTLEY, T. E., *Enoch Powell. The Man and his Thinking*, Kimber, London 1968.

WOOLTON, LORD, *Memoirs*, Cassell, London 1959.

YOUNG, K., *Sir Alec Douglas-Home*, Dent, London 1970.

(D) MAGAZINES AND PERIODICALS

1 CUCO
Notes on Current Politics.
Weekly Newsletter.
Onlooker, 1943–7 (ceased publication).
Tory Challenge, 1947–53 (ceased publication).
Onward, 1953–7 (ceased publication).
Objective, 1950–8. CPC Quarterly.

2 Young Conservatives
Advance, 1946–53.
Rightway, 1954–5.
Impact, 1964–8.

3 Bow Group
Crossbow, 1957– (quarterly).

4 Monday Club
Monday World (quarterly).
Newsletter (monthly).

5 Other
Cambridge Journal.
Encounter.
New English Review.
Political Quarterly.

Politics and Money.
Spectator.
Truth.

II Secondary sources

(A) BOOKS AND ARTICLES

The following is a list of the works that have most influenced me in writing this book.

ANDERSON, P., 'Origins of the present crisis', *New Left Review*, 23, Jan.–Feb. 1964.

BARRATT BROWN, M., *After Imperialism*, Heinemann, London 1963.

BEER, S., *Modern British Politics*, Faber, London 1965.

BLAKE, R., *The Conservative Party from Peel to Churchill*, Eyre & Spottiswoode, London 1970.

BRITTAN, S., *Steering the Economy*, Penguin, Harmondsworth 1971.

BULMER-THOMAS, I., *The Growth of the British Party System*, John Baker, London 1965.

BUTLER, D. E. and STOKES, D., *Political Change in Britain*, Macmillan, London 1969.

DOWNS, A., *The Economic Theory of Democracy*, Harper, New York 1955.

GLYN, A. and SUTCLIFFE, R., *British Capitalism, Workers, and the Profits Squeeze*, Penguin, Harmondsworth 1972.

GOLDSWORTHY, D., *Colonial Issues in British Politics, 1945–61*, OUP, London 1971.

GRAINGER J. H., *Character and Style in English Politics*, Cambridge 1969.

GUTTSMAN W. L., *The British Political Élite*, Heinemann, London 1963.

HARRIS, N., *Competition and the Corporate Society*, Methuen, London 1972.

HOBSBAWM, E., *Industry and Empire*, Penguin, Harmondsworth 1969.

HOFFMAN, J. D., *The Conservative Party in Opposition*, MacGibbon & Kee, London 1964.

HOROWITZ, D., *From Yalta to Vietnam*, Penguin, Harmondsworth 1967.

JACKSON, D., TURNER, H. A. and WILKINSON, F., *Do Trade Unions cause Inflation?*, Cambridge 1972.

KORNHAUSER, W., *The Politics of Mass Society*, Routledge & Kegan Paul, London 1960.

LEVIN, M. B., *The Compleat Politician*, Bobbs Merrill, New York 1962.

LIPSET, S. M. and ROKKAN, S. (eds), *Party Systems and Voter Alignments*, Free Press, New York 1967.

MCKENZIE, R. T., *British Political Parties*, Heinemann, London 1963.

MCKENZIE, R. T. and SILVER A., *Angels in Marble*, Heinemann, London 1968.

MACPHERSON, G. B., *The Real World of Democracy*, CBC, Toronto 1965.

MARSHALL, T. H., 'Citizenship and social class', in *Sociology at the Crossroads*, Heinemann, London 1963.

MATTICK, P., *Marx and Keynes*, Merlin, London 1971.

MILIBAND, R., *The State in Capitalist Society*, Weidenfeld & Nicolson, London 1969.

MOSCA, G., *The Ruling Class*, New York 1939.

NAIRN, T., 'British nationalism and the EEC', *New Left Review* 69, Sept.–Oct. 1971, pp. 3–28.

PARKIN, F., 'Working class Conservatives; a theory of political deviance', *British Journal of Sociology*, vol. 18, no. 3, Sept. 1967, pp. 278–90.

PINTO-DUSCHINSKY, M., 'Central Office and power in the Conservative party', *Political Studies*, vol. 20, no. 1, March 1972, pp. 1–16.

POLLARD, S., *The Development of the British Economy*, Arnold, London 1967.

ROSE, R., *Influencing Voters*, Faber, London 1967.

SCHUMPETER, J. A., *Capitalism, Socialism, and Democracy*, Allen & Unwin, London 1950.

SHONFIELD, A., *Modern Capitalism*, OUP, London 1969.

SKIDELSKY, R., *Politicians and the Slump*, Macmillan, London 1967.

URRY, J. and WAKEFORD, J. (eds), *Power in Britain*, Heinemann, London 1973.

VINCENT, J. R., *The Formation of the British Liberal Party*, Constable, London 1966.

(B) WORKS OF REFERENCE

Nuffield Election Studies

MCCALLUM, R. B. and READMAN, A., *The British General Election of 1945*, Oxford 1947.

NICHOLAS, H. G., *The British General Election of 1950*, Macmillan, London 1950.

BUTLER, D. E., *The British General Election of 1951*, Macmillan, London 1952.

BUTLER, D. E., *The British General Election of 1955*, Macmillan, London 1955.

BUTLER, D. E. and ROSE, R., *The British General Election of 1959*, Macmillan, London 1960.

BUTLER, D. E. and KING, A., *The British General Election of 1964*, Macmillan, London 1965.

BUTLER, D. E. and KING, A., *The British General Election of 1966*, Macmillan, London 1966.

BUTLER, D. E. and PINTO-DUSCHINSKY, M., *The British General Election of 1970*, Macmillan, London 1971.

BUTLER, D. E. and FREEMAN, J., *British Political Facts*, Macmillan, London 1969.

CRAIG, F. W. S. (ed.), *British General Election Manifestos, 1918–66*, Chichester 1970.

——*British Parliamentary Election Statistics, 1918–70*, Chichester 1970.

(C) UNPUBLISHED THESES

HARRIS, N. *Conservatism: State and Society*, University of London 1970.

KOPSCH, H. *The Approach of the Conservative Party to Social Policy during World War II*, University of London 1970.

Index

Amery, J.: on American imperialism, 162; and imperial preference, 170; on Labour's imperial policy, 168–9; and 1963 Leadership crisis, 88; and Suez crisis, 173, 275n.; on United Europe, 184

Amery, L. S.: attacks dominance of finance capital, 136–7; attacks GATT, 170; on Empire and the class war, 166; and Empire Industries Association, 172; makes final plea for Empire policy, 171; on perils of European Union, 185–6; his political perspective, 99

Astor, W. W.: analyses Conservative predicament after 1945, 42

Atlantic Alliance: breakup of US cold war strategy, 163; Britain's subordination to America in, 162, 188; cold war, 161–2, 273n.; containment of Communism, 161f; elimination of old colonial Empires, 162; European Union, 184; GATT, 162, 168, 170–2, 185, 214, 274n.; Imperialists, 214; Marshall Aid, 162; strains in, 220, 221–2; Washington Loan Agreements, 167, 214; *see also* World market

Baldwin, S.: and General Strike, 26; his handling of Labour party, 25, 27, 211, 212–13; and Wind of Change, 276n.

Bank of England, 22, 131, 172

Barber, A.: on the enveloping crisis, 219; on trade unions, 146

Berkeley, H.: on Heath's leadership, 263n.; and procedure for election of leader, 262n.

Biggs-Davison, J.: on creeping socialism, 106–7; and Scramble for Africa, 273n.; on special role of the Monday Club, 107

Birch, N.: on EEC and the Commonwealth, 192; on Lenin and inflation, 139; on public expenditure, 269n.; resigns from Government, 130

Boothby, R.: and European Movement, 277n.; as Right Progressive, 35, 36

Bow Group: attacks New Right, 101; and Common Market, 189, 278n.; compared with Monday Club, 106; and competition policy, 92; criticizes Hogg, 75–6; *Crossbow*, 74f; endorsement of planning, 76, 77; and Enoch Powell, 117; formation, 74; and ideology of economic growth, 75, 77; irrelevance of Labour party, 98; and level of government spending, 137; policy and attitudes, 74f, 90, 91, 260n.; and popularity of Labour's wage freeze, 100; reactions to 1961 crisis, 76; reform of Tory party, 76–7; and social services, 64, 135; support for big firms, 100; and support for Conservative party, 99, 100–1; and trade union reform, 156; and welfare consensus, 214; as workshop for Tory leadership, 75

Bowden, A.: on EEC, 190–1